W9-BHT-616

THE GREAT BOOK OF
CHINESE
COOKING

Piero Antolini
The Lian Tjo

THE GREAT BOOK OF CHINESE COOKING

Foreword by Edoardo Fazzioli

International Culinary Society
New York

Acknowledgments
The publishers wish to thank Eileen and Edoardo Fazzioli for their kind
assistance in the transliteration of Chinese names. Special thanks are also
due to chef Pang Kim Poo for help with the recipes.

Editor: Maria Luisa Viviani
Editor English-language edition: Anna Bennett
Art director: Giorgio Seppi
Designed by Brunhild Kindermann
Jacket designed by Bill Akunewicz
Photographs of the dishes by Adriano Brusaferri

Copyright © 1990 Arnoldo Mondadori Editore S.p.A., Milan

English translation copyright © 1990 Arnoldo Mondadori Editore S.p.A.,
Milan

Translated by Sara Harris

This 1990 edition published by
International Culinary Society,
distributed by Outlet Book Company, Inc.,
a Random House Company,
225 Park Avenue South,
New York, New York 10003

All rights reserved.

ISBN 0-517-0 33 16-X

8 7 6 5 4 3 2 1

Typeset in Great Britain by Tradespools Ltd, Frome, Somerset
Printed and bound in Italy by Arnoldo Mondadori Editore, Verona

CONTENTS

Note

As a rule, all recipes serve 4, except where
the main ingredient is used in its entirety.
Many recipes serve more than 4 people if part
of a typical Chinese menu comprising a wide
selection of dishes.
An asterisk after the recipe title indicates that
the recipe is illustrated.
Chinese names are given in Pinyin, the
official system for the transliteration of
Chinese names into the Roman alphabet
internationally adopted on 1 January 1979.

CONFUCIUS: SCHOLAR, PHILOSOPHER AND DISCRIMINATING GOURMET

It is remarkable how often the great names of Chinese history, art, and literature chose to write on culinary matters. They considered food and, more importantly, its preparation to be significant within a far wider cultural context; it was therefore their duty and pleasure to explore the subject with erudition and enthusiasm.

Precious information about Confucius (Kong Fu zi), the Great Master, who lived from 551 to 479 B.C. and his thoughts on food, is recorded in *The Discourses and Dialogues* compiled by his disciples.

In chapter seven of the fourth book of this work we read: "Confucius said: 'I never refused to teach anyone who came to me bearing a gift of dried meat.'" Teachers would therefore appear to have been paid in kind, the most modest payment admissible being ten slices of dried meat. A few lines further on, the great man's simplicity and wisdom are revealed: "Confucius said: 'Plain food to eat, pure water to drink and one's own folded arm as a pillow, these bring joy. Ill-gotten riches and undeserved honors are like fleeting clouds to me.'"

Chapter 10 describes his behavior and attitudes, his preferences and tastes, particularly as regards food. It is said that: "He liked plain, wholesome rice and very finely chopped meat. He would not eat bad or sour rice (damaged by heat or damp) and only the freshest fish and soundest meat. He refused to eat discolored or malodorous foods, or anything not cooked to just the right degree, nor foods which were out of season." These were intelligent choices which showed how much importance Confucius attached to a wholesome, well cooked diet. The immensely influential Sage of China also thought the appearance of food important, as well as the quantity served, the proportions of, and relationship between the various courses, and their taste. As an ancient Chinese proverb says: "A good meal is eaten first with the eyes, then with the nose and finally with the mouth." Different types of satisfaction but all intense are to be derived from admiring the way in which the food is presented, savoring both the aroma and scent as well as the taste. Mindful of the Master's precepts, the Chinese remember to enjoy each stage in turn.

"He would not eat badly cut meat or meat cooked with unsuitable seasonings. Even when meat was in plentiful supply, he maintained that the rice content of a meal should always be preponderant. He placed no limit on the amount of wine served, but never drank to the point of intoxication.

"It was inadvisable to drink wine or eat dried meat that had been bought at a market. There should always be some dishes cooked with ginger (he believed that it sharpened the intelligence and eliminated impurities). He never ate to excess."

The wine referred to here did not come from grape vines (first brought to China by an ambassador, Zhang Qian, in 116 B.C.) but would have been the liquor made from fermented cereals, rice among them, which is called Chinese wine, and much used for cooking to add extra flavor. A few lines underline the important role food played in ceremonial and domestic ceremonies. "When he (Confucius) went to the Prince's sacrifices, he was careful not to keep meat longer than overnight, to avoid losing the favor of the spirits, and meat used for domestic sacrifices was never kept longer than three days: once these three days had passed, he took care not to eat it, as he considered it no longer fit for consumption. . .He did not talk while he ate. . .Even when enjoying the simplest meal of vegetable or bean soup, he always remembered to make a respectful offering."

RECIPES AND BANQUETS IN CHINESE HISTORICAL DOCUMENTS

One of the most valuable original sources of information on recipes, diet, cooking methods and banquets is found in the *Shu King* or *Book of Historical Documents* (chronicles of the dynasties).

These books were compiled by highly educated civil servants appointed especially for this task and generously remunerated by the kings and emperors of China, so that a record would be made for posterity of the important events of their reigns; several pages are concerned with cookery. In the *Zhou Li*, also known as the *Li Ki* or *Book of Rites and Ancient Ceremonies and Institutions of the Zhou Dynasty*, written during the Warring States Period (453–222 B.C.), we learn that the rulers of the Zhou Dynasty (1121–222 B.C.) had adopted a seasonal diet. In spring they ate lamb and suckling pig cooked with butter. In summer, sun-dried chickens and dried fish cooked in dog's fat. When the fall came, it was time for veal, venison, and fawn cooked in pork fat or lard. Winter was the season for fresh fish and wild geese cooked in mutton fat.

During the Han Dynasty (206 B.C.–A.D. 220) the technique of extracting oil from various cereal seeds was discovered. This new substance revolutionized cooking methods and opened the way for techniques which are recognizably the precursors of those used in Chinese cooking today. The three basic

8

techniques of cooking in oil were classified as: slow-frying (jian), deep-frying in very hot oil (zha); and stir-frying (chao). Each of these techniques has several variations which, when combined with water-cooking methods, add up to a total of at least 50 different cooking processes, each with its own name and every one processing the food in a distinctive different way.

In both the *Zhou Li* and in the *Li Ji* (*Records of Ceremonies*) which is attributed to Confucius, eight "precious foods" are listed, prepared for the ruler's table. These might refer to eight special dishes or eight different ways of cooking food for the emperor. One of these concerns roast mutton, and is a more elaborate version of an extremely complicated and famous recipe for lacquered suckling pig, the proud boast of the inhabitants of Peking. For lacquered mutton the meat is first roasted, then fried, and finally stuffed. Among the ingredients listed are rice flour, a thick soybean paste, Chinese vinegar, and many spices. Such were the counsels of perfection followed by the imperial court's cooks and the degree of skill achieved 2,000 years ago.

POETRY IN THE KITCHEN

The great poet Qu Yuan (340–278 B.C.) was active in the Chu kingdom, during the Warring States Period (Zhanguo 453–222 B.C.); apart from his masterpiece *Li Sao* (*The Lament*), he also wrote many other poems, one of which is called *Summons to the spirits*. This takes the form of a tribute to the generals and soldiers who lost their lives in defence of the Chu kingdom; some Sinologists prefer to interpret it as an invitation and invocation to his king, Huai, held prisoner in the kingdom of Qin, to return to his homeland.

In ancient China it was believed that if a person became sick it was because his spirit had distanced itself from his body, endangering the unfortunate's life. The sick man's closest relatives and dearest friends would gather together around midnight, to sing dirges, begging the wayward spirit to return to the patient's body before irreparable damage was done to his health.

Every effort was made to tempt the spirit back, including a mouthwatering banquet of many courses, each comprising many delicious dishes:

...Come back, oh spirit...
The banquet is prepared, with many good
    dishes,
Steaming millet and rice, tender wheat;
With salt and vinegar and appetizing aromas,
Ginger and honeyed pepper, all display'd.
Thick, juicy meat has been brought to table,

And exquisite sharp-flavored broths, too;
Followed by roast lamb and turtle soup,
Juicy sugar cane to quench your thirst;
Swans cooked in vinegar and flocks of wild
    duck;
Succulent black cranes and roast wild geese;
Whole cooked chickens and rare turtles,
A wondrous feast, to tempt your appetite.
Cakes, honey and sweetened malt all wait to
    be sampled.
And pure hydromel has been poured into
    wingéd cups...

This seems enough to summon even the most wayward spirit, and also provides us with a fascinating glimpse of the culinary refinement of the time. Such variety would appeal to the most discriminating palate, and the rare and highly prized meats would be those enjoyed by the rich people of the day.

THE FIRST FLOWERING OF THE CULINARY ART IN CHINA

Toward the end of the Warring States Period, in 239 B.C., the *Spring and Fall Annals of Master Lu* (*Lu Shi Chun Qiu*) were published. A whole book or *zhuan* (commentary) on this work is devoted to "natural flavors" where the author explores the theory that the control of heat or the flame during cooking, the appropriate use of flavorings and seasonings, an understanding of the ageing process (in the sense of ripening, to improve flavor) are indispensable in good cooking.

This is the first surviving example in ancient Chinese documents of a writer stating that controlled flame, accurate timing, and the marinating of meats are vital for the best results.

During the Han dynasty (206 B.C.–A.D. 220) many unfamiliar foodstuffs were imported into China for the first time by soldiers returning from military expeditions: nuts, beans, carrots, onions, and cucumbers and, for the first time, mention is made of "soybean flour cake" or "soybean curd" often erroneously called "soybean cheese," since no milk is used.

This humble ingredient was to become a very important staple in China; while almost tasteless it is rich in nutritional value and has a high lecithin content, an important dietary factor in lowering cholesterol.

Another book, concerned with agriculture and cooking, was published in the years 533 and 534 during the northern Wei dynasty (384–534), written by Jia Sixie, a famous man of letters who was also an erudite agronomist. Entitled *Qi Min Yao Shu* (*Important skills for the well-being of the people*) this contained many previously unrecorded ingredients and recipes.

In the four previous centuries great

migrations of people had brought different ethnic groups into China and caused a mingling of races. This meant that new ingredients and new ways of cooking came to be introduced to China.

From Xinjiang came the custom of dry-frying or dry-roasting (briefly searing very thinly sliced meat); from Hunan and Szechwan came the use of chili oil and oyster sauce; from Fujian and Guangdong roast pork and raw fish while from the southeastern coast came delicious seafood dishes, made with crustaceans and many types of fish.

Under the Tang Dynasty (618–907) China became the dominant power in east Asia. Wealth, power, and an advanced culture and civilization were reflected also in the art of cooking. It was not enough for a dish to be wholesome, nourishing, and flavorsome. The color, aroma, scent, taste, shape, and design had also to satisfy exacting standards. Each course was a performance, a work of art, both in taste and appearance.

Wi Quyan's book *Recipes* has left a record of this flowering of culinary skill.

Many works on fine cooking were published during the Song Dynasty's reign (960–1279), among the more noteworthy: *Yu Gong Pi* written by the head cooks at the Imperial Palace, and *Zhong Ku Lu* written by Wu Shi.

SWALLOWS' NESTS AND SHARK'S FINS

It was the cooks of the Ming Dynasty (1368–1644) and the Qing Dynasty (1644–1911) who were to benefit from improvements in transport and maritime trade, enabling them to use an impressively wide range of ingredients for their fabulously expensive and renowned culinary masterpieces. Swallows' nests (yan wo) and shark's fins (yu chi) are dried so that they keep well and can be easily transported; both need long and meticulous preparation which the master cooks at the Ming and Qing courts developed and perfected.

Both these raw materials have a delicacy and subtlety of flavor that only the best cooks manage to bring out and enhance, transforming unusual ingredients into unforgettable dishes.

One of the cornerstones of Chinese culinary literature and one of the last great classics on the subject was the *Menu of the Sui garden*, written by the scholar Yuan Mei (1716–1798). This not only contains recipes but also describes various cooking techniques, an opinion on the dish and the salient difficulties involved in its preparation. The author states that all the recipes in his book have been tested under his supervision and that he has personally tasted each one.

CI XI: THE EMPRESS WHO LOVED GOOD FOOD

The Empress Ci Xi reigned over China for nearly half a century and proved a wise, firm, though fairly unscrupulous ruler. An iron lady with a weakness for good food, she first entered the Imperial Palace in 1852 as a fifth-grade concubine. Over the next four years, however, Lan Gui Fei (Little Orchid) had not only given birth to an heir for the Emperor but she had also been promoted to the rank of Second Grade Concubine with the name Huang Gui Fei (Imperial Favorite).

Ci Xi was only 20 years old but already she felt she was edging ever closer to the Dragon's Throne. Her dreams came true in 1861, when during the course of a single night she became at once Empress Regent on behalf of her son, the heir, friend to the Empress Dowager (widow of Emperor Xian Feng), and the richest woman in China. She would parade through the imperial gardens or the more extensive grounds of the Summer Palace carried in a litter or sedan-chair and accompanied by hundreds of high functionaries, soldiers, ladies in waiting, concubines, and eunuchs. In summer the eunuchs would bring all that was necessary to prepare a meal with them: little ovens, pots and pans, food and dishes, so that at any time the Empress wished, in any spot which took her fancy, she could order them to prepare a meal.

Hundreds of dishes were served at these impromptu meals, many of which were pre-prepared and transported in special containers so that they could be reheated quickly. Ci Xi was not only a gourmet, she was also a glutton. She loved wheatflour bread, which was baked in all sorts of shapes for her: flowers, fruit, dragons, and butterflies, seasoned with salt, pepper, covered with seeds, steamed or fried in oil. She was not overfond of Chinese wine and drank a great deal of tea, scented with flower petals such as chrysanthemums, roses, jasmine, and honeysuckle. She took great pleasure in inventing new jams and conserves and woe betide the eunuchs if they could not carry out her recipe instructions to her satisfaction. One of her more bizarre recipes involved frying the tender young leaves of lotus and magnolia in butter.

Among the most outstanding dishes included in her menus were swallows' nests, shark's fins, sea cucumbers, and an unfamiliar addition to the repertoire of the palace kitchens: steamed duck's feet and tongues. (In one meal, she managed to eat no less than 30 of these.) The Empress was also fond of pork, her particular weakness being for "tinkling bells" (pig's skin cut into tiny pieces and fried so that they were crisp on the outside, soft and tender inside). She liked to

10

end a meal with winter melon, filled with fruit, lotus and other seeds, pine nuts, cured raw ham, and chicken. This combination of ingredients was steamed for several hours. One of her ladies in waiting wrote: "Her majesty's appetite has never ceased to amaze me."

Surprisingly, portraits of Ci Xi, especially the one painted by Katherine Carl in 1903 and exhibited at the World Fair that year in St. Louis, show the Empress, aged 68, as slim with a fine complexion.

PROFLIGACY AT THE LAST EMPEROR'S COURT

According to the tradition established under the Qing dynasty (1644–1911) the Emperor usually ate alone. Meals were prepared in three different imperial kitchens: the tea kitchen supplied drinks and beverages, notably a butter tea made with milk, cream, salt, and yellow tea; the patisserie kitchen produced cookies and cakes made with flour; the main kitchen was responsible for all the dishes served at mealtimes. There was also a further kitchen, in the "Inner Court," always ready to satisfy sudden whims or fancies. These three official kitchens served breakfast at 6–7 a.m., lunch at 1 p.m., and dinner at 6 p.m. These mealtimes are still observed in China today. The Chinese breakfast (and the Emperor's was no exception) was, unlike a Western breakfast, a very substantial meal. The Emperor Qian Long reigned from 1735 to 1796 and his son Jia Qing (1796–1820) recorded one of his breakfasts in the fourth year of his reign. One morning in 1799 at 7.30 in the morning, Qian Long went to the Yang Xing dian (Palace of Nourishment of the Character.) On the table 40 dishes awaited him: swallows' nest soup, duck, chicken, deer's tail, pork, rice flour cakes, pies, small pastries and dumplings, hot and peppery vegetable conserves...

"The water for cooking the ingredients for the dishes and for making the tea was brought fresh daily to the Palace from the spring at Yuquan Shan (the Hill of the Jade Fountain) in the purple Bamboo Park, to the north of the capital. Two ministers were responsible for the smooth running of the kitchens and the high standards of imperial meals. In that year more than 30,000 silver taels were spent on purchases of chickens, duck, pork, fish, and vegetables; all the rest was "donated" by various provinces. This wild extravagance had continued during the short reign of the last Emperor of China, Pu Yi, and he criticized it himself in his autobiography, written when he was in prison. After describing the procession of dozens of eunuchs, each one bearing a dish sent from the imperial kitchen to the dining room, Pu Yi remembers that there were three tables laden with pies, rice, and porridge and another small table on which were spread out a variety of salt-pickled preserved vegetables. These were only the appetizers and the final course. The main selection of dishes was paraded before the Emperor so that he could make his choice.

Pu Yi's wife, the Empress Long Yu, had followed the example of her predecessor Ci Xi and could choose from a hundred dishes at each meal, spread out on six tables. All this abundance was even more wasteful than was at first apparent since none of it was, in fact, eaten by the Emperor. The imperial meal was prepared in the Empress's private kitchens by superb cooks who prepared about 20 exquisite dishes for the Son of Heaven's every meal. Why all this waste? Firstly, it was an exhibition, to be interpreted as proof of wealth, magnificence, and plenty; secondly, such customs were written in the imperial protocol and tradition demanded it. It is not surprising that the lamentable state of the imperial purse deteriorated further. The deposed Emperor recounted how: "According to palace records, in the second year of my reign, the Empress Regent Long Yu, the four imperial wives and I consumed 3,960 cattes of meat [more than two tonnes], 388 chickens and ducks; I was recorded as having accounted for 810 cattes of the meat total [about half a tonne] and 240 of the chicken and duck total. All this was supposed to have been eaten by a child of four!" Perhaps the eunuchs took their tasting duties a little too seriously.

While the empire was crumbling and China was suffering from famine, in the Forbidden City the imperial family was squandering nearly 15,000 silver taels on food alone. This was inexcusable waste and profligacy yet it cannot be denied, in very slight mitigation, that the court cooks had been encouraged to achieve a degree of perfection in their culinary art which has left its mark on Chinese cooking. After many bleak years, the national cuisine has started to flower again. There is bound to be tremendous variety in the cooking of a nation composed of 56 ethnic groups which has the products of a vast country, ranging through very many different climatic conditions and an immensely industrious population to provide raw materials. This book aims to give a selection of dishes which are representative of the national and regional cuisine yet are sufficiently straightforward to be prepared at home.

Edoardo Fazzioli

The subdivision of China into four geographical areas, North, East, South, and West, indicates the differences in climate and tradition that prevail in this vast country. In spite of this, food is a unifying spirit throughout China, synonymous with fellowship, pleasure, and culture.

CONTINUITY AND VARIETY IN CHINESE COOKING

12

The expression "Chinese cooking" is a broadly descriptive term for the food we in the West associate with this vast country, an area covering about 2.5 million square miles, stretching across many latitudes and longitudes, its landscape changing from coast to inland plain, to the harsh mountains of the Roof of the World, from swamps and marshlands to deserts, and with a different climate in each region. This enormous country is peopled by nearly one billion inhabitants, a total which accounts for about one quarter of all humanity.

The foodstuffs, both primary and secondary, used by all these people are almost infinitely varied. This is not so surprising when we remember what an important part food and the ritual of eating plays in the Chinese philosophy of life. Food, its preparation and consumption, fulfills a vitally important bonding role between family members, their friends, and those with whom they work. The type of food consumed, the cooking techniques, and the ambiance in which it is eaten are all thought by the Chinese to be contributory factors to physical, mental, and spiritual well-being.

Concepts of good manners, tradition, and enjoyment of life are handed down from father to son and these may be heavily influenced by religious considerations. Many customs apparently inspired by religion are, in fact, rules for good health based on knowledge gained from centuries of experience and observation; certain foods or practices could be dangerous, whereas others promoted physical fitness and freedom from disease. Some of these customs did, however, spring from deeply held beliefs, such as those of animists (Buddhists among them) who felt that killing and eating other sentient beings was wrong on several counts.

The Chinese never lose sight of the fact that food has two main roles: it is essential to maintain life (and with China's history of dreadful famines, the people are unlikely to forget this) and it is also the source of stability and harmony for the individual and for society at large.

Eating the correct foods has a beneficial effect on the mind and the emotions and is thought to promote good behavior at the same time as increasing strength and determination. The object is to achieve a balance between two apparently contrasting but actually complementary elements, Yin and Yang, which can be identified in the differences between the sexes, in the

relationship between mind and body and in the coexistence of altruism, unselfishness, kindness, cheerfulness, and good manners with courage, power, and decisiveness.

To a Westerner there is something contradictory in this high-minded theory and the reality of everyday life in China. There have always been extreme contrasts between the unfortunate lot of the masses in China and the comparatively few, prosperous élite sections of society. This was far more marked

Rice is a staple food in China. The plates on these pages are taken from Ben Cao's imperial pharmacological encyclopedia (sixteenth century).

in the past but inequalities still persist to this day, often due to the differences in population density and in the fertility of different regions of China and to a low average per capita production and income by Western standards. Many of China's millions cannot afford any but the simplest foods and insufficient of even these to eat to satiety and their dishes will often be low in protein content, and comparatively plainly cooked. However, even the Chinese peasant subsisting largely on cereals such as rice, noodles, corn or sweet potatoes will try to acquire a few extra ingredients to add savor to the plain fare, such as salty sauces, spices, dried fish or vegetables. For special occasions, such as weddings or other important celebrations, a poor man will get himself deeply in debt to be able to treat his family to the more expensive foods such as pork.

Chinese food reflects a search for balance and contrast not only in its ingredients but also in tastes and textures: "opposites" are combined in the same dish, in sweet-sour sauces and sweet-salty flavors. Sometimes the actual foodstuffs will provide the contrast either in taste, such as sweet or mild mixed with bitter, or in texture, combining softness with crispness, and in color, using dark and pale ingredients. Besides such contrasts within an individual dish, a wider contrast is provided by the variety of dishes all served at the same time; a meal can thus consist of a juxtaposition of simple and complicated dishes, sweet and mild versus sour flavors, bitter versus salty, bland versus hot and peppery, or simply hot versus cold in temperature. Modern Western cooks observe certain taboos which would simply not occur to the Chinese, such as mixing fish and meat in the same dish, or serving the same vegetable in more than one guise at the same meal. Although there are many obvious differences in serving and eating conventions between East and West the most fundamental difference lies in the absence of limitations and constraints in Chinese cooking as to what can be eaten and in the omnipresent Chinese respect for tradition. This is still very strongly rooted in the Chinese mentality, although perhaps somewhat weakened for a while by the Cultural Revolution which swept away all the old traditions for several years, among them the love of fine cooking and all it had symbolized down the ages.

Foreigners experiencing Chinese cuisine for the first time are often taken aback, not only by some of the ingredients used, rarely or never seen on tables in the West (such as jellyfish, sea cucumbers, swallows' nests and dried shark's fin) but also because even familiar ingredients acquire totally different tastes when prepared in the Chinese way. A Westerner may be accustomed to eating pork spareribs but will hardly recognize them when they have been roasted with honey; he will react similarly to fish when cooked with ginger or braised in rice wine and soy sauce.

Equally unusual, treatments include stuffed dumplings, "candied" pork fritters, lamb cutlets boiled and flavored with star anise, ginger, cinnamon, garlic, and chili pepper, chicken with sesame seeds, chicken with soy sauce and rose petal liquor. The differences are produced by the choice of certain ingredients, the method of preparation, the cooking technique, even the way in which the raw materials are cut (there are 16 methods of cutting and 11 distinctive shapes in the Chinese repertoire).

Swallow's nests are a gourmet Chinese dish. The birds glue the nests together with a gelatinous liquid secreted from their beaks.

Nearly all writers on China stress the importance of historical background and the effects of thousands of years of civilization, with particular reference to the influence of the many imperial dynasties that ruled China

14

and the effects of invasion and conquest. This prompts the question of when a national, distinctive type of cooking began to evolve, and how far it is possible to attribute this to historical events. The primary sources consulted by most researchers date back to 3,000 years before Christ, when Europe was passing through its Iron and Bronze ages, when the great Mediterranean and Middle Eastern kingdoms were being established, during eras when Nineveh and Babylon, Crete and Mycenae were founded and prospered. Certain parallels can therefore be drawn between the development of the southern Europeans, the peoples of the Middle East, and those of Asia. Many historians maintain that during this period, at the very beginning of recorded history, some regions of greater China, and particularly those around Peking in the north, culinary skill and knowledge was already highly developed.

Boiling and, more particularly, steaming are known to have been used as a cooking method in China from very ancient times but were only introduced into European cooking relatively recently in archaeological and anthropological terms.

Looking at the hypotheses of those who have studied the ancient narrative texts and their painstaking reconstruction of how life may have been lived in those far-off times, we are left with the impression that what we think of as strange and baffling customs and techniques are logical steps in man's development of his skills, which sooner or later occur in most societies. This occurred in the Far East before the West, and perhaps not at random.

The social and political events during the reigns of the imperial dynasties may well have been determining factors in the evolution of Chinese cooking. From the earliest times, the rulers of China and their political and economic fortunes must have had considerable influence on the type of crops grown, the animals reared for meat, and the wildlife and fish that were hunted. The ethnic origins of these dynasties must also have counted for something. The great Shang dynasty is a good example; this is the first to have left some records and concrete evidence of its existence, after an era described only in myth and legend, telling of monarchs with symbolic names. Tales from this dynasty, 2,000 years before Christ, conjure up a picture of great tiger and elephant hunts; evidence that the very early varieties of millet and other ancient varieties of cereals were already being sown and cultivated, while the ancient inhabitants of China fished for giant carp; all these activities provided them with raw materials which were already undergoing relatively sophisticated cooking techniques. Archeologists have found elegant bronze and ceramic artefacts

Top: red Yangshao terracotta bowl dating from the Neolithic period (fifth–fourth century B.C.). Above: bronze tripod of the Ting type, dating from the Shang-yin dynasty (twelfth–eleventh century B.C.). Museo Nazionale d'Arte Orientale, Rome.

which suggest that food preparation and presentation had already achieved some splendor. Yet it is only informed guesswork, inferred from archeological excavations, that links the birthplace of this dynasty with the people who inhabited the Hunan region and possibly the Shandong peninsula at that time. It must also be remembered that there is no written evidence to confirm the dates of these ancient reigns and provide information about the earliest dynasties: all we have so far to tell us about them are the traces they left behind. As to the events which are said to have taken place, the names and the deeds, the borderline between legend and history is blurred until the compilation of the first

Chinese chronicles in the eighth century B.C., in the middle of the Zhou dynasty's reign. Confucianism spread through China during this era and the borders of the empire were extended southward and westward. The first insurgencies of the nomadic peoples across what were then China's northern borders convulsed this highly developed Chinese society.

The Xiung Nu barbarians, who originally came from Siberia, and who are mentioned by the chroniclers toward 300 B.C., have been identified by some historians as belonging to the Huns, the same race that swept through Europe laying to waste everything in their path. The Great Wall of China was built as a barrier to keep these barbarians out; Prince Gin Shihuang Di of the Qin or Ch'in dynasty is believed to have been responsible for its construction which started in 221 B.C. The influence of the various barbarian invasions which the Great Wall was only partially successful in preventing was significant but patchy; around A.D. 1200 Genghis Khan's invading hordes finally swept over the wall and overran China. It was during the Qin dynasty that China assumed roughly its present form under one ruler, and encompassed the Szechwan basin, an area vitally important for its fertile land and as a rich source of many foods and raw materials, and the southern plains of Guangdong within its borders, leading the way to the development and exploitation of the coastal regions.

These frontiers were consolidated by the following Han dynasty, making it possible to open up trade routes; their reign saw flourishing commercial activity and relative political stability on the northwestern frontiers once they had achieved a decisive victory in the long fight with the Xiung Nu. During the third century B.C. Chinese ideas and customs were adopted by the nomads, spreading along the trade routes, just as later on, in the early years of our millennium the religion and moral philosophy of Buddhism were brought by nomads along trade routes into China, and with them a vegetarian diet and meat-free dishes.

During this period in Chinese history, a respite between turbulent times of grave social unrest, the imperial civilization became increasingly refined and highly civilized: paper is thought to have been invented then, making it possible for ideas to be disseminated far more widely. The pursuit of luxury among the privileged classes led to far greater variety and elaboration in culinary matters. Progress in the use of wheat is recorded, and in improvements in milling, the development of the technique of extracting liquid from the soybean and curdling this to make tofu (bean curd) as were the earliest known cultivation of vines, garlic, and other vegetables and plants not known to have been grown earlier.

Weighed against these instances of progress was the hardship and abject poverty suffered by the peasants. This led to popular uprisings, to civil wars and a political dislocation which lasted for nearly three centuries, weakening China and making her vulnerable to invasion by the Turco-Mongol nomadic peoples. These invading hordes extended the influence of the Xiung Nu power southward, along the inside of the great bow of the Yellow River as far as the Shani region, with the Chinese emperors hemmed in within the southern part of today's China.

These barbarians must have left their mark on the eating habits of the indigenous Chinese, converting them to the consumption of lamb, mutton, and goat's meat and, perhaps, kumiss (fermented sheep's milk).

The last of the six dynasties which followed one another in comparatively quick succession was the Sui dynasty, who were originally northerners: in A.D. 589 they conquered the southern imperial kingdom, unified all the Chinese provinces, and eventually extinguished Turkish territorial ambitions, reaffirming Chinese supremacy in central Asia. The Su dynasty was short-lived but left many lasting monuments in the form of their public works. Apart from these, marvelous culinary innovations are attributed to this period, such as fried rice Yang-chow or Canton style and the widely adopted custom of dim sum, an amazing variety of hot delicacies which were to become one of the glories of Chinese cuisine. These had probably been eaten in some form or other before this period, since few dishes or food preparations are invented out of the blue, but by this time they were probably recognizable as the delicious little tidbits we eat today.

The accession to power of the Tang dynasty (618–907) was to signal China's unification and greatly strengthened power as well as exceptional prosperity and population growth and the development of China's administrative system or civil service. This dynasty's capital was the city of Xian (formerly Chang) and the records of the time tell us that life at their court reached dizzying heights of luxury and refinement, mirrored by the great cities of the south which became very important cultural and commercial centers as well as meccas of fashion.

The Tang emperors spread Chinese civilization as far away as Tibet, and to Iran and the Indian subcontinent. Subsequently, however, they were confronted by a new Mongol power, in one of the surges in the ebb and flow of supremacy in these regions, during which the triumph of Chinese civilization would alternate with other customs being assimilated when her

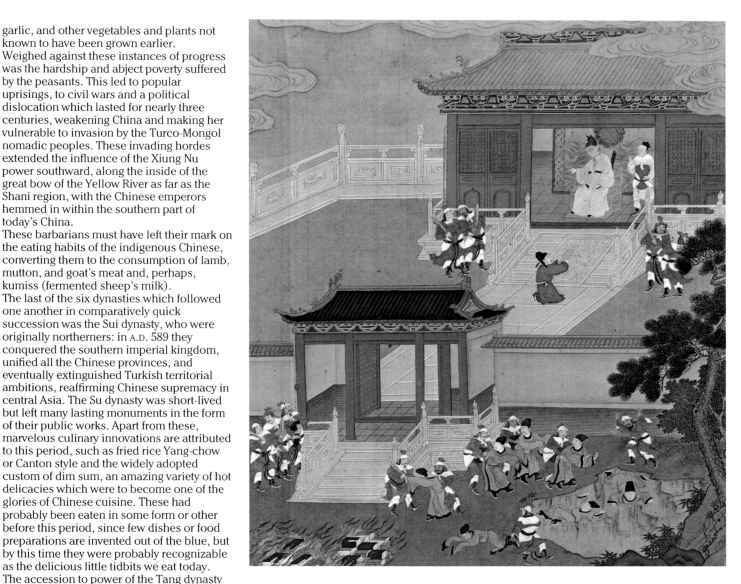

barbarian neighbors were victorious; first Chinese tradition and culture would prevail, then another wave of invasions would bring more alien ways and customs into China, further enriching the great variety of Chinese cooking among other facets of everyday life. These vicissitudes had a less positive, fragmenting effect on political power during the first half of the tenth century, leading indirectly to rebellion in the southern region of Vietnam which gained its independence from China in A.D. 939, becoming an autonomous state which has survived in one form or another to this day and it is interesting to see how, despite the comparatively recent secession of the country from China, Vietnam's cooking has developed a distinctive character and repertoire of dishes very much its own. In the year 960 a military coup brought the Song

Shih Huang Di, who built the famous Great Wall, waged a savage campaign for the destruction of books (from Traits . . . des Empereurs Chinois, *thirteenth century.)*

rulers to power and their dynasty was to last for just over 300 years until 1279 when it succumbed in turn, overwhelmed by a series of Mongol invasions. The Song emperors had attempted to restore the "civil empire" of earlier rulers, reviving ancient traditions, entrusting important governmental roles to the high echelons of their civil service, the Mandarins, who belonged to the most highly educated class. Unfortunately their attempts at economic reforms and encouragement of trade (the tea trade in particular) were not

16

successful. The agrarian crisis of the ninth century gradually deepened, and by the eleventh century it had become chronic. After years of savagely fought wars, bringing with them massacre and destruction, Kubla Khan (nephew of Genghis Khan who had united all the Turco-Mongol tribes under his command by 1206) managed to reunify China under Mongol rule; he proclaimed himself emperor and founded the Yuan dynasty (1280–1368).

Kubla Khan found himself ruling over a vast territory whose decimated and exhausted population looked to the new emperor to revitalize the country, and Kubla Khan did carry out public works such as the planning and construction of a network of great highways, the building of the Imperial Canal which links the two great rivers of China, the Yangtze (the Blue River) to the Huang Ho (the Yellow River) linking these with Tientsin and joining up with the Hai Ho.

This Mongol dynasty also tried to improve the lot of slave workers, peasants, and small farmers, large numbers of whom were dying of starvation; many reforms were put in the statute book but were never implemented.

Eventually, the destitute masses rebelled against the rich and this developed into an uprising against the Mongols, bringing a new order, the Ming dynasty, to power.

It appears that the Mongols were resistant to the civilizing influence of their subjects and they retained their dietary customs, eating a good deal of raw meat with a preference for horse meat, donkey meat, and mutton, their favorite drink being fermented sheep's milk. The Mongols and Tartars have left their mark on Chinese cooking, especially in the north, where the population still eat these meats, less readily consumed elsewhere in China, the last example of a significant influx of barbarians' customs being absorbed by the native Chinese population.

The Ming dynasty (1368–1644) is considered the last truly Chinese dynasty. It played an important role in the development of what we could call modern Chinese cuisine, when Chinese food became recognizable in approximately its present form.

Certain events must have had some bearing on how the culinary tradition developed during the centuries that followed. Peking was chosen as the new capital in preference to the old capital of Nanking; early in the reign foreign trade flourished, promoting an interchange of customs and products with other countries. Other, much less constructive trends also affected China: the scourge of Japanese piracy which was to plague the Chinese until the end of the fifteenth century and class warfare which, between them, first sapped and, in the sixteenth century, destroyed a flourishing maritime trade with the Moslem countries, east Africa, central America and even with neighboring India.

European penetration of China started in the early sixteenth century with the establishment of trading posts and Catholic missions and increased as the Ming reign progressed.

Opulence and conspicuous wealth and refinement were still the order of the day among the privileged classes in China, exciting the greed and envy of neighboring barbarians who threatened her frontiers; as a result the Chinese, once the arbitrators between the warring tribes of Manchuria, promoting the formation of the Manchu League, had to appeal to the Manchu for help in fighting the barbarians and in suppressing the peasant revolts. Thus the Ming dynasty, originally seen as the answer to the grievances of the poor and the solution to social unrest, gradually adopted their

Ming painting depicting the everyday life of ladies at court. From Ch'in Ying, sixteenth century. British Museum, London. The Ming period produced many examples of decorative art.

predecessors' aristocratic and conservative ethos; it was already beset by grave political crises, weakened by popular unrest and finally succumbed to the Manchu invasion. The Manchus supplanted the Ming ruler of the day and founded the Qing dynasty (1644–1911).

This foreign dynasty has gone down in history as the most open to the appreciation of the arts and the finer things in life, and the most deeply imbued with the love of pleasure which is synonymous with being Chinese; the early Manchu rulers were ready and willing to favor indigenous Chinese being appointed as important public servants and were ready to learn from them in cultural matters. This new dynasty was to adopt the hedonism which was traditional in Chinese imperial and aristocratic circles, and pursued both with the utmost dedication.

We have all heard tales of their capricious extravagance and the lengths to which these emperors and their courtiers would go to bring delicacies from the four corners of the empire to Peking by the fastest possible means to ensure they arrived in good condition, of their opulent banquets in the Forbidden City where the court was set apart from the outside world in the heart of Peking, the capital chosen by the preceding dynasty, but the Manchus also brought some of their own customs and retained them, such as use of the Mongolian hotpot, which was to become part of the Chinese culinary repertoire. Their reign was punctuated by violent attempts to break up the vast estates held by aristocratic landowners and by the invasion of Tibet culminating in the occupation of Lhasa in 1720. Conflicts with the Siberians and the Russians were followed, toward the end of the eighteenth century, by the breaking up of the Manchu empire, mainly as a result of the Manchu loathing of all things European, exacerbated by the increasingly frequent intervention of the European powers into China's affairs. By this time we can assume that Chinese cooking and the Chinese attitude to food were very much as we know them now. They remained largely untouched and unchanged by all the events and changes which took place during the nineteenth century: the cession of Hong Kong to the British; the trading concessions granted to the United States and France; the treaties concluded with Japan under duress, resulting from the Sino-Japanese war. This unhappy century for the Chinese also brought attacks on China by certain European powers and encouragement by them of elements and trends harmful to her people in order to weaken her and enrich themselves, which led to xenophobic revolts, such as the Boxer Rebellion and the launching of a joint European expeditionary force to end it, leading to the sack of Peking (1900). The Manchus steadfastly refused to alter their way of life or to temper the legendary magnificence of their court and in particular of the imperial table. It seemed that nothing could subdue the mind, heart, and stomach of the legendary "dragon" of China. There was, however, another side to the coin. Political turmoil, chronic famine, and uncertainty because of mismanagement and foreign incursions all contributed toward the decision of many Chinese to emigrate. Many went to Australia, to North and Central America, to Malaya, South Africa, and to European countries. Most, but by no means all, were peasants and workers, soldiers who had left the army, people of modest means who filled low-paid jobs. Large numbers of these emigrants were to work as cooks, preparing the food of their country of adoption, often for workers almost as poor as themselves (many took such jobs in newly settled areas and remote outstations in the United States, Canada, Australia and

elsewhere) while others worked in Chinese restaurants owned by their better educated and more prosperous fellow immigrants, cooking Chinese food for their fellow countrymen and, later on, making a good living serving Chinese food to the inhabitants of their adopted country, from the ubiquitous Chinese takeouts. Others owned shops selling Oriental foodstuffs.

From being a culinary art shrouded in mystery, Chinese cuisine thus spread all over the world. The cooking of two regions was to predominate in this export of culinary skills: that of the south, known as Cantonese cooking, by far the most widely known, and that of the northern, or Peking school, less widely known, while Western connoisseurs of Chinese cooking and old China hands have long maintained that the western school, Szechwan cooking was greatly undervalued, an acquired taste which only the discriminating had learned to appreciate. The much more delicate, subtle, and refined tastes of the east of China, typified by Shanghai cooking, was also not nearly so highly renowned as it should be. Many of the expatriate Chinese who cooked in small restaurants had very little knowledge or experience and theirs were often less than authentic versions of traditional Chinese recipes. Foreigners were not always being introduced to genuine Chinese cuisine and sometimes they judged (and condemned) the whole culinary tradition after sampling these travesties of Chinese gastronomy.

The Revolution transformed China into a People's Republic in this century after power had alternated between moderate nationalists and radical communists, with such milestones as the Long March of the Communist army (1934–5) and the retreat of the Nationalist army to Taiwan (1949). The long grim years of World War II and the need to survive the Japanese invasion showed how adept the Chinese were at living at subsistence level. This was certainly not an era in which the niceties of ancient gastronomic customs were likely to be greatly regarded and this neglect must have reached its nadir during Mao's Cultural Revolution. The Chinese people's potential for recovery, however, is lengendary and a visitor to Shanghai who searches out the food stalls and humbler eating houses where the workers take their midday meal, from among the myriad restaurants and cafés, will not find that their fast food consists of hamburgers or French fries but the far more healthy and nourishing steamed stuffed buns and a very wide choice of dim sum.

In such a vast country, where climate and basic foodstuffs vary greatly, it is inevitable that the cooking will differ from province to province. Although a more complicated classification of the differing areas might be

17

more meticulously accurate (many cookery experts divide China into eight parts for this purpose: Peking, Shandong, Jiangsu, Anhvi, Guangdong, Fujian, Szechwan and Henan) the more generalized, large-scale division into four large geographical sectors gives a good general impression of the food one is likely to encounter in these regions.

EATING CHINESE STYLE

Ingredients and recipes are only half the story when it comes to teaching the novice how the Chinese take their meals. The first step is to learn what form these meals take and how the dishes are served.

The selection of dishes is not only important from a nutritional point of view, to ensure that the correct proportion of carbohydrates, proteins, fats, and vitamins are present; when the Chinese prepare an elaborate meal, they also take an enormous amount of trouble to make sure that it satisfies aesthetic and other criteria. There is a great deal of poetic and symbolic meaning implicit in food preparation and the considerations of balancing foods in the context of the principles of Yin and Yang are constantly borne in mind. Chinese recipes are interesting from a dietician's point of view because the method of ensuring a well-balanced diet is different from ours, their distinction between sources of essential nutrients more subtle. We grow up with the idea that one component of a main course will be meat for our protein, another potatoes for carbohydrates and, say, green vegetables for vitamins, roughage, trace elements etc. The Chinese will combine many, and sometimes most, of the elements needed for a good diet in one dish. The same approach applies to the composition of a meal: while we are used to having clear distinctions drawn between courses and between the type of dishes served for certain courses, the Chinese custom is to serve all or most of the dishes at the same time and much more mixing of different types of food is practised: meat or tofu or soy flour noodles will be combined with vegetables in one dish, while a dish in which the principal ingredient is meat may also include vegetables, fruit, or vegetable broth. Chinese vegetarian dishes often comprise sprouts and beans and vegetables or fruit with a high lipid content, thus amply fulfilling the requirements for protein and fat. A revealing convention, showing just how much Western and Chinese attitudes to meals differ, is that of increasing the number of different dishes as the number of eaters rises: one or two dishes, each a composite dish, will be served if there are only one or two people to be catered for; if the number increases, then so will the variety of dishes: four, five, six or eight (or more) different ones will be placed in front of the assembled eaters. In the West we increase the quantities but still restrict ourselves to one, two or at most three or four courses. For everyday eating, most people in China expect to sit down to a meal consisting of one dish, or at most one main dish with a couple of side dishes. This main dish will be based on the time-honored bowl of rice or noodles with accompaniments of salty or spicy sauces and a little meat or vegetables, traditional peasant fare and still served to workers and students all over China, varying a little from region to region but basically a cereal of one type or another providing bulk and the additional ingredients depending on what is available, affordable and, in many cases, what is permitted by the consumer's religion. In the West our staple, and most symbolic, food has usually been bread; in China it is rice or noodles. These are also cheap, abundant, and filling.

Although rice is only one of the cereals grown and consumed in China, and cultivated only in certain areas, it has nevertheless always been understood there as the synonym for food and nourishment, invested with an almost sacred quality: "fan" is Chinese for "rice" but has also come to mean "food" and "a meal." "Have you eaten your rice?" is a greeting to friends and acquaintances which means "How are you?" or "Is all well with you?" "The lid has been taken off the rice dish" is the announcement which means that a meal is ready, when inviting guests to sit down to a meal.

Chinese meals acquire a very strong feeling of intimacy and fellowship from the custom of all those present helping themselves to a little food from a variety of dishes with their own chopsticks, and a code of good manners has of necessity been developed: if a guest is present, he will be offered to help himself first. It is considered bad manners to take one's favorite item without considering the other people at the table; since each person must consider other people's preferences, everyone can be sure of having at least some of the choicest foods. It is considered good form (within reason) to have a good appetite, as a sign of appreciation of the dishes which have been placed on the table. Such rituals assume much greater importance on special

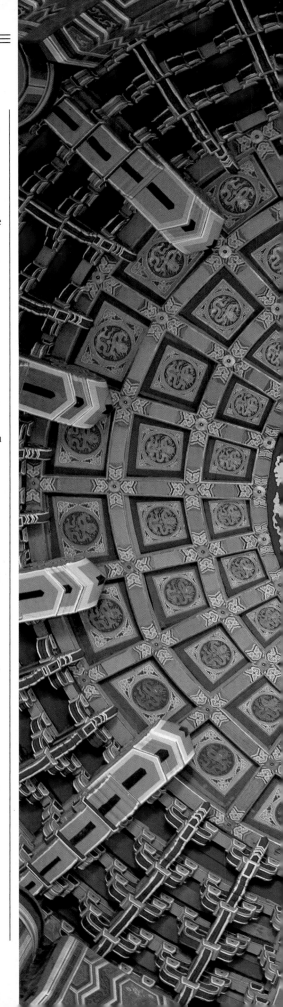

Wooden ceiling from the Altar of Heaven, Peking. The architectural features of this temple in the Forbidden City have a symbolic meaning: the columns represent the seasons and months, and the circular shape of the building suggests the sky. Here, during the Ming period, the emperor would celebrate the spring ritual for a faborable grain harvest.

occasions, when many people have been invited to a meal; the host or hostess will want to make a good impression and give pleasure to everyone by making sure that a wide variety of dishes are served. However elaborate and copious the feast, it is good form for hosts to be self-deprecating, apologizing that there are not more delicacies.

There is a golden rule in the Chinese code of good table manners: the host and his wife sit in the least desirable place (near a draughty door, if there is one, or with their backs to a window) while all the consideration is for the comfort of their guests, to whom every care and attention is shown.

The dishes served on special occasions and for celebratory feasts will depend on the wealth of the hosts, the rank or position of the guests, and on whether the occasion is a very formal one or more of a friendly, informal affair. If relatives or friends are invited, then things will be kept simple, with a big dish of rice (or noodles) in the center of the table with, perhaps, a large bowl of steaming soup (which those present will ladle into their bowls and drink to refresh themselves before, during and after the meal, without using a spoon). Fairly simple dishes will add interest and variety to these basic items.

At official or ceremonial dinners no rice, noodles, bread or buns await the diners as they take their seats at table. At least eight elaborate dishes will be served and often twelve or many more. On such occasions each guest has a full place setting laid out: cup, plate, bowl, spoon, and chopsticks; not the everyday utensils and dishes but made of fine china, while the chopsticks will probably be ebony.

Cold dishes and appetizers will have been arranged on the table ready for the banquet to begin; soup will not only be served at the beginning of the meal but also after each set of dishes.

A round table is the favored shape, often with a lazy Susan (a revolving stand) in the center to make it easy for each guest to take a selection of foods. The meal will get under way with toasts of warmed rice wine drunk to the health of the guests. Reciprocal toasts are drunk at various stages during the meal.

At the end of the meal, when everyone seems to have eaten their fill, the host will have a magnificent whole fish dish placed on the table, representing a superfluity of food, a subtle way of suggesting that there is no end to his prodigality; fried rice, noodles and steamed buns may be placed on the table with the fish or instead of it, to underline by their simplicity just how different from ordinary, everyday food the preceding, magnificent meal has been, and how full of unusual and prized delicacies.

As we have seen, when it comes to less grand

occasions, the number of different dishes served will depend on how many guests are present and it is important to remember this when you are following a Chinese recipe: usually these recipes will only be sufficient for four people, provided other dishes are served at the same time. When the recipe calls for a large fish, duck, a lamb leg or other large pieces of meat, then obviously this does not apply. Amounts of ingredients are calculated to achieve the correct visual and gastronomic effect and it is better not to increase quantities; do as the Chinese do and add another recipe or several more to your menu: each person will take a little less of each dish but will still have plenty to eat. If, however, you prefer not to go to the trouble of preparing a wider variety of dishes (which sometimes daunts Western cooks) then it is hardly a crime to apply Western habits to Chinese food and, say, double the ingredients while using a little discernment. Many Chinese restaurants make a concession to Western usage and go against their own traditions by serving larger portions. The order in which the recipes are listed in this book would not be recognizable to the Chinese: the division of dishes into soups, fish dishes, poultry and meat dishes, vegetables, desserts etc. would seem incomprehensibly arbitrary to them. Some concessions have to be made for international tastes, however. In most countries, there are some dishes which are synonymous with traditional celebrations and special occasions; nowhere is this more true than in China, where certain foods and recipes are highly symbolic and so closely linked to certain events that it would be unthinkable to leave them off the menu (worst of all, their omission might bring bad luck). We have indicated the recipes that are associated with festivals and with famous myths and folklore.

The Chinese have retained their conception of food as a sacrificial and propitiatory offering to the dead, to their ancestors, and to the gods: ever practical and pragmatic, these votive offerings remain symbolic, for the food is usually consumed by the donor after it has been offered. The scents, smoke, and replicas of food are enough to satisfy the dead; it is the intention that counts. Chinese wisdom maintains that we are what we eat; this idea dates back thousands of years and means that many of the dishes served today are made to ancient recipes, which are reputed to furnish particular benefits for the physical, mental and spiritual well-being of those who eat them, and induce a sense of balance and serenity (in accordance with the theory of Yin and Yang). Wisdom, sensuality, mysticism, and culinary prowess are often personified by symbolic characters of Chinese mythology, to whom legend

attributes miraculous inventions and amazingly clever solutions to problems that once upon a time vexed emperors and rulers, heroes and martyrs, lovers, and poets. This may account for the skill with which Chinese cooks can shape any foodstuffs, be they rice, flour, vegetables or tofu, into a phoenix, dragon, serpents and birds, or symbolic, abstract shapes, all full of auspicious symbolism, for the esthetic dimension of cooking provides allusions to desirable virtues and moral strengths at the same time as providing nourishment and promoting equilibrium.

DRINKING CHINESE STYLE AND THE TEA CEREMONY

Where alcoholic beverages are concerned, the Chinese have apparently patterned their drinking habits on the simple and logical application of certain fundamental principles. Religious or moral considerations may necessitate abstinence, or this may be imposed involuntarily due to poverty. Choice may be limited by restricted local supplies but, like most of us, the Chinese do not drink just to slake their thirst, but to enjoy themselves, to celebrate the joys of friendship, and to observe the rites of hospitality.

At table, the Chinese drink when they wish, without feeling they have to observe hard and fast gastronomic rules; some drink only clear soups or light broths during a meal. Many Westerners believe, wrongly, that the Chinese drink tea with their meals but this is not the custom. Most Chinese who can afford it, however, do enjoy tea after the end of the meal and at intervals between meals. All this talk of broths and tea might seem to suggest that the Chinese are very abstemious; not so: many drink warmed rice wine throughout the meal, taking tea only at the meal's conclusion. There is a growing tendency to drink spirits at mealtimes: in the north, during the icy winters, some drink Kaoliang, a spirit with a very high alcohol content; elsewhere hard liquor or spirits may also be drunk, often Western style, such as brandy and Cognac distilled from wine, or whisky made with malted barley or rye, or even vodka. These are usually diluted with water but are taken straight sometimes. At more formal meals, repeated toasts are usually drunk and the most suitable drink for these occasions is warmed Shao Xing lao jiu, or rice wine, poured from little porcelain bottles or flasks into minute cups; such very small quantities are advisable as the wine is hot, strong, and very quickly goes to the drinker's head. It is, moreover, considered good form for all those present ostentatiously to empty their cups when the first toast is

given at the beginning of a meal. Succeeding toasts do not have to be drained in one mouthful, and often going through the motions of lifting the cup to one's lips is enough, without actually emptying it.
The history of wine production from the alcoholic fermentation of various musts made with certain strains of rice dates back to antiquity in the Orient, at least as far as wine production from grapes in the West, and has been traced back to about 2000 B.C. Rice is not the only material which the Chinese use to make alcohol. Many liquors are distilled from aromatic sugary solutions made with cereals, tubers, bamboo or fruit, such as Szechwan's renowned specialty of gooseberry wine, or the very strong Moutai, made from millet. Mei gui you (well known throughout the world through its popularity with Chinese restaurateurs for their foreign customers in the West) is distilled from fermented grains and scented with rose petals; the Chinese not only drink this spirit as a beverage but also use it to flavor certain dishes. There are plenty of full-blooded

Chinese who like to drink a lot, following the example of some of their most famous poets who (in common with some Western poets) found that alcohol procures the freedom from inhibition sometimes necessary to give inspiration a free rein. The most commonly cited example, Li Bai, is said to have drowned when drunk but perhaps the legend was correct when it said that he threw himself from a boat when in the grip of a hallucination, managed to grasp the moon, mirrored in the deep waters of a lake, and sank to the bottom only to be reunited with the beautiful young girl who had been his muse. Poets were not the only ones to try to achieve a state of ecstasy through drinking alcohol; monks and taoist divines were also wont to attempt it: the antithesis of followers of the Buddhist and Moslem faiths which prohibit alcohol and condemn drunkenness, taking copious draughts of pure water to purify themselves, and infusions of stimulating leaves and herbs for mental concentration and the capacity to endure long hours of prayer.

An interior in a small agricultural village, Majinbao, in Xishuangbanna province. This family meal, traditionally including many vegetables, is consumed in individual bowls around a small bamboo table.

It is a fairly common belief in the West that the Chinese do not drink wine made from grapes and that consequently this type of wine should never be served during an authentic Chinese meal. This is incorrect and goes against the Chinese attitude of eschewing hard and fast rules for matching drink with food. In northern China, many years before the Christian era, the emperors already had vineyards near Peking, and the knowledge of vines and wine making is said to have been introduced to China by Middle Eastern merchants from the Mediterranean basin. It is not clear why vines were relegated to a very minor source of wine for nearly 1,000 years. The European penetration of

22

A table elaborately set for a ritual meal, with chopsticks resting on the appropriate rests so as not to stain the cloth, traditional Chinese dishes, and the inevitable teapots.

China in the nineteenth and early twentieth centuries, in particular of the Catholic missionaries, brought about a revival in the grape's fortunes and wine production was brought up to date. Large vineyards of European varieties of grape were planted, many of which survive to this day. Also in the north, German influence led to beer being brewed and it is still produced on a large scale today. One of the best beers is Yingdao, made in the city of that name. So China even has its grape wine and beer producing regions and consumes the products. Beers and wines are also drunk in the larger cities elsewhere in China.

As a result, beer and wine consumption is rising and imports of these into China are also increasing. In view of this, it seems slightly pedantic to throw up one's hands in horror at the idea of serving beer, or wine made from grapes with Chinese foods in those countries where they are commonly drunk with meals. We cannot talk about Chinese beverages, however, without touching on the hot infusions of flower petals, such as chrysanthemum tea and jasmine-flavored tea, for which we Westerners are sometimes slow to acquire a taste.

Tea is the Chinese beverage *par excellence*, playing an important role in public and private life, and punctuating everyday life: tea after meals, tea as an indispensable sign of hospitality, being both the accompaniment and inspiration for a ritual of courtesy and consideration toward guests, involving careful preparation, pouring, and serving. Perhaps it was purely by chance that the ancient Chinese discovered the agreeably refreshing and stimulating properties of the dried leaves of numerous varieties of the *Camellia sinensis* when infused in freshly boiling water. This plant has been cultivated for thousands of years. An infusion of tea leaves is one of the remedies in the age-old Chinese pharmacopaeia; Buddhist holy men, part monks, part doctors, adopted the habit of drinking tea before they embarked upon protracted periods of meditation, and prescribed the infusion as an antidote to sleep. Tea was certainly consumed in great quantities and had become very popular by the time the poet Lu Yu was active, around the middle of the eighth century. Lu Yu was inspired by pantheistic beliefs and chose tea as the symbol of universal order and harmony, dedicating a treatise to it: *Cha Ching or The Sacred Book of Tea* in three volumes, divided into ten chapters, recording and promulgating rules and ideals which were to stand the test of time, despite many subsequent changes in usage and ritual. As time went by tastes were also bound to change. Tea prepared according to Lu Yu's methods would certainly not be to the taste of Westerners, nor to contemporary Chinese tea drinkers, although it is fascinating to read of the 24 utensils he deems indispensable for correct infusion, the detailed preparation, the types of water that make the best tea, and so on. Nowadays a good deal of the old ritual has been discontinued due to changes in everyday life. Modern methods of transport meant that there was no longer a need for the Masters of Tea, the knowledgeable and flamboyant purveyors of plentiful supplies of freshly brewed tea to the thousands who once traveled by ferry boat or sampan, once the only means of transport in certain areas of China. Their disappearance does not mean that no Masters of Tea remain: the art is still practised by artists, poets, and craftsmen who honor the ritual connected with this noble Oriental beverage.

The cultivation of tea (*cha*) is carried on in many areas of China but is particularly important in the south; in the southeastern province of Yunnan, the physical geography and climate is particularly well suited to the production of very fine tea. There are many different types and these are classified in meticulous detail by the Chinese. As a broad outline the method of preparation provides one way of categorizing them: black (fermented) tea which is strong tasting and reddish in color; green (unfermented) tea, exquisitely fragrant and full-flavored; aromatic or scented tea (mixed with flowers, jasmin being one of the most usual); oolong (semi-fermented) tea, prized as one of the finest of teas because of its full, strong flavor and aroma; white tea (when some of the normal processes are omitted), with a delicate aroma and pale color; and block tea (compressed tea), made with powdered green and black teas that are steamed, then pressed into various shapes and which retain their original fragrance.

It is difficult to give a very detailed account of the tea trade in China. But the Chinese take great care to ensure that production, from the growing stages through harvesting, drying and fermentation, are all carried out to the highest possible standards. They manage to produce teas with delicious aromas, and these are not confined to the two main types of tea (black tea and green tea) but are also made by storing the tea leaves with aromatic plants for a while before they are packed. While Lu Yu's dictates are no longer obeyed, today's Chinese still feel passionately enough about their national drink to follow well-proven rules and rituals which have been copied all over the world. Use freshly boiling water; make the tea in a china teapot and serve it in china cups; allow one teaspoon of tea for each person, plus "one for the pot" when making fairly large quantities. The teapot should be heated by filling it with boiling water before making the tea; as soon as the fresh water for making the tea nears boiling point, the teapot is emptied, the tea placed in it, and then the fast boiling water poured into the pot. An average of 3 minutes' infusion time is allowed for many Chinese teas, but this may vary and the tea drinker's

eye, nose, and palate are probably the best guide to the time needed. In Chinese houses water is always ready for tea-making, showing how this beverage and its preparation is woven into the fabric of everyday life and has assumed an importance beyond that of providing a fragrant, refreshing and invigorating drink for all times of day and all occasions.

CHINESE COOKING UTENSILS

Some people try a few Chinese recipes just for curiosity and for fun, others are perfectionists and determined to do things properly, using all the right equipment for a really authentic end result. Use of the correct kitchen utensils obviously has some effect on the finished dish, just as the choice of instruments has in the interpretation of a piece of music. It is difficult to fry foods successfully in aluminum skillets and impossible to whisk egg whites with a spoon. A wok is really indispensable for some Chinese recipes, being particularly well suited to their techniques of food preparation, just as earthenware casseroles will give the best results for long, slow, and gentle cooking.

There are many types of equipment, manual or automatic, available in kitchen shops and stores, which make light work of certain processes which may seem very difficult. Some gadgets will enable novice Western cooks to copy Chinese techniques: shaped cutters are invaluable when it comes to turning raw vegetables into decorative shapes such as flowers, or slicing the typical oblique sections, julienne strips or cubes and other shapes, tasks at which Chinese cooks are expert. These masters of the art of sculpting raw vegetables are skillful enough to use just a very sharp knife for this visually important aspect of Chinese dishes (the four classic components a master chef will make sure his dishes possess are shape, color, fragrance, and flavor).

In China's fascinating eating houses and on market or street foodstalls customers can marvel at the variety of food and drink prepared while they wait and watch; it is worth having a good look at the utensils being used: very large cooking pots, barbecues or broilers, large steaming ovens, enormous woks and bamboo steamers as well as cast-iron griddles or dry fryers. The old-fashioned cast-iron or bronze water pot is still part of the kitchen equipment in many private houses, sitting on the hotplate of the solid-fuel stove, although electric and gas kettles and cookers are gradually replacing them, together with mass-produced heatproof glass or stainless steel utensils. The Mongolian barbecue or griddle on which

lamb or mutton kabobs are traditionally cooked, the enormous earthenware cooking pot in which soups are made, the sets of bamboo compartments placed over cauldrons of boiling water, used for steaming stuffed buns, rice cakes and puddings, and all the other intriguing, old pieces of traditional equipment are still very much part of the *batterie de cuisine*; they may be relics of bygone ages but they still serve their purpose efficiently and the Chinese rightly see no justification for replacing them just for the sake of change.

First in order of importance comes the *wok*, the most traditional being iron or bronze with a domed lid. The wok is round, with a curved base and sides, almost as though it had been sliced off a sphere. Some have two handles, one on each side, with or without a section of the handle made of wood which is non-conductive and therefore cooler to grasp, or the wok may have one long handle, again either in iron or bronze so that an oven cloth must be used, or with a wooden handle. Woks come in three sizes: small, medium, and very large but the standard size for home use will be about 14 in in diameter and certainly not more than 16 in wide. In a Chinese kitchen the wok rests securely in a hole over the stove or is used over a gas flame; in both cases the flames hug the sides of the wok and this shape therefore promotes even distribution of the heat, and also makes it easy to cook very small quantities, or larger amounts, for four or even six or more people. Besides its lid, the wok may come with a round stand to give stability when it is not being held by the cook. Another accessory for the wok is a grid, usually made of wood, placed inside it and which rests against its sides, on which wood, bamboo or ceramic steamer compartments are placed, keeping them above the water. The shape of the wok dates back hundreds of years and the design must have evolved as the most effective partly through experience, partly from the materials available all those years ago and how they behaved when subjected to heat. Good conductivity was vital so that the cooking vessel would heat up quickly, easily, and with comparatively little fuel; the wok is particularly well suited to fast cooking at very high temperatures.

Tremendously versatile, the wok can be used for making broths or for boiling food; as the water containing base of a steamer; as a skillet for plain broiling; or to sauté, fry or deep-fry, equally effective when large or small quantities of oil or fat are used. When it comes to braising and very slow cooking, for making soups or blanching, it is probably better to use earthenware cooking pots or casseroles, or stainless steel pans. It is a good idea to use Western style stainless steel pans as containers of the boiling water when

steaming as they are more stable, and if you already have stainless steel steaming inserts which slot into one another, with a lid fitting snugly into the top one, then these can also be used instead of buying the more traditional Chinese steamers. A flat-bottomed cast-iron pan can be used for semi deep-frying instead of the wok. An electric deep-fryer is safest for deep-frying. But when it comes to quick frying, shallow-frying, and above all stir-frying, especially when several different ingredients have to be stir-fried separately or added one after the other and then combined in typically Chinese cooking techniques, then the wok is unsurpassed.
A wok should be heated well before the oil is added, then tipped carefully this way and that for the oil to coat the hot sides of the wok; the food to be cooked should be added immediately afterward and, in the case of stir-frying, quickly stirred and turned.
A similar treatment applies to seasoning a new, unused wok before you cook in it for the first time: heat the wok, brush it all over the inside with oil, rinse the oil off with very hot water (never use detergent or any type of abrasive); wipe the inside and outside of the wok with kitchen towels, using fresh towels, and continue to wipe the wok until it is absolutely dry and wiping the inside no longer leaves marks on the towels. After cooking rinse the wok with very hot water and dry off very thoroughly with kitchen towels. Store it in a dry place. If you wish to use your wok as the container for the boiling water under your steaming compartment, choose a suitable size of grid and steamer to allow them to be above the boiling water but not so high that you cannot fit the lid of the wok securely in place. You may prefer to buy a set of steamers, however, the topmost one with a lid on it.
Ladles and spatulas, whether slotted or unperforated metal, or made of wire mesh (large-gauge or very small, rather like sieves or strainers), can be bought cheaply at Chinese hardware stores and differ in appearance and shape from their Western counterparts. Ordinary, Western style utensils which you will have in your kitchen can of course be used instead. The advantage of some Chinese ladles and scoops is that they are slightly concave and ideal for using with a wok, hugging the inside of its concave shape neatly. Some of these utensils, especially those made in bamboo (some only have bamboo handles, the rest being metal) are very attractive.
Chopsticks for kitchen use are very practical and are longer than the ones used for eating at table. Once you have mastered the not too difficult art of handling them, you will find them particularly practical for handling fried foods, especially when fairly small pieces have to be turned one by one. Chopsticks are

described in greater detail later in this section.

Knives, cleavers, choppers etc. It will be worth your while to purchase one or two extra if you intend doing a lot of Chinese cooking, but if you already have good, strong, and above all very sharp knives, use these until you decide that a Chinese steel cleaver could be helpful and you will gradually become accustomed to using it for all sorts of tasks. With its rectangular blade and rather stubby wooden handle, the cleaver provides enough weight to make it invaluable for chopping and slicing to various degrees of fineness; the flat of the blade is ideal for pounding and flattening and very handy for scooping up the ingredients you have chopped or pounded. With a good cleaver you can cut up your meat and fish and cut right through the flesh and bones of poultry as is the custom in the Chinese style. Chinese cleavers are, however, heavy and must be treated with care, although they are probably no more dangerous than any other large, sharp kitchen knife. The normal blade size is about 8 in long and 4 in wide. Lighter cleavers, easier for the novice to handle but obviously less effective for certain tasks, are also available. Always keep your cleaver razor-sharp and wipe the blade thoroughly after each cooking session with a dry cloth to prevent it rusting; hang up the cleaver by the handle from a hook to prevent the blade coming in contact with other metal, which would help to dull the cutting edge. Keep it in a safe place, away from children. If you decide to do a lot of Chinese cooking, you could buy the three basic Chinese knives: a chopper, a slicer, and a dual-purpose knife. If you use a cleaver you will need a thick, strong chopping and cutting board, preferably end-grain wood. Chinese cooks use a cross-section of a tree trunk, several inches thick (for domestic and restaurant use) and you can buy these in Oriental hardware shops. Most home cooks will have to think twice before going to the expense of buying a traditional and decorative brass version of the Mongolian hotpot and opt for a modern, stainless steel equivalent. Chinese earthenware, clay or stoneware cooking pots are attractive cooking vessels and come in many different sizes; many are squat, almost conical in shape, some with just one handle, some with two, glazed or unglazed on the outside and always glazed inside; their snugly fitting lids are usually convex. They are often placed in a water bath

Some implements used in Chinese cookery. From left to right: bamboo steamer, Mongolian hotpot, bamboo grater, a wok with a steel rack for draining, vegetable brush, cleavers, a bamboo sieve for washing rice and vegetables, and an assortment of small brushes.

(*bain marie*) for very gentle, slow cooking. Porcelain is of course the only material suitable for tea cups and teapots and it is also used for the little bottles containing warmed rice wine served with meals, as well as the tiny cups from which the wine is drunk. Soup bowls and spoons, other bowls, dishes, and serving plates, chopstick rests and small bowls for sauces, all are made of porcelain and used for most meals when a table is to be laid properly. These may have very simple decoration, but you can buy dishes cheaply that are good quality china and look typically Chinese, with their patterns of dragons, phoenixes, pagodas, and brightly colored symbolic animals reminiscent of Chinese vases. Porcelain has two great advantages: it keeps food hot for a long time and gives the appearance, often misleading, of being extremely fragile, symbolizing refinement and delicacy.

Another important material used for making utensils and other kitchen equipment is bamboo. This plant, with its long, reed-like stems, is one of the most typical and evocative sights in the Chinese countryside where it grows in profusion, cultivated widely, no part of the plant being wasted. The stems are very strong and pliable and can be split lengthwise very evenly and easily, making it an ideal material for making all sorts of objects including fishing rods, furniture, baskets, and mats. The young shoots of the bamboo plant also make delicious eating.

Bamboo makes very good kitchen equipment: steaming compartments or baskets; grids; slotted, perforated or mesh ladles and spatulas (often just the handles are made of bamboo); sieves, colanders (some types of which prevent meat, fish or vegetables from sticking to the bottom of the wok or pans); chopsticks. The list is endless. Utensils made with bamboo (including steamers) can be boiled and are therefore very hygienic, besides being hardwearing and practical.

There are, however, Western equivalents for most of the utensils and equipment mentioned above, some of which have been copied from the Chinese (e.g. the conical sieve, known as a *chinois* or "Chinese" sieve). And some tasks can, of course, be carried out in your electric food processor.

CHOPSTICKS (KUÀI ZI)

Hardly any mention is made in Chinese culinary literature or other texts of the origin of chopsticks, the eating tools which the inhabitants of East Asia have used for so many centuries. Mystery surrounds their invention and adoption as everyday utensils, but mention is made of them as far back as the Shang dynasty (1650–1026 B.C.). It can, however, be safely inferred from what little evidence is available that their shape and use has changed very little over the centuries. They are a good example of the Chinese tendency to continue using the old, traditional methods so long as these are the most practical and effective.

The shape of chopsticks is that of a very elongated cone, with smoothly rounded ends. Chopsticks used for eating are usually about 10 in long, the cooking variety being considerably longer. Ask someone who is expert at eating with chopsticks to show you how to hold and use them: basically it is a question of holding one of them between the inside of your thumb and the tip of your fourth, or ring, finger while the other chopstick is held like a pencil between the thumb, index, and middle finger. When pausing to drink or while waiting for a new selection of dishes or course to be placed on the table, the chopsticks should be placed, side by side, to the right of the dish or bowl from which you have been eating, and on their rest if there is one to avoid soiling the table cloth.

Almost anything can be, and is, eaten with chopsticks; soups are obviously eaten with the porcelain spoon provided. When eating rice, the rice bowl is held close to the mouth and the chopsticks used to ferry the rice the short remaining distance. Materials used to make chopsticks and decorative embellishment have varied greatly; in the past high-ranking Chinese spent large sums on precious chopsticks and had them made by craftsmen who transformed them into minor works of art.

Very beautiful and valuable chopsticks are still made today but normally they will be in wood or plastic (both of which, the latter in particular, are hygienic and do not retain odors) and mass-produced. Wooden, throw-away chopsticks are sold in sterile packets to be used just once. More expensive chopsticks, made of the ubiquitous bamboo or of wood and lacquered in decorative patterns, are also widely available. Very prosperous families may well eat with chopsticks made of agate, jade or ivory, this last considered the best of all by the Chinese (but not by the Japanese). Chopsticks can also be made of gold or silver; the latter used to be very popular with politicians, high-ranking civil servants, rich aristocrats, and the privileged classes in general. Silver was prized for its reputed property of turning black when in contact with arsenic, protecting intended victims from their poisoners. As for stories that attribute the traditional use of chopsticks to the fact that no one can cut or wound with them (thus protecting the guest under the strict code of Chinese hospitality), this can be discounted as manufactured folklore as can the "tradition," allegedly full of symbolism, that a child holds the chopsticks by their pointed ends and as he grows older, holds them further up, progressing toward the handles with advancing years and wisdom.

CHINESE METHODS OF PREPARATION AND COOKING TECHNIQUES

Methods of preparing the raw materials and the cooking techniques of Chinese cooks can seem odd and complicated to the uninitiated, especially when the implements used are unfamiliar. Expert Western cooks will soon recognize processes which have a lot in common with those of so-called international cooking; the basic techniques have simply evolved somewhat differently over the centuries. Often the techniques are less unexpected than cooking times, and never more so than when several successive cooking processes are involved, for some dishes are startlingly elaborate. A few methods demand some experience, daunting for someone new to Chinese cooking, but it is worth a little perseverance to acquire the skill. These techniques are not only followed because they are the most practical way: artistic considerations are also very important, whether these are expressed in the appearance of the dish, through simple color and form, or whether the food is made to look like something else which has a symbolic meaning for the Chinese, such as when food is arranged cleverly to look like fishes, dragons etc. Many vegetarian dishes eaten by Buddhist monks or by the devout laity are arranged so that they show precisely those foods that are forbidden, and which the eater has renounced, such as game birds or poultry etc. The act of eating these dishes after admiring their appearance underlines the self-denial and self-sacrifice involved in giving up all flesh and serves as a reminder of their religious beliefs: the heart, mind, and spirit take precedence over the appetite and senses. This artistry even expresses itself in the combination of unexpected tastes and textures, introducing great variety and interest into a single dish.

Many Chinese culinary traditions and habits have been invented through hard necessity and are harshly practical. One example is the widespread use of oil made from seeds (such as sesame seed oil or sunflower seed oil). These should not be subjected to high temperatures since these result in the formation of toxic polymers (Chinese cooks usually take care to cook sesame seed oil as little as possible, which is why it is usually added when a dish is in its final stage of preparation). Another is the widespread use of monosodium glutamate which, while

Some of the many varieties of Chinese tea, including the famous green tea (Hoang Shian).

certainly a very effective and efficient flavor enhancer, can be harmful in large or very frequent doses. Then there is the somewhat undiscriminating inclusion of sugar in a great number of dishes, some of which may well taste better without it (when sugar was first discovered the Chinese took to it with great zeal). In some regions of China the use of salt, spices, scallions, garlic, and ginger can be said perhaps to be a little over-enthusiastic. More recently, in areas in close contact with Western and other influences, the use of commercially prepared sauces, such as ketchup, Worcestershire sauce, bottled chili sauce, and indifferent blends of curry powder has not always been judicious. Chinese cooks employ all the known cooking techniques and use utensils and cooking vessels ideally suited to the task in hand. The most popular cooking methods are steaming, stir-frying, and deep-frying. Broiling and roasting are considered rather primitive and rudimentary forms of cooking, but they are widely used and methods differ little from

Western usage. Boiling entails different preparatory stages for the ingredients and the water is usually left unsalted. Steaming is an alternative method to roasting many foods; the result is obviously moister and softer, usually with a more subtle taste, and retaining more of the original flavor. The Chinese think steaming particularly well suited to very fresh foods, such as freshly caught fish and freshly picked vegetables. Other foods, such as the famous stuffed steamed buns, acquire their soft, featherlight consistency from the steaming process and the same gentle treatment works wonders with dumplings and all sorts of dim sum. Foods to be steamed are often marinated beforehand; they are usually placed in heatproof dishes in the steamer, or the steamer compartment is lined with cabbage

or lettuce leaves or parchment, waxed paper or a cloth.

Deep-frying needs care and practice. The wok is a development of the most basic and traditional vessel used for frying, the iron skillet; without the traditional Chinese stove, however, with the hole into which the wok fits so neatly and securely over the glowing charcoal, deep-frying in a wok can be a little dangerous, even with a stand; an electric deep-fryer is a sensible substitute. Chinese cooks blanch their foodstuffs in hot oil, a process rarely encountered in other schools of cooking. Sometimes shortening or lard is used, sometimes oil, to seal the items before they undergo other cooking processes. This means that under their thin, cooked outer layer, they are still juicy; the following cooking stages take less time, and often the pre-fried food will swell or puff up attractively when it undergoes a second, hotter deep-frying. Pieces of vegetable, meat and fish can be fried just as they are, or marinated first, or coated with batter or flour. Most people agree that the cooking technique most readily associated with Chinese cooking is stir-frying: using just a little oil or fat, the ingredients are cut into small pieces and fried rapidly and very briefly over very high heat while they are constantly stirred and turned. The wok's shape is particularly well suited to this method. Care must be taken to use very small quantities of oil and speed and good timing is of the essence. Often several different ingredients have to be fried, each requiring a longer or shorter cooking time; when they are cooked together in the wok, the cook must obviously work out which needs the most cooking, and will add this first to the wok, the rest being added one after the other, according to their texture. You will soon realize just how much (or, rather, how little) stir-frying is needed for various ingredients, bearing in mind that foods cooked this way should be slightly undercooked rather than well done.

NORTHERN CHINA

華
北
菜

THE NORTH, PEKING, AND THE SHANTUNG PHENOMENON

30

It is customary to divide Chinese cookery into four great schools: those of the north, south, east, and west. Some critics hold that this is rather an arbitrary division, that the so-called northern school of cooking does not faithfully reflect the indigenous cooking of the region and is not an accurate collection and codification of the original Chinese dishes and culinary traditions of northern China. The recipes we see grouped under this heading did not necessarily originate in northern China but were brought there and developed by the cooks of the Manchu imperial dynasty. Some maintain that Peking and the northern provinces have almost spuriously acquired the reputation as a center for fine cuisine as a result of relatively recent developments in their culinary traditions, dating back only to the reigns of the Manchu imperial family (or the Qing dynasty, a period which lasted from the middle of the seventeenth century until the early twentieth century). To support their argument these critics contend that these hedonistic rulers "imported" their favorite foods and dishes from all over China, superimposing them onto the native cooking of the north and to a certain extent eclipsing this by adopting a vast number of methods and foodstuffs which had originated elsewhere.

The school is thus called "Imperial cooking" by some. However well founded this theory may be, many other strong influences which can be traced down the centuries are of equal relevance: a great many of the oldest and most traditional dishes are based on products for which northern China has always been famed and which are unavailable in other regions. The fact remains that the cooking of Peking and the north has become internationally famous and is the next best known among Westerners after southern Chinese or Cantonese cooking. It is not too arbitrary to group together the following areas: Manchuria; Inner Mongolia (where even the Great Wall failed to keep out the Tartar hordes before the Mongol ascendency in the fourteenth century); Hopei; Shantung and, to the south of the region, Honan; to its west Shansi and Shensi. All these areas have some aspects of culinary tradition in common. It is, however, perhaps more valid to draw a distinction between the inland and the coastal regions: between the colder, poorer plains and those areas which are temperate and fertile. The Yellow River (Huang Ho) provides a link and, to some extent, a unifying element between Inner Mongolia and the provinces of Honan and Shantung. The decisive factors, however,

have to be those connected with climate, the foods which can be grown.

A good example, as always, is provided by the staples: cereals such as wheat, millet, barley, and corn are cultivated instead of rice, for which the northern climate is totally unsuited. Adverse weather conditions, which modern agro-technology is beginning to alleviate in some measure, such as long, bitterly cold winters, followed by spring sandstorms blowing in from the Gobi desert all the way to Inner Mongolia and the area surrounding Peking, and short, frequently drought-ridden summers have led to distinctive treatments for certain products: the custom of drying an immense variety of ingredients, vegetables in particular, to preserve them; the extensive use of root vegetables such as the long white radish or daikon root which can be stored successfully for long periods, as can sweet potatoes, also grown in the area and which were originally imported from South America and, of course, the ever-present Chinese cabbage. During the

Dressed in traditional costume, this young couple of nomadic shepherds are pictured near the salt lake of Qinghai, nearly 10,000 feet above sea level.

summer months, the most is made of the abundance of fresh vegetables and fruits. Peanuts and soybeans are produced on a very large scale, and can be processed in a variety of ways to result in products such as cooking oils and sauces; large quantities of fresh pork fat and shortening are also used, except by the Buddhist minority groups. Pig rearing is, however, carried out on a fairly small scale and most dishes can be made with oil instead of pork fat products.

The fierce cold of the long winters has left its mark on the cooking and presentation of many dishes: the celebrated Mongolian hotpot is a good example. In its original form, the hotpot containing the broth in which each person cooked his or her food would be kept boiling on top of a brazier full of glowing charcoal, radiating plenty of warmth for those seated round it. Steam-cooked, often flour-based foods such as dumplings, with or without meat or vegetable fillings (both the soft, fluffy dumplings with a light consistency and the dough dumplings, eaten piping hot straight from the steamer), are nutritious and filling, as are the ribbon noodles served with all sorts of flavorings and dressings that accompany various dishes. The Yellow River, feared and venerated as a capricious demon, has long been notorious for its extremes of flood and very low water resulting in a surprisingly small population of fish. It has now been partially restrained by engineering works to curb flooding and regulate its flow so that it can be used for managed irrigation. The river's influence on the region dominates the customs and recipes of the inland areas, but this tyranny holds less and less sway as the river makes its way to the sea, until it finally reaches the gulf of Po Hai in eastern Shantung and runs into the sea, teaming with fish in a province blessed with a temperate climate.

Shantung is exceptional among the northern Chinese provinces not only for its abundance of fish and seafood (among them the giant shrimp of the Yellow Sea), but also for its viticulture: its vines produce good white wines (such as Riesling and Chardonnay grape wines), while other white and red wines are made from varieties of vines which grow particularly well in this area. Good beer production, using German methods, was started by German tenant farmers who developed the industry in the region over a period of 25 years, ending with the beginning of World War I in 1914.

The plentiful supply and consumption of wine in Shantung, long confined to this area, is a remnant of an ancient Chinese custom which is now being revived: that of drinking wine and beer with meals, giving the lie to the generally accepted belief that tea is usually drunk with Chinese meals; this is in fact far more commonly drunk either at the end of a

Woman in the courtyard of her tufa construction house near Sanmenxia between Zhenghou and Xi'an.

meal or, more frequently, between meals and the whole tea-making and tea-drinking process is invested with much ceremony. In the more "typical" regions of the north fish is seldom served, with the exception of carp and a few other freshwater fish, caught in the

Yellow River and also in Peking's rivers, the Young Tsing and the Pai and in some other rivers and streams. In the various meat dishes, ancient Mongolian cooking methods are still discernible, as well as the Moslem influence with a heavy dependence on

Looking past the prow of a boat built in traditional, vernacular style, across the Hwang Ho (Yellow River).

mutton, lamb, goat, and kid; horse meat and donkey meat also feature. Pork and beef are often highly flavored with garlic, onion, scallions and, of course, the ubiquitous preserved cabbage and other pickled greens, as well as sweet peppers and spices, some very strong. Imperial cuisine at the Qing (or Manchu) dynasty's court in Peking is said to have owed its predilection for pronounced flavors to the influence of high functionaries at the capital who were natives of Shantung and had brought their tastes to court with them. Whether this was true, or whether the real cause was the climate, other outside influences or simply the availability of certain foodstuffs, northern cooking is full-flavored, robust, and varied, making use of the entire range of tastes: sweet, salty, sour, spicy, and peppery-hot. Some methods of preparation are unique to this area and are reflected in the recipes of the region.

Perhaps the most famous Peking dish is the classic Peking duck, also called lacquered duck. Not only does the dish's excellence stem from its unique form of preparation, cooking, and method of serving; the duck used is of quite exceptional quality, the famous white Peking duck, flocks of which are raised in the plains surrounding Peking.

By its very nature as a national and regional capital city, a political and industrial center, and the destination for millions of vistors through the centuries, Peking has adopted much of the best cooking from the south, east, and west and added them to its own. This is reflected by its wide variety of restaurants but is also found, to a lesser extent, in other very important regional centers, underlining the fact that there is a broader, national cuisine which coexists with the distinctive regional schools of cooking.

34

SESAME BUNS *

烧饼

shāo bǐng

6 cups all-purpose unbleached flour
1¹/₂ cups hot water
¹/₂ cup cold water
1¹/₂ cups peanut oil
1 tbsp salt
¹/₂ cup white sesame seeds

Time: 1¹/₂ hours

Sift half the flour in a mound in a large mixing bowl or onto a pastry slab; make a well in the middle, pour in the hot water, and gradually mix this into the flour by hand or with a wooden spoon. Add just enough cold water to make a smooth, fairly firm dough.

Leave to stand while making the second portion of dough as follows: sift the remaining half of the flour in the same way and mix in as much of the slightly warmed peanut oil to make a dough similar in consistency to the first dough. Place in a bowl in the barely warm oven for 10 minutes with the door left ajar. Using the palms of your hands, roll and shape the two pieces of dough separately into long cylinders 1¹/₂ in in diameter. Slice into 1¹/₂-in sections. Assemble the buns as follows: place a disk of water dough flat on the work surface, press to flatten evenly or roll lightly with the rolling pin into a disk; sprinkle lightly with salt; roll a piece of the oil dough to the same dimensions as the water dough disk and place it on top of the first piece. Press firmly to make the two layers adhere. In order to make a triangle, fold thirds of the disk's edges toward the center (folding both layers at once); flatten out the center where the edges overlap and roll the triangles lightly. Fold the apex of the triangle over to rest in the middle of the edge opposite it. Sprinkle the surface liberally with sesame seeds, then roll lightly to flatten out and lengthen somewhat, which will also push the seeds into the dough a little. Place in the oven, preheated to 300°F and bake for 5 minutes; turn and bake for a further 5 minutes.

STEAMED BUNS

馒头

mán tóu

7 cups all-purpose unbleached flour
2¹/₂ tbsp sugar
2 cups warm water
1 tbsp compressed yeast or 1 tsp dried yeast
3 tbsp shortening

Time: 1 hour + rising time

Mix the sugar and yeast gently with the lukewarm water; when it foams it is ready to use. Dried yeast will take a little longer to reactivate.

Melt the shortening and mix into the flour, stirring thoroughly to distribute it evenly. Make a well in the center, pour the yeast mixture into it, and gradually mix into the flour until very smooth and soft. Knead for up to 10 minutes. Cover the dough with a clean, damp cloth and leave in a warm place until tripled in bulk (this

can take up to 4 hours). Knock down the dough, knead briefly, and shape into a sausage $1^1/_2$ in in diameter; cut into $1^1/_2$-in sections and roll each piece into a ball; press each ball with the heel of your hand to flatten slightly.

Place a disk of waxed paper in the bottom of the steamer compartment and place the buns on it; cover and steam over gently simmering water for about 10 minutes.

STEAMED BUNS WITH PORK STUFFING *

猪 肉 包
zhū ròu bāo

$3^1/_2$ cups very finely chopped pork
2 tung ku (dong gu) mushrooms
$2^1/_2$ tbsp very finely chopped scallions
1 medium-sized onion, very finely chopped
2 cloves garlic, very finely chopped
6 tbsp oil

For the sauce:
3 tbsp sweet soy paste
3 tbsp soy sauce
pinch monosodium glutamate (optional)
1 tbsp sugar
1 tbsp rice wine
1 tbsp sesame seed oil
generous pinch salt
generous pinch freshly ground pepper
1 heaping tbsp cornstarch or potato flour

For the dough:
See Steamed Buns on p. 14–15

Time: $1^1/_2$ hours + preparation time for the dough

Make the dough as directed on p. 14–15 and leave to rise. Soak the dried mushrooms in warm water for 20 minutes or longer, until soft and plumped up. Drain the mushrooms, cut off their stalks and discard them. Chop the caps. Fry the scallion, onion, and garlic briefly, then add the meat and stir-fry; add the mushrooms and stir-fry all together for 5 minutes.

Add all the sauce ingredients, stir well, and cook to allow some of the liquid to evaporate; stir in the thickening agent mixed with a very little cold water. Set aside. Use the prepared dough to assemble and cook the buns, with this filling, as directed for Steamed Buns with Chicken Filling and cook as directed in that recipe.

STEAMED BUNS WITH CHICKEN FILLING

鸡 肉 包
jī ròu bāo

10 tung ku (dong gu) mushrooms
$1^3/_4$ lb chicken meat
1 tbsp salt
1 tbsp rice wine
$^1/_2$ tsp monosodium glutamate (optional)
1 heaping tbsp cornstarch or potato flour
$^1/_4$ lb bamboo shoots
$^1/_4$ lb button mushrooms
1 tbsp very finely chopped scallion
1 tbsp very finely chopped fresh ginger
$^1/_3$ cup peanut oil

For the sauce:
1 tbsp rice wine
1 tbsp sugar
$2^1/_2$ tbsp soy sauce
1 tbsp salt
1 tsp monosodium glutamate (optional)
generous pinch freshly ground pepper
1 tbsp sesame seed oil
1 tbsp cornstarch or potato flour

For the dough:
See Steamed Buns on p. 14–15

Time: $1^1/_2$ hours + preparation time for the dough

Soak the dried mushrooms in warm water to soften. Make the dough and when it has only a short time left to finish rising, make the filling for the buns. Cut the chicken flesh into very small dice and mix with the salt, wine, monosodium glutamate (if used), and the cornstarch or potato flour. Cut off and discard the stalks of the drained mushrooms; chop the caps coarsely; chop the fresh button mushrooms and the bamboo shoots.

Heat the oil in the wok and fry the scallion and ginger briefly, then add the meat and cook for 1–2 minutes, stirring and turning. Add the vegetables and continue cooking for 5 minutes, stirring frequently. Add the sauce ingredients: wine, sugar, soy sauce, salt, monosodium glutamate (if used), pepper, and sesame seed oil. Stir and cook for a short time to reduce the liquid. Stir in the thickening agent mixed with a very little cold water and simmer for 1–2 minutes. Set aside to cool.

Roll out the dough into a fairly thick sheet and cut out disks 4–$4^3/_4$ in in diameter with a plain round cookie cutter. Place a little of the filling in the center of each disk. Bring the edges of the disk up and over the filling pinching them together gently as you do so. Steam these little buns as directed in the recipe for Steamed Buns on p. 14–15.

YELLOW SOY FLOUR BUNS *

窝窝头
wō wō tón

36

4¹/₂ cups all-purpose unbleached flour
4¹/₂ cups yellow soy flour
hot water

Time: 1 hour

Sift the two types of flour together into a large mixing bowl or onto the work surface. Make a well in the center of the flour and pour in a little hot water. Gradually mix the water into the flour, adding a very little more at a time when necessary; the dough should be smooth, firm, and homogeneous.

Shape this dough into little pagoda or cone shapes; insert your little finger into the middle of the base of each pagoda and push until the tip of your finger is halfway up the center of the pagoda: this will ensure that the bun cooks evenly right through.

Line the steamer compartment with a circle of waxed paper and place the buns on it; cover and steam over gently simmering water for 30 minutes.

MANDARIN PANCAKES

薄饼
báo bǐng

Makes 12 pancakes:
2¹/₂ cups all-purpose flour
1 cup boiling water
sesame seed oil or peanut oil

Time: 20 minutes + 1 hour standing time

Sift the flour into a large mixing bowl and make a well in the center. Stir 1 tsp of oil into the water and keep it simmering in a small saucepan. Pour a little of the water into the well and gradually mix into the flour with a wooden spoon or cooking chopsticks; add more water a little at a time, using only as much as is needed to make a smooth, soft dough just firm enough to hold its shape. Leave to stand for 1 hour. Divide the dough into three equal portions and shape each of these into a sausage or cylinder; divide each of these sausages into four equal sections; flatten each portion and then roll into neat thin disks; brush the surface of the disks lightly with oil, assemble them in pairs, oiled sides together, and press or roll lightly to make them adhere. You will end up with 6 pairs of pancakes. Place on a floured pastry board and with a lightly floured rolling pin roll them a pair at a time until they are much thinner and measure approx. 6 in in diameter. Heat a non-stick skillet over moderate heat and cook the

pancakes one pair at a time. When bubbles start to form slowly on the surface (after one or two minutes) turn the pancake and cook until the underside starts to color very lightly. Take the pancake out of the skillet and very carefully separate the two layers. The pancakes can then be folded ready to serve: fold loosely in half, then in half again, forming triangular shapes, and serve. If they are not to be used at once, keep flat, covered with a cloth or foil, and warm just before using. They can also be steamed for a further 5 minutes (or longer), wrapped inside a fine-weave cloth or foil and will keep well until you are ready to serve them. Traditionally served with Peking lacquered duck (also known as crispy duck), these pancakes can also be served with fillings of pork, egg, shellfish, and vegetables.

Good, readymade Mandarin pancakes are sold in many Oriental foodstores.

WONTON DUMPLINGS

饺子

jiǎo zǐ

For the dough:
1³/₄ cups all-purpose unbleached flour
warm water

For the filling:
5 oz pork
5 oz beef
7 oz spinach or Savoy cabbage
7 oz Chinese white cabbage
1 leek
1 medium-sized onion
1 walnut-sized piece fresh ginger
1 tbsp soy sauce
2 tbsp cornstarch or potato flour
2 tbsp sesame seed oil
pinch salt
pinch monosodium glutamate (optional)

Time: 2 hours + 12 hours standing time

The sheet of dough used for these dumplings should be so thin as to be almost transparent; this is not as difficult as it sounds. The secret is to knead the dough very thoroughly and then let it rest for several hours; this means you can prepare the dough in advance and leave it to stand overnight, ready for use the next day.

Sift the flour and a pinch of salt in a mound on the pastry board or into a large mixing bowl. Gradually mix in sufficient lukewarm

Ethnic Tibetan women busy making yak's milk butter inside one of their tents, in the Qinghai region. Most of the inhabitants of this northern area of China (who number about three million) are of Tibetan origin. This is one of the harshest and most inhospitable parts of China; the hostile climate and landscape have made the people tough and resourceful, jealously defending their traditional ways of life and their right to live in their mysterious and fascinating adopted homeland.

Apart from herding yaks, native to the high

(over 16,000ft) barren steppes of southern Tibet, these women weave woollen textiles and rugs for the tents they live in and make elaborate and beautiful silver jewelry with which to bedeck themselves.

Apart from butter, yak's milk is used to make cheese and yoghurt, and a by-product is used as fuel for the votive lamps that burn in the temples.

Wild yak belong to a vanishing species; when domesticated they are also prized as working animals and beasts of burden.

water to make a smooth, firm dough. Knead the dough for at least 15 minutes to develop the gluten in the flour. Place in a bowl, cover with a clean cloth, and leave to stand in a cool place for 12 hours or a little longer. When you have made the filling for the dumplings, knead the dough again for about 15 minutes, then roll out on a lightly floured board or marble slab to a very thin sheet, thin enough to see your hand dimly when placed immediately below the sheet of dough. Use a cookie cutter or a glass to cut out disks approx. 2³/₄ in in diameter or, if preferred, cut into 2¹/₂-in squares.

Make the filling: rinse and dry the vegetables, chop them very finely, and place in a mixing bowl. Add the peeled and finely grated fresh ginger, a pinch of salt, the monosodium glutamate (if used), soy sauce, cornstarch or

potato flour, the very finely chopped pork and beef and 2¹/₂ tbsp sesame seed oil. Mix thoroughly. Take heaping teaspoons of this mixture from the bowl and roll into balls between the palms of your hands, place in the center of each circular or square wrapper, moisten along the edges and fold in half, enclosing the ball of filling. Press the edges to make them adhere.

These dumplings are best steamed: line the steamer compartment with a clean, damp piece of cloth and place the dumplings on it. Steam for about 10 minutes or until the dough has become almost transparent (do not allow the water to come anywhere near the wontons as it boils).

Slightly thicker, readymade wonton skins or bean curd wrappers may be bought in Oriental foodstores.

PEKING FRIED DUMPLINGS *

锅 贴
guō tiē

38

For the dough wrappers:
1 cup all-purpose unbleached flour
warm water

For the filling:
5 oz very finely chopped pork
14 oz Chinese white cabbage (or ordinary
crisp white cabbage)
1 scallion
2 thin slices fresh ginger
1 clove garlic
$^1/_2$–1 tsp salt
$1^1/_2$ tsp soy sauce
1 tbsp rice wine
$3^1/_2$ tbsp peanut oil
generous pinch freshly ground white pepper
water and oil for cooking

Time: $1^1/_2$ hours

Make the dough for the wrappers a little while in advance: sift the flour into a mound on the pastry board or in a large mixing bowl, make a well in the center, and pour a little warm water into it; gradually mix into the flour, adding a very little water in instalments as you blend the moisture and flour together. The dough should be fairly soft, very smooth, and dry enough to leave the sides of the bowl cleanly. Knead for 15 minutes then leave to stand, covered with a clean cloth.

Rinse the cabbage, trim where necessary, and blanch in boiling water for 2 minutes. Drain well, chop finely, and wring out any remaining moisture by placing in a clean cloth and twisting the ends of the cloth.

Chop the scallion, peeled ginger, and the garlic very finely and mix thoroughly with the meat, cabbage, and all the other ingredients listed above for the filling. Knead the dough briefly, place on a lightly floured pastry board or marble slab and roll out into a very thin sheet. Cut out into disks approx. $2^3/_4$ in in diameter. Place 1 tsp of the filling in the center of each disk, dampen the edges of the disk lightly and then fold in half, enclosing the filling; press firmly all round the edges to seal. Heat the wok or a nonstick skillet and brush the inside surface with a cloth dipped in sesame seed oil. Add $2^1/_2$ tbsp peanut oil or other vegetable oil and when very hot, add the dumplings in a single layer. As soon as they are all in the wok, pour in $^1/_2$ cup boiling water (lean back a little as you do so: as the oil may spatter). Cover and cook for 2 minutes, then check whether you need to add more boiling water yet; the same quantity should be added as soon as the previous amount has been almost completely absorbed. Do not move the

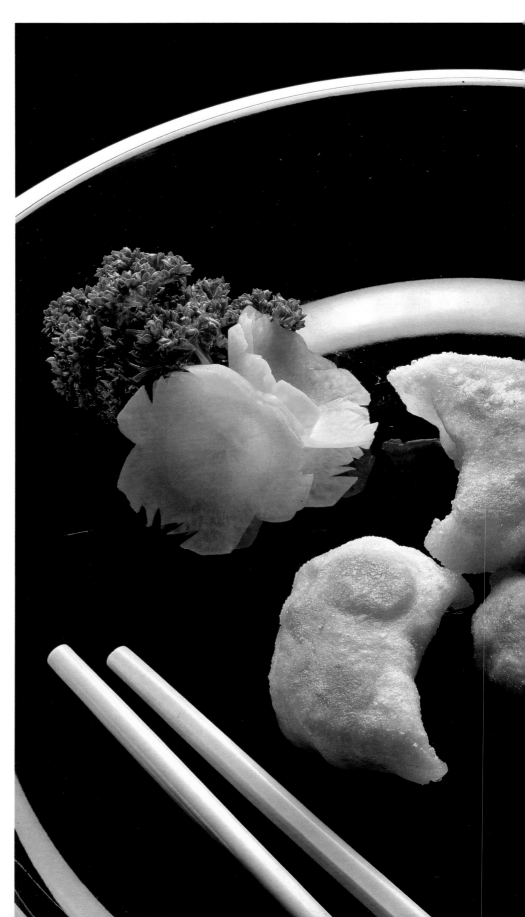

dumplings at any stage during cooking. Cover again and continue cooking until the second instalment of water has been absorbed completely, then sprinkle 1 tbsp more oil into the wok and fry the dumplings until their undersides are crisp (check one to see).

Transfer the dumplings carefully to a hot serving plate, with their crisp undersides uppermost.

DUMPLINGS WITH CURRY FILLING

咖 哩 酥 饺
gā lí sū jiǎo

For the wrappers:
see Peking Fried Dumplings on p. 18

For the filling:
2 cups very finely chopped pork or beef
2¹/₂ tbsp cornstarch or potato flour
¹/₂ cup peanut oil
2 small onions or shallots, very finely chopped
1 clove garlic, very finely chopped
1 tbsp Chinese curry powder
1 tsp salt
1 tbsp sugar
pinch monosodium glutamate (optional)
1¹/₂ tsp soy sauce
oil for frying

Time: 1¹/₂ hours

Mix the meat with the cornstarch or alternative to coat well. Heat the peanut oil in the wok and fry the onions and garlic until tender. Add the meat, stir-fry, sprinkle with the curry powder, salt, sugar, monosodium glutamate (if used), and the soy sauce. Mix well and cook for 5 minutes.

Roll out the dough into a very thin sheet and cut out into disks about 2³/₄ in in diameter, using a cookie cutter or a glass. Place a little of the filling in the center of each disk, fold the disk in half, enclosing the filling, and press the edges together to seal securely (dampen slightly if wished).

Heat plenty of oil in the wok or a skillet to about 285°F or a little hotter. Fry the dumplings in the oil for 5 minutes; remove with a slotted spoon, draining well, and transfer into another large saucepan (or preferably a deep-fryer) containing plenty of oil heated to 350°F and fry the dumplings until light, crisp, and pale golden brown.

WONTON SOUP *

水 饺
shuǐ jiǎo

For the wrappers:
1³/₄ cups all-purpose unbleached flour
warm water

For the sauce:
1 small piece peeled fresh ginger, cut into fine matchstick strips marinated for about 30 minutes in mixture of ¹/₄ cup dark rice wine vinegar (hei jiu) and ¹/₄ cup dark soy sauce
few drops sesame seed oil

For the filling:
14 oz Chinese white cabbage (pai ciai) or ordinary crisp white cabbage
¹/₂ cup ground pork tenderloin
¹/₂ cup ground pork belly
1 scallion or 1 small onion, finely chopped
2 thin slices fresh ginger
1 tsp salt
1 tbsp sesame seed oil
1 tbsp rice wine
pinch monosodium glutamate (optional)

Time: 1¹/₂ hours

Prepare the dough in advance (see Peking Fried Dumplings on p. 18). Alternatively, wonton wrappers can be purchased readymade. Mix together the sauce ingredients.

Blanch the cabbage in boiling water for 2 minutes; drain, squeezing out excess moisture, and chop finely. Mix all the ingredients listed for the filling. When the dough has rested for some time, knead again for 5–10 minutes, then roll out on a lightly floured board until fairly thin (not as thin as for the previous dumpling recipes). Cut out into disks measuring approx. 2³/₄ in in diameter. Place a little filling in the center of each disk, then fold the wrapper in half, enclosing the filling. Moisten the edges if wished and press together to seal tightly. Pour 2 quarts water into a very large saucepan; bring to a fast boil; add 8–10 dumplings, cover the pan, and when the dumplings float to the surface of the water, add ¹/₂ cup cold water; allow the water to return to a boil again and then remove the dumplings with a ladle, taking some of the cooking liquid with them as you do so; keep hot in the liquid or broth while you boil the next batch in exactly the same way. These dumplings must be served very hot. Beat a little sesame oil to taste into the sauce, and pour a little into individual small bowls for each person to dip the wonton dumplings into.

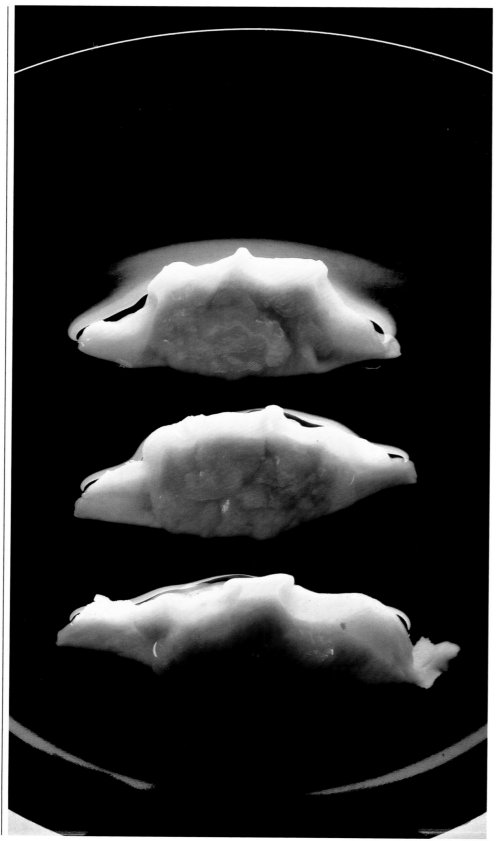

RIBBON NOODLES WITH EIGHT FLAVORS

什锦炒面

shí jǐn chǎo miàn

¹/₂ lb egg noodles
2 eggs
7 oz lean pork (e.g. tenderloin)
¹/₂ cup peeled shrimp
¹/₄ lb bamboo shoots
¹/₄ lb spinach (fresh or frozen)
2 leeks
1 tbsp light soy sauce
2¹/₂ tsp cornstarch
¹/₂–1 tsp sugar
6 tbsp oil
generous pinch salt

Time: 35 minutes + 25 minutes marinating time

Cut the meat into short matchstick strips and place in a bowl containing the mixed soy sauce, sugar, and cornstarch; stir well and leave to marinate for 20 minutes. Break the eggs into a bowl, add a pinch of salt, and beat lightly with a fork. Heat a very little oil in a wide skillet and pour in the eggs to make a thin, firm omelet. When the omelet is completely set, slide it onto a plate and leave to cool; cut into thin strips. Bring a large pot of water in which to cook the noodles to a boil. If using fresh spinach, wash the leaves thoroughly and shred into thin strips. If using frozen, thaw then shred or boil briefly and chop coarsely. Finely slice the bamboo shoots; wash the leeks well and slice into thin rounds. If using dried noodles, add them to the boiling water now and while they are cooking heat 1¹/₂ tbsp oil in the wok or skillet and stir-fry the marinaded meat to cook very lightly and color evenly; remove the pork from the wok and set aside. Heat the remaining oil and stir-fry the leeks until just tender; add the bamboo shoots and the spinach, cook for 2 minutes over slightly higher heat before adding the shrimp, the pork and the omelet. Stir-fry briefly and gently, add a little more salt if necessary, and allow the ingredients to heat through. As soon as the noodles are tender but still have a little "bite" left to them, drain well and add to the contents of the wok (fresh noodles will take only 2 or 3 minutes to cook). Stir well and serve at once.

FRIED NOODLES

炸 面

zhà miàn

4¹/₂ cups all-purpose unbleached flour
3 eggs
cold water
1 clove garlic
oil for frying
salt

Time: 1 hour

Sift all but ¹/₂ cup of the flour into a mound on the work surface or into a large mixing bowl. Break the eggs into a liquidizer or food processor, add 1¹/₂ tbsp warm water and the reserved flour and process until the flour has completely and smoothly blended with the eggs. Pour this liquid into the well in the center of the mound of flour and, using your slightly cupped hand (fingers held together) or a wooden spoon, stir the liquid round and round, gradually working the flour. Knead the resulting dough for 10 minutes until firm and elastic but homogeneous and smooth; add a very little more water at a time until it is the right consistency. Shape the dough into a ball and leave to stand for 15 minutes, covered with a damp cloth. Knead the dough for about 5 minutes, then roll out on a lightly floured board into a very thin sheet with a rolling pin (or use a pasta machine). Dust the dough sheet very lightly with flour, roll up and cut by hand (or use the machine) to your preferred width (very narrow, medium or broad). Add the noodles to a large pan of boiling salted water and cook for 2–3 minutes, or until done. Drain thoroughly.

Heat plenty of oil for deep-frying (or semi deep-frying if you are using a wok). Add the noodles a small amount at a time and fry each batch until pale golden brown and crisp; remove each batch with a slotted ladle when done and drain well; finish draining on paper towels.

Chinese fried noodles are always eaten with another dish, never on their own: serve with fish, meat or vegetable dishes which are simmered in liquid or cooked with a sauce. Each person takes a helping of the crispy fried noodles and adds them to the moist dish, providing a pleasing contrast of textures.

NOODLES WITH MEAT SAUCE *

酱 肉 面

jiàng ròu miàn

14 oz ribbon noodles
1³/₄ cups finely chopped lean pork
5 tbsp oil
2¹/₂ tbsp rice wine
2¹/₂ tbsp soy sauce
1 medium-sized onion, very finely sliced
6 tbsp chicken or vegetable broth
pinch sugar
1 large cucumber
5 cloves garlic, finely chopped
salt

Time: 40 minutes

Heat 2¹/₂ tbsp oil in the wok or a large skillet and brown the meat lightly, stir-frying for a few minutes. Add the wine and cook until it has evaporated. Add the onion, the soy sauce, and the sugar. Stir well. Pour in the broth and cook until this has also evaporated. Turn off the heat and cover to keep hot. Cut the cucumber lengthwise in half, scoop out the seeds, and cut into fine matchstick strips; mix these with the very finely chopped garlic and the remaining sliced onion and transfer to a serving dish. Cook the noodles in plenty of boiling salted water, drain well, mix in 2¹/₂ tbsp oil to coat them lightly all over. Place in a heated serving dish. Transfer the meat to a third, heated, serving dish and serve.

41

42

A section of the Great Wall, to the north of Peking. The wall is 1,400 miles long, stretching from the Yellow Sea to Gansu, on the edge of the Gobi desert. It was the idea of a Ch'in dynasty ruler, Shih Huang-ti, who unified China, suppressed all opposition and became the first emperor (third century B.C.). Shih Huant-ti embarked upon a colossal program of change, dividing the country into provinces and districts and standardizing the ideogrammatic Chinese script (thus establishing a universal bureaucratic language for his new, highly organized and effective civil service). Henceforth, he decreed, there was to be only one army; a unified legal system, and a single, national currency.

This centralized and highly organized nation state was surrounded by barbarians; the Great Wall was to be both a product and casue of the yawning gap that developed between a highly evolved society of cultivators and China's neighbors, nomadic peoples from the Steppes and central Asia.

The pace of unification was forced too hard, however, leading to peasant revolts, the death of many scholars, and the destruction of sacred texts.

minutes, stirring continuously, then place a tight-fitting lid on the pan, turn down the heat to low so that the water boils but does not boil over and cook for 8 minutes without lifting the lid. The rice should be nearly done when the water has been absorbed and the surface of the rice has a series of "dimples" on its surface (which the Chinese call "fish eyes"). When this point is reached, replace the lid, turn off the heat and allow to stand to finish cooking for a further 5 minutes.

Soak the dried mushrooms in warm water for 20 minutes to soften and reconstitute them. Cut the shrimp in half unless tiny ones are used. Break the eggs into a bowl and beat lightly with a fork. Heat 1 tbsp oil in the wok or a skillet, pour in the eggs, and cook them into a thin, firmly set omelet, scrambling them lightly with a fork as you do so. Remove from the pan and set aside. Drain the mushrooms, cut off their stems and discard; dice the caps and stir-fry in $2^1/_2$ tbsp fresh oil. Add the meat, stir-fry to color it evenly, then add the ham and the shrimp. Mix well. Cook for 2 minutes before adding the soy sauce (and a small pinch of monosodium glutamate if wished). Transfer this mixture to a plate and keep warm. Boil the peas until tender in lightly salted water; drain. Wipe the inside of the wok or skillet and heat 6 tbsp fresh oil; fry the onion until pale golden brown. Add the rice, another small pinch of monosodium glutamate if wished, and stir thoroughly. Return all the prepared ingredients to the pan, stir-frying them and breaking up the omelet as you do so. Add a little more salt and freshly ground pepper if wished and serve.

PORK AND NOODLE SOUP *

汤面

tāng miàn

4 tung ku (dong gu) mushrooms
$^1/_2$ lb lean pork
$^1/_2$ lb noodles
2 scallions or small leeks
$^1/_4$ lb bamboo shoots
$2^1/_2$ cups chicken broth
1 tbsp soy sauce
1 tbsp rice wine
generous pinch sugar
$^1/_4$ cup peanut oil
salt

Time: 1 hour 10 minutes

Soak the mushrooms in warm water for 20 minutes. Meanwhile, shred the pork very finely (if wished, put the meat in the freezer for

FIVE-COLOR FRIED RICE

什锦炒饭

shí jǐn chǎo fàn

*Approx. 4 cups boiled Chinese or any long-grain rice (*pai fan*)*
$^1/_4$ cup pork, finely diced
$^1/_4$ cup Yunnan or York ham, finely diced
$^1/_4$ cup peeled small shrimp
2 eggs
3 tung ku (dong gu) mushrooms
1 small onion, very finely chopped
$^1/_3$ cup fresh or frozen peas

1 tbsp light soy sauce
pinch monosodium glutamate (optional)
$^1/_2$ cup oil
salt and freshly ground pepper

Time: 40 minutes

Boil the rice. Use Chinese rice (when buying, stipulate that it is for plain boiled rice; do not use glutinous rice or any good long-grain rice); place the rice in a sieve, rinse well under running cold water; if you have time, soak the rice for 1–2 hours in cold water, then drain. To cook 2 cups rice, heat $2^1/_4$ cups water in a pan until it boils; sprinkle in the rice and boil for 5

about 30 minutes beforehand to make it easier to slice) and place in a bowl; sprinkle the shredded pork with the soy sauce, rice wine, and sugar. Mix well, then leave to marinate for 30 minutes. Drain the softened mushrooms, then remove their stalks and discard them; cut the caps into thin strips. Trim the scallions and cut into ³/₄-in lengths. If leeks are used, wash thoroughly and dry. Cut the bamboo shoots into thin strips the same length. Heat half the oil in the wok and stir-fry the pork until evenly colored all over. Remove the meat from the wok or pan and set aside. Bring a large pan of salted water to a boil and add the noodles. Heat the remaining, fresh, oil in the wok, add the scallions, stir-fry briefly, then add the mushrooms and the bamboo shoots. Stir-fry briefly, then return the meat to the wok and add a little salt. Cook for a further 5 minutes or until the ingredients are tender, moistening with a little hot water or broth as necessary. Heat the chicken broth in a small saucepan. Drain the noodles when done and place a small quantity in each person's individual bowl. Add a portion of pork and pour the boiling chicken broth into the bowls. Serve at once.

SWEET PEANUT SOUP *

花生汤
huā shēng tāng

1¹/₄ lb peanuts in their shells or approx.
1 lb shelled, unroasted peanuts
1 cup sugar
3–4 drops pure vanilla extract (optional)

Time: 1 hour

Shell the peanuts and place in a large bowl. Add sufficient boiling water to cover and leave to stand for 5 minutes (this will make it easier to remove the thin papery skin which covers the nuts). Drain and place the nuts in a clean cloth and rub to help loosen the skins. Bring 2 quarts water to a boil in a large pan, add the nuts, and boil for 40 minutes. When the nuts are cooked, stir in the sugar and vanilla until the sugar has completely dissolved. Serve hot.

EGG AND TOMATO SOUP

番茄蛋花汤
fān qié dàn huā tāng

6 cups chicken broth
2¹/₂ tsp salt
pinch monosodium glutamate (optional)
2 large, ripe tomatoes
2 oz tofu (bean curd)
2 large, very fresh eggs
2¹/₂ tbsp very finely chopped scallions
generous pinch freshly ground pepper
1 tbsp rice wine

1 tbsp sesame seed oil (optional)

Time: 15 minutes

Bring the broth to a boil with the salt and monosodium glutamate (if used). Blanch and peel the tomatoes, remove their seeds and cut them roughly into strips. Add to the broth. Cut the tofu into small cubes and also add to the broth. Simmer for 5 minutes. Beat the eggs lightly in a bowl and pour into the soup; turn off the heat as you add them and stir very vigorously with a balloon whisk. Add the scallion, pepper, rice wine, and sesame seed oil to taste.

EGG AND SOY FLOUR NOODLE SOUP

榨菜粉丝蛋花汤

zhà cài fěn sī dàn huā tāng

6 cups chicken broth
1 tsp salt
pinch monosodium glutamate (optional)
2 zucchini
1 carrot
2 oz bamboo shoots
1¹/₂ tbsp fresh or frozen peas
2 oz salt-pickled Chinese greens (za zai)
2 oz soy flour noodles
2 eggs
2¹/₂ tbsp finely chopped scallion
pinch freshly ground pepper
1 tbsp sesame seed oil
1 tbsp rice wine

Time: 30 minutes

Bring the chicken broth to a boil and add the salt and monosodium glutamate (if used). Wash and trim the zucchini, the carrot, and bamboo shoots (drain if canned) and cut all these vegetables into fine matchstick strips. Rinse the Chinese greens in a sieve under running cold water to eliminate excess salt, drain well, and shred into thin strips. Add all these vegetables to the broth and boil for 10 minutes. Meanwhile, soak the noodles in warm water for 10 minutes, then add to the soup. Cook for 2 minutes, then stir in the lightly beaten eggs.

Turn off the heat, stir in the scallion, pepper, sesame seed oil, and rice wine.

CHICKEN AND MUSHROOM SOUP

冬菇炖鸡

dōng gū dùn jī

1 oven-ready roasting or boiling chicken
weighing 3¹/₄–3¹/₂ lb
10 tung ku (dong gu) mushrooms
2 leeks
2 sticks celery
1 large piece fresh ginger approx. 2 in long
1 tbsp rice wine
salt

Time: 2¹/₂ hours

Soak the mushrooms in warm water for 20 minutes and drain, squeezing out excess moisture. Remove and discard the stalks and keep the caps whole. Bring a large, deep pan of water (about two-thirds full) to a boil, add the whole chicken and boil for 5 minutes. Remove the chicken from the pan, rinse thoroughly under running cold water and then place in a large, heavy-bottomed saucepan with a very tight-fitting lid. Add the cleaned, trimmed, and finely sliced leeks, celery, peeled ginger, the rice wine, and sufficient water to completely cover the chicken. Add a generous pinch of salt. Bring to a boil, cover, and lower the heat so that the liquid simmers very slowly; cook for 2 hours, then remove the lid and skim any scum from the surface. Take the chicken out of the pan and remove the flesh off the bone, and chop it into fairly small, neat pieces with a light cleaver or very sharp knife. Place all or some of the chicken pieces into individual bowls and ladle the boiling hot chicken broth over them.

BEEF AND EGG SOUP

牛肉蛋花汤

niú ròu dàn huā tāng

¹/₂ lb lean beef
7 cups beef broth
2 sticks celery
1 scallion
2 large, very fresh eggs
salt and freshly ground pepper

Time: ³/₄ hour

Cut the beef into very small pieces. Trim and wash the celery and slice very thinly. Trim off the extreme ends of the scallion and remove the outer layer. Cut off the green, leaf section and chop very finely. Cut the white part into thin rings. Keep these two parts separate. Break the eggs into a bowl, remove the membranous white thread (chalaza), and beat lightly with a fork. Bring the beef broth to a boil in a large pan; add the meat, celery, the white part of the scallion and a pinch of salt. Simmer for 20 minutes, remove from the heat, and beat in the egg using a balloon whisk. Work fast so the eggs have no chance to scramble but thicken the soup slightly instead. Ladle the soup into individual bowls, sprinkle the surface with the chopped scallion leaves, add a little pepper if wished, and serve.

Make your own beef broth by simmering a shin of beef for several hours in a large pan of water with an onion, carrot and bay leaf or use 3 cans good-quality canned beef consommé, each can diluted by an equal volume of water.

TOFU SOUP PEKING STYLE *

肉丸豆腐汤

ròu wán dòu fǔ tāng

10 oz firm tofu (bean curd) (i.e. not silken
tofu)
3 fairly thin slices pork belly
3 tung ku (dong gu) mushrooms
5 cabbage leaves
¹/₂ cup finely chopped lean pork
1 tbsp rice wine
2¹/₂ tsp finely chopped leek
1 tsp grated fresh ginger
1¹/₂ tbsp soy sauce
2¹/₂ tsp salt
1 heaping tbsp cornstarch or potato flour
monosodium glutamate (optional)
freshly ground pepper
1 tsp sugar

Time: 45 minutes

Dice the tofu cake and allow any excess liquid to drain off. Cut the pork belly into narrow strips, cutting across the lines of fat and lean. Soak the mushrooms in warm water until softened and reconstituted, drain, cut off the stalks and discard; cut the caps into quarters and then slice each quarter finely. Shred the cabbage. Place the meat in a large mixing bowl with the leek, ginger, cornstarch or potato flour, rice wine, a few drops of soy sauce, a pinch of monosodium glutamate (if used), a small pinch each of salt and freshly ground pepper, and 2¹/₂ tbsp cold water. Mix all these ingredients together very thoroughly. Break off small pieces and shape into balls about 1 in in diameter. Bring 4¹/₂ cups water to a boil in a wide saucepan and add the meatballs, mushrooms, and pork belly. Boil gently for 5 minutes, then stir in 1 tbsp soy sauce, the sugar, a pinch of salt, a pinch of monosodium glutamate (if used), a little pepper, and the cabbage.

Cook, stirring gently for 1–2 minutes, then add the tofu and simmer for 5 minutes. Serve very hot.

FISH FILLETS PÁ CHǍO

扒 炒 鱼 片

pá chǎo yú pián

1¹/₄ lb white fish fillets
¹/₂–1 tsp salt
1¹/₂ tsp rice wine
1 heaping tbsp cornstarch or potato flour
oil for frying

For the sauce:
2¹/₂ tbsp oil
1 tbsp very finely chopped scallion
1 tbsp very finely chopped fresh ginger
¹/₄ cup fish stock or chicken broth
1 tsp salt
¹/₂–1 tsp sugar
¹/₂ tsp monosodium glutamate (optional)
1 tbsp sesame seed oil
1 tbsp cornstarch or potato flour

Time: ¹/₂ hour

Cut the fish fillets into pieces measuring about 1¹/₄ × ³/₄ in. Mix the rice wine with the salt in a bowl large enough to accommodate the fish; stir in the cornstarch mixed with a very little water. Dip the fish pieces in this, coating all over. Heat plenty of oil until very hot in a skillet and fry the fish pieces a few at a time for 1 minute; remove, draining well. Heat 2¹/₂ tbsp oil in the wok, stir-fry the scallion and ginger briefly, then add the broth, salt, sugar, and monosodium glutamate (if used). Stir briefly, add the fish pieces, and cook, uncovered, for a few minutes to reduce the liquid a little. Mix the cornstarch with a very little cold water and stir into the wok to thicken the sauce slightly. Turn off the heat and sprinkle in the sesame seed oil.

Pa ciao is a cooking technique said to have been invented by a cook at the imperial court: an empress who was partial to fish fillets found this recipe particularly delicious and asked its name so that she could order it again. The cook made up a name on the spur of the moment: "pa ciao yu pian," which describes the technique of dipping the fish in this special coating mixture before cooking it.

FISH WITH VINEGAR AND PEPPER

醋 椒 活 鱼

cù jiāo huó yú

1 very fresh whole fish (e.g. porgy, trout or
  similar) weighing approx. 1³/₄ lb
2¹/₂ tbsp shortening or butter
¹/₂–1 tsp freshly ground white peppercorns
1 tbsp very finely chopped fresh ginger
1 tbsp finely chopped scallion
¹/₂ cup chicken broth
¹/₂ cup milk
1 tbsp rice wine
2¹/₂ tbsp white rice wine vinegar or ordinary
  white wine vinegar
1 tsp salt
1 tbsp sesame seed oil
1 sprig parsley

Time: 45 minutes

Trim the fins off the fish, remove all the scales if present, and gut through the gill opening; rinse well inside and out and dry. Make 6 deep, oblique slashes down each side, then 6 more, crossing the other slashes to form a lattice effect. Melt the shortening in the wok or in an oval skillet large enough to take the whole fish, add the pepper, ginger, and scallion and stir-fry briefly, then add the broth, milk, rice wine, vinegar, and salt.

Place the fish in fast boiling water for 2 minutes, drain, and transfer to the wok; cook over fairly low heat for 5 minutes, then turn carefully and cook for a further 5 minutes or until done. Sprinkle with the sesame seed oil just before removing from the wok.

Place the fish on a serving plate, keeping it whole, sprinkle the liquid from the wok all over it, and garnish with chopped parsley.

Cu jiao (vinegar and pepper) is a cooking method which originates in Shantung (where all fish are only killed just as work begins on the dish); the combination of these two flavors is pleasantly astringent and spicy.

FISH FILLETS ZĀO LIŪ

槽 溜 鱼 片

zāo liū yū pián

4 mo ha mushrooms (tree ear fungus), sold
  dried
1¹/₄ lb fillets of white fish
1 egg white
1 tsp salt
1 heaping tbsp cornstarch or potato flour
¹/₂ cup oil for frying
1 tbsp finely chopped fresh ginger
1 tbsp finely chopped scallion
3 tbsp fish stock or chicken broth
1 tsp sugar
¹/₂ tsp salt
pinch monosodium glutamate (optional)
6 tbsp rice wine (Shian ciao type)
2¹/₂ tbsp cornstarch or potato flour

Time: 30 minutes

Soak the mushrooms in warm water (20–30 minutes), trim off and discard any tough, fibrous pieces, and cut into thin strips.

Cut the fish fillets into short strips measuring ³/₈ × 1¹/₄ in. Beat the egg white, mix with the salt and cornstarch, add the fish pieces, and blend well. Leave to marinate for 10 minutes.

Heat the oil in a skillet until very hot and fry the fish pieces in two or three batches for 1 minute only (alternatively, deep-fry). Drain the fish well and set aside. Heat 2¹/₂ tbsp fresh oil in the wok and stir-fry the ginger and scallion until they release their aroma; add the broth, sugar, salt, monosodium glutamate (if used), and the wine and cook until reduced a little. Return the fish pieces to the wok, add the mushrooms, and cook for 2 minutes, turning once. Mix the cornstarch with a little cold water and add to the wok; stir and cook for 1–2 minutes. Serve.

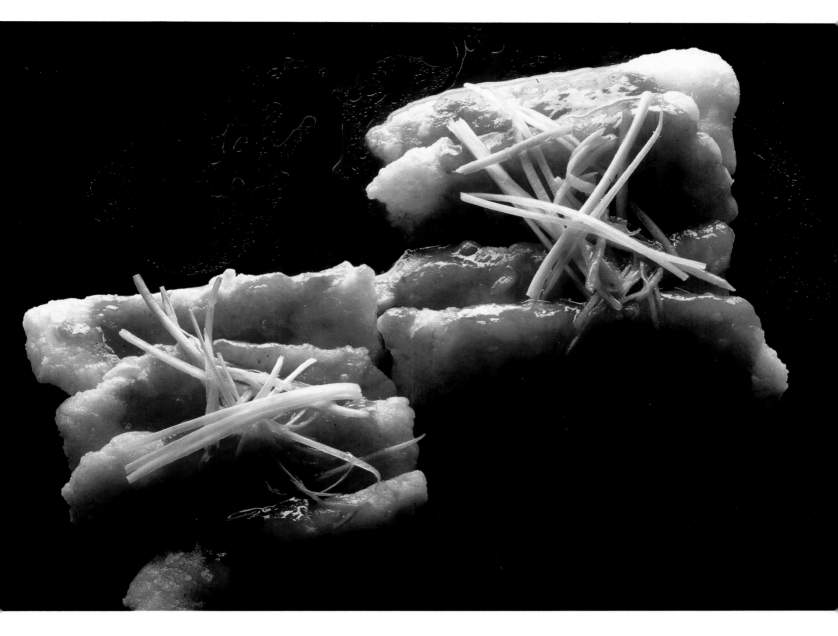

PEKING SWEET-SOUR FISH *

京式糖醋鱼

jīng shì táng cú yú

1³/₄ lb fillets of flounder, sole, porgy or trout
2 scallions
5 thin slices fresh ginger
1 tbsp very finely chopped garlic
oil for frying

For the coating batter:
1 large egg
¹/₂ cup all-purpose flour

For the sauce:
3 tbsp oil
¹/₃ cup sugar
¹/₃ cup red or white rice wine vinegar
3 tbsp rice wine
1 tbsp salt
pinch monosodium glutamate (optional)
generous pinch freshly ground pepper
3 tbsp tomato ketchup
1¹/₂ tbsp cornstarch or potato flour

Time: 40 minutes

Cut the fish fillets into rectangular pieces about 1 × 2 in. Beat the egg lightly, then beat in the flour and just enough water to make a creamy batter (alternatively, process these in-gredients in the liquidizer). Heat plenty of oil in the wok for semi deep-frying or use a deep-fryer. When very hot, dip the fish pieces in the batter to coat and fry a few at a time until gol-den brown. Remove with a slotted spoon, draining well, and place on paper towels. Slice the trimmed and peeled scallions and ginger into very thin strips, crush the garlic, and stir-fry these 3 ingredients gently in 3 tbsp fresh oil. Add the sugar, vinegar, wine, salt, monosodium glutamate (if used), pepper, and ketchup, simmer for 1–2 minutes, then thicken by stirring in the cornstarch mixed with a little cold water.

Transfer the fish pieces to a serving plate, pour the sauce over them, and serve.

the fish on paper towels.

Wipe the inside of the wok and make the sauce: heat $^1/_4$ cup fresh oil and stir-fry the scallion and ginger; add the Szechwan pepper, stir well, and return the fish to the wok. Fry briefly, turning the fish once carefully, then mix the salt, rice wine, and sesame oil and sprinkle all over the fish. Cook for a further minute and serve.

SWEET-SOUR FISH WITH CRISPY FRIED NOODLES

糖醋鱼焙面

táng cù yú bèi miàn

1 whole white-fleshed freshwater fish (e.g. perch, tench, carp etc.) weighing approx. 1$^1/_4$ lb
1 cup red wine vinegar
2 tbsp dark soy sauce
3$^1/_2$ tbsp light soy sauce
1 cup fish stock or chicken broth
4 cloves garlic, very finely chopped
2 small fresh red chili peppers, finely chopped or generous pinch ground chili
1 onion, finely chopped
$^1/_4$ cup oil
$^1/_2$ cup sugar
1 cup cornstarch
oil for frying

Time: 1 hour

Trim the fish removing head, tail, and fins; descale and gut it by slitting down the belly; make a deep incision down to the backbone all along its length and work the flesh neatly off the bones with a very sharp pointed knife. Rinse and dry the fillets.

Prepare the sweet-sour sauce: mix all the sauce ingredients in a small bowl and set aside. Heat $^1/_4$ cup oil in the wok (or a skillet), add the sugar, and cook watching it carefully, until the sugar turns pale golden brown; pour in the contents of the bowl and boil until the sauce has reduced and thickened a little.

Make the batter: mix the cornstarch very thoroughly with just enough cold water to make a fairly thick coating batter. Coat the fish fillets with this batter. Heat plenty of oil for deep semi-frying in a pan (or use a deep-fryer). When the oil is at about 360°F (very hot but not smoking hot) add the first fish fillet and fry until golden brown all over. Remove, draining well, and allow the oil to return to the correct temperature before frying the next fillet. Transfer the cooked fillets to a heated serving dish, pour the sweet-sour sauce over them, and serve.

Accompany with crispy fried noodles, served in a separate dish (see recipe on p. 21).

FRIED ANCHOVIES WITH SZECHWAN PEPPER *

五香鱼

wǔ xiāng yú

2$^1/_4$ lb fresh anchovies or silversides
1 tsp very finely chopped scallion
1 tsp very finely chopped fresh ginger
2 tbsp sesame seed oil
$^1/_2$ tbsp ground Szechwan pepper
oil for frying

For the coating batter:
1 large egg
$^1/_2$ cup all-purpose flour

For the sauce:
$^1/_4$ cup oil
1 tsp very finely chopped scallion
1 tsp very finely chopped fresh ginger
2 tsp salt
1 heaping tsp Szechwan pepper
5 tbsp rice wine
1 tbsp sesame seed oil

Time: 1 hour

Trim off the anchovies' tail fins. Carefully pull off their heads and the entrails should come out too (or leave the heads on and snip their bellies open with scissors to gut). Rinse and dry. Mix together the scallion, ginger, sesame oil, and Szechwan pepper. Roll the fish in this mixture to flavor them all over and leave to stand for 30 minutes.

Beat the egg with the flour and add sufficient cold water to make a fairly thick batter. Pour this over the fish, turning them to coat evenly and then fry them a few at a time in 3 tbsp oil in the wok (add more oil when necessary) until golden brown. Drain well and place

TROUT TIENTSIN STYLE

天津鱼

tiān jīn yú

1 trout weighing approx. 2¹/₄ lb
¹/₂ cup very finely chopped lean pork
*   (e.g. shoulder)*
1 tbsp soy sauce
1 tbsp finely chopped scallion
1 tbsp finely chopped fresh ginger
1 tbsp cornstarch or potato flour
¹/₂ cup all-purpose flour
oil for frying

For the side salad:
1 large carrot
1 large, long white radish (Daikon root)
2 scallions
6 thin slices fresh ginger
4 cloves garlic
1 tsp ground Szechwan pepper
¹/₄ cup soy sauce
1 tsp sugar
1 tsp salt
pinch monosodium glutamate (optional)
3 tbsp rice wine
1 tbsp sesame seed oil

Time: 1¹/₂ hours

Trim and clean the trout, gutting it through the gill opening; rinse well and dry. Mix the chopped pork with the soy sauce, finely chopped scallion and ginger, and the cornstarch and use to stuff the ventral cavity of the fish. Heat 3 tbsp oil in the wok and shallow-fry the trout until a good golden brown on both sides. Remove carefully from the wok and set aside.

Peel the long white radish and the carrot and cut into thin matchstick strips; blanch for 1 minute in boiling water. Drain well. Finely chop the peeled and trimmed scallion and ginger; heat 3 tbsp oil in the wok and stir-fry them briefly with the crushed garlic and the Szechwan pepper. Once they have started to release their aroma, add the soy sauce, sugar, salt, monosodium glutamate (if used), wine, sesame seed oil, and the shredded carrot and radish; stir-fry for 1 minute and then add 2 cups water, allow to return to a simmer, and cook for 20 minutes, uncovered. Place the whole trout on top of the vegetables in the wok and cook slowly for 25–30 minutes, making sure that the liquid does not completely evaporate.

Transfer the trout to a serving dish, surround with the vegetables, and pour the remaining liquid over the fish.

FILLETS OF FISH MANDARIN STYLE *

锅锟鱼

guō kūn yú

14 oz fillets of perch
¹/₄ cup light soy sauce
1 cup chicken broth
3 tbsp rice wine
1 tbsp fresh ginger juice (see method)
salt
1 cup shortening
¹/₂ cup all-purpose flour
2 lightly beaten eggs

Time: 40 minutes

Pound the fillets very lightly with a meat bat; sprinkle with 1¹/₂ tbsp light soy sauce.

Pour the chicken broth into a bowl and stir in the remaining soy sauce, the rice wine, ginger juice (to obtain this, mince the ginger in a garlic crusher) and a pinch of salt.

Heat the shortening in the wok or a skillet; coat the fish fillets with flour, shaking off excess, and dip in the egg to cover all over. Heat the shortening to very hot (not smoking hot), draw the wok or pan off the heat and slide the fillets into the fat down the side of the wok or pan; leave in the fat to fry (cook in several batches, reheating the fat and removing from the heat each time as above); drain and place in a fireproof casserole dish or pan.

Pour the contents of the bowl into the casserole containing the fish and simmer very slowly for 20 minutes.

STIR-FRIED SHRIMP *

清炒虾仁

qīng chǎo xiā rén

1¼ lb shrimp, heads removed
1 egg white
pinch monosodium glutamate (optional)
1 tsp salt
1 tbsp cornstarch or potato flour
2½ tbsp rice wine
oil for frying
⅓ cup fresh or frozen peas

For the sauce:
3 tbsp oil
pinch monosodium glutamate (optional)
pinch salt
1½ tbsp rice wine

Time: 30 minutes

Peel the shrimp, remove the black alimentary tract which runs down the center of their backs, rinse, and dry. Beat the egg white, adding the monosodium glutamate (if used), salt, cornstarch, and rice wine; add the shrimp, stir, and leave to marinate. Boil the peas until tender and drain. Heat ½ cup oil in the wok or a skillet and when very hot add the shrimp and peas, fry for 1 minute, drain well, and set aside. Empty the oil out of the wok and heat 3 tbsp fresh oil with a pinch of salt and monosodium glutamate (if used) and 1½ tbsp rice wine. Return the shrimp and peas to the wok and stir-fry for 2 minutes, allowing the liquid to reduce. Serve.

PEKING FRIED SHRIMP

京式虾球

jīng shì xiā qiú

1¼ lb jumbo or large shrimp, heads removed
1 tbsp light soy sauce
1 tbsp rice wine
1 tsp sugar
2 tsp red wine vinegar
salt
freshly ground pepper
2½ tbsp shortening
1 onion
3 slices fresh ginger
1 cup cornstarch
oil for frying

Time: 30 minutes

Peel the shrimp, removing the black thread-like alimentary tract which runs down their backs; rinse and dry with paper towels.

Mix the soy sauce in a bowl with the rice wine, sugar, vinegar, a pinch of salt, and a pinch of freshly ground pepper; set aside.

Heat the shortening in the wok and stir-fry the very finely chopped onion and ginger for 1 minute; add the contents of the bowl, stir well, and bring to a gentle simmer. Turn off the heat while frying the shrimp; reheat when they are ready.

Heat enough oil for deep semi-frying, or use a deep-fryer. Mix the cornstarch with sufficient cold water to make a fairly liquid coating batter; dip the shrimp in this (stir the batter well at frequent intervals to prevent the cornstarch sinking to the bottom) and fry one or two at a time for 1–2 minutes or until golden brown. Drain well then add to the simmering sauce. Cook, turning once or twice, for just long enough to flavor; serve.

KOREAN FRIED SHRIMP *

高丽凤尾虾

gāo lí fèng wěi xiā

2¹/₄ lb jumbo shrimp, heads removed
pinch freshly ground pepper
1 tsp salt
pinch monosodium glutamate (optional)
pinch sugar
oil for frying

For the batter:
1 egg white
¹/₂ cup cornstarch or potato flour
1 tbsp oil
1 tbsp wine vinegar

For the sauce:
1 tbsp soy sauce
1 tbsp wine vinegar
1 tbsp finely chopped scallion
1 tbsp finely chopped fresh ginger
1 tsp sugar

1 tsp sesame seed oil
1 tsp ground chili pepper

For the condiment:
1 tbsp five-spice powder
6 tbsp salt
2 tsp monosodium glutamate (optional)

Time: 30 minutes

Peel the shrimp; use very sharp, pointed scissors to make a fairly deep cut straight down the center of the shrimp's backs, extract the black alimentary tract, rinse, dry, and open the shrimp out along the incision so that when pressed with the palm of your hand they lie almost flat (keep the extreme ends of the tail intact, with the last section of shell and flippers still attached). Season with pepper, salt, monosodium glutamate (if used), and sugar. Mix well, and leave to flavor.

Beat the egg white and mix with the cornstarch, oil, and vinegar, adding a very little cold water if necessary to make a smooth, fairly thick coating batter. Add the shrimp to this batter, making sure they are coated all over. Heat plenty of oil in the wok or skillet (to about 325°F or a little hotter) and fry the shrimp until golden brown.

Mix all the sauce ingredients together in a bowl and mix the condiment ingredients in a second bowl.

Each person dips the fried shrimp in the sauce and condiment as wished.

SHRIMP PÁ CHĂO

扒炸虾仁
pá chǎo xiā rén

1¼ lb peeled shrimp
1 tbsp rice wine
1 tsp salt
½ tsp monosodium glutamate (optional)
1 tbsp sugar
1 egg
2½ tbsp cornstarch or potato flour
oil for frying

For the sauce:
3 tbsp oil
1 tsp finely chopped scallion
1 tsp finely chopped fresh ginger
3 tbsp rice wine
3 tbsp fish stock or chicken broth
1 tsp sugar
1½ tsp cornstarch

Time: 30 minutes

Mix the shrimp with the wine, salt, monosodium glutamate (if used), and sugar. Beat the egg lightly, dip the shrimp in it, and then coat with a batter made by mixing the cornstarch with scant ¼ cup cold water, allowing any excess to drip off. Heat the oil in the wok and when very hot, fry the shrimp for 1 minute (in several batches), and drain well. Empty the wok, heat 3 tbsp fresh oil and stir-fry the ginger and scallion until they release their aroma; return the shrimp to the wok, add the wine, fish stock or broth, and the sugar. Cook for a few minutes, allowing the liquid to reduce. Stir in the cornstarch mixed with a very little cold water.

STIR-FRIED SHRIMP IN TOMATO SAUCE

茄汁虾仁
qié zhī xiā rén

1 lb shrimp
1 egg white
1 tsp salt
1 tbsp cornstarch or potato flour
1 tbsp finely chopped fresh ginger
1 tbsp finely chopped scallion
⅓ cup fresh or frozen peas
1 large, ripe tomato
¼ cup oil

For the sauce:
3 tbsp tomato ketchup
½ cup chicken or vegetable broth
½ tsp monosodium glutamate (optional)
2½ tbsp sugar
1 tbsp wine vinegar
½ tbsp salt
1 tsp sesame seed oil
1½ tbsp cornstarch or potato flour

Time: 40 minutes

Peel the shrimp, remove the black thread which runs down their backs, rinse and dry them, then coat in the mixture of beaten egg white, salt, and cornstarch.

Heat 1½ tbsp oil in the wok and stir-fry the shrimp for 1 minute. Remove and drain.

Wipe the inside of the wok, heat 3 tbsp fresh oil and stir-fry the ginger and scallion; add the peas and tomato. Stir in the ketchup, broth, monosodium glutamate (if used), sugar, vinegar, and salt. Return the shrimp to the wok and cook for 2 minutes. Mix in the cornstarch combined with a little cold water, stir well, turn off the heat, and sprinkle with the sesame seed oil before serving.

BUTTERFLY SHRIMP *

炸明虾段
zhà míng xiā duàn

12 jumbo shrimp
3 tbsp all-purpose flour
oil for frying
1 scallion

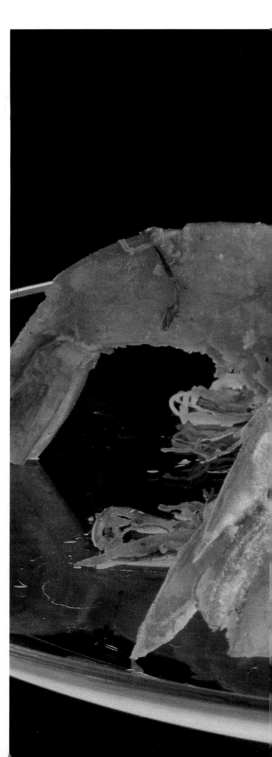

8 thin slices fresh ginger
1 tsp salt
pinch monosodium glutamate (optional)
1 tbsp rice wine
1 tsp sesame seed oil

Time: 35 minutes

Snip off the shrimp's legs and feelers; use the scissors to cut right down their backs, remove the black alimentary canal and then deepen the cut you have already made and cut them lengthwise in half. Rinse, dry, and coat with the flour. Heat 3 tbsp oil in the wok and stir-fry the shrimp until golden brown; drain on paper towels and keep hot.

Trim and peel the scallion and the ginger slices; shred both finely, then stir-fry in 2 tbsp fresh oil in the wok; once they start to release their aroma, add the salt, monosodium glutamate (if used), wine, and sesame oil. Stir. Return the shrimp to the wok, mix well, and simmer for 1–2 minutes to reduce the liquid a little.

RUNAWAY CRABS

赛螃蟹

sài páng xiè

14 oz fillets of white fish
5 eggs
6 tbsp oil
1 tbsp finely chopped scallion
1 tsp finely chopped fresh ginger
1 tsp salt
pinch monosodium glutamate (optional)
2¹/₂ tbsp rice wine
2¹/₂ tbsp chicken broth
1 heaping tsp cornstarch or potato flour
1 tbsp melted chicken fat

Time: 30 minutes

Make sure there are no bones left in the fish, then cut the fillets into squares or small cubes if thick. Break the eggs into a bowl and beat lightly with a fork. Heat 6 tbsp oil in the wok; stir-fry the scallion and the ginger briefly, add the fish, cook for 1–2 minutes then pour in the beaten egg to one side so that you can scramble it with a fork or chopsticks as it cooks and sets. Once the eggs are set, add the salt, monosodium glutamate (if used), wine, and broth and cook until the liquid has reduced a little. Mix the cornstarch with a little water and stir into the sauce in the wok to thicken slightly. By this time the fish should be completely cooked. Sprinkle the melted chicken fat into the wok, stir gently, and serve.

In this deceptively named dish, the white fish represents the white crabmeat and the eggs the brown meat.

STUFFED STEAMED CRABS *

清蒸蟹肉

qǐng zhěng xiè ròu

8 small freshwater or sea crabs
1 tbsp very finely chopped onion
¹/₂ tbsp very finely chopped fresh ginger
1¹/₂ tsp red wine vinegar
1¹/₂ tsp sugar mixed with 1 tsp salt

Time: 1 hour

Rinse the crabs, pull the lower section away from the upper shell, and remove the gray feathery gills ("dead men's fingers") and the small, leathery stomach sac. Remove all the meat (brown and white) from the body shell and from the legs and claws, placing it in a

bowl. Mix the crabmeat thoroughly with the onion, ginger, wine, vinegar, and the sugar and salt mixture.

Rinse out the empty top halves of the crab shells, dry and pack the flavored crabmeat firmly back into them; line the steamer compartment(s) with a clean cloth or cloths and place the crab shells, with the open side showing the stuffing uppermost, in the steamer. Place a sheet of waxed paper on top of them, cover, and steam for 15 minutes.

When cooked, transfer to a serving plate and decorate with fresh flowers or flowers made out of white or small red radishes, carrots, tomatoes etc.

SQUID YOU BAO

油爆鱿鱼

yóu bào yóu yú

1¼ lb squid
2 cloves garlic
1 tbsp finely chopped scallion
2½ tbsp rice wine
1 tsp salt
1 tbsp sesame seed oil
1 tbsp wine vinegar
pinch monosodium glutamate (optional)
1 tbsp cornstarch or potato flour
oil for frying

Time: 40 minutes

Buy prepared squid if you can; you will use only the empty bodies (looking like long white bags) for this recipe; if the thin skin is present, rub it off under running cold water. Slit the body down one side and open out flat; cut into rectangles measuring 1 × 1½ in and make a fairly deep incision in the form of a cross on one side of each rectangle.

Add the squid pieces to a saucepan of boiling water and blanch very briefly until they curl up (without the incision they will not do this). Drain well, then semi deep-fry or deep-fry for a few seconds in very hot oil; remove from the oil, draining well. Heat 2½ tbsp fresh oil in the wok and stir-fry the peeled and very thinly sliced garlic and the scallion lightly; add the squid, followed by the wine, salt, sesame oil, vinegar, and monosodium glutamate (if used); stir and simmer to reduce the liquid a little. Mix the cornstarch with a little cold water and stir into the wok to thicken the liquid.

"You bao" describes the technique of blanching meat or fish before deep-frying or stir-frying in oil and then adding the sauce ingredients. The term "len bao" describes a similar process but the saucing is omitted and the ingredients are eaten "dry."

CHRYSANTHEMUM CHICKEN *

菊花鸡

jú huā jī

1/2 medium-sized oven-ready chicken
1 egg white
1 tsp salt

1 tbsp cornstarch or potato flour
2 medium-sized onions
2¹/₂ tbsp oil
oil for frying

For the sauce:
2¹/₂ tbsp soy sauce
¹/₂ tsp salt
1 tsp sugar
pinch monosodium glutamate (optional)
1 tbsp rice wine

1 tsp sesame seed oil
2 cups chicken broth

Time: 1 hour 10 minutes

Take all the chicken flesh off the bone, remove the skin, and dice the flesh (you should have approx. 1 lb). Beat the egg white and mix thoroughly with the salt and cornstarch, add the diced chicken, mix to coat thoroughly, and leave to stand. Peel the onions, removing the first, tougher layer underneath the brown papery skin; use a very sharp, serrated knife to cut from the top of the onion downward, stopping short of the base: have the point of the knife in the center of the onion and pivot the point as you gradually work round the onion slicing downward to within $1/2$ in of the base, each cut being about $1/4$ in apart: the result will be a "feathery" look reminiscent of a chrysanthemum flower.

Heat enough oil to semi deep-fry or deep-fry the chicken in a skillet or deep-fryer; when very hot but not smoking, fry the chicken for 1–2 minutes; remove, draining well. Heat $2^1/2$ tbsp fresh oil in the wok, stir-fry the onions for 1 minute over gentle heat, add the chicken and cook for another minute. Add the soy sauce, salt, sugar, monosodium glutamate (if used), the rice wine, and sesame seed oil. Pour in the broth and simmer, uncovered, until the onion is tender and the liquid has considerably reduced.

This is one of the many examples in Chinese cooking where foods are fashioned to look like a different, beautiful natural object, part of the strong aesthetic inspiration in food preparation.

CHICKEN AND CHESTNUTS

栗 子 鸡
lì zǐ jī

$1/2$ oven-ready chicken weighing $2^1/4$ lb
20 or 30 dried chestnuts
3 shallots or scallions, finely chopped
$2^1/2$ tbsp finely grated fresh ginger
$1/4$ cup rice wine
$1/4$ cup light soy sauce
$2^1/2$ tbsp sesame seed oil
$1/4$ cup chicken broth
1 tsp sugar
salt

Time: 2 hours 20 minutes + 24 hours soaking time for the chestnuts

A full 24 hours before you intend to prepare this dish, place the dried chestnuts in a bowl of water to soak and reconstitute; the following day, drain and remove any remains of the thin inner skin still clinging to them. Place the chestnuts in a saucepan, cover with water, add a generous pinch of salt, and boil until they are tender. Drain and set aside. While the chestnuts are cooking, take all the chicken flesh off the bone, remove the skin and cut into small bite-sized pieces. Make the marinade: mix the wine with the soy sauce, sugar, ginger, scallion, and a pinch of salt. Place the chicken pieces in a fairly deep dish, pour the marinade all over them, mix, and leave to stand for 30 minutes, turning occasionally. Drain the

chicken pieces, reserving the marinade, and stir-fry in the sesame seed oil in the wok or skillet. Add the reserved marinade and the broth. Bring to a boil, then reduce the heat and add the chestnuts. Simmer for 20 minutes, seasoning with a little more salt if necessary.

SESAME CHICKEN *

芝 麻 鸡
zhī má jī

$1/4$ lb bamboo shoots
1 cucumber
10 oz chicken breasts
1 tbsp finely chopped scallion
1 tbsp finely chopped fresh ginger
1 tsp salt
1 tbsp rice wine
pinch monosodium glutamate (optional)
1 tbsp cornstarch or potato flour
3 eggs
$1/2$ cup white sesame seeds
3 tbsp all-purpose flour
oil for frying

Time: $1^1/2$ hours

Peel the cucumber, cut lengthwise in half, and scoop out all the seeds; cut into fairly small pieces, sprinkle with salt, and place in a colander with a plate and a weight on top to express as much moisture as possible (this should take about 15 minutes); rinse under running cold water and dry thoroughly, then mince or process in the food processor to a thick purée. Drain off more liquid if possible. Grind the chicken meat finely and do the same with the drained bamboo shoots (or use a food processor to reduce to a fairly smooth paste). Mix the chicken, bamboo shoots, cucumber, scallion, ginger, salt, rice wine, monosodium glutamate (if used) and the cornstarch until very well blended. Beat 2 of the eggs lightly and make the thinnest possible omelets, using a 6-in omelet pan if possible; 2 large eggs should yield about 12 wafer-thin omelets. Beat the remaining egg with the flour and just enough cold water to make a thick coating batter.

Place a small quantity of the chicken mixture in the center of each omelet and roll up into parcels approx. $3/4$ in thick, $1^1/4$ in wide and about $2^1/4$ in long. Coat the outside of the parcels carefully with the thick batter and sprinkle all over with the sesame seeds. Heat about $1/2$ cup oil in the wok or a very wide skillet and fry the parcels gently for 5 minutes, then turn very carefully, increase the heat, continue frying, and serve when golden brown.

58

CHICKEN WITH WALNUTS *

炸鸡饼

zhà jī bǐng

1 lb chicken breasts
1 egg white
1 tsp salt
1 tbsp soy sauce
2¹/₂ tbsp cornstarch or potato flour
1 cup shelled walnut halves
¹/₄ cup sugar
¹/₄ cup sweet soy paste
1 tbsp rice wine
1 tbsp sesame seed oil
peanut oil

Time: 1 hour

Remove the skin and cut the flesh into strips measuring about ³/₈ × 1¹/₄ in; beat the egg white and mix with the salt, soy sauce, and cornstarch; add the chicken to this mixture and stir. Leave to stand.

If you have bought shelled and skinned walnut halves, place these in a bowl, pour in sufficient boiling water to cover them, and leave to stand for 5 minutes. Remove any small remaining pieces of thin skin, dry well, and fry in ¹/₂ cup hot oil until golden brown. Stir in 2¹/₂ tbsp sugar and stir over moderate heat until all the sugar has dissolved.

Heat ¹/₂ cup oil in the wok and stir-fry the chicken pieces for 10 minutes. Drain and set aside. Tip the oil out of the wok and heat 2¹/₂ tbsp fresh oil in it; stir in the soy paste with the remaining sugar. After a few minutes add the rice wine and sesame seed oil and stir well; return the chicken to the wok, add the wal-

nuts, mix well, and serve.

This is a delicious and typically Pekinese method of cooking various meats, the soy paste and added sugar imparting a rich warm color and pleasant, uncloying sweetness to them.

FEATHERLIGHT CHICKEN SLICES *

软炸鸡

ruǎn zhà jī

1 lb chicken breasts
1 tsp salt
1 tbsp rice wine
1 tsp sugar
1 tsp monosodium glutamate (optional)
1 egg
1 tbsp cornstarch or potato flour
oil for frying

Time: 20 minutes

Place the chicken breasts flat and cut horizontally in half and then into rectangles measuring approximately $1^1/_4 \times 2^3/_4$ in. Mix the salt, rice wine, sugar, and monosodium glutamate (if used) in a bowl, add the chicken, and mix well. Beat the egg white, dip the chicken pieces in it and then coat with the cornstarch. Heat the oil in the wok (or use a deep-fryer) until very hot but not smoking and fry the chicken in several batches; they will take 2–3 minutes to cook and brown lightly.

CHICKEN WITH MUSTARD

鸡 丝 粉 皮

jī sī fěn pí

2 chicken quarters (leg and thigh)
4 mo ha mushrooms (tree ear fungus)

1 cucumber
1 carrot
2 eggs
1 tbsp oil
$^1/_2$ lb dried fried tofu (bean curd)

For the sauce:
$2^1/_2$ tbsp sweet soy bean paste
$2^1/_2$ tbsp strong Chinese or ordinary mustard
pinch monosodium glutamate (optional)
1 tbsp sesame seed oil

Time: 30 minutes

Rinse the tree ears under running cold water then soak in warm water for 20 minutes to soften; when they are soft, trim off any woody or fibrous pieces.

Boil the chicken legs and tree ears together gently in water for 20 minutes. Remove the chicken skin, take the flesh off the bones and shred into thin strips. Shred the tree ears. Peel the cucumber and carrot and cut into matchstick strips about $1^1/_2$ in long. Beat the eggs lightly; heat 1–2 tbsp oil in the wok, pour in the eggs, tipping the wok this way and that so that you have a very thin omelet. When firmly set, slide the omelet out of the wok and cut into thin strips.

Soak the tofu in hot water to soften; squeeze out excess water and place the cakes on a serving plate, place the chicken, mushrooms, omelet strips and vegetables on top; mix the sauce ingredients thoroughly and pour over the contents of the serving dish.

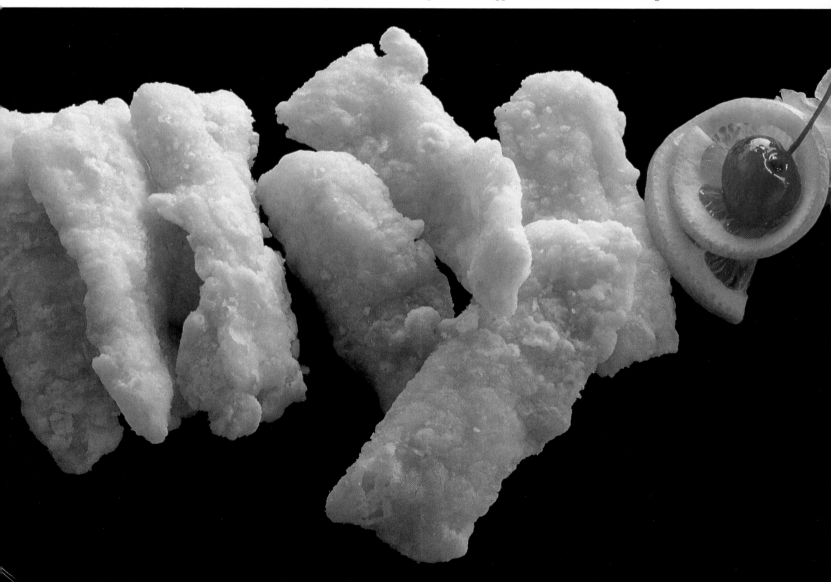

PEKING DUCK *

北京烤鸭
Běijīng kǎo yā

1 duck weighing 4¹/₂ lb
1¹/₄ cups boiling water
¹/₄ cup molasses (or clear, runny honey)
2¹/₂ tsp salt
1 tsp ground ginger
6 tbsp sugar
6 tbsp sweet soy paste
2¹/₂ tbsp sesame seed oil
¹/₂ cup water
8 thin leeks or scallions

Time: 3 hours + up to 12 hours for drying the lacquered duck

It is best to buy a duck that has not been dressed for this recipe but you can omit some stages if only oven-ready duck is available (see alternative in this method). Cut off the duck's wing tips and feet and singe the surface of the skin all over with a lighted taper to burn off any remaining feathers left behind after plucking. Snip open the vent, making as small an incision as possible to enable you to draw the bird; avoid rupturing the intestines as you pull them out. Discard all the entrails, saving only the liver and gizzard for other recipes. Cut off the head but leave a good length of neck attached; make a slit in the underside of the neck close to where it joins the body (i.e. on the breast side of the duck) and extract the windpipe and the esophagus. Rinse the duck inside and out very thoroughly; dry the outside surface of the duck very meticulously. If using an oven-ready duck, wash and dry, and join the recipe here.

If wished, place the duck in a colander and pour a kettleful of boiling water all over the skin; this will help it to shine later on. Allow to dry very thoroughly. Sprinkle a little salt inside the duck. Insert a straw through the neck slit, between the skin and the flesh and cartilage of the neck, with the straw pointing toward the body of the duck; blow steadily into the straw, holding the neck tightly just below the straw in between breaths; this process makes the duck puff up and separates the skin from the flesh so that it will be really crisp when cooked. (This may be impossible to do with an oven-ready duck but is not vital.) Bind the neck tightly as you remove the straw, just below the slit. Sew the vent and neck openings closed with a poultry needle and kitchen string; hang the duck up by its neck from a hook over a large bowl (not practicable for oven-ready duck which should be placed on a grid in a roasting pan). Mix the molasses or honey with the boiling water, add the salt and ground ginger, and stir well. Use a pastry brush to "paint" the entire surface of the duck with this mix-

ture. Collect all the mixture which has dripped off the duck. Let the first layer dry for a little while, then repeat the painting (or "lacquering") operation. Collect the remaining liquid from the bowl or pan and when the previous layer is dry paint the duck once again. Hang the duck in a dry, airy larder for at least 2 hours or place in a larder refrigerator. Lacquered duck is often left to dry for up to 12 hours for the best results. When the duck has completely dried, heat the oven to 400°F, place a large roasting pan about one third full of water in the bottom of the oven, and place the duck on a grid above it, the grid standing well clear of the water (or directly on the oven grid shelf placed two shelf positions above the pan). Roast the duck on the grid, breast uppermost for 30–45 minutes (the skin must not brown too deeply at this early stage; if it is browning too quickly turn the oven down to 350–375°F). Turn the duck and cook breast side downward for 30–45 minutes; take care not to puncture or tear the skin at all. If the skin is not quite crispy enough when the duck is nearly cooked (it should be well done) turn up the heat to finish crisping. While the duck is roasting make the sauce, mixing the sugar with the soy paste and water; heat the sesame oil in a saucepan, stir in the soy paste mixture, and cook until thickened; transfer to a bowl or several very small bowls. (Use commercially prepared hoisin sauce instead if preferred.) "Top and tail" the leeks or scallions and cut across into 2³/₄-in lengths, then hold these upright and slice into each of them lengthwise from the top about ³/₄ in deep, making several cuts very close together; repeat at the other end and place in iced water; the cuts you have made at their ends will open out to look like little brushes. Drain well just before serving.

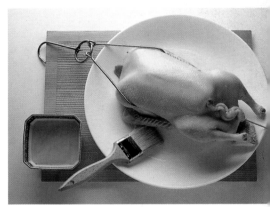

Use a very sharp knife to carve the duck, cutting neatly through the skin, holding the knife at an oblique angle to the surface of the duck; place all the pieces which have skin attached on top of any which do not, with the skin uppermost on a very hot serving plate. Place Mandarin pancakes on another plate (see recipe on p. 16, or buy readymade). Each person takes a pancake, spreads a little hoisin sauce on it by dipping a leek or scallion brush in the sauce, places a piece of duck on top, and rolls up the pancake which is then eaten with the fingers.

In China the whole duck would very probably be brought to the table by the cook, there to be carved and distributed to the diners amid expressions of praise and anticipation. On such an occasion the crisp, succulent skin would be served first and eaten with pancakes and sauce before doing the same with the flesh beneath which might be eaten with different accompaniments.

The frugal Chinese would probably serve a soup to round off the meal, made with the duck giblets, vegetables, and broth.

60

SALTY DUCK

盐 水 鸭

yán shuǐ yā

1 duck weighing approx. 4¹/₂ lb
7 cups chicken broth
3 thin slices fresh ginger
1 scallion
1 tsp ground Szechwan pepper
2¹/₂ tbsp rice wine
1 tbsp salt

Time: 1 hour 50 minutes

Wash and dry the duck, pulling off any large pieces of fat inside the carcass. Place in a large fireproof casserole dish and add sufficient cold water to cover; bring to a boil and then simmer for 30 minutes. Remove from the casserole and bone (or simply take all the flesh off the carcass, leaving it in large pieces at this stage).

Place the duck pieces in the wok with the chicken broth, ginger, scallion, pepper, rice wine, and salt; bring to a boil and immediately lower the heat and simmer for 30 minutes by which time the duck pieces should be well cooked and very tender. Use slotted spoons or ladles to remove the duck from the wok or pan and slice; arrange on a serving plate and moisten with a little of the cooking liquid.

This dish is excellent warm or cold.

BRAISED DUCK *

红 扒 鸭
hóng pá yā

1 oven-ready duck weighing approx.
  4^1/$_2$lb
^{1}/$_2$ cup soy sauce
2 scallions
6 thin slices fresh ginger
^{1}/$_4$ cup rice wine
10 oz bamboo shoots
^{1}/$_2$–1 tbsp sugar
^{1}/$_2$ tbsp monosodium glutamate (optional)
^{1}/$_2$ tbsp salt
1 tbsp sesame seed oil
1 heaping tbsp cornstarch or potato flour
oil for shallow-frying

Time: 4 hours

Wash the duck, removing any remaining large pieces of fat from inside the cavity; add the duck to a large, deep pan two thirds full of boiling water and blanch for 5 minutes; take out of the pan, drain well, and dry. Brush liberally all over with soy sauce and leave to stand for 20 minutes.

Heat approx. ^{1}/$_2$ cup oil in the wok or a large skillet; add the duck and brown all over, cooking over high heat. Remove the duck and place in a large, heavy-bottomed fireproof casserole dish (enameled iron or earthenware). Add the finely chopped scallions and ginger, 2^1/$_2$ tbsp soy sauce and the rice wine; pour in enough water to come about one third of the way up the side of the duck, cover tightly once the water has come to a boil, and simmer over low heat for 2 hours. Add a little hot water if necessary at intervals during this time. Remove the duck and strain the cooking juices. Clean the casserole dish and heat

2½ tbsp oil in it; dice the bamboo shoots and stir-fry in the oil. Return the duck to the casserole dish, pour the cooking liquid all over it, and stir in 1 tbsp soy sauce, the sugar, monosodium glutamate (if used), salt, and sesame seed oil. Cover and simmer for a further 30 minutes. About 25 minutes through the simmering time mix the cornstarch with a very little cold water and stir into the cooking liquid to thicken.

Take out the duck; carve into fairly small pieces, place these on a serving platter, and sprinkle with the sauce from the casserole dish.

BRAISED DUCK LIVERS ZĀO LIŪ

糟 溜 鸭 肝

zāo liū yā gān

6 mo ha mushrooms (tree ear fungus)
12 duck livers
1 tbsp oil
1 tsp finely chopped fresh ginger
1 tsp finely chopped garlic
2 cups chicken broth
½ cup rice wine (Shian ciao type)
1 tbsp sugar
2½ tsp salt
½ tsp monosodium glutamate (optional)
1 heaping tbsp cornstarch or potato flour

Time: 40 minutes

Rinse the mushrooms well under running cold water then soak in hot water for 20 minutes. Rinse the livers, trim off any pieces of membrane etc., and slice thinly.

Bring a saucepan of water (unsalted) to a full boil, add the duck liver slices, and boil gently for 10 minutes. Drain. Drain the mushrooms, snip off any tough parts with kitchen scissors, and slice into thin strips. Heat 1 tbsp oil in the wok and stir-fry the ginger and garlic very briefly; add the broth, wine, sugar, salt and monosodium glutamate (if used), mix well then add the liver and mushrooms. Simmer, uncovered, to allow the liquid to reduce somewhat. Stir in the cornstarch mixed with a little cold water and cook for 1–2 minutes. Serve.

Shantung province is famous for this "zao liu" method of cooking. The Shian ciao rice wine used in the sauce is flavored with sugar and flowers and is blended with Chinese yellow wine; its sweet yet slightly acidulated taste imparts a distinctive flavor to dishes.

DUCK GIZZARDS AND PIG'S KIDNEY YÓU BÀO

油 爆 双 脆

yóu bào shuāng cuì

63

4 duck gizzards
1 pig's kidney
1 tbsp finely chopped scallion
1 tbsp finely chopped garlic
1 tsp finely chopped fresh ginger
oil

For the sauce:
1½ tbsp soy sauce
1½ tbsp rice wine
1½ tbsp wine vinegar
1 tsp salt
1 tsp sugar
1 tbsp sesame seed oil
pinch monosodium glutamate (optional)
½ tsp freshly ground pepper
1 tbsp cornstarch or potato flour

Time: 45 minutes

Blanch the gizzards in boiling water then cut away the tough muscular lining and discard. Wash the gizzards and cut into quarters; make two fairly deep incisions bisecting one another on one side of each piece (this is to help the gizzards cook quickly as otherwise they will be tough). Remove the thin membranous skin from the surface of the pig's kidney, lay it flat on the work surface, and cut it horizontally in half; use scissors to trim away the small pieces of gristle, then dice the kidney. Heat a little oil in the wok and stir-fry the gizzard and kidney pieces over high heat for a few seconds; drain and set aside. Empty the wok, wipe the inside, and heat 2½ tbsp fresh oil to stir-fry the scallion, garlic, and ginger briefly; return the gizzard and kidney pieces to the wok, with the soy sauce, wine, vinegar, salt, sugar, sesame seed oil, monosodium glutamate and the pepper. Simmer until the sauce has reduced and the meat is tender (the gizzards will remain a little chewy); stir in the cornstarch mixed with a very little cold water to thicken the remaining liquid.

"Pao" is a Pekinese technique in which the basic or main ingredients are briefly pre-fried in oil (almost equivalent to blanching and sealing) and then cooked in the sauce. This treatment, particularly well suited to variety meats and giblets, ensures that they retain their original color and are tender and juicy.

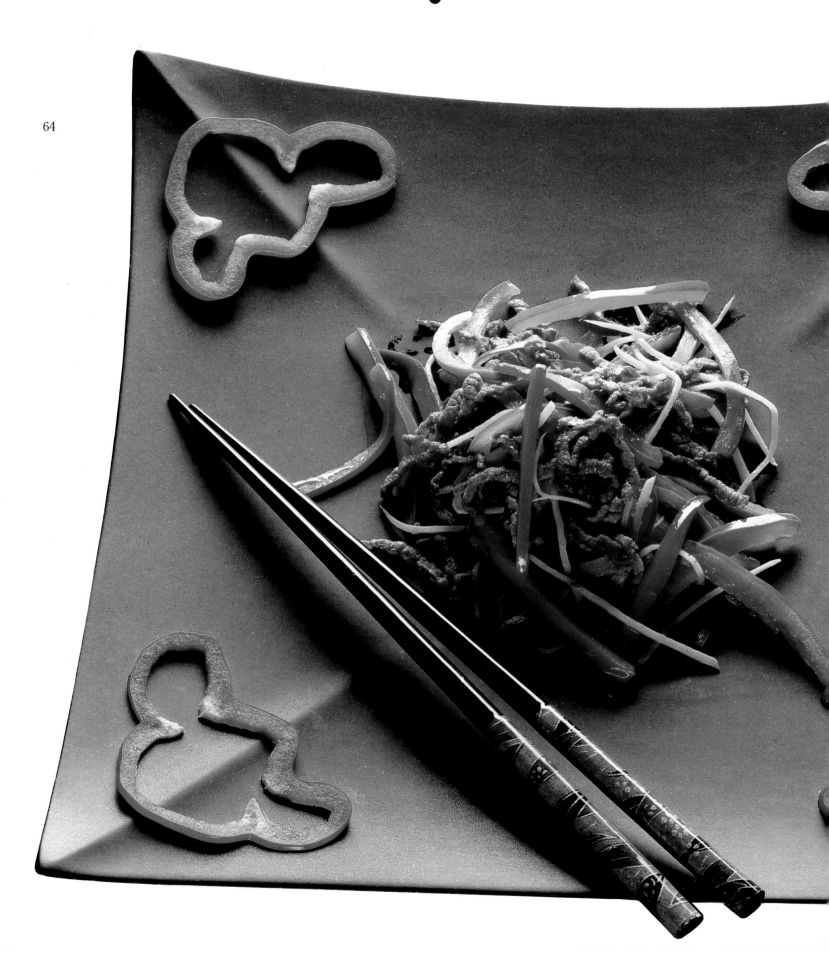

DUCKS' FEET IN MUSTARD SAUCE

芥 末 鴨 掌

jiè mò yā zhǎng

10 ducks' feet
$^1/_2$ tbsp wine vinegar
$^1/_2$ tbsp soy sauce
pinch monosodium glutamate (optional)
1 tbsp mustard oil or strong mustard sauce
1 tbsp sesame seed oil

Time: 1 hour

Scrub the ducks' feet very thoroughly indeed under running cold water then add them to a large pan of fast boiling water; boil gently for 40 minutes. Take the skin and flesh (both of which can be eaten) off the bone; remove and discard all the tendons. Cut the skin and flesh into thin strips.

Mix all the remaining ingredients listed above and stir the shredded skin and meat thoroughly with the resulting dressing.

IMPERIAL TOFU

仿 膳 豆 腐

fǎng shàn dòu fǔ

10 oz firm tofu (bean curd)
10 oz chicken breasts
10 oz crabmeat (fresh or frozen)
1 tsp monosodium glutamate (optional)
1 tbsp salt
pinch freshly ground pepper
1 tbsp cornstarch or potato flour
4 egg yolks
oil

Time: 1 hour

Place the tofu in a clean cloth, gather up the edges, and twist round to expel as much moisture as possible; chop finely. Mince the chicken. Flake the crabmeat with a fork. Mix these three ingredients with the monosodium glutamate, if used, and the salt, pepper and cornstarch or potato flour.

Line one or more molds (ideally 2$^1/_2$ in deep), which will fit in the compartment of your steamer, with waxed paper, pack the prepared mixture into the mold, sprinkle the top with a little oil, and press a piece of waxed paper on top. Place the mold in the steamer, cover, and steam for 20 minutes. Remove the paper covering, turn out the mold (or molds) and cut the cooked mixture neatly into 2$^1/_2$-in

cubes. Beat the egg yolks lightly in a fairly shallow plate, coat the cubes carefully all over with yolk, then fry in oil over fairly high heat until golden brown. Slice and serve.

LAMB WITH BAMBOO SHOOTS AND RED BELL PEPPER *

清 椒 羊 肉

qīng jiāo yáng ròu

14 oz lamb tenderloin
2 egg whites
$^1/_4$ cup cornstarch
1 tsp salt
generous pinch freshly ground pepper
$^1/_4$ lb drained canned bamboo shoots
1 red bell pepper (capsicum)
3 onions
1 large, thick piece fresh ginger (approx.
    2$^1/_2$ in long)
3 tbsp rice wine
oil as required

Time: 50 minutes

Remove any pieces of fat and gristle (especially the cream-colored smooth thin strip which is sometimes left on the tenderloin, as this is very tough). Cut the meat into thin slices and then into strips about 1$^1/_2$ in long and $^3/_4$ in thick. Beat the egg whites lightly, beat in the cornstarch, salt, and pepper and mix well with the lamb; leave to marinate for 30 minutes.

Cut the bamboo shoots into matchstick strips; do likewise with the red pepper, peeled onion, and peeled ginger. Heat sufficient oil to semi deep-fry in the wok or use more oil and deep-fry; when very hot but not smoking add the lamb; the meat pieces should rise to the surface almost immediately; fry for 1$^1/_2$ minutes, separating them if they stick to each other (use cooking chopsticks to do this effectively if you have them).

Remove the lamb from the oil, using a slotted ladle, and drain well; set aside. Drain off all but 6 tbsp of the oil if using a wok, or heat this amount of oil in a skillet; stir-fry the bamboo shoots and red pepper for 2 minutes; add the onion and ginger and stir-fry for 30 seconds more.

Add the pre-fried lamb, stir-fry over high heat, add the rice wine, and stir briefly before transferring to a heated serving plate. Serve at once.

STEAMED LAMB

白 切 羊 肉
bái qiē yáng ròu

2¹/₄ lb boned lamb shoulder
2 scallions
6 thin slices fresh ginger
1 tsp salt
1 tbsp Szechwan pepper
1¹/₂ tbsp oil
1 tbsp soy sauce

For the sauce:
1¹/₂ tbsp rice wine
6 tbsp sweet soy paste
1 tbsp finely chopped garlic
2 tbsp finely chopped parsley

Time: 2 hours + 24 hours marinating time

Cut the lamb shoulder into three equally-sized pieces and place these in a deep dish. Trim and shred the scallion; peel and mince the ginger (use a garlic crusher or smash with a rolling pin).

Buy whole Szechwan peppercorns if possible and grind just as much as you need; fry the coarsely ground pepper in a little oil until the pepper starts to release plenty of spicy aroma; add the oil and pepper to the lamb, followed by the scallion, ginger, salt, and soy sauce; mix and coat well to flavor and place in the refrigerator for 24 hours. The next day, place the meat in a heatproof dish that will fit in your steamer compartment, cover, and steam for 1 hour or until very tender.

Leave to cool then slice thinly and arrange on a serving platter.

Mix the sauce ingredients thoroughly and serve in a bowl with a spoon.

LAMB WITH SCALLIONS

酱 爆 羊 肉
jiàng bào yáng ròu

14 oz lean lamb
6 tbsp oil
2 cloves garlic
6 large scallions
1 tbsp sesame seed oil
For the marinade:
2¹/₂ tbsp soy sauce
2¹/₂ tbsp rice wine

For the sauce:
1 tsp salt
¹/₂–1 tbsp sugar
2¹/₂ tbsp dark soy sauce
2¹/₂ tbsp rice wine
1 tbsp sesame seed oil

Time: 45 minutes

Trim any fat or gristle off the lamb and place it in the freezer for 1–2 hours to make it firm enough to slice wafer-thin (use a very sharp knife or a slicing machine). Dry the slices with paper towels if necessary.

Mix the marinade ingredients, combine thoroughly with the sliced lamb in a bowl or deep dish, and marinate for at least 15 minutes.

Trim the scallions and slice into very long thin strips; peel the garlic and cut into wafer-thin slices.

Mix the sauce ingredients. Heat the wok slowly until it smokes, pour in the oil, and tip the wok this way and that so that the oil merely coats the very hot surface thinly (you can use a large nonstick skillet but do not overheat). Fry the garlic slices until they just begin to color; add the lamb slices and stir-fry for only 30 seconds (use a spatula or Chinese flat scoop to prevent the slices tearing and sticking as you move or turn them). Add the sauce and the scallions; continue stir-frying carefully until the liquid has almost evaporated: there should be no liquid slopping around in the wok. Transfer the lamb to a serving dish and sprinkle with a little more sesame seed oil.

NOMAD'S LAMB CUTLETS *

白 切 羊 肉
bái qiē yāng ròu

4¹/₄–4¹/₂ lb loin of lamb (on the bone)
2 quarts water
2¹/₂ tbsp rice wine
1 fresh red chili pepper, thinly sliced
2 onions, coarsely chopped and peeled
1 large, thick piece fresh ginger approx. 2¹/₂ in
    in length, peeled and thinly sliced
1 tsp salt
2 star anises
2 cloves garlic, minced
1 1¹/₂–2-in piece cinnamon bark

For the salad or relish (optional):
1 scallion or small leek
fresh ginger
fresh chili peppers
fresh coriander leaves, chopped

Time: 2 hours + 6 hours marinating

Ask your butcher to cut the loin into pairs of double chops; trim off excess fat and expose the long, thin rib bones so that you can use these as "handles" if you intend to eat them with your fingers.

Place the chops in a deep dish; mix all the ingredients (but not the water, which will be

used later) and add to the lamb; mix thoroughly so that all the meat is covered; leave to stand for about 6 hours in a cool larder or refrigerator for the flavors to penetrate. Three or four hours before you wish to serve the lamb, bring the water to a boil in a very large saucepan; add the chops and all the spices etc. used for its flavoring; allow the water to return to a boil, reduce the heat, and simmer for 1 1/2 hours.

Leave the chops to cool in the cooking liquid, then drain and serve with a salad made with the ingredients listed above, served finely chopped in separate plates.

KID CŌNG BÀO

葱爆羊肉

cōng bào yáng ròu

1 lb kid (baby goat) meat
2 1/2 tbsp oil
2 1/2 tbsp soy sauce
pinch salt
pinch ground Szechwan pepper
2 1/2 tbsp rice wine
2 scallions
2 cloves garlic
1/4 cup sesame seed oil
1 tbsp wine vinegar

Time: 40 minutes

Cut the meat into very small pieces; trim and finely slice the scallions; crush the garlic cloves. Mix the meat and scallions with the oil, soy sauce, salt, pepper, and wine and leave to stand and marinate for 10 minutes to flavor. Heat 2 1/2 tbsp oil in the wok, fry the garlic gently and add the meat and all the marinade; stir-fry over high heat for 5 minutes. Sprinkle with the vinegar and the remaining sesame seed oil and serve.

"Cong bao" describes the technique of cooking both the meat and its marinade in oil.

BRAISED LAMB BREAST

扒羊肉条

pá yāng ròu tiáo

1 3/4 lb lamb breast
6 tbsp oil
2 scallions
5 thin slices fresh ginger
4 star anises
1 small piece cinnamon bark
1 fresh chili pepper
6 tbsp dark soy sauce
1 tsp freshly ground pepper
1/4 cup rice wine
1 tsp sugar
1/2 tsp monosodium glutamate (optional)
1 tsp salt
1 cup meat, chicken or vegetable broth
1/2 cup sesame seed oil

Time: 1 1/2 hours + steaming time

Cut the lamb breast into pieces measuring 4 × 2 1/2 in, add these to a large saucepan of boiling water, and simmer for 30 minutes; drain the lamb and dry. Heat plenty of oil in the wok or a skillet and semi deep-fry the lamb for a few minutes over high heat to brown lightly all over. Remove the meat and drain well; cut into slices 3/4 in wide; keep these neatly lined up side by side where possible and transfer to a heatproof dish (arranging them skin side down) that fits in the steamer compartment. Heat 6 tbsp oil in the wok and fry the chopped scallion and the peeled, crushed slices of ginger; add the star anise and cinnamon, and the shredded chili pepper and stir-fry briefly. Stir in the soy sauce, pepper, rice wine, sugar, monosodium glutamate (if used), salt, and broth.

Boil this mixture gently for 10 minutes, then pour all over the meat and place the dish containing the meat in the steamer compartment; cover and steam for 2 hours (check the water level at intervals to make sure it does not boil dry but do not allow the water to come anywhere near the steamer compartment).

When the meat is done, transfer to a serving dish; pour the cooking juices and liquid from the dish into a small saucepan, stir in the sesame oil and heat through; pour over the meat.

Spinach stir-fried briefly in oil goes very well with this dish.

LAMB TĀ SÌ MÌ

塌斯蜜

tā sī mì

1 3/4 lb lean lamb
1 lightly beaten egg
1 tbsp sweet soy paste
1/2–1 tbsp cornstarch or potato flour
oil for frying

For the sauce:
2 1/2 tbsp oil
1 tsp finely chopped garlic
1/2–1 tbsp sugar
1 tbsp soy sauce
1 tsp sweet soy paste
pinch monosodium glutamate (optional)
1 tbsp rice wine

Time: 30 minutes

Cut the meat into thin slices and mix with the egg, soy paste, and cornstarch or potato flour. When thoroughly and evenly coated, fry the slices in a little oil over moderate heat for 10 minutes, turning occasionally; remove from the wok and set aside.

Wipe the wok clean or use another skillet; heat 2 1/2 tbsp oil and fry the garlic and sugar gently. When the sugar has completely dissolved, add the remaining sauce ingredients, stir, then return the meat to the wok or skillet, mix well, and simmer for 1 minute to heat the meat through and allow the liquid to reduce a little more. Serve.

CRISPY LAMB

羊肉炸焦

yáng ròu zhà jiāo

1 3/4 lb lean lamb
2 scallions
4 thin slices fresh ginger
2 star anises
2 cups soy sauce
1/2 cup rice wine
1 tbsp sugar
2 1/2 tbsp all-purpose flour
4 slices crunchy rice cakes (sold as dried rice cakes in Oriental foodstores)
oil for frying

For the condiment:
6 tbsp salt
1 heaping tbsp five-spice powder
1 tsp monosodium glutamate (optional)

Time: 1 hour 10 minutes

A Buddhist monk in one of the many dwellings which cluster round the monastery. The religious community is entirely self-sufficient: the lamas (from the Tibetan bla-ma, meaning chief) are responsible for cultural work such as the printing of books; they carry out ritual duties, are present during births, deaths, and marriages and paint pictures inspired by religious subjects. The ordinary monks are entrusted with manual tasks, such as joinery and everything that concerns everyday, practical life at the monastery.

It is probably true to say that the vast majority of the Chinese are not religious in the way we in the West would understand the term. No religious organization remotely comparable to the Christian church in the West has ever existed in China, even though many of her citizens are devout followers of Buddhism, Confucianism, Taoism, and other creeds. The Buddhas carved on the walls off Lung Men caves near the cradle of Buddhism, Loyang, between A.D. 589 and 681, are world-famous.

MONGOLIAN BARBECUE

蒙古烤肉

měng gǔ kǎo ròu

¹/₄ lb pork tenderloin
¹/₄ lb skinned chicken breasts
¹/₄ lb lean beef
¹/₄ lb lean lamb
¹/₄ lb tender young carrots
1 large scallion
1 large red bell pepper (capsicum)
2 firm, ripe tomatoes
¹/₄ lb Chinese white cabbage
¹/₄ lb bean sprouts

For the dipping sauces and condiments
place the following in separate small bowls:
1 tbsp chili pepper;
6 tbsp soy sauce (divided between several bowls)
3 finely chopped, peeled garlic cloves
1 scallion, trimmed and finely chopped
2–3 tbsp sesame seed oil
2–3 tbsp chili oil
juice of 1 lemon, strained
1–2 tbsp ginger juice (chop fresh ginger very coarsely and express the juice with the garlic crusher)
2–3 tbsp rice wine
2–3 tbsp thick sugar syrup

Time: 1¹/₂ hours

Place the meat in the freezer for 1–1¹/₂ hours to make it very firm and easy to slice wafer-thin by hand (or use a slicing machine). Scrape the carrots, trim, and cut lengthwise into thin slices; trim the scallion and cut with the knife held diagonally into slanting sections; remove the stalk, seeds, and inner pith from the red bell peppers and cut into thin strips; slice the tomatoes into rounds, removing the seeds; trim the cabbage, take the leaves off one by one, rinse and dry, then slice very thinly (across the leaves). Rinse the bean sprouts, pick off all the empty or ungerminated green seed cases and discard.

Ideally, you should have a griddle for this dish or a griddle pan; failing this, it will work well with a cast-iron skillet, lightly greased by rubbing a cloth dipped in oil all over the surface; if using a modern griddle or nonstick skillet you will probably not need to grease it first. Heat the griddle or skillet and grease with oil or not as required. Place the vegetables on the griddle and cook briefly, turning several times and mixing them with one another. When tender but still crisp, transfer the vegetables to heated plates.

Cook the various meats next in the same way, turning once, and then transfer to the plates (this barbecue can be eaten as several courses rather than all at once). The cooked

Cut the meat into strips measuring ³/₈ × 1¹/₂ in. Blanch in boiling water for 2 minutes; drain well.

Place the meat in a large saucepan with 4 cups water, the trimmed and rinsed scallions, ginger, star anise, soy sauce, rice wine, and sugar. Bring to a boil and simmer for 20 minutes. Drain the meat once more and coat with flour. Semi deep-fry or deep-fry the meat in plenty of very hot oil until crisp and golden brown; remove from the oil, draining well, then fry the rice cakes.

Mix the condiment ingredients and place a little in tiny bowls for each person to dip the lamb as wished.

ingredients are dipped as wished into the various sauces and condiments.

When feasible, an electric griddle (along the lines of a Japanese teriyaki griddle) can be placed in the center of the table, within reach of all those present, for each person to cook his own selection of ingredients.

70

MONGOLIAN HOTPOT *

蒙古火锅

méng gŭ huŏ guó

1¹/₂ lb lean lamb
5 tung ku (dong gu) mushrooms
¹/₂ lb spinach
1 lb Chinese white cabbage
¹/₄ lb soy flour noodles
¹/₂ lb firm tofu (bean curd)
¹/₂ lb fillets of white fish (optional)
2 cloves garlic
1 leek
1 oz fresh ginger
¹/₄ cup hoisin (or barbecue) sauce
3 tbsp fresh chili peppers, pounded to a paste
2¹/₂ tbsp soy sauce
1 tbsp sesame seed oil
9 cups chicken broth

Time: 20 minutes

Soak the noodles in cold water for 10 minutes to soften. Soak the dried mushrooms in warm water for 20–30 minutes. Wash the spinach and the Chinese cabbage thoroughly, trimming where necessary. Cut both into broad strips. Cut the tofu into cubes. Slice the fish fil-

lets into bite-sized pieces. Drain the noodles and if they are very long, snip in half or into approx. 4-in lengths. Arrange all these prepared ingredients attractively on large serving plates, e.g. the tofu, vegetables, and noodles on one plate to give a green and white color scheme and the fish pieces in a fairly deep dish on their own. Slice the meat very thinly (part-freeze beforehand to make this easier, if wished) and spread out to cover a large serving platter so that the slices do not have to overlap. Have 4 bowls ready to take the sauces and dressings. Peel the ginger and garlic and chop very finely. Trim, wash, and take the outer layer off the leek, and slice into very thin rounds. Mix the ginger, garlic, and leek in one bowl. Spoon the hoisin sauce into the next bowl, the chili paste into the third. Mix the soy

72

sauce and sesame oil together and place in the last bowl. Place the hotpot in the center of the table; a large fondue pot and burner will keep the dish hot at table. Fill the hotpot (or fondue pot) with chicken broth and bring to a boil. Place the plates with all the ingredients around it. Each person mixes a dipping sauce to their individual preference, taking a little from some or all of the condiment and sauce bowls and mixing them in a very small bowl. Poach the ingredients of your choice in the hot broth using chopsticks or fondue forks and then dip in the sauce for extra flavor. Have a little extra hot broth ready in case the hotpot liquid needs topping up. Once all the meat and fish has been eaten (there is no particular order in which the ingredients should be cooked) any leftover vegetables can be added to the broth, cooked for a few minutes and then ladled into individual bowls with the delicious broth for a suitable end to the meal.

The Mongolian hotpot would be traditionally cooked in a magnificent, intricately decorated brass pot sitting over a brazier that would radiate heat on cold winter nights from its glowing charcoal embers, enhancing the diners' pleasure at this truly communal method of cooking and eating. This is an opportunity for people to gather together and enjoy hospitality and good fellowship; indeed, some aspects of the occasion used to have an almost ceremonial air to them.

Each region of China has developed its own, distinctive types of preserved meat, but sausages are produced throughout the country. These are usually for cooking, rather than slicing for cold meats, and they are fresh or wind dried, in all sorts of shapes, sizes, flavors, and textures, varying from the pink, leaner meat varieties, to paler, fatty pork, while others are darker, made with pig's or duck's liver or a mixture of both.
Some local specialties have become very sought after. The hams are particularly good. One of the best is Jinhua (after the city of that name, south of Shanghai, in eastern China). These delicious rosy red hams are moist, sweet, and succulent; they are exported all over the world.

SHEEP'S STOMACH SHUǏ BÀO

水 爆 肚 仁

shuǐ bào dù rén

1¹/₄ lb sheep's stomach

Sauces and condiments:
1 tbsp salt
2¹/₂ tbsp soy sauce
1 tbsp sesame seed oil
1 tbsp wine vinegar
1 tbsp finely chopped scallion
1 tsp finely chopped chili pepper
1 tbsp chopped parsley
2 tbsp chili oil
2¹/₂ tbsp oil

Time: 1 hour + 1 hour soaking time

Wash the sheep's stomach, soak in cold water for 1 hour, turn inside out, and scrape the inner, tough surface with a very sharp knife; trim off the lower part and any pieces of fat, then cut into pieces measuring ³/₈ × 1¹/₄ in.

Bring plenty of water to a boil in a large saucepan, add the pieces of stomach to it, and boil until they turn creamy white and curl up. Meanwhile bring another, smaller saucepan of water to the boil (or use a kettle, see below). Remove the pieces of sheep's stomach from the first pan, using a slotted spoon so that they drain well; place them in 4 separate bowls and pour sufficient boiling water from the second saucepan over them to cover. Serve at once.

Have each of the items listed under sauces and condiments ready in separate small bowls and arrange these on the table. Place a very small bowl beside each place setting: each person will mix their dipping sauce to taste, using their choice of flavorings from the little bowls. The pieces of sheep's stomach are taken out of the hot water one by one and dipped in the sauce.

The "shui bao" cooking technique (blanching in boiling hot water followed by immersion in fresh hot water) cooks the special texture of variety meats such as sheep's stomach sufficiently but avoids the toughening effect of very prolonged cooking.

LAMB IN ASPIC

羊糕

yáng gāo

1¹/₄ lb boneless lamb leg
7 cups meat, chicken or vegetable broth
4 thin slices fresh ginger
2 scallions
2 cloves
1 small piece cinnamon bark
2 star anises
4 cloves garlic
6 tbsp rice wine
1 tbsp salt
1 tsp sugar
1 tbsp soy sauce
¹/₂ tsp monosodium glutamate (optional)
7 oz fresh pork skin, washed, with all bristles
   or hairs removed
2 white radishes (Daikon roots)

Time: 2 hours

Add the meat to a large pan of boiling water; allow to return to the boil and simmer for 10 minutes. Drain and cut into small cubes. Place the meat in a wok with the broth, ginger, trimmed scallions, cloves, cinnamon, anises, peeled garlic, rice wine, soy sauce, monosodium glutamate (if used), the pork skin cut into small pieces, and the peeled, coarsely chopped radishes.

   Simmer gently until the liquid has reduced to one third of its original volume and both the lamb and the pork rind are very tender.

   Take the lamb and pork rind out of the pan, place them neatly in a rectangular loaf pan or mold, and strain the liquid all over the meat (to fill to the brim). Leave to cool completely, then chill in the refrigerator until completely set. Slice and serve.

STIR-FRIED VARIETY MEATS AND SHRIMP

全爆

quán bào

¹/₄ lb chicken gizzards
¹/₄ lb pig's stomach
¹/₄ lb lamb's (or kid's) stomach
¹/₄ lb lean pork
¹/₄ lb lean chicken
¹/₄ lb lean lamb (or kid)

¹/₄ lb peeled shrimp
2 egg whites
2¹/₂ tbsp cornstarch or potato flour
oil for frying
2¹/₂ tbsp oil
1 tbsp finely chopped scallion
1 tsp finely chopped fresh ginger
1 clove garlic
2 oz bamboo shoots
2¹/₂ tbsp rice wine
¹/₂ tsp monosodium glutamate (optional)
pinch ground Szechwan pepper
1 tsp salt
2¹/₂ tbsp broth
extra cornstarch or potato flour
2¹/₂ tbsp sesame seed oil

Time: 1 hour

Trim the stomachs (see previous recipe) and blanch for a few minutes in boiling water, drain, and scrape away the inner surface and remove any pieces of fat, using a very sharp knife. Cut away the inner muscular layer of the chicken gizzards. Cut into small cubes. Cut all the meat into small cubes, keeping the various types separate, and coarsely chop the shrimp. Whisk the egg whites and fold in the cornstarch (having first mixed the latter with a little water). Dip each of the pieces of variety meat, meat (including the chicken) and the shrimp in this mixture and set aside. (Keep separate.) Chop the bamboo shoots coarsely.

   Heat plenty of oil in the wok or a skillet for semi deep-frying (or use a deep-fryer) and fry the various meats and the shrimp in separate batches until pale golden brown. Drain well and set aside. Heat just 2¹/₂ tbsp fresh oil in a wok or skillet, fry the ginger, scallion, crushed garlic, and bamboo shoots briefly, add the fried ingredients, starting with the variety meats, then the other meat and chicken and lastly the shrimp.

   Stir in the wine, monosodium glutamate (if used), Szechwan pepper, salt, and broth and simmer until reduced a little; if necessary, thicken with a little of the extra cornstarch mixed with a very small amount of water. Stir well, then sprinkle in the sesame seed oil.

   This is an exceptional dish even for the eclectic Chinese cuisine; it is rare to find so many different types of meat in one recipe. The pre-frying allows the meats to seal and retain all their juices and natural flavors, even when they are added to the sauce. This method is not unlike braising in principle; here all the oil is drained off with the result that the finished dish has a surprisingly low-fat content.

BEEF WITH SCALLIONS

酱爆牛肉

jiàng bào niú ròu

1 lb lean beef (fillet, sirloin tip or
   eye of round)
1 tbsp soy sauce
1 tsp salt
¹/₂–1 tbsp sugar
pinch monosodium glutamate (optional)
1 tbsp rice wine
1 tbsp sesame seed oil
1 egg white, lightly beaten
1 tbsp cornstarch or potato flour
2 large scallions
3 thin slices fresh ginger
¹/₂ chili pepper
¹/₄ cup oil
salt, sesame seed oil, and soy sauce to
   taste for extra flavoring

Time: 30 minutes

Cut the beef into very thin slices measuring about 1¹/₄ × 1¹/₂ in. Mix the soy sauce, salt, sugar, monosodium glutamate (if used), wine, sesame oil, egg white, and cornstarch. Add the meat, mix well, and leave to stand.

   While the meat is marinating, trim the scallion and cut into 1-in lengths; shred the ginger and the chili pepper.

   Heat 3 tbsp oil in the wok and stir-fry the beef slices briefly over high heat for only about 30 seconds (the meat will toughen if cooked for longer). Remove the meat from the wok, tip out any oil and wipe the inside, then heat 2¹/₂ tbsp fresh oil over lower heat and fry the scallions and ginger until they start to release their aroma; return the beef to the wok, adding a very little extra salt, sesame seed oil and soy sauce (depending on how pronounced a flavor you prefer) and cook for 1 minute longer, stirring and turning. Garnish with the shredded chili pepper and serve.

   Lean lamb may substitute the beef in this recipe.

BEEF IN SOY SAUCE

酱牛肉

jiàng niú ròu

1¹/₄ lb beef brisket, or any good boiling cut
3 scallions
4 thin slices fresh ginger
1¹/₂ cups soy sauce
¹/₂ cup hot soy paste
¹/₂ tsp monosodium glutamate (optional)
1 tsp salt

2¹/₂ tbsp sugar
6 tbsp rice wine
1 tsp five-spice powder
2 star anises
2 tsp ground Szechwan pepper

74

Time: 4 hours

Fill a fairly large saucepan (large enough to accommodate the meat easily) three quarters full with water, add all the remaining ingredients listed above (trim the scallions and peel the fresh ginger slices) and bring to a boil; boil gently for 30 minutes.

Rinse the beef, place in the pan with the flavored, boiled water and bring back to a boil; reduce the heat, cover, and simmer gently for 3 hours or until the beef is very tender.

Remove the beef carefully from the saucepan, place on a board, and leave to cool. When cold, slice thinly with a very sharp knife and arrange the slices on a serving platter. Strain 2 cups of the cooking liquid into a saucepan and boil hard until reduced by half; pour into a bowl or jug and hand round as a sauce for the meat.

PORK WITH CUCUMBERS

滑溜里脊

huá liū lǐ jǐ

1¹/₄ lb pork tenderloin
1 egg white
¹/₂–1 tsp salt
1 tbsp cornstarch or potato flour
2 cucumbers
1 scallion
2 slices fresh ginger
¹/₃ cup oil
2¹/₂ tbsp rice wine
1 tsp cornstarch or potato flour

Time: 45 minutes

Cut the pork into slices ³/₄ in thick, then cut these slices into pieces measuring ³/₄ × 1¹/₄ in.

Whisk the egg white fairly stiffly then fold in the salt and cornstarch; coat the pork all over with this mixture. Peel the cucumber and cut into ¹/₄-in thick slices (in rounds or in the Chinese rolling oblique cut, turning the cucumber one half turn between each cut). Trim the scallion and slice very thinly; fry in ¹/₄ cup oil in the wok; add the meat and stir-fry for 5 minutes. Remove and set aside, draining off the oil. Heat 2¹/₂ tbsp fresh oil in the wok and fry the shredded ginger briefly, add the cucumber and stir-fry for 1 minute over high heat.

Return the meat to the wok and add the rice wine; mix the cornstarch with a little cold water and stir into the wok. Serve.

BEEF CROQUETTES
TIÁN DĀN *

田单复齐

Tián Dān fù jì

10 oz lean chicken (breast or leg meat)
1 tbsp cornstarch
2 eggs
3 water chestnuts
¹/₄ lb Chinese gold coin ham, Westphalian
    ham, Virginia ham or any good raw, cured
    ham
5 oz spinach
1 tbsp wine vinegar
salt
10 oz lean beef
¹/₂ cup all-purpose flour
fine breadcrumbs
oil for frying
few coriander or parsley leaves

Time: 1 hour 10 minutes

Mince the chicken finely, blend in 1 egg, the cornstarch, and a pinch of salt; set aside. Drain and finely chop the water chestnuts; wash the spinach thoroughly and chop very finely. Chop or mince the ham finely; place the water chestnuts, spinach, and ham in a mixing bowl and stir in the vinegar and a pinch of salt. Part-freeze the beef briefly if wished to make it easier to slice it very thinly. Spread a layer of the spinach and ham mixture on each slice, roll up quite tightly and spread a thin covering of the chicken mixture all over the surface of each roll, making sure it sticks securely to the meat. Beat the second egg lightly, dip all the rolls in this to coat evenly all over and then roll in the breadcrumbs, pressing lightly so that they adhere.

Semi deep-fry or deep-fry the croquettes in plenty of very hot (but not smoking) oil; fry them in several batches and remove each batch when golden brown with a slotted ladle, set aside to finish draining on kitchen paper. Transfer the croquettes to a heated serving dish and decorate with the coriander or parsley leaves. Deep-fried crispy vegetables (in batter or not as preferred) can be served with this dish.

The Chinese name for this dish, roughly "Tian Dan's feat of reconquest," recalls a general of the Combatants' reign who was famous for having freed his home state Qi, one of the seven fighting states, from the yoke of an oppressor; this was partly achieved by mounting the first wave of his assault with a herd of maddened bulls (their tails having been plunged into boiling oil beforehand).

75

BRAISED OXTAIL *
红烧牛尾
hóng shāo niú wěi

4¹/₂ lb oxtail
¹/₂ cup oil
2 scallions
4 thin slices ginger
1 clove garlic
1 chili pepper
¹/₂ cup soy sauce
3 tbsp rice wine
1 tbsp sugar
1 tsp monosodium glutamate (optional)
1 tsp salt
4 star anises
1 small piece cinnamon bark (or pinch
   ground cinnamon)
4 cloves
2 small pieces dried tangerine peel

Time: 3 hours

Cut the oxtail into 2-in sections (most butchers will have already done this). Trim off excess fat. Rinse these pieces thoroughly and then add to a large pan of boiling water to pre-cook for 10 minutes; remove from the boiling water, place in a colander or sieve and rinse under running cold water. Heat the oil in the wok or in a large, heavy-bottomed fireproof casserole dish; fry the trimmed and sliced scallions, the peeled and shredded ginger, the minced garlic and the chopped chili pepper. Add the meat and stir-fry for a few minutes. Add all the other ingredients and sufficient hot water to cover the oxtail; simmer for 2 hours, turning now and then.

PORK IN PEKING SAUCE
京酱肉丝
jīng jiàng ròu sī

1 lb pork tenderloin
1 tbsp rice wine
1 tsp salt
1 tbsp soy sauce
1 tbsp cornstarch or potato flour
2 scallions
oil for frying

For the sauce:
¹/₄ cup sweet soy paste
1 tsp salt
pinch sugar
pinch monosodium glutamate (optional)
1 tsp sesame seed oil
3 tbsp broth

Time: 1 hour

Cut the pork into thin strips; mix the wine, soy sauce, and cornstarch thoroughly in a large

bowl. Add the pork, mixing well. Heat 3 tbsp oil in the wok and stir-fry the pork briefly, just enough to make it turn a paler color and partly cook it. Remove, draining well, and set aside. Add a very little fresh oil to juices left in the wok if necessary and fry the trimmed and finely sliced scallions over lower heat until they are tender; do not allow to brown at all. Remove from the wok, draining well, and set aside.

Tip away any oil left in the wok, wipe the inside with paper towels and return the pork to it; add the soy paste, salt, sugar, monosodium glutamate (if used), the sesame seed oil, and the broth. Cook, uncovered, until the liquid has reduced a little, stirring and turning, then return the scallions to the wok and stir while cooking for a minute or two longer.

This is also a popular dish in western China (Szechwan).

CHOPPED MEAT IMPERIAL STYLE

仿膳肉末

fǎng shàn ròu mò

2 tbsp ground Szechwan pepper
1/4 cup peanut oil
2 tbsp finely chopped scallions
1/2 tsp finely chopped fresh ginger
4 water chestnuts, finely chopped
14 oz pork tenderloin
7 oz fresh pork belly
1 tbsp rice wine
1 tsp soy sauce
pinch sugar
pinch monosodium glutamate (optional)
1 tbsp sesame seed oil

Time: 30 minutes

Heat 2 tbsp of the oil in a small saucepan and fry the Szechwan pepper for 1 minute. Pour in the rest of the oil, allow to come up to temperature, then fry for 30 seconds more. Transfer 3 tbsp of this flavored oil into a wok or skillet and use it to fry the scallion, ginger, and water chestnuts. Chop the pork and the pork belly very finely (do not grind as this does not give the desired texture for this dish) and add to the contents of the wok. Stir-fry for 5 minutes. Add the wine, soy sauce, sugar, monosodium glutamate (if used), sesame seed oil, and the remaining pepper-flavored oil. Continue cooking and stirring until the liquid has reduced a little. Serve.

Freshly made sesame buns are delicious with this dish (see recipe on p. 14).

FRIED SPARERIBS *

酥炸猪排

sū zhà zhū pǎi

8 pork spareribs
2 scallions
5 thin slices fresh ginger
2 cloves garlic
oil for frying

For the sauce:
1 scallion
2 fresh chili peppers
3 tbsp oil
1/4 cup soy sauce
1 tbsp soy oil or sesame seed oil

1 tsp salt
pinch monosodium glutamate (optional)
pinch sugar

Time: 45 minutes

Have your butcher saw the spareribs in half so that they are not too long or chop them in half yourself. Chop the scallions coarsely, mince the ginger and the garlic, place in a bowl with the spareribs, and stir to flavor; leave to stand for a short time. Bring a large saucepan of water to a boil, add the spareribs and all the flavorings and simmer for 10 minutes. Remove the spareribs and drain well.

Heat sufficient oil to semi deep-fry in the wok or use a deep-fryer; fry the spareribs until golden brown, take out of the oil, draining well, and set aside.

Having emptied the oil out of the wok, heat 3 tbsp fresh oil and fry the shredded scallion and chili peppers. Add the soy sauce, soy oil or sesame seed oil, salt, monosodium glutamate (if used), and the sugar; stir well. Add the spareribs and coat with the sauce to flavor and moisten, cooking for a few minutes over moderate heat to reduce and thicken the sauce.

HAM WITH HONEY SAUCE
蜜汁火腿
mì zhī huǒ tuǐ

1 piece raw ham, skin removed, weighing 1 lb
3 tbsp clear, runny honey
3 tbsp sugar
3 tbsp rice wine
2¹/₂ tsp rose water, fruit cordial or liqueur of choice, e.g. Kirsch, Grand Marnier, peach or pear cordial
fresh fruit (to match the cordial or liqueur)
2¹/₂ tsp cornstarch

Time: 2¹/₂ hours + 12 hours soaking time

Soak the ham in cold water for 12 hours, changing the water once or twice; drain, dry well and place in the steamer compartment, cover, and steam for 2 hours. While the ham is cooking, prepare the fruit garnish: pit and slice your chosen fruit as required, cutting them, if wished, into decorative shapes: triangles, stars etc. If using fruit which can discolor, dip in water mixed with lemon juice to prevent this. When the ham is cooked, remove from the steamer and allow to cool a little; cut into slices just under ¹/₄ in thick and spread out on a serving platter. Mix all the sauce ingredients (honey, sugar, rice wine, rose water or liqueur, and cornstarch) in a small saucepan over low heat; continue stirring as the mixture thickens and comes to a boil; when the sugar has completely dissolved, pour the hot sauce all over the sliced ham and decorate with the prepared fruit. Serve at once.

PORK WITH MÙ XI
炒木犀肉
chǎo mùxi ròu

¹/₂ oz dried mu er mushrooms (cloud ear fungus)
1 oz mù xi golden needles (dried lily flower buds)
10 oz lean pork
4 eggs
¹/₂ cup oil
¹/₂–1 tbsp salt
1 tbsp soy sauce
1 tsp sugar
4 scallions
1 tbsp rice wine
2¹/₂ tbsp sesame seed oil

For the marinade:
1 tbsp salt
1 tbsp sugar
1 tbsp light soy sauce
1 tbsp dark soy sauce
pinch freshly ground pepper
1 tbsp rice wine
1 tbsp cornstarch or potato flour
1 tbsp water
1 tbsp oil

Time: 1³/₄ hours

Soak the mushrooms or fungus in warm water for 20 minutes; drain, dry, and trim off any tough pieces; soak the golden needles for the same length of time (or longer if necessary); chop roughly. Cut the pork into very thin slices (if wished, place in the freezer beforehand for 1–2 hours to make this easier).

Mix all the marinade ingredients in a bowl, add the meat, stir well, and leave to stand for 20 minutes. Heat 3 tbsp oil in the wok and stir-fry the pork briefly over high heat. Remove and set aside.

Beat the eggs lightly with 1 tbsp oil and a pinch of salt. Wipe the inside surface of the wok clean with paper towels, heat until very hot (it may smoke slightly) and then pour in 3 tbsp oil; tip the wok carefully this way and that to coat evenly with oil; stir-fry the mushrooms, reducing the heat if they are cooking too fiercely. Add the golden needles, stir well, season with salt, soy sauce, and sugar, and set aside.

Wipe the wok clean, heat again, repeating the same process of coating the hot wok with oil; pour in the egg mixture and scramble; when firm and set, remove from the wok and set aside. Trim the scallions and cut both the green leafy part and the white, holding the knife blade on the slant so that you cut diagonally, into small pieces; keep the green leafy part separate.

Wipe the wok again, heat once more, pour in the remaining oil and coat as before; stir-fry

the white part of the scallions briefly, add the meat, and stir-fry for 1 minute; stir in the wine and cook gently for 1–2 minutes.

Add all the other ingredients and stir-fry for a further minute to finish cooking the meat and heat the ingredients through thoroughly. Sprinkle in the green part of the scallions, transfer the contents of the wok to a heated serving dish, and sprinkle with the sesame seed oil. Serve at once.

PORK KABOBS WITH HONEY *
串烧猪肉
chuàn shāo shū ròu

14 oz pork tenderloin
7 oz goose liver or pig's liver
1¹/₄ lb pork belly
1 egg white
¹/₄ cup rice wine
¹/₄ cup sugar
1 tbsp dark soy sauce
1 tsp five-spice powder
salt
¹/₂ cup clear, runny honey
¹/₂ cup peanut oil

Time: 1 hour 20 minutes

Cut the pork, liver, and the pork belly into ¹/₂-in thick slices and then cut into pieces close to disk (circular) shape, preferably 1¹/₂–2 in in diameter.

Mix a marinade for the pork and liver, using the lightly beaten egg white, 1¹/₂ tbsp rice wine, 2 tbsp sugar, the dark soy sauce, the five-spice powder, and a pinch of salt; add the sliced pork and liver, stir and turn and leave to marinate for 30 minutes. Make a separate marinade for the pork belly, using the remaining rice wine and sugar and 1 tsp salt; stir well and then mix with the pork belly slices and leave to marinate for 30 minutes.

Thread all these marinated slices onto skewers in the following order: pork, pork belly, liver, pork belly, pork, etc. Barbecue these kabobs or broil at a moderately hot setting, turning frequently and basting when turned with the honey and the oil to keep the meat moist and juicy. Alternatively, roast in the oven at 400°F, reducing the heat to 350°F if they brown too quickly; turn and baste frequently. Serve the kabobs at once, freshly cooked and very hot.

PORK TENDERLOIN IMPERIAL STYLE

烧 子 盖
shāo zǐ gài

1¹/₄ lb pork tenderloin
2 eggs
2 cups all-purpose flour
oil for frying

For the marinade:
1 tbsp salt
1 tbsp sesame seed oil
1 tbsp rice wine
generous pinch freshly ground pepper
pinch monosodium glutamate (optional)

For the condiment:
3 tbsp salt
¹/₂–1 tbsp five-spice powder
pinch monosodium glutamate

Time: 1 hour 40 minutes

Add the meat to a pan of unsalted boiling water, allow to return to a boil, and simmer for 30 minutes; leave to cool in the water, then drain, cut into ³/₈-in thick slices; cut these slices into strips ³/₈ in wide (so you will have strips with a ³/₈-in square section).

Mix the marinade ingredients thoroughly in a bowl; add the meat, and mix well to flavor all over.

Beat the egg with the flour and just enough cold water to make a coating batter; dip the meat in this, coating all the pieces thoroughly, then semi deep-fry or deep-fry (in several small batches) in very hot oil until crisp and golden brown on the outside. Mix the condiment ingredients and place in a bowl or tiny bowls for each person to dip the pork morsels if wished.

STIR-FRIED VENISON

滑 溜 鹿 里 脊
huá liū lù lǐ jǐ

1 lb lean venison
pinch monosodium glutamate (optional)
2 tsp salt
¹/₂–1 tsp freshly ground pepper
3 tbsp rice wine
1 tbsp soy sauce
2¹/₂ tbsp cornstarch or potato flour
1 egg white
6 water chestnuts
¹/₂ scallion
oil for frying
2¹/₂ tbsp oil
1 tbsp melted chicken fat (optional)

Time: 30 minutes

Cut the meat into very thin slices (if wished, place in the freezer for 1 hour beforehand to make this easier). Rinse these slices under running cold water; dry thoroughly. Mix the monosodium glutamate (if used) with 1 tsp salt, the wine, soy sauce, lightly beaten egg white, and 1 heaping tbsp of the cornstarch. Add the meat to this mixture, stirring and turning to coat evenly, and leave to stand.

Slice the water chestnuts and shred the trimmed scallion. Heat plenty of oil in the wok or a skillet (or a deep-fryer) and when very hot, add the meat and sear for 2 minutes, keeping the pieces from sticking to each other with cooking chopsticks or a long-handled fork. Remove from the oil, draining thoroughly.

Heat 2¹/₂ tbsp fresh oil in a wok or skillet and stir-fry the water chestnuts and scallion gently. Add the venison and sprinkle with a pinch of salt and some freshly ground pepper. Mix the remaining cornstarch with a little cold water, stir into the wok, and cook for a few minutes more. Stir in the melted chicken fat, if wished. Turn off the heat and serve.

CARAMELIZED PORK FRITTERS *

冰 糖 肉
bīng táng ròu

7 cups chicken broth
14 oz fairly fat pork (e.g. breast or boned shoulder)
2 egg whites, lightly beaten
¹/₂ cup all-purpose flour
¹/₂ cup very fine cornmeal
oil for frying
¹/₄ lb Chinese rock sugar, also called yellow lump sugar (ping tan)
1 tsp finely chopped fresh chili pepper
1 tsp finely chopped onion

Time: 2 hours

Bring a large saucepan two-thirds full of water to a boil, add the meat (in one piece), allow to return to a boil, and simmer for 1 hour or until very tender; leave to cool in the cooking liquid and when cold remove from the saucepan and trim off as much fat as possible.

Make a batter by mixing the flour and cornmeal or cornstarch very thoroughly with the egg whites. Cut the meat into even-sized rectangular pieces no longer than 2 in; dip these pieces in the batter. Heat plenty of oil in the wok or a heavy-bottomed skillet for semi deep-frying (or deep-fry) and when it reaches 340°F or a little hotter, lower the batter-coated pieces of meat into it a few at a time and fry until crisp

and golden brown all over. Remove each batch from the oil and drain well.

Place the Chinese sugar (ordinary sugar can be substituted if necessary) and $1/2$ cup water in the top of a double boiler (or in a heatproof bowl over fast boiling water) and heat until pale golden brown; immediately stir in the chili pepper and onion. Turn off the heat below the pan but keep the top compartment or bowl over the hot water. Dip the pork fritters in this savory caramel, coating completely, and transfer one by one to a lightly oiled serving plate. If the caramel starts to set in the pan before you have finished dipping, reheat it briefly to soften and liquefy again.

PORK XIANG ZAO

糟肉

zāo ròu

1¹/₄ lb pork tenderloin
2¹/₂ tsp salt
3 tbsp rice wine (lao jiu)
1 scallion
3 tbsp rice wine (Shian ciao [Xiang zao])
1 tbsp sugar

Time: 1 hour + 12 hours chilling time

Stir 1 tsp salt into the lao jiu rice wine until it has dissolved; sprinkle this all over the meat, cover with Saran wrap and place in the refrigerator to marinate for 12 hours; turn several times during this time.

When the meat has finished marinating, bring plenty of water to a boil in a large pot and add the meat; boil gently for 10 minutes, then take out of the pot and place in a heatproof dish that will fit in the steamer compartment and sprinkle with 1 tsp salt, the trimmed and chopped scallion, the sugar, and the Shian ciao rice wine; cover the dish tightly with foil, place in the steamer, cover, and steam for 30 minutes.

Remove the dish from the steamer and when the meat is completely cold, slice thinly.

The deliciously aromatic Shian ciao (Xiang zao) wine gives this dish its name.

STEAMED EGGS WITH PORK

肉末炖蛋

ròu mò dùn dàn

2 tung ku (dong gu) mushrooms
$1/2$ cup finely chopped pork tenderloin
$1/2$ cup finely chopped pork belly
1 finely chopped scallion
1 tbsp rice wine
1 tbsp light soy sauce
pinch salt
pinch monosodium glutamate (optional)
4 eggs

Time: 40 minutes

Soak the dried mushrooms in warm water for 20 minutes, then drain, remove and discard the stalks, and chop the caps finely.

Mix the chopped meat (this should not be ground, as fine chopping gives a better texture) with the mushrooms, scallion, rice wine, soy sauce, salt, and monosodium glutamate (if used). Beat the eggs lightly and mix with the meat. Place this mixture in a fairly deep heat-proof dish (small enough to fit into your steamer compartment but large enough to leave sufficient room when the mixture rises during cooking).

Cover and steam for 10 minutes. Serve hot or cold, with sauce and seasonings to taste.

THREE-COLOR EGG PIE

三色蛋糕

sān sè dàn gāo

6 eggs
1 tsp salt
1 tbsp rice wine
3 tbsp chopped Chinese gold coin ham, Virginia ham or Westphalian ham
2 scallions, finely chopped
2 tung ku (dong gu) mushrooms
1 tbsp fresh or frozen peas
oil

Time: 40 minutes

Soak the mushrooms in warm water for 20 minutes, then drain, remove and discard the stalks, and chop the caps. Beat the eggs lightly with the salt and wine; stir in the ham, scallions, and the mushrooms. Grease a pie dish lightly with oil, pour the mixture into it, and place in the steamer compartment. Cover and steam; after 2 minutes, uncover the dish and sprinkle the peas over the surface. Cover and continue steaming for a further 6 minutes or until the mixture has set and has risen slightly in the dish.

Remove from the steamer, slice like an ordinary pie and serve. Sprinkle each serving with a little more of the ham, also finely chopped, if wished.

THREE-FLAVOR OMELET

三鲜炒蛋

sān xiān chǎo dàn

$1/4$ lb pork tenderloin
$1/4$ lb dried shrimp (scia mi) or fresh or frozen peeled shrimp
4 tung ku (dong gu) mushrooms
$1/4$ lb fine French beans
4 bamboo shoots
1 scallion
1 tbsp rice wine
1 tsp salt
pinch monosodium glutamate (optional)
1 tsp soy sauce
1 tsp sesame seed oil
7 eggs
oil for frying

Time: 45 minutes

Cut the pork into matchstick strips. If using dried shrimp, soak these in hot water for 30 minutes. Do likewise with the mushrooms, then remove and discard their stalks, and cut the caps into matchstick strips. If the shrimp are on the large side, chop coarsely. Rinse and trim the beans and cut into lengths which roughly match the pork strips. Cut the bamboo shoots and the scallion into thin strips. Beat the eggs lightly.

Heat $1/4$ cup oil in the wok, stir-fry the mushrooms and the vegetables with the meat, add the rice wine, salt, monosodium glutamate (if used), and the soy sauce and then simmer over lower heat for 8–10 minutes (the beans should still be quite crisp when the dish is ready). Sprinkle in the sesame oil and turn off the heat, before briskly stirring in the eggs (if cooking on an electric hob, draw the wok aside from the heat before adding the eggs).

Grease the inside of another wok or a skillet with oil, heat and then add the contents of the first wok; cook for 1 minute over high heat and turn the omelet very carefully. Cook for 1 minute more, then serve at once.

If wished, serve a sauce with the omelet: in a small saucepan mix 1 cup chicken broth with a pinch of salt and 1 heaping tbsp cornstarch or potato flour; heat, stirring continuously until thickened, simmer for 1–2 minutes, and serve with the omelet.

QUAIL'S EGGS ON TOAST

象眼鹌鹑蛋

xiàng yǎn ān chún dàn

10 quail's eggs at room temperature
1 small white pan loaf (rectangular shape)
$1/4$ cup all-purpose flour
$1/4$ lb chopped shrimp
$1/4$ cup finely chopped lean pork
$1/4$ lb finely chopped pork belly
1 egg white
$2^1/2$ tbsp cornstarch or potato flour
1 tbsp rice wine
pinch salt
1 tsp light soy sauce
pinch sugar
$2^1/2$ tbsp finely chopped scallion
1 heaping tbsp finely chopped fresh ginger
1 tbsp sesame seed oil
$1/2$ cup oil

For the garnish:
2 tbsp minced or chopped gold coin Chinese ham, Virginia ham or Westphalian ham
1 sprig parsley
1 tbsp cornstarch or potato flour

Time: 50 minutes

Boil the quail's eggs for 3–4 minutes; cool quickly under running cold water and then peel. Cut each egg lengthwise in half. Cut 20 slices of bread $1/2$ in thick, cut off the crusts, and trim to oval shapes (considerably larger than the eggs).

Mix just enough water with the flour to form a smooth spreading mixture; spread this over the top surface of the oval bread slices, then place a half egg in the center of each (wider end pointing toward the wider end of the slice) cut side downward. Mix all the remaining ingredients thoroughly to form a paste and spread this over the egg halves.

Sprinkle each slice with the garnish or topping, pressing this gently to make it adhere, press small sections of the parsley leaves onto the surface, and dust evenly with the remaining cornstarch or potato flour.

Heat the oil in a very wide skillet and fry the slices (with the egg side uppermost) for 2 minutes. Serve hot.

SHRIMP- AND PORK-STUFFED EGG ROLLS

虾仁蛋饭

xiā ròu dàn jiǎo

$1/4$ lb peeled shrimp
$1/2$ cup finely chopped pork tenderloin

On the outskirts of Xi'an, in Shanxi province, a makeshift market gives the peasants an opportunity to sell eggs and vegetables; this timeless scene could date from almost any age, were is not for the billboard in the background on which the advertisment apes Western publicity methods. The Chinese long ago perfected a method of preserving eggs, which involves covering them thickly all over when fresh with an alkaline mixture of lime, salt,

ashes, bicarbonate of soda, and tea; they are then stored in clay pots for up to six months before they are ready to eat.
Historically long, bitterly cold winters meant that large amounts of food had to be preserved efficiently and so the tradition evolved. The inhabitants of this part of China are expert at sun- and wind-drying, among other methods, many of which entail the plentiful use of spices.

1/3 cup sweet soy paste

Time: 1 1/2 hours

Rinse the mushrooms well under running cold water and then soak in hot water for 20 minutes. Soak the soy flour noodles in water for 10 minutes. Shred the meat and vegetables. Drain the mushrooms, trim off any tough or fibrous parts, and slice into thin strips.

Heat 1/4 cup oil in the wok and stir-fry the meat, noodles, bamboo shoots, mushrooms, and vegetables for up to 10 minutes. Add the salt, monosodium glutamate (if used), pepper, and rice wine, stir well then mix in the cornstarch mixed with a very little cold water Transfer to a large, round heated serving dish.

Beat the eggs lightly, grease a very wide, preferably nonstick skillet, pour in the eggs and cook until set.

Keep the pancakes hot until needed. Trim the scallion and cut into thin strips.

To eat, spread a pancake with a little sweet soy paste, sprinkle with a few strands of scallion and place about 1 tbsp of the vegetable mixture and a little chopped omelet on top. Roll up and eat with the fingers.

SCRAMBLED EGGS MÙ XŪ
蛋炒木耳肉
dàn chǎo mù ěr ròu

1/4 lb finely chopped pork tenderloin
2 1/2 tbsp finely chopped scallion
pinch finely chopped fresh ginger
6 mo ha mushrooms (tree ear fungus)
4 bamboo shoots
3 eggs
1 tbsp rice wine
1/2 tbsp salt
pinch monosodium glutamate (optional)
pinch freshly ground pepper
1 tbsp light soy sauce
oil as required

Time: 40 minutes

Rinse the mushrooms under running cold water then soak in hot water for 20 minutes.

Heat 1/4 cup of oil in the wok and stir-fry the meat for 2 minutes; remove and set aside. Wipe the wok, heat 6 tbsp fresh oil in it and fry the scallion and ginger gently until they start to release their aromas; add the drained and trimmed mushrooms and the bamboo shoots, both cut into thin strips, and fry for about 30 seconds. Return the meat to the wok; lightly beat the eggs with the rice wine, salt, monosodium glutamate (if used), pepper, and soy sauce and mix briskly into the wok to scramble the eggs. When the eggs have set, serve.

1 1/2 tbsp finely chopped pork belly
1 tsp rice wine
1 tsp light soy sauce
2 1/2 tsp cornstarch or potato flour
pinch salt
pinch monosodium glutamate (optional)
6 eggs
oil as required

Time: 1 hour

Chop the shrimp finely and mix with the chopped tenderloin and pork belly, rice wine, soy sauce, cornstarch, salt, and monosodium glutamate (if used). Beat the eggs lightly. Use a 6-in omelet pan and grease it with oil. Spoon in about 1 1/2 tbsp of the beaten egg and tip the pan a little from side to side to make the egg cover the bottom of the pan with a wafer-thin layer. Turn carefully and cook briefly on the other side then slide gently out of the pan. Continue until all the beaten egg has been used up, stacking the wrappers on a plate. Spread a little filling in the center of each wrapper, fold in half and fry briefly.

VEGETABLE OMELET
合菜戴帽
hé cài dài mào

2 oz lean pork
2 oz bean sprouts
2 oz bamboo shoots
2 oz mo ha mushrooms (tree ear fungus)
2 oz scallion
1 medium-sized carrot
1 oz soy flour noodles
6 tbsp oil
1 tsp salt
pinch monosodium glutamate (optional)
pinch freshly ground pepper
1 tbsp rice wine
1 tbsp cornstarch or potato flour
3 eggs

Serve with:
12 Mandarin pancakes (bought or
   homemade, see recipe on p. 16)
1 scallion

THREE-COLOR VEGETABLES

扒三素

pá sān sù

12 baby corn cobs (frozen or canned)
10 oz broccoli tops
2 carrots
10 tung ku (dong gu) mushrooms
pinch salt
pinch monosodium glutamate (optional)

For the sauce:
1 tbsp rice wine
2¹/₂ tbsp chicken broth
1 tsp cornstarch or potato flour
pinch salt
pinch sugar
small pinch monosodium glutamate
    (optional)

Time: 1 hour

If frozen baby corn cobs are used, cook from frozen. Steam fresh or frozen cobs for 20 minutes; if canned corn is used, drain the cobs thoroughly and rinse under running cold water. Rinse the broccoli and blanch in a large pan of boiling water for 1 minute; drain in a colander and refresh immediately under running cold water. Slice the peeled carrots finely. Soak the tung ku dried mushrooms in warm water for 20–30 minutes to soften and reconstitute, then drain well. Cut off and discard the stalks. Place all the vegetables in a dish and sprinkle with the salt and monosodium glutamate.

Arrange the vegetables in sections on a circular plate that will fit in your steamer: three sections of corn cobs with three sections of broccoli separating them; heap up the carrots in a ring around the middle of the plate and place the mushrooms in the center. Place in the steamer, cover, and steam for 20 minutes.

Make the sauce by mixing together the wine, broth, cornstarch or potato flour, salt, sugar, and monosodium glutamate (if used). Sprinkle all over the vegetables just before serving them.

CARROT AND WHITE RADISH CROQUETTES WITH SCALLOPS

干贝萝卜球

gàn bèi luó bo qiú

3 or 4 dried Chinese scallops
2 or 3 large, crisp carrots
2 medium-sized long white radishes (Daikon
    roots)
1 tsp salt
¹/₂ tsp monosodium glutamate (optional)
1 scallion
1¹/₂ tsp fresh pork fat or shortening
1 tbsp rice wine
2¹/₂ tbsp chicken broth
1 tbsp cornstarch or potato flour

Time: 3 hours

Place the dried scallops in a heatproof (i.e. metal) colander or in one of the bamboo steamer compartments with the lid on, place in a saucepan, and add sufficient water to just cover the scallops. Bring to a boil and simmer for 1 hour. Trim and peel the carrots and radishes and use a melon baller to cut them into small balls.

Take the scallops out of the saucepan when cooked, draining well; reserve the cooking liquid. Chop the scallops coarsely and place in a heatproof bowl; place the carrot and radish balls on top, well mixed up. Flavor the reserved cooking liquid with salt and monosodium glutamate (if used), pour this into the bowl, cover tightly with foil, and steam in the steamer for 1¹/₂ hours.

Strain the cooking liquid into a small saucepan and stir in the finely chopped scallion, the rice wine, fat or lard and the chicken broth; leave to boil fast and reduce for a few minutes. Place a serving plate upside down on top of the bowl, holding the two tightly together, turn the plate the right way up and release the contents of the bowl onto the plate. Mix the cornstarch with a very little cold water and stir into the small saucepan to thicken the sauce; simmer for a few minutes longer then pour over the scallops and vegetables on the dish.

EGGPLANT IMPERIAL STYLE

清宫茄段

qǐng gōng qié duàn

3 medium-sized eggplant
1¹/₄ cups very finely chopped pork
    tenderloin
¹/₂ cup finely chopped pork belly
6 tbsp finely chopped scallions
2¹/₂ tbsp finely chopped garlic
2¹/₂ tbsp soy sauce
¹/₂ tsp monosodium glutamate
    (optional)
¹/₂ tsp salt
¹/₂ tsp sugar
2 red bell peppers (capsicums)
¹/₄ cup oil
oil for frying

Time: 1 hour

Peel the eggplant and cut into ³/₄–1-in cubes; semi deep-fry or deep-fry in very hot oil for 5 minutes; drain well. Heat ¹/₄ cup fresh oil in the wok, stir-fry the scallions and garlic briefly, add all the meat, cook for 1–2 minutes then add the fried eggplant cubes, followed by the soy sauce, monosodium glutamate (if used), the salt, and the sugar.

Stir-fry briefly, then add the finely shredded red bell peppers; stir-fry over high heat for 1 minute then serve.

STIR-FRIED TIENTSIN CABBAGE WITH SOY FLOUR NOODLES

粉丝焖津白

fěn sī mèn jīn bái

1 Tientsin (or Peking) cabbage
1 scallion
2 thin slices fresh ginger
1 clove garlic
3 tbsp oil
3 cups chicken broth
pinch salt
small pinch monosodium glutamate
    (optional)
1 tbsp soy sauce
2 oz soy flour noodles
2 tbsp melted pork fat (optional)

Time: 50 minutes

Soak the soy flour noodles in warm water for

15 minutes.

Rinse the cabbage well and cut into thin strips about 2 in long. Cut the trimmed scallion and the peeled ginger slices into thin strips and stir-fry them gently, with the lightly minced garlic clove, in 3 tbsp oil in the wok. Add the cabbage and stir-fry until it wilts; add the chicken broth, salt, monosodium glutamate (if used), and the soy sauce. Simmer, uncovered, for 10 minutes over low heat.

Drain the noodles and add to the wok, stir well, and simmer, still uncovered, over slightly higher heat for 10 minutes. If wished, the pork fat can be stirred in just before serving.

KIDNEY SALAD *

凉拌腰花

liáng bàn yāo huā

1 pig's kidney (or calf's kidney)
2 cucumbers
$^1/_2$ oz agar-agar strands
2 sticks celery

For the sauce:
$2^1/_2$ tbsp sugar
$^1/_4$ cup wine vinegar
1 tbsp soy sauce
1 tbsp mustard sauce or mustard oil
1 tsp sesame seed oil
pinch monosodium glutamate (optional)

Time: 30 minutes

Peel off the thin membrane covering the kidney; slice in half horizontally and remove the white gristly parts and any discoloration, fat, etc. Cut down the length of these two thin kidney halves to yield strips approx. $^3/_8$ in wide. Add the kidney strips to a pan of boiling water to blanch for 3 minutes only; drain well and immediately refresh by placing in a sieve and holding under cold water (these two last steps make sure the kidney loses any pungent taste or smell). Dry the kidney pieces and cut each strip into half its original length and half its width, to give very thin, shorter strips. Tease out the hank of agar-agar strands, place in a colander, rinse thoroughly under running cold water, drain, squeeze out excess moisture, and snip into pieces the same length as the kidney strips. Cut the cucumbers diagonally into thin slices then cut these into thin strips. Remove any tough strings from the celery and then cut diagonally into thin slices. Place the kidney, agar-agar, cucumber, and celery in a large salad bowl. Blend the sauce ingredients thoroughly and pour over the salad as a dressing. Mix well and serve.

BRAISED BAMBOO SHOOTS

干烧笋

gàn shāo sǔn

$^1/_4$ lb bean sprouts
$2^1/_4$ cups water
14 oz fresh or canned bamboo shoots
$^1/_2$ cup cornstarch
$2^1/_4$ cups oil
1 $1^1/_4$-in piece fresh ginger, peeled and thinly sliced
1 tbsp dark soy sauce
$1^1/_2$ tsp rice wine
1 tsp sugar
1 red bell pepper (capsicum) (or use 1 piece each red, green, yellow, and black peppers for color effect)
$^1/_4$ cup sesame seed oil

Time: $1^1/_4$ hours

Make a vegetable broth: remove and discard any little green empty seed cases from the bean sprouts before you use them as these are bitter, then rinse and drain the sprouts well. Fry the bean sprouts in $1^1/_2$ tbsp oil in a large pan. Add the water and boil until reduced to less than half its original volume; strain the broth and reserve, discarding the bean sprouts. Drain the canned bamboo shoots, or trim and wash if fresh, then blanch in boiling water for 8 minutes. Drain and cut into thin, flat rectangular slices. Alternatively, the bamboo shoots may be shredded. Heat the oil in the wok or a heavy-bottomed pan; coat the bamboo shoots all over with cornstarch and semi deep-fry in the very hot oil until pale golden brown; remove with a slotted ladle or spoon and drain well.

Heat $1^1/_2$ tbsp fresh oil in a clean wok or skillet, stir-fry the ginger slices for 30 seconds or until they start to give off a distinctive aroma; remove the ginger and discard; add the fried bamboo shoots to the flavored oil, together with the prepared broth, the soy sauce, rice wine, and sugar; simmer, stirring occasionally, until the bamboo shoots are just tender.

Shred the peppers, add to the wok or pan, and cook until tender but still slightly crisp; stir in the sesame seed oil and serve at once.

86

The road to Lanzhou, not far from Xining, to the southwest of Peking and near Lake Qinghai. Peasants have set up stalls by the roadside, with baskets of fruit and vegetables to sell to passers by. These makeshift markets are once more to be found all over China and large quantities of fresh produce are sold during the short growing season which are then preserved, mainly by drying and brining, ready for the cold

winter months.
For many years such free markets were forbidden but with the reintroduction of market forces, food production has soared and the variety of basic foodstuffs has increased enormously, marking a shift from collective farming to a mixture of state control and private, often family, enterprise.

lowed by the rice wine, chicken broth, and monosodium glutamate (if used). Continue cooking until the liquid has evaporated; meanwhile reheat the oil (semi deep-fry or deep-fry) until very hot but not smoking and transfer the vegetables (use a slotted or wire ladle) to the oil to deep-fry for 2 minutes, when they should once more be crisp. Drain thoroughly, transfer to a serving plate, and sprinkle with the mixed salt and sugar. Eat while very hot and crisp.

ASPARAGUS KUO TA

锅 锟 芦 笋

guō kūn lú sǔn

2¼–2½ lb asparagus spears
¼ cup oil
3 tbsp chicken broth

For the marinade:
2½ tbsp rice wine
pinch monosodium glutamate
½–1 tbsp salt
1 tbsp oil

For the batter:
2 eggs
1¾ cups all-purpose flour

Time: 30 minutes

Cut the top 3 in from the asparagus, discarding the paler, tougher stalk section. Steam for 10 minutes (less if very young and tender) and then take out of the steamer, place in a dish, and pour the marinade all over them. Leave to stand.

Mix the flour into the lightly beaten eggs (use a blender if wished) and add just enough water to make a smooth, thick coating batter. Dip the asparagus in the batter, coating them all over. Heat ¼ cup oil in the wok or a very wide skillet and arrange the asparagus in the oil in a single layer: cook over low heat for 2 minutes, turn, and cook for a further 2 minutes. Add the broth, cook until this has reduced, and serve.

STIR-FRIED PEAS WITH SOY SAUCE *

青 豆 肉 丁

qīng dòu ròu dīng

5 oz lean pork
14 oz fresh or frozen peas
2½ tbsp melted fresh pork fat or shortening
2 scallions

TWICE-FRIED BAMBOO SHOOTS

干 烧 冬 笋

gàn shāo dōng sǔn

14 oz bamboo shoots (fresh or canned)
¼ lb brine-pickled Chinese greens (she li hon)
1 scallion
2 thin slices fresh ginger
1 tbsp rice wine
3 tbsp chicken broth
pinch monosodium glutamate (optional)
salt
sugar
3 tbsp oil
oil for frying

Time: 45 minutes

Cut the bamboo shoots into thin, rectangular pieces measuring about ⅜ × 1¼ in. Rinse the pickled vegetables thoroughly under running cold water to eliminate excess salt (the brine they are preserved in is very salty), removing and discarding the larger stalks: you will use all the leaves and the tiny, tender stalks; cut them into strips. Heat the oil for semi deep-frying in the wok or a heavy-bottomed saucepan (or deep-fry in a deep-fryer) and when very hot add the bamboo shoots and the pickled green vegetables and fry until very crisp. Remove from the oil, draining very thoroughly.

Cut the trimmed scallion and the peeled ginger into thin slices and stir-fry in 3 tbsp oil in the wok; once they release their aroma and have flavored the oil well, remove and discard; add the fried vegetables to the flavored oil, fol-

1 1½-in piece fresh ginger
¼ cup dark soy sauce
1 tbsp rice wine
2½ tbsp chicken broth
1 tsp sesame seed oil
½–1 tbsp salt

Time: 45 minutes

Trim and finely chop the scallions; peel and finely chop the ginger. Cut the meat into small dice. Bring a saucepan of lightly salted water to a boil and add the peas; cook until only just tender; drain in a sieve, refresh by holding the sieve under running cold water and set aside. Heat the pork fat or shortening in a wok or skillet and stir-fry the meat until it loses its pink color and turns pale; add the scallion, ginger, and soy sauce and stir-fry for a further 1–2 minutes. Add the peas, wine, and broth and stir-fry until all the ingredients are well mixed and very hot. Sprinkle with the sesame seed oil and immediately remove from the heat. Serve piping hot.

STIR-FRIED BAMBOO SHOOTS AND SEAWEED

干烧冬笋

gàn shāo dōng sǔn

1 lb bamboo shoots (fresh or canned)
pinch salt
1 tbsp rice wine
1 oz dried Wakame seaweed
oil for frying

Time: 50 minutes

If canned bamboo shoots are used, drain well; if fresh, trim, wash well, and cut away the hard lower parts; cut each bamboo shoot in quarters, place these on a plate, and sprinkle with salt and the wine.

Soak the seaweed in a bowl of cold water until soft; drain well and cut away the large, hard ribs; blanch the leaves for 1–2 minutes in boiling water, drain, dry, and cut into small pieces.

Heat sufficient oil to semi deep-fry in the wok or a skillet or use more oil and deep-fry in a deep-fryer; heat to 325°F and fry the bamboo shoots until they are crisp on the outside but tender inside; remove from the oil with a slotted or wire ladle and place on paper towels.

Add a little more oil if necessary and allow to come up to temperature. Deep-fry the seaweed, taking care not to overcook: they are done when bright green and crisp. Transfer the bamboo shoots and the seaweed to a heated serving plate and serve without delay.

88

WALNUT AND CANDIED FRUIT MERINGUE BREAD PUDDING

雪花豆泥

xuě huā dòu nī

¹/₂ lb white pan loaf
¹/₄ lb shelled walnuts
6 tbsp oil
¹/₃ cup seedless white raisins
2 oz candied pineapple (or other fruit of choice)
2 oz dried apricots or peaches
3 eggs
2¹/₂ tbsp shortening or clarified butter
6 tbsp sugar
assorted candied or glacé fruits for decoration

Time: 1¹/₄ hours

Cut the crusts off the bread and crumble; moisten thoroughly with a cupful of water, squeeze hard to eliminate excess moisture, and place in a mixing bowl.

Blanch the walnuts in fast boiling water for 3–4 minutes, then drain and peel off any of the brown papery skin adhering to them.

Heat the oil in a wok or skillet and fry the walnuts, turning frequently, for about 3 minutes or until they are lightly browned, then drain them thoroughly, chop finely, and mix with the breadcrumbs. Chop the candied and dried fruit very finely and add to the mixing bowl; separate the egg yolks from the whites and stir the yolks very thoroughly into the other ingredients in the bowl.

Heat the shortening (or clarified butter) in the wok or a skillet, add the mixture from the bowl, and fry over high heat for 5 minutes; add the sugar and continue stirring over high heat until the mixture acquires a translucent look. Spoon quickly into a mold or heatproof bowl, packing it very firmly, then turn out onto a serving dish.

Beat the egg whites stiffly, transfer to a heatproof dish that will fit in the steamer compartment, place a piece of foil loosely on top of the egg whites, cover the steamer compartment and steam for 6 minutes by which time the whites should have set. Spread the egg white all over the unmolded bread pudding and decorate with small pieces of candied or dried fruit.

SWEET PEANUT AND SESAME SEED SOUP

花生奶蛋

huā shēng nǎi lù

3 tbsp sesame oil
¹/₂ cup white sesame seeds
2 cups unroasted, unsalted shelled peanuts
¹/₂ cup sugar
1¹/₂ tbsp cornstarch or potato flour
¹/₂ cup milk

Time: 30 minutes

Heat 3 tbsp oil gently in a small saucepan or skillet and add the sesame seeds; stir continuously over moderate heat until the seeds turn a very pale golden brown and you can smell their distinctive aroma. Add the peanuts and continue cooking for a few minutes, stirring continuously. Allow to cool a little, then reduce to a very smooth, soft paste in the food processor with 1 cup water. Spoon this mixture into a heavy-bottomed saucepan and stir in 5 cups water and the sugar. Cook over moderate heat, stirring continuously, until the sugar has completely dissolved. Mix the cornstarch with a very little cold water, then stir into the mixture in the saucepan; continue stirring as it thickens slightly. Draw aside from the heat and immediately stir in the milk.

Serve at once. This dish can also be eaten cold.

SWEET ROASTED SESAME SEED CREAM SOUP *

芝麻糊

zhī má hù

4 cups sesame seeds (black or white)
3 tbsp oil
¹/₂ cup sugar
¹/₄ cup cornstarch or potato flour

Time: 30 minutes

Stir-fry the sesame seeds in the oil until they give off a pleasant, nutty aroma, add 1 cup water, cook for a few more minutes, then allow to cool a little before processing them in the liquidizer with the sugar and 4 cups more water (liquidize in several batches if you do not have a large-capacity blender). Pour the mixture into a heavy-bottomed saucepan and cook, stirring frequently, for 10 minutes. Turn off the heat and immediately stir in the cornstarch mixed with a very little cold water.

Serve at once, hot, or allow to cool and serve cold.

CHINESE TOFFEE APPLE SLICES *

拔丝苹果

bá sī píng guǒ

4 large apples
1 cup fine white cake flour or all-purpose flour
1 egg
oil for frying
2¹/₂ tsp sesame seed oil
1 tbsp shortening or clarified butter
2¹/₂ tbsp water
¹/₂ cup sugar
1 large bowl iced water

Time: 1 hour

Choose a firm-fleshed variety of apple for this recipe. Peel and core the apples; cut them into quarters and cut each quarter lengthwise in half; coat these segments thoroughly with the flour, shaking off excess. Set aside. Mix the lightly beaten egg with all the flour that is left over (including that shaken off the segments) and only just enough water to make a fairly thick coating batter.

Heat plenty of oil in the wok or a deep saucepan, or use a deep-fryer; heat the oil to 325°F. Working quickly, add the apple segments to the batter, making sure they are coated all over. Add half the sesame seed oil to the hot oil and immediately lower the first small batch of apple segments into the oil, using a wire ladle or frying basket; when they are crisp and golden brown, remove with a slotted or wire ladle, draining well, then fry the next batch. Place each completed batch on paper towels. Heat the shortening or clarified butter in another saucepan with the 2¹/₂ tbsp water and the sugar; continue cooking until the sugar melts and turns pale golden brown; immediately draw aside from the heat and start dipping the apple fritters to coat with this toffee mixture; place each dipped piece onto a serving plate, lightly greased with the remaining sesame seed oil.

If you want to make sure that the toffee sets to a pleasant crunchy consistency, dip the coated slices in the iced water before placing them on the oiled serving dish, or place a small bowl of iced water by each person's table setting. The hot, freshly cooked toffee apples can then be dipped in the iced water one at a time and eaten.

90

WHITE SEAWEED IN SYRUP *

冰糖木耳

bīng táng mù ěr

2 oz dried white seaweed
1 cup sugar
canned fruit of choice

Time: 30 minutes

Soak the seaweed in a bowl of hot water for 10 minutes; drain well and trim off the stalk. Mix the sugar with 6 cups hot water and heat until the sugar has dissolved and a syrup formed; add the seaweed and cook over moderate heat for 10 minutes. Transfer the seaweed to a serving dish and decorate with canned fruit (preferably canned in a syrup).

This dish can be eaten hot or cold.

GLUTINOUS RICE AND SWEET SOY PUDDING

豆沙糕饼

dòu shā gāo bǐng

3 cups glutinous rice flour
1/2 cup cake flour or all-purpose flour
1/2 cup sweet soy flour

Time: 30 minutes

Mix the three types of flour thoroughly, then gradually stir in 1 cup hot water, adding a little at a time, followed by 1/4 cup cold water. Line the steamer compartment with waxed paper, spoon the mixture into the lining, and smooth the surface level. Cover and steam for 10 minutes.

Remove the pie or pudding from the steamer, turn upside down and remove the waxed paper. Serve cold.

STEAMED BUNS WITH SWEET RED BEAN PASTE

豆沙包

dòu shā bāo

For the dough:
See Steamed Buns on p. 14

1 1/4 lb red bean flour or sweet red bean paste
red food coloring (optional)
2 1/2 tbsp shortening (optional)

Time: 1 hour + dough preparation time

Prepare the dough and leave to rise.

If using red bean flour, moisten by gradually adding 1/2 cup warm water, stirring well to make a soft paste (use a food processor if wished). Melt the shortening in a small saucepan and stir in the red bean and water paste. You can omit this stage of adding the fat if wished. Commercially-prepared red bean paste can also be used.

Knock down the risen dough and roll out into a fairly thick sheet; cut out into 4–4½-in disks; place a little of the paste in the center of each disk, then enclose this in the dough, shaping into round buns. Use chopsticks or skewers to press indented lines radiating from the center top of the buns; use the tines of a fork to prick along these lines and sprinkle the buns with red food coloring powder.

Steam as directed for Steamed buns on p. 14.

FLUFFY EGG CHIFFON MOUSSE *

三不粘

sān bù zhān

15 egg yolks
½ cup sugar
½ cup cornstarch or potato flour
½ cup water
¼ cup oil

Time: 40 minutes

Bring the water to a boil then stir in the sugar until it has completely dissolved; set aside to cool. Beat the egg yolks (use the bowl and whisk of your food mixer if wished for this recipe or use a balloon whisk) and continue beating while adding the syrup in a very thin stream. Mix the cornstarch with a very little cold water and beat a little of this at a time into the egg and syrup mixture.

Grease the inside of the top of a double boiler with oil (or use a heatproof bowl over a pan of simmering water), pour 2 tbsp more oil into the receptacle used, before adding the egg mixture. Cook over the gently simmering water, stirring continuously with a wooden spoon, until the mixture becomes very thick and creamy. It should not stick to the sides of the pan or to the spoon (or cooking chopsticks if used).

Serve hot or cold in small dishes.

"LONG LIFE" BUNS *

寿桃
shòu táo

For the dough:
See Steamed Buns on p. 14

*1¼ lb marrons glacés (candied sweet
    chestnuts)*
2½ tbsp shortening (optional)
green and red food coloring

Time: 1 hour + time for making the dough

Make the dough and leave to rise.

Chop the marrons glacés very finely and moisten with ½ cup warm water, stirring this in very thoroughly with a wooden spoon, or use a food processor. Melt the shortening (if used) in a saucepan and add the chestnut mixture, stirring and cooking for a short time (omit this stage if you do not choose to use any fat). When the dough has risen, detach one quarter of it and knock down, then knead with a little green food coloring, working this in well with the dough. Knock down and briefly knead the rest of the dough, roll out into a fairly thick sheet, and cut out into 4–4½-in diameter disks; place a little of the chestnut paste in the center of each disk, then enclose with the dough, shaping each one gently into the shape of a peach (take care that the filling remains completely enclosed in the center).

Roll out the green dough and cut into elongated "leaves" pressing with the back of a knife to imprint the design of the leaf ribs on the surface; dust each "peach" lightly on one side with a little red food coloring powder, then place the leaves in position, moistening slightly on the underside to make them stick and pressing gently onto the peach. Place in the steamer (lined with waxed paper) and steam as for Steamed Buns on p. 14.

This dessert is a symbol of long life and is prepared and served as a sign of well-wishing; particularly popular as part of old people's birthday celebrations.

If you prefer not to use commercial food colorings, use spinach juice for the green color, boiled and concentrated red fruit juice for the red, or use liqueurs (green Chartreuse and Maraschino or Alkermes).

ALMOND PUDDING *
杏仁豆腐
xìng rén dòu fǔ

¹/₂ oz agar-agar
2¹/₂ cups cold water
1³/₄ cups milk
1¹/₄ cups sugar
2¹/₂ tsp pure almond extract

Time: 45 minutes + 8 hours soaking time + setting time

Snip the agar-agar strands into 1-in lengths with scissors. Soak in the cold water in a bowl for 8 hours (there is no need to stir) then transfer the agar-agar and water to a saucepan and bring to a boil. Simmer until the agar-agar has completely dissolved. Stir in the heated milk to boiling point, and stir it into the agar-agar together with the sugar. Cook gently for a further 10 minutes. Stir in the almond extract, draw aside from the heat, and pour into one of several shallow (about 1¹/₄ in deep) molds, filling these up to their rims. Agar-agar will set at room temperature; when firm, cut into cubes and serve.

RED SOY PASTE GRAPES
GĀO LÌ *
打泡高力豆沙
dǎ pào gāo lì dòu shā

¹/₄ lb sweet soy paste
2 egg whites
¹/₄ cup all-purpose flour
¹/₄ cup cornstarch or potato flour
1¹/₂ tbsp confectioner's sugar
oil for frying

Time: 40 minutes

Shape the soy paste into little balls about 3/8 in in diameter. Whisk the egg whites stiffly and gradually whisk in the flour and cornstarch or potato flour, adding a little at a time. Dip the soy paste balls in this mixture, coating them thickly; heat plenty of oil in the wok for semi deep-frying or use more oil and cook in the deep-fryer and when very hot but not smoking, add the dipped balls; turn down the heat slightly once they have been added, cook until they start to turn golden yellow, then increase the heat for about 30 seconds; remove the "grapes" with a slotted ladle or spoon, draining well, and place them on a serving dish. Sprinkle with a fine dusting of confectioner's sugar, shaking this over the grapes with a fine mesh sieve.

WONTONS WITH SWEET SOY PASTE FILLING

炸馄饨
zhà hún tún

For the wonton wrappers:
1³/₄ cups all-purpose unbleached flour
1 egg
pinch salt
cold water

(or 1 packet commercially prepared fresh wonton wrappers)

For the filling:
1¹/₂ cups dates
¹/₄ lb shelled walnuts
finely grated peel of ¹/₄ orange
2¹/₂ tbsp fresh orange juice
oil for frying

Time: 1¹/₄ hours + 2 hours resting time for pastry dough (unless wonton wrappers are purchased)

If you make your own wonton skins, prepare the dough at least 2 hours before you intend using it. Sift the flour into a mound on the working surface, make a well in the center, and place the lightly beaten egg, the salt, and a very little water in it. Gradually stir the liquid and incorporate the flour slowly; add a very lit-

tle more cold water if necessary; the dough should be firm, smooth, and easy to handle and knead (if you mix it in a mixing bowl, it should leave the sides of the bowl cleanly). Shape into a ball, cover with a clean cloth, and leave to rest at room temperature for 2 hours. When you need to use the dough, knead it briefly, then roll out with a rolling pin into a very thin sheet; cut out into 12–16 rectangles measuring 2³/₄ × 4 in. If you buy wonton skins, these may be square, but this does not matter.

Chop the dates and walnuts very finely, place in a bowl and mix with the grated orange peel and juice. Use a teaspoon to break off a little of this mixture, shape into little sausages, and place these on the rectangles, leaving a good margin of dough all round, especially at the ends. Wrap the filling in the skins as if they were candies or boiled sweets, with the paper ends twisted round. Deep-fry until crisp and golden. Drain well.

EASTERN CHINA

華東菜

THE SHANGHAI EXPERIENCE AND TRADITIONAL EASTERN CHINESE COOKING

The provinces to the east of central China, Kiangsu, Hanwei and Chekiang, with their coastlines on the Pacific Ocean (better known as the East China Sea) share more or less the same climate and growing conditions. The cuisine of these areas well to the north of the Tropic of Cancer, irrigated by the long Yangtze river (or Yang-Tze Kiang or Changjiang as the Chinese call it) is usually defined as the Shanghai school of cooking and differs so markedly from that of the rest of the eastern region that it merits a section to itself.

The numerous water courses, lakes, rivers, and lagoons not only lead to efficient irrigation but also provide an abundance of delicious freshwater fish and crustaceans, as highly prized as the plentiful saltwater fish and seafood caught along the coastline. Rearing of livestock and poultry provides a reliable supply of many types of meat, especially pork, chicken, and duck (Nanking is famous for its ducks). Mutton is conspicuous by its absence and the southern and southeastern Chinese actually dislike the smell and taste of this meat beloved by the northern Chinese.

This region is by no means unique in China in having such a rich and varied cuisine; Peking, like Shanghai, has also developed excellent cold weather dishes with plenty of pork fat for calories and warming hot stuffed rolls, steamed dumplings, and other foods high in carbohydrates such as noodles. This does not alter the fact that the eastern Chinese school has many dishes which are very much its own, either because the raw materials used are only found in this part of China or because the methods of preparation and presentation are unique to the cooks of the area.

The richness and diversity of Eastern Chinese cooking was not only stimulated by the plentiful supply of excellent raw materials but also has historical causes. The region's love of display, sumptuousness, and decoration is a legacy from the time when Nanking was the imperial capital. This has left its mark in the lavish but refined cooking with its subtle tastes, with sweet flavors frequently introduced into otherwise savory dishes, and with a restrained and discriminating use of

One of the Shanghai opera's traditional characters during one of the many street performances in cities and villages. According to Chinese theatrical convention, white stage make-up signifies treachery.

spices and strong flavors. Comparatively little use is made of garlic: wine, soy sauce, and rice wine vinegar are preferred as flavoring agents. The cooks of this area are renowned for their skill in preparing elaborate, beautifully presented cold dishes.
Perhaps this subtlety and need for great skill in preparation is the cause of Eastern Chinese and Shanghai cooking not being better known outside the region: it tends to be oily, with sweetness introduced in unexpected contexts; many of the methods are time-consuming and some of the most highly prized culinary delicacies call for local foods which are difficult to purchase elsewhere such as Shanghai hairy crabs, which are caught in the inland lakes of this region but nowhere else. Being in short supply, they are greatly sought after; some find their way to

Hong Kong where they fetch staggeringly high prices. Certainly, there is never a surplus to be shipped abroad for gourmets further afield. Certain types of carp and other fish from the Western Lake and the many brooks and streams are also unique to this area. Some products of eastern China are widely known, however, such as Shao Xing rice wine, Chinhua ham, dark vinegar from Chinkiang and many preserved foods such as Ningpo salt-pickled fish; pickled, dried or fermented vegetables and the so-called "hundred-year eggs." Other very famous dishes include crispy fried shrimp; various recipes for eels cooked in oil, and Yang-Chow fried rice with plenty of shrimp, very small pieces of meat, and other additions. Cantonese rice was probably inspired by this recipe and is often confused with it. Then

Hangzhou market. The large placard in the foreground says: "wholesale seafoods." The other signs, with their red ideograms, indicate the product, its price, and its quality: on this particular day dried cuttlefish, shrimp, oysters, dried salt fish, and other delicacies are being sold.

there are "lions' heads" (delicious large meat balls) and fish in sweet-sour sauce. Hung-shao stews made with meat, chicken or fish originated in the East, but this cooking method with its use of dark soy sauce and rice wine has now become part of China's wider, national culinary tradition.
Shanghai is one of the great cities of the world and its growth was fostered by foreign

100

interests; situated at the mouth of the
Huangpu, within sight of the Yangtze delta,
Shanghai was a far smaller, typically Chinese
town up to the end of the nineteenth century.
It has given its name to a school of cooking
but other eastern towns and cities are
renowned for their cuisine, such as Yang-
chow, Nanking and Hang-chou. Shanghai is
famous for its innumerable restaurants and
small eating houses, as well as hundreds of
food stalls selling the original, tasty and
nutritious, version of fast food. The city's
enormous population provides a brisk
demand for all types of Chinese cooking, not
just the native Eastern cuisine. Hong Kong's
culinary tastes have much in common with
those of Shanghai whose specialties are also
much appreciated in Taiwan (Formosa).

An island on Lake Xihu, near Hangzhou with a profusion of lotus leaves.

TURNIP OR WHITE RADISH PASTRIES

萝卜丝饼

luó bo sī bīng

1¼ lb white radish (daikon root)
1 tsp salt
¼ lb Chinese Gold Coin ham, Virginia ham or Westphalian ham
¼ lb pork belly
1½ tbsp chopped scallion
pinch Szechwan pepper
1 tsp sugar
pinch monosodium glutamate (optional)
1¾ cups all-purpose flour
½ cup shortening
1 cup milk
2 tbsp sesame seeds
few sprigs Chinese or ordinary parsley
1½ tbsp oil
1 tbsp dried shrimp (optional)

Time: 1½ hours

Peel and grate the turnips or radish or chop very finely, place in the middle of a clean cloth, gather up the edges, and twist round firmly to squeeze out any moisture. Coarsely chop the ham and pork belly and mix with the radish, scallion, pepper, ½ tsp sugar and the monosodium glutamate (if used). For a more pronounced flavor, stir in 1 tbsp dried shrimp, pre-soaked in warm water for 20–30 minutes (available from most Oriental foodstores and some delicatessens).

Mix 1¼ cups of the flour with the melted (but not hot) shortening or pork fat to make a smooth, firm pastry dough. Mix the remaining flour and sugar with just enough milk to form a fairly firm dough. Roll these two pieces of pastry dough out separately into two sheets of equal size and place the thinner, milk dough sheet neatly on top of the thicker sheet. Roll up like a jelly roll; roll out with the rolling pin into a neat rectangle, and roll up again into the jelly roll shape. Roll out once more into a fairly thin sheet. Use a 4-in diameter cookie cutter to cut out as many disks as possible from this sheet. Spread a small spoonful of the prepared filling in the center of each disk and fold the disks in half, moistening the edges and pressing together firmly to seal securely. Sprinkle with sesame seeds and press a sprig of parsley flat onto the surface of each pastry. Line one or two large cake pans with waxed paper, brush very lightly with oil and arrange them in a single layer, covering each batch with a sheet of waxed paper, the lightly oiled side in contact with the pastries. Bake in a preheated oven at 350°F for 20 minutes.

If preferred, these pastries can be shallow-fried in oil over moderate heat for 15 minutes, turning once during cooking.

RICE PARCELS

端午粽子

duān wǔ zòng zǐ

1¼ lb lean pork
10 oz pork belly
⅓ cup soy sauce
1 tbsp salt
1½ tbsp rice wine
pinch monosodium glutamate (optional)
2½ tsp sugar
5 cups glutinous rice
4 tung ku (dong gu) mushrooms
½ cup dried shrimp
30 dried bamboo leaves
3 tbsp oil

Time: 2¾ hours + soaking and standing time

Chop all the meat very finely and mix with all but 1½ tbsp of the soy sauce, the salt, wine, monosodium glutamate (if used), and half the sugar.

Rinse the rice in a sieve under running cold water; leave to soak for 2 hours in a bowl of cold water. Drain well and mix with the remaining soy sauce and sugar; leave to stand for 1 hour.

Meanwhile, make the following preparations: soak the mushrooms in warm water for 20–30 minutes, cut off the stalks and discard; slice the caps into small pieces. Place the shrimp in a small bowl of hot water and soak for 30 minutes. Drain well. Mix together the meat, mushrooms, and shrimp. Soak the bamboo leaves in hot water for 5 minutes, drain, spread out flat on the working surface, and brush lightly with oil. Place a small quantity of rice in the center of each leaf, cover with a little meat mixture, then top with rice.

Roll up the leaves rather as you would spring rolls but make the bundles short, squat, and securely but not too tightly wrapped as the rice will expand considerably during cooking; fasten with kitchen string. Place in the wok, add sufficient boiling water to cover, and simmer very slowly for 2 hours or longer, until done.

YANGZHOU (CANTONESE) RICE *

扬州炒饭

Yángzhōu chǎo fàn

1⅓ cups long-grain rice
5 dried tung ku (dong gu) mushrooms
2 eggs
oil for frying
⅓ cup peas
½ cup shelled small shrimp
2 scallions
7 oz chicken breasts (optional)
6 tbsp oil
7 oz lean pork
pinch sugar
2½ tbsp soy sauce
1 tbsp sesame seed oil
2½ tsp cornstarch or potato flour
1 egg white
generous pinch freshly ground white pepper
pinch salt
2½ tbsp rice wine
oil for frying

Time: 45 minutes

Boil the rice. Drain off any remaining moisture and leave to cool. Soak the mushrooms in warm water for 20 minutes. Beat the two eggs lightly together, pour into a lightly oiled wok or skillet, and cook as a thin omelet. Leave to cool. Cook the peas until tender in boiling salted water. Drain. Slice the scallions into thin rounds. Cut the meat (and chicken if used) into very small cubes. Drain the mushrooms, cut off their stalks, dice the caps, and mix with the sugar, soy sauce, and sesame seed oil.

Beat the egg white until frothy and stir in the cornstarch. Use half this mixture to mix with the shrimp, drain off excess, and fry them in hot oil in the wok or skillet until golden brown. Remove with a slotted ladle, draining well. Repeat this operation with the other half of the egg white mixture and the chicken cubes (if used). Cut the omelet into small squares.

Heat 6 tbsp oil in the wok and fry the pork cubes over fairly high heat.

Add the mushrooms, scallions, peas and, after a few minutes of stirring and turning, the shrimp, chicken, omelet and, finally, the rice. Stir-fry for a few minutes. Season with the pepper and salt, add the rice wine, and continue stir-frying over high heat until all the wine has evaporated. Serve.

This rice dish originated in Yangchow and although originally belonging to the Shanghai or Eastern Chinese school of cooking, it has become a classic rice dish throughout China. Although internationally known as Cantonese rice, this only refers to the fact that the South Chinese were the ones to make it internationally popular, but they did not create the dish. Cantonese rice often appears as a plainer, side dish, without shrimp or mushrooms.

Dried leaves from bamboo shoots (gán cài sǔn). Sold in bundles or boxes at markets all over China, these have a scent reminiscent of some types of mushroom or fungus and should be soaked for about 30 minutes in warm water to soften and reconstitute them before use in much the same way as dried fungi. They are then cut into small pieces and added to soup or meat dishes; they are particularly good with seafood such as abalone and shark's fin. The bamboo is an invaluable source of food; its cone-shaped shoots peep out round the base of the plant, valued as vegetables in their own right and as an additional ingredient in many dishes. Both shoots and leaves are canned when fresh, besides being packaged in small plastic bags in their dried form, ready trimmed and only needing soaking before use. Some varieties of bamboo contain silicious deposits inside the hollow sections of their woody stems; these are extracted for use as medicines in China and India.

Ancient Chinese books were made of bamboo leaves. The stems are manufactured into chopsticks, utensils, furniture, and even used for construction and building of equipment and materials.

coat lightly all over with the remaining cornstarch. Heat plenty of oil in the wok (or use an electric deep-fryer) and when very hot add the slices to the oil. Fry for about 1 minute or until crisp and golden. Remove, drain well, and sprinkle with the sesame seed oil.

The dish derives its name from the fried disks' resemblance to pagoda bells.

SHANGHAI DUMPLINGS *

小笼包

xiǎo lóng bāo

For the pasta dough:
3¹/₂ cups all-purpose flour
1 cup very hot water
¹/₂ cup cold water

For the filling:
1 cup ground lean pork
¹/₂ cup ground pork belly
2 finely chopped scallions
1 tbsp finely chopped fresh ginger
¹/₂–1 tsp salt
¹/₂–1 tsp sugar
¹/₂–1 tsp monosodium glutamate (optional)
1¹/₂ tbsp soy sauce
1¹/₂ tbsp rice wine
2¹/₂ tbsp sesame seed oil
pinch freshly ground pepper
1¹/₂ tsp cornstarch

Time: 1¹/₂ hours

Put the flour into a very large bowl and stir the hot water into it adding a little at a time while mixing with a fork. Leave to stand for a minute or two, then work in just as much as you need of the cold water to make a firm dough. Knead briefly until smooth and homogeneous. Replace in the bowl, cover with a clean, slightly damp cloth and leave to stand while you prepare the filling.

Mix all the filling ingredients together; if too stiff and heavy, add a very little water.

Roll out the dough into a thin sheet on a lightly floured working surface and cut out into disks approx. 2¹/₂ in in diameter. Place a little heap of filling in the center of each disk and bring the edges up around the filling, gathering them together so that you form a little bag, the filling being enclosed in the "bag" with just a little visible in the neck of the bag. Pinch the neck folds to make the pastry stay in position. Place a pea in the center of the little bag's gathered top, on the visible meat filling, for a touch of color and decoration. Line the steamer with a piece of cheesecloth, place the dumplings in the steamer, leaving a little space between them, cover with a lid and place over boiling water. Steam for 15 minutes.

FRIED BELLS

炸响铃

zhà xiǎng líng

6 dried tofu sheets (bean curd skins)
²/₃ cup very finely chopped pork belly
²/₃ cup very finely chopped pork tenderloin
3 egg whites
¹/₂–1 tsp monosodium glutamate (optional)
2¹/₂ tbsp cornstarch or potato flour
oil for frying
1 tbsp sesame seed oil

Time: 45 minutes + soaking time

Soak the bean curd skins in hot water for 30 minutes until soft and pliable, drain, blot any excess moisture with paper towels, and spread out flat; trim off any hard edges and cut into rectangles measuring 3 × 1¹/₂ in. Alternatively, use very thin, vacuum-packed bean curd skins (sold in Oriental foodstores); these require no pre-soaking. Mix the pork and pork belly with 2 beaten egg whites, the salt, monosodium glutamate (if used), and half the cornstarch.

Place a little of this mixture in a thin line, lengthwise along the middle of each rectangle and roll up to form fat, filled cylinders (do not roll too tightly as the meat mixture swells as it cooks). Cut these stuffed rolls into short lengths just under ¹/₂ in long. Beat the remaining egg white and dip the rolls in this, then

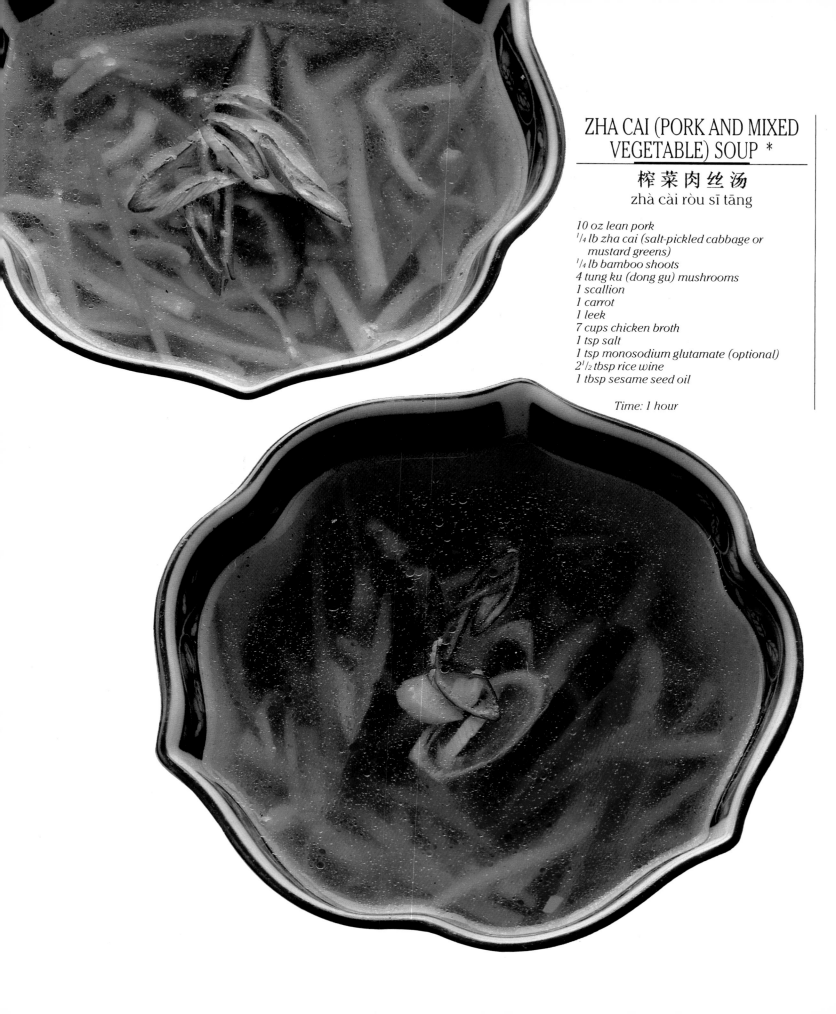

ZHA CAI (PORK AND MIXED VEGETABLE) SOUP *

榨菜肉丝汤

zhà cài ròu sī tāng

10 oz lean pork
1/4 lb zha cai (salt-pickled cabbage or
    mustard greens)
1/4 lb bamboo shoots
4 tung ku (dong gu) mushrooms
1 scallion
1 carrot
1 leek
7 cups chicken broth
1 tsp salt
1 tsp monosodium glutamate (optional)
2 1/2 tbsp rice wine
1 tbsp sesame seed oil

Time: 1 hour

Soak the mushrooms in warm water for 20 minutes, then drain well (do not use the liquid), cut off the stalks, and discard; slice the caps into thin strips.

Meanwhile, shred the pork and vegetables. Bring the chicken broth to a boil in a large pan and add all the vegetables and the other ingredients listed above. Simmer for 25 minutes, removing any scum which rises to the surface.

MEAT BROTH WITH YELLOW SOYBEANS

肉丝黄豆汤
ròu sī huáng dòu tāng

10 oz yellow soybeans
1/4 lb tenderloin of pork
5 oz pork belly (with the skin on)
9 cups chicken broth
1 tbsp soy sauce
1 tsp salt
1/2 tsp monosodium glutamate (optional)
1 tbsp melted pork fat or shortening
1 scallion, finely chopped

Time: 4 hours + soaking time for the beans

Soak the beans in cold water for 3 hours. Drain well. Slice the pork belly (skin and flesh) very thinly or ask your butcher to machine-slice it if you prefer and cut into rectangles 1 1/4 in long and 3/4 in wide. Do likewise with the pork tenderloin.

Pour the broth into a large, deep pan or cooking pot, add the beans, bring to a boil and then simmer slowly for 2 hours. Add the pork belly and continue simmering for a further hour. Skim any scum from the surface; add the pork fillet, soy sauce, salt, monosodium glutamate (if used), and the pork fat. Simmer, uncovered, until the soup reduces and thickens a little. Serve in bowls, sprinkled with the chopped scallion.

CAULIFLOWER SOUP

菜花羹
cài huā gěng

1 cauliflower
7 oz chicken breasts
7 cups chicken broth
2 eggs
1 sprig fresh coriander or parsley
salt

Time: 30 minutes

Wash the cauliflower, trim off the outer leaves, and remove the hard, central stem. Cut the cauliflower into small florets. Cut the chicken into small, thin strips. Pour the broth into a large pan, add the cauliflower and chicken, and bring to a boil; simmer for 15 minutes. Add a little salt halfway through this cooking time. Break the eggs into a bowl and beat lightly with a fork. Snip the coriander or parsley leaves into fairly small pieces, and stir them into the eggs. When the soup has simmered for the required time, draw aside from the heat and beat in the eggs vigorously so that they thicken the soup before they have a chance to set and scramble. Serve at once.

JASMINE FLOWER AND CHICKEN SOUP

茉莉鸡片汤
mò li ji pián tāng

7 oz chicken breasts
1 egg white
1 tbsp cornstarch
pinch salt
24 fresh jasmine flowers
7 cups chicken broth

Time: 30 minutes

Shred the chicken; beat the egg white with the salt and cornstarch and dip the chicken strips in this. Bring the broth to a boil in a large pan, add the chicken, and blanch for 3 minutes; skim off all the scum which rises to the surface. Remove the chicken with a slotted ladle and divide equally between 4 small bowls or soup plates.

Rinse the jasmine flowers briefly under running cold water and place in the bowls. Bring the broth back to a boil, add a little salt if necessary, and pour over the chicken and flowers. Serve at once.

SHARK'S FIN SOUP

鱼翅汤
yú chì tāng

5 oz dried shark's fin
1 chicken breast
3 1/2 cups chicken broth
2 leeks
2 small slices fresh ginger
4 tung ku (dong gu) mushrooms
2 oz boiled (or canned) bamboo shoots
2 1/2 tbsp peanut oil
1 tbsp rice wine
1–1 1/2 tsp wine vinegar
2 1/2 tbsp light soy sauce
pinch sugar
pinch salt
1–1 1/2 tsp cornstarch

Time: 3 hours

Fill two large pans with water (about two thirds full); bring the first pan to a boil. Place the dried shark's fin in it. After about 20 minutes, bring the second pan of water to a boil. Drain all the water from the pan containing the shark's fin and discard; transfer the shark's fin to the second pan. Refill the first pan with cold water. Bring this to a boil after a further 20 minutes and repeat the draining and boiling process, in fresh water, at least 4 times (this preparation stage will take about 2 hours). Bring 1 3/4 cups chicken broth to a boil with the thoroughly cleaned leeks and the peeled ginger slices. Add the drained shark's fin. Simmer for 15 minutes once the broth has returned to a boil, then drain off and discard the broth. Soak the mushrooms in warm water for 30 minutes, drain, remove and discard the stalks, and shred the caps. Shred the chicken breasts, slicing lengthwise along the grain of the meat. Thinly slice the bamboo shoots. Heat the oil in a deep cooking pot or pan, stir-fry the chicken, add the bamboo shoots and the shark's fin and continue stir-frying briefly. Sprinkle with the wine and the vinegar and continue cooking until the wine and vinegar have evaporated. Pour the remaining broth into the pan; add the soy sauce, sugar, mushrooms, and a little salt if needed. Mix the cornstarch with 2 1/2 tbsp cold water and stir into the soup to thicken slightly. Cook, stirring continuously, for a few minutes more. Serve very hot.

SHANGHAI FISH SOUP

特别黄鱼羹

tè bié huáng yú gěng

1 lb white fish (sea fish)
1¹/₂ oz lean pork
1¹/₂ oz chicken breast
¹/₄ cup peeled shrimp
1 dried sea cucumber (optional)
1¹/₂ oz bamboo shoots
2 tung ku (dong gu) mushrooms
¹/₄ cup fresh button mushrooms
3 tbsp fresh or frozen peas
3 tbsp oil
1¹/₂ tsp finely chopped scallion
1 tsp finely chopped or minced fresh ginger
7 cups chicken broth
2¹/₂ tbsp rice wine
1 tbsp salt
pinch monosodium glutamate (optional)
generous pinch freshly ground pepper
3 tbsp shucked clams (fresh or canned)
1 egg
1¹/₂ tbsp oil, melted pork fat or lard
1¹/₂ tbsp melted chicken fat
1¹/₂ tbsp cornstarch or potato flour
1¹/₂ oz Chinese Gold Coin ham, Westphalian ham or Virginia ham

Time: 1 hour + soaking time if sea cucumber is used

Sea cucumbers (little sea creatures which the Chinese consider a delicacy, an opinion which some Westerners do not share) are sold dried and need a thorough rinsing and 3–5 days' soaking in several changes of cold water. Slit the sea cucumber down its smooth section, gut it, and place in a pan of cold water. Bring to a boil and simmer for 2 hours or until very tender and gelatinous. You may well consider it an ingredient which you can omit.

Soak the tung ku mushrooms in warm water for 20–30 minutes, drain off the liquid then cut off their stalks and discard. Wipe and trim the fresh mushrooms.

Dice the fish, meat, and chicken, sea cucumber, bamboo shoots, and both types of mushrooms. Coarsely chop the shrimp. Heat the oil in the wok, fry the scallion and ginger briefly, then add all the other prepared ingredients and the peas.

Stir-fry briefly, then pour in the broth (this should cover the ingredients). Add the wine, salt, monosodium glutamate (if used), and the pepper. Stir well. Bring to a boil, skim off any scum from the surface, reduce the heat, and simmer for 5 minutes.

If using fresh clams, blanch in boiling water 1–2 minutes then drain. Lightly beat the egg and beat it into the soup, increasing the heat. Mix the cornstarch or potato flour with a very little cold water (or with some of the clam juice if canned clams are used) and stir into the soup to thicken slightly. Beat in the oil or melted pork fat and the chicken fat. Add the clams, stir briefly, and serve, sprinkling each serving with finely chopped ham and a little more pepper if desired.

Eastern Chinese cooks use locally caught Yellow Croaker fish for this recipe but any firm, flavorsome white fish will do: sole and flounder are excellent.

VEGETABLE SOUP WITH MEATBALLS *

肉丸子白菜汤

ròu wánzi bái cài tāng

¹/₂ cup finely chopped lean pork
¹/₂ cup finely chopped pork belly
1 tbsp finely chopped fresh ginger
1 tbsp finely chopped scallion
1 tsp salt
¹/₂ tsp monosodium glutamate (optional)
1¹/₂ tbsp rice wine
1 tbsp sesame seed oil
generous pinch freshly ground pepper
2¹/₂ tbsp cornstarch or potato flour
¹/₄ lb Chinese cabbage
4 tung ku (dong gu) mushrooms
1 carrot
2 oz bamboo shoots
2 oz leek
7 cups chicken broth
extra salt, pepper, rice wine, and sesame seed oil to taste

Time: 1 hour 10 minutes

Soak the mushrooms in warm water for 20 minutes. Meanwhile, mix the meat very thoroughly with the ginger, scallion, salt, monosodium glutamate (if used), rice wine, oil, pepper, and cornstarch or potato flour. Shape by hand into firm meatballs a little smaller than ping-pong balls. Cut the stalks off the mushrooms and discard; slice the caps into 2 or 3 pieces; shred the washed and dried cabbage, the peeled carrot, the bamboo shoots, and well-washed leek. Bring the broth to a boil, add the meatballs, and cook for 15 minutes over gentle heat. Remove with a slotted ladle and keep warm. Add the vegetables to the broth and simmer for a further 15 minutes. Return the meatballs to the soup and simmer for a final 15 minutes. Add salt and pepper to taste with a little more rice wine and a little sesame seed oil if wished.

XUE CAI AND CHICKEN SOUP *

雪菜鸡丝汤

xuě cài jī sī tāng

1¹/₄ cups shredded chicken, firmly packed
¹/₄ lb salt-pickled cabbage or mustard greens (Xue cai)
¹/₄ lb bamboo shoots
1 leek
1 scallion
7 cups chicken broth
¹/₂ tsp salt
1 tbsp rice wine
1 tsp monosodium glutamate (optional)
1 tbsp sesame seed oil

Time: 1 hour

Chicken breast or darker, leg and thigh meat can be used for this recipe. Rinse the pickled cabbage under running cold water to eliminate excess salt (it is pickled in brine). Cut the bamboo shoots, leek, and scallion into thin strips. Place all the ingredients in a large pan, bring to a boil, skim off any scum with a slotted ladle or spoon, and reduce the heat to a simmer; cook for 30 minutes. Serve.

Xu cai is called "flower of the snow" because its leaves shoot up through the surface of the last snow in springtime, especially in Chekiang province.

PIGEON'S EGG AND CHÁI BǍ SOUP

柴把鸽蛋汤

chái bǎ gē dàn tāng

2 tung ku (dong gu) mushrooms
¹/₄ lb chicken breast
3 scallions
1 small bunch chives
¹/₂ tsp salt
2¹/₄ cups chicken broth
1 tbsp rice wine
1 tbsp melted pork fat or shortening
12 very fresh pigeons' eggs
2¹/₂ tbsp oil
1 sprig of parsley
2 oz raw, sweet-cure Chinese ham (Jin Jua Huo Tui), Westphalian or Virginia ham

Time: 2 hours

Soak the dried mushrooms in warm water for 20 minutes; cut off the stalks and discard. Poach the chicken breast in water for 10 min-

utes. Cut the ham into strips measuring about 2¼ in × 1¼ in; do likewise, keeping the strips separate, with the chicken, 2 of the scallions, and the mushroom caps (these strips may have to be shorter). Carefully select a few strips from each batch, form into a bundle and tie up securely but not too tightly by winding a chive round each bundle and tying it. (Ciai pa is Chinese for bundle.) Choose a deep heat-proof dish which will fit easily into the steamer with room to spare round the sides, place the bundles in it, sprinkle with the salt, the remaining scallion cut into rings, the broth, wine, and pork fat. Place in the steamer, cover and steam for 1 hour.

If pigeons' eggs are unavailable, use pullets' or bantams' eggs, or triple the number of quails' eggs. Break each raw egg (3 if quails' eggs are used) into a lightly oiled small porcelain bowl or glazed earthenware or pyrex ramekin dish. Arrange a leaf of parsley and a thin strip of ham on each egg yolk, place in the steamer, cover, and cook for 2 minutes. Remove and set aside.

Arrange the vegetable bundles carefully in the center of a serving dish and surround with the eggs. Strain ½ cup of the chicken broth and sprinkle over the eggs and bundles.

FIVE-COLOR SOUP

什锦汤
shí jǐn tāng

4 chicken wings
3 tung ku (dong gu) mushrooms
12 scallops
3 slices cured pork belly about ⅛ in thick
8 quails' eggs
1–1½ tbsp soy sauce
¼ lb boiled fresh or canned bamboo shoots
    (tung shoun)
4 whole leaves Chinese cabbage
½ leek
1½ tbsp oil
1 tbsp rice wine
pinch monosodium glutamate (optional)
salt
pinch freshly ground pepper
oil for frying

Time: 50 minutes

Soak the mushrooms for 20 minutes in warm water. Drain. Cut off the stalks and discard; slice the caps into thin strips. Thaw the scallops if frozen, clean, and prepare. Shred the belly of pork. Place the quails' eggs, which

should be at room temperature, in the steamer, cover, and steam for 5 minutes. Cool under running cold water; peel. Cut off the tips of the chicken wings and discard; blanch the wings in boiling water for 5 minutes; drain and place in a bowl with the quails' eggs, sprinkle with 2 1/2 tsp of soy sauce, stir, and turn. Heat approx. 1/2 cup oil in the wok and fry the chicken wings and quails' eggs over high heat for about 5 minutes. Drain well and set aside. Thinly slice the bamboo shoots and the cabbage. Slice the leek into thin rings.

Heat 1 1/2 tbsp oil in a wide, heavy-bottomed (or nonstick) pan and sauté the leek and belly of pork. Sprinkle with the remaining soy sauce and with the wine, add monosodium glutamate (if used), and pour in 2 1/4 cups boiling water. Add all the other ingredients except for the scallops. Bring back to a boil and simmer for 10 minutes. Add the scallops, simmer for about 4 minutes, season with a little salt and pepper if needed, and serve.

SWEET-SOUR CARP

糖 醋 鲤 鱼
táng cù lǐ jú

1 carp weighing approx. 3 1/4 lb
2 tung ku (dong gu) mushrooms
2 1/2 tbsp red wine vinegar
1/2 carrot
1 small bamboo shoot
1/2 leek
approx. 1 oz fresh ginger
1 clove garlic
1 chili pepper (preferably fresh)
2 1/2 tbsp oil
2 1/2 tbsp cornstarch or potato flour
1 egg white
salt
1 tbsp rice wine
pinch freshly ground black pepper

For the sauce:
5 tbsp oil
5 tbsp sugar
5 tbsp white wine vinegar
2 1/2 tbsp light soy sauce
pinch ground or crumbled chili pepper
5 tbsp water
1 1/2 tbsp cornstarch

Time: 1 hour

If you can buy it, you can use water chestnut powder instead of cornstarch. Descale the carp, trim off the fins, and gut. Rinse the fish thoroughly inside and out under running cold water. Dry with paper towels. Mix the red vinegar with a little cold water and sprinkle all over the ventral cavity. Drain. Place in the refrigerator to chill thoroughly: this will make it easier to cut and prepare later.

Soak the dried mushrooms in warm water for 20 minutes, drain, and gently squeeze out excess moisture; cut off the stalks and slice the caps into thin strips.

Prepare the carrot, bamboo shoot, leek, and ginger, peeling where necessary; cut all these into very thin strips about 3/4–1 1/4 in long. Cut the stalk and hard end off the chili pepper, remove and discard the seeds, and chop the chili finely. Peel and finely chop the garlic.

Stir-fry all these prepared ingredients together with the mushrooms in 3 tbsp oil in the wok or a skillet. When tender but still crisp remove and set aside.

Make deep diagonal cuts about 1 in apart on both sides of the carp with a very sharp knife or cleaver as far as (but not through) the backbone, working from tail to head.

Mix 2 1/2 tbsp cornstarch with the egg white, 1 tsp salt, the wine, black pepper, and 1 1/2 tbsp cold water. Brush the fish all over with this mixture, paying particular attention to the cut surfaces of the deep gashes in the fish's sides. Sprinkle plenty of cornstarch or potato flour onto a large plate and coat the fish completely (gashes included) with this. Shake off excess. Heat plenty of oil in a deep, heavy pan or wok (have the wok on a stand for stability).

When the oil is very hot, grasp the fish very tightly by its tail, using rubber gloves or a dry cloth for a better grip or alternatively thread a strong wood or metal skewer right through the flesh toward the tail end. Carefully hold the fish above the hot oil and use a small ladle to scoop up some oil and pour it into the gashes down the side of the fish. Continue ladling the oil into all these incisions until the cut surfaces are slightly crisped and browned.

Lower the fish carefully into the hot oil and fry until crisp and golden brown on the surface. Remove from the wok or fryer and drain well on paper towels. Keep warm, uncovered, in a fairly deep, oval serving dish.

Make the sauce: heat the oil, sugar, vinegar, soy sauce, pepper, and water together quickly in a small saucepan. Add the reserved vegetables and heat through, stirring continuously. Thicken a little by stirring in the cornstarch mixed with a little cold water and cook for a few minutes more. Pour the sauce all over the fish.

CARP SHANGHAI STYLE

鲤 鱼 划 水

lǐ yú huá shuǐ

1 carp weighing approx. 1 lb
1/4 cup pork fat, shortening or lard
1 tbsp finely chopped scallion
1 tsp finely chopped fresh ginger
1/4 cup rice wine
1 tbsp soy sauce
red food coloring
pinch monosodium glutamate (optional)

1 1/2 tbsp cornstarch or potato flour
1 tbsp sesame seed oil
1 leek

Time: 1 hour

Wash, trim, and descale the fish. Cut off the head just behind the gills with a very sharp knife. Split the underside of the head just enough to flatten slightly by pressing down between the eyes against the chopping board.

Slit the fish body right down its belly, leaving the very end of the body and tail uncut and the neatly trimmed fins in place. Starting at the "head" end, cut about 1/2 in deep along the backbone, i.e. right down to the backbone, again stopping short of the tail. Return to the wider, head end and gradually lift the fillet from the backbone and from the bones which are attached to it, carefully freeing it with a sharp, narrow cleaver or knife. Do likewise with the other side. Now you have the backbone and bones on either side only attached by the backbone to the tail. Snip across the backbone and discard the bones (or reserve to use for broth). The tail is still attached to the filleted body. Open the fish out flat, skin side downward. Press the fish fillets gently to flatten. Melt the pork fat or shortening in the wok, stir-fry the scallion and ginger very briefly, add the filleted fish and the head and fry for 30 seconds, then turn carefully and fry for a further 30 seconds. Add the wine, 2 1/4 cups water, the soy sauce, coloring, sugar, monosodium glutamate (if used) and allow to return to boiling point. Simmer gently, uncovered, for 5–6 minutes. Turn the fish fillets carefully and shake the wok gently as they cook to make sure they do not stick. Remove the fish and set aside. Reduce the liquid to just over half its original volume by boiling, uncovered, over high heat. Mix the cornstarch or potato flour with a little cold water and stir into the liquid to thicken. Return the fish to this sauce, simmer for 1–2 minutes, turn, and sprinkle with the sesame seed oil.

Shred the well-washed leek. Place the head of the fish at one end of an oval serving dish, place the filleted fish behind it to "reassemble" the fish in a flattened form. Scatter the leek over the fish and sprinkle with the sauce.

CARP WITH CLAM BROTH

蛤 蜊 鱼 汤

há lí yútāng

1 cup very small clams in the shell or 1/2 cup shucked clams
1 carp or any firm-textured white fish weighing approx. 1 1/4 lb
2 1/2 tbsp rice wine

1 tbsp salt
6 thin slices fresh ginger
2 scallions
pinch freshly ground pepper

Time: 30 minutes + 2 hours soaking time if fresh clams are used

Leave the clams in a bowl of cold water with cold water trickling into it for 2 hours to eliminate any sand. Canned clams can be substituted, shucked or unshucked. Descale, trim, gut, and wash the carp. Place it in a fish kettle or large pan with the clams (if fresh unshucked clams are used). Add enough water to cover. Add all the other ingredients and bring to boiling point, reduce the heat, and simmer very gently for 10 minutes. If canned clams are used, drain off their juice and add it to the poaching liquid; add the clams themselves for the last 5 minutes' poaching. Transfer the whole carp carefully to a serving platter, surround with the clams, and sprinkle with a little of the cooking liquid.

LAKE SHIU FISH WITH RICE WINE VINEGAR

西 湖 醋 鱼

xī hú cù yú

1 carp weighing approx. 1 1/4 lb
2 1/2 tbsp oil or shortening
1 scallion, cut lengthwise into thin strips
1 tbsp very finely chopped fresh ginger
1 1/2 tbsp rice wine
1 1/2 tbsp soy sauce
2 1/4 cups chicken broth
1/2–1 tbsp sugar
1 1/2 tbsp wine vinegar
1 1/2 tbsp cornstarch, water chestnut powder or potato flour
1 tbsp sesame seed oil

Time: 30 minutes

Fishing at Wuxi. Freshwater fish and crustaceans are an important natural resource of this area and one of its main money earners. They are not only superlative (among the best in the world) but there is a tremendous choice of species and varieties. The crabs are the star attraction, but the shrimp, salmon trout, and shad (similar to herring but larger and more rounded) are also outstanding.

There are more than 2,000 lakes in China; Wuxi is on the north shore of Lake Taihu which covers an area of 865 square miles, one of the country's five largest lakes with more than 90 islands. Wuxi is justly famed as "the city of fish and rice" and is renowned throughout China for its specialties. Among the greatest delicacies are local roast eels and Taihu crabs.

The local fish is usually eaten fresh; salted or brine-pickled fish is much more expensive and reserved for special occasions.

Fish are farmed in lagoons constructed round the edges of the lakes by the local peasants; it is a seasonal industry. When the time comes to "harvest" the fish, large-gauge nets are used so that the small, immature fish are not destroyed. The Chinese take care to cook their fish lightly to preserve its flavor (it is usually killed just before cooking), most often steamed with scallion and fresh ginger and served with the head and tail left on, so that the guests can see how fresh it is.

Apart from its gastronomic attractions, Wuxi is a spa, with hot springs, and has a very pleasant climate.

Clean and prepare the fish; fillet it, cutting the fillets into small pieces approx. 1¼ in × ½ in. Heat the oil or shortening in the wok and stir-fry the onion and ginger very briefly. Add the fish, stir-fry briefly, then add the wine, soy sauce, and broth.

Simmer for 5 minutes. Increase the heat, add the sugar and vinegar, and stir in the cornstarch or chosen thickening agent mixed with a little cold water. Stir in the sesame seed oil.

Lake Shiu is considered the most beautiful lake in China and this dish is inspired by an eleventh-century legend. At that time China was ruled by the Song dynasty from their capital in this Eastern region. The Song emperor of the day was attacked and killed while he was fishing at one of the many lakes or lagoons in the area with his wife and his favorite brother. His terrified widow, fearing lest her brother-in-law be assassinated in his turn, persuaded him to flee but first she cooked him a fish fresh from the lake, with a vinegar and sugar sauce, signifying her attempt to sweeten the bitter sorrow of parting. The dish is also called "su sao yi" (brother-in-law's fish).

"BUNCH OF GRAPES" FISH

葡萄鱼
pú táo yú

1 carp weighing approx. 2¼ lb
1 tbsp finely chopped fresh ginger
1 finely chopped scallion
1 tsp salt
generous pinch freshly ground black pepper
oil for frying

For the sauce:
1 cup fresh grape juice (preferably from black grapes)
1 tbsp red wine vinegar
2½ tbsp light soy sauce
½ tsp salt
1 tsp sugar
2½ tbsp cornstarch, water chestnut powder or potato flour
1 tbsp sesame seed oil

Time: 1 hour

Descale and trim the carp; cut off its head and the tail end. Cut the fish open right along its belly, open out, and carefully remove the backbone and all the attached bones. Rinse, dry and, with the opened fish skin side down, make deep diagonal incisions in the exposed flesh just over 1 in apart; repeat this scoring (take care not to puncture the skin on the underside) in the opposite direction to achieve a lattice effect.

Mix together the ginger, scallion, salt, and pepper and sprinkle them over the lattice side of the carp. Leave to stand for 30 minutes. Heat enough oil to cover the fish in a pan wide enough to take it still opened out flat. When very hot (315–320°F), place the fish in the pan, scored side uppermost, and fry until done without turning. As the fish cooks, the skin on the underside will contract and the lattice will expand and curl to look like a bunch of grapes. Transfer the fish carefully to a serving dish. Heat the grape juice in the wok with the vinegar, soy sauce, salt, and sugar until the sugar has dissolved; mix the thickening agent (either cornstarch, water chestnut powder or potato flour) with a little cold water and stir into the liquid to thicken a little. Stir in the sesame seed oil, pour over the fish, and serve at once.

STIR-FRIED EEL

清炒鳝糊
qīng chǎo shàn hú

1¾ lb eel
6 tbsp oil
1 tbsp finely chopped scallion

1 tbsp finely chopped fresh ginger
2¹/₂ tbsp rice wine
¹/₂ tsp monosodium glutamate (optional)
1 tbsp sugar
¹/₂ tsp salt
1¹/₂ tbsp light soy sauce
¹/₄ cup dark soy sauce
1 tbsp sesame seed oil
pinch freshly ground pepper
1 tbsp cornstarch, water chestnut powder or
    potato flour
1 small bunch Chinese parsley, coriander or
    chervil
1¹/₂ tbsp finely chopped York ham

Time: 35 minutes

Have your fishmonger skin and gut the eel for
you. Use without delay. Blanch for 1 minute in
fast boiling water. Cut into 1-in sections and
take the flesh off the bones.

Heat the oil in the wok, stir-fry the scallion
and ginger briefly, add the eel, the wine,
monosodium glutamate (if used), sugar, salt,
light and dark soy sauces, sesame oil, and
pepper. Stir and turn. Add ¹/₂ cup water, return
to a boil, and simmer for 3–4 minutes. Mix the
thickening agent (cornstarch or chosen
alternative) with a little cold water and stir into
the wok.

Transfer to a serving dish, sprinkle with the
Chinese parsley (or substitute) and the ham
and serve.

CRISPY FRIED EEL *

炸 鳝
zhà shàn

1³/₄ lb eel
oil for frying

For the sauce:
3 tbsp oil
8 wafer-thin slices fresh ginger
1 scallion
1 tsp sugar
3 tbsp soy sauce
3 tbsp rice wine

generous pinch freshly ground pepper
¹/₂ tsp salt
1¹/₂ tbsp cornstarch, water chestnut powder or
  potato flour

114

Time: 45 minutes

Skin and gut the eel (see previous recipe). Blanch for 1 minute in fast boiling water. Cut into 1-in sections; take the flesh off the bone. Finely shred the ginger and scallion.

Heat plenty of oil in the wok or deep-fryer until very hot. Lower the eel pieces into the oil and fry until crisp on the outside and golden brown. Remove with a slotted spoon and drain on paper towels. Transfer to a serving plate.

Make the sauce: heat the oil in another saucepan or wok and fry half the scallion and half the ginger; add the sugar, soy sauce, wine, pepper, salt, and 6 tbsp water. Boil gently to reduce a little, then stir in the thickening agent mixed with a little cold water. Draw aside from the heat, pour over the eel and decorate with the remaining shredded ginger and scallion.

TIGER TAIL EEL

炝 虎 鱼
qiàng hǔ wěi

Approx. 3¹/₄ lb small, live or freshly killed
  young freshwater eels
scant ¹/₂ cup wine vinegar
4 thin slices fresh ginger
2 scallions

For the sauce:
1 tbsp finely chopped garlic
5 tbsp sesame seed oil
3 tbsp soy sauce
1 tsp salt
1 tsp sugar
generous pinch freshly ground pepper
1 cup chicken broth
1¹/₂ tsp cornstarch

Time: 1 hour

Bring 4¹/₂ quarts water to a boil in a very large pan with the salt, vinegar, ginger, and trimmed, sliced scallions to make a *court bouillon*. Kill the eels yourself by chopping their heads off just below the gills with a swift blow of the heavy cleaver (or ask your fishmonger to kill them for you; be sure to cook them soon afterward). Add the eels to the boiling *court bouillon*, cover, and cook for 3 minutes. Stir, add 1 quart cold water, bring back to a boil, reduce the heat and simmer for a further 8 minutes. Take the eels out of the cooking liquid (reserve this) and immediately plunge them in a large bowl of cold water. Cut into 1¹/₂-in sections.

Take the flesh off the bones (you can work it away from the bones in fairly neat sections). Cut into strips just under ¹/₂ in wide. Heat these strips in the simmering *court bouillon*, remove with a slotted ladle, and arrange side by side, curving diagonally across a serving platter.

Heat all the sauce ingredients in the wok or small saucepan; boil until slightly reduced, then stir in the cornstarch mixed with a little cold water. Cook for a minute or two and pour over the eel. Sprinkle with pepper.

LOBSTER SALAD *

沙 拉 龙 虾
shā lā lóng xiā

1 cooked lobster weighing 2 lb
1 medium-sized waxy potato
2 small young carrots
1 crisp dessert apple
2 slices fresh pineapple

1 cucumber
2¹/₂ tbsp chopped (not ground) fresh peanuts
1 cup homemade mayonnaise
1¹/₂ tbsp fresh lemon juice

Time: 1¹/₂ hours

Split the lobster lengthwise in half and take out all the flesh, reserving the shell halves. Cut the flesh into small pieces. Boil the prepared potatoes and carrots. Dice the vegetables and fruit and mix with the chopped peanuts.

Beat the lemon juice into the mayonnaise and mix one third of it with the lobster pieces, and one third with the diced mixture. Spoon the vegetable and mayonnaise mixture in a fairly long shape on the serving plate and cover with the lobster and mayonnaise. Place the lobster head at one end, the tail at the other. Pipe the remaining mayonnaise decoratively over the salad.

The illustration shows a dramatic, Chinese-style presentation of the dish.

SHRIMP WITH SEAWEED

苔条拖虾仁
tái tiáo tuō xiā rén

2 cups peeled shrimp
1 tsp salt
1¹/₂ tbsp rice wine
1 tsp finely chopped scallion
1 tsp finely chopped fresh ginger
pinch monosodium glutamate (optional)

generous pinch sugar
5 egg whites
1 cup glutinous rice flour powder
$^{1}/_{2}$ oz dried tai ciao seaweed
oil for frying

For the garnish:
2 tbsp salt
1 tsp ground Szechwan pepper
$^{1}/_{2}$ tsp monosodium glutamate (optional)

Time: 30 minutes

Mix the salt, wine, scallion, ginger, monosodium glutamate (if used), and sugar; mix the shrimp with this mixture and leave to stand. Stiffly beat the egg whites; fold in the rice flour and the finely chopped seaweed.

Heat plenty of oil in the wok (on its stand) or in a deep-fryer (to about 300°F or a little hotter). Dip the shrimp in the fluffy seaweed and rice flour mixture to coat completely and lower into the hot oil to fry for 3 minutes, then increase the heat to make them crisp and crunchy on the outside. Fry in several batches. Drain each batch well on paper towels.

The season for gathering tai ciao seaweed lasts from late winter to early spring: when dried it turns dark green and has a very distinctive, pungent scent.

FRIED SHRIMP WITH PEAS

青豆虾仁

qīng dòu xiā rén

14 oz small shrimp
1$^{3}/_{4}$ cups fresh or frozen small peas
1 egg white
2$^{1}/_{2}$ tbsp cornstarch
6 tbsp oil
1 small slice fresh ginger, approx. $^{1}/_{2}$ in thick
1 tsp salt
1 tsp sugar
2 tbsp rice wine
freshly ground pepper

Time: 20 minutes + 20 minutes marinating
time

Peel the shrimp, place in a bowl; mix with the egg white and cornstarch and place in the refrigerator for 20 minutes. Heat the oil in a wok or skillet, add the shrimp, and stir-fry for a few minutes over gentle heat. Remove with a slotted ladle and set aside. Turn up the heat and fry the finely chopped, peeled ginger; as soon as this gives off a good strong aroma, add the peas, salt, and sugar and stir-fry for 2 minutes. Add the shrimp, the wine, and a generous pinch of pepper and cook for 1–2 minutes more. Serve very hot.

CRABS WITH SOY SAUCE *

油酱螃蟹

yóu jiàng páng xiè

2 crabs weighing 1$^{3}/_{4}$ lb each or approx. 2$^{1}/_{4}$ lb
crab claws
cornstarch, water chestnut powder or potato
flour
oil for frying

For the sauce:
$^{1}/_{4}$ cup oil
3 tbsp finely chopped scallion
1 tbsp finely chopped fresh ginger
3 tbsp rice wine
$^{1}/_{4}$ cup dark soy sauce
1 tsp salt
1 tsp sugar
$^{1}/_{2}$ cup water

Time: 1 hour

If you have bought live crabs, kill them by pushing a skewer right into each crab, underneath the eyes and just above the mouth. For both raw and pre-cooked crab, break off the large claws, place them between several sheets of newspaper, and crack them open with a hammer. Do not hit them too hard, the object is to remove all the hard outer shell and leave the flesh still in position on the cartilage (thin, semitransparent framework in the center of the claw). Break open the body (it should come apart easily if you grasp the hard, top part of the shell in your left hand, with the crab's eyes downward, and push the crab's underside along the suture at the back, downward and away from the top with the fleshy heel of your thumb) then insert your thumb and push apart (the legs will come away attached to the underside). Remove and discard the grayish feathery gills (the so-called "dead men's fingers"), the stomach sac, and intestine. Use a cleaver to chop each crab body (top and bottom, shell and all) into 4 pieces.

If only claws are used, prepare as described above. Coat lightly with cornstarch (or alternative), shaking off excess. Heat plenty of oil in the wok on its stand or in a deep-fryer (to approx. 340°F) and fry the crab in 2 or 3 batches for 2 minutes or until crisp and pale golden brown on the outside. Remove with a slotted ladle, draining well, and keep warm on paper towels.

Heat $^{1}/_{4}$ cup oil in the wok or a saucepan; sauté half the scallion and all the ginger briefly, then add the crab pieces. Pour in the rice wine and soy sauce then add the sugar and water. Stir, then leave to simmer over low heat for 10 minutes. Mix the thickening agent with a very little cold water and stir into the crab mixture to thicken slightly. Serve, sprinkled with the remaining chopped scallion.

This is an excellent recipe for almost any type of crustacean: freshwater scampi or crayfish, lobster and, perhaps best of all, softshell crabs when they are in season.

SWEET-SOUR SHRIMP

糖醋虾

táng cù xiā

1$^{1}/_{4}$ lb peeled shrimp (raw or cooked)
$^{1}/_{4}$ cup oil
1 tsp cayenne pepper

For the sauce:
1 large, hot green chili pepper
$^{1}/_{2}$ cup water
3 tbsp cornstarch
2$^{1}/_{2}$ tsp soy sauce
3 tbsp oil
3 tbsp sugar
3 tbsp wine vinegar
1 tsp minced or grated fresh ginger
$^{1}/_{2}$ cup grapefruit juice

Time: 20 minutes

Heat the oil in the wok and stir-fry the shrimp with the cayenne pepper for 5 minutes (3 minutes if pre-cooked).

For the sauce: have the chili pepper ready shredded into very thin strips $^{1}/_{2}$ in long (seeds, stalk and inner pith should be discarded). Use only half the chili if you do not like your food too fiery. Mix the cornstarch and water. Place all the other sauce ingredients in a small saucepan and bring to a boil while stirring; add the chili pepper, reduce the heat, cover, and simmer for 3 minutes. Stir in the cornstarch and water and continue stirring over moderate heat until the sauce has thickened and the cornstarch has lost its starchy taste and texture when tasted. Transfer the shrimp to a serving plate, pour the sauce over them, and serve with fried or boiled rice.

SHRIMP IN GREEN TEA *

龙井虾仁
Lóng jǐng xiā rén

1 lb peeled shrimp (raw or cooked)
1/4 cup oil
1 tbsp Longjing tea leaves
1 cup freshly boiling water

For the marinade:
1 egg white
3 tbsp rice wine
1 1/2 tbsp cornstarch or alternative
1 tsp salt

Time: 40 minutes

Place the tea leaves in a cup or small heat-proof bowl and pour 1 cup freshly boiling water from the kettle over them. Leave to stand to allow the green, lanceolate leaves to reconstitute.

Rinse the shrimp if wished and pat dry with kitchen towels; beat the egg white and mix it with the marinade ingredients. Add the shrimp, stirring and turning to coat evenly. Leave to stand for 15 minutes.

Heat the oil in the wok and if raw shrimp are used stir-fry them briefly, then remove with a slotted ladle, and set aside. Discard the oil. Pour the tea (including the leaves) into the wok, add the shrimp, cook briefly, uncovered, to reduce the liquid somewhat, then serve.

Longjing tea is a sought-after product of Eastern China: it has a very light, subtle taste and is delicately scented.

SHRIMP WITH APPLES

苹果虾
píng guǒ xiā

1 cup peeled and finely chopped large
    shrimp (raw or cooked)
1/2 cup finely chopped pork belly
7 oz chicken breasts, skinned and finely
    chopped
1 tsp salt
pinch monosodium glutamate (optional)
2 egg whites
3 tbsp milk
1/4 cup cornstarch or potato flour
3 tung ku (dong gu) mushrooms
2 crisp apples
2 tbsp peas (fresh or frozen)
12 jumbo shrimp or saltwater crayfish
    (scampi)
12 coriander leaves
1/4 cup finely chopped Chinese Gold Coin
    ham, Virginia ham or Westphalian ham
oil for frying

Time: 1¹/₂ hours

Soak the dried mushrooms in warm water for 20 minutes. Mix the chopped meats and shrimp with the salt, monosodium glutamate (if used), and beaten egg whites and fold in the mixed milk and cornstarch thoroughly.

Drain the mushrooms, slice off their stalks, and discard; cut the caps into very small pieces. Peel the apples and cut into small dice. Mix the mushrooms, apples, and peas. Peel the jumbo shrimp except for the last section of tail and tail flippers; slit carefully down their backs just deep enough to extract the black alimentary tract. If raw, blanch in boiling water for 30 seconds and drain well.

Lightly oil the inside of 12 muffin pans or cylindrical molds (the shape is relatively unimportant but they must be deep and approx. ¹/₂–³/₄ cup in capacity; place a coriander leaf flat against the bottom of each, sprinkle a very little chopped ham around the leaf. Fill one third full with the meat and egg white mixture. Cover with a layer of the apple and vegetable mixture. Fill to the rim with more of the meat and egg batter.

Place the molds in the steamer, cover, and steam for 15 minutes. Turn each mold out and, when it is no longer too hot to handle, shape into a ball. Push a jumbo shrimp into each ball just beside the coriander leaf, leaving the end of the tail and flippers showing.

Heat plenty of oil until very hot in the wok or deep-fryer and fry the balls briefly, 2–3 at a time until golden brown.

SHANGHAI SHRIMP *

蟠珍虾
pán zhěn xiā

12 jumbo shrimp or saltwater crayfish
(scampi)
1 tbsp finely chopped scallion
1 tbsp finely chopped fresh ginger
1 tbsp sugar
6 tbsp tomato ketchup
1 tbsp chili oil
3 tbsp rice wine
1 tsp salt
¹/₂ tsp monosodium glutamate (optional)
1¹/₂ tsp soy sauce
¹/₂ cup fish stock or chicken broth
1¹/₂ tsp cornstarch, water chestnut powder or
*   potato flour*
oil for frying

Time: 30 minutes

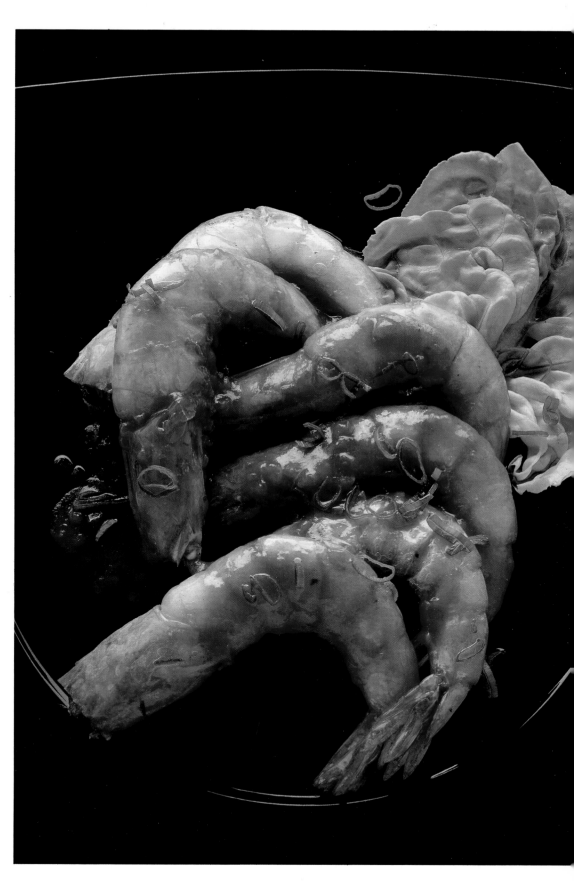

Snip off the feelers and legs from the shrimp; heat plenty of oil until very hot and fry the shrimp for 30 seconds. Remove with a slotted spoon and set aside. Heat 3 tbsp oil in the wok and sauté the scallion and ginger briefly. Add all the other ingredients, stirring well, add the shrimp, stir, and then simmer for 10 minutes. Mix the cornstarch with a very little water and stir into the wok to thicken the sauce a little.

FRIED SHRIMP

油爆虾
yóu bào xiā

2¼ lb fairly large shrimp
oil for frying
1 tbsp finely chopped scallion
1 tsp finely chopped fresh ginger
1½ tbsp light soy sauce
3 tbsp rice wine
1 tbsp sugar
1 tsp salt

Time: 30 minutes

The shrimp may be left unpeeled for this recipe. Trim off the feelers and legs from the shrimp (use scissors) and remove the black "vein" or alimentary tract which runs down their backs. Rinse, if wished, and dry in paper towels. Heat plenty of oil to 340°F for deep-frying, either in the wok using the special stand for stability or, preferably, in a deep-fryer. Cook in batches, frying for 1½ minutes. Alternatively, shallow-fry for 1 minute on each side. Remove, draining well, and set aside. Heat 3 tbsp fresh oil in the wok, sauté the scallion and ginger briefly, add the soy sauce, wine, sugar, and salt, then add the fried shrimp and stir-fry over the usual high heat for 30 seconds. Serve immediately.

SHRIMP PARCELS *

纸包明虾
zhǐ bāo míng xiā

12 jumbo shrimp
6 candied or glacé cherries
2 egg whites
½ cup fresh or frozen peas
3 tung ku (dong gu) mushrooms
oil for frying

Coating for the jumbo shrimp:
1 egg white
pinch salt
1½ tbsp cornstarch

Time: 1 hour

Soak the dried mushrooms in warm water for 20 minutes. Peel the shrimp, carefully make a shallow slit down their backs and remove the black intestinal tract. Beat the egg whites stiffly with the salt then beat in the cornstarch. Dip the shrimp in this mix. Deep-fry until pale golden brown, then lay 3 shrimp flat on their sides, close together, on each piece of paper.

Cut the stalks off the softened and drained mushrooms and discard; chop the caps coarsely. Cook the peas until just tender in boiling lightly salted water. Sprinkle the peas and mushrooms over the shrimp and top with the halved cherries. Fold up the paper as if making envelopes, folding the point facing you over the shrimp first of all, then fold over the sides, roll the entire filled part of the packet away from you; this should leave a pointed triangle of paper furthest away from you. Tuck this flap securely into the "space" or slot below the bulging, filled main part of the envelope. Deep-fry in boiling hot oil for 2–3 minutes.

SCALLOPS WITH ASPARAGUS *

干贝芦笋
gàn bèi lú sǔn

12 scallops
½ lb fresh or frozen asparagus tips
4 tung ku (dong gu) mushrooms
2 oz bamboo shoots
1 carrot

4 thin slices fresh ginger
1 cup oil
½–1 tsp salt
½–1 tsp monosodium glutamate (optional)
generous pinch freshly ground pepper
3 tbsp rice wine
1½ tbsp sesame seed oil
3 tbsp fish stock or chicken broth

Time: 1 hour

Soak the dried mushrooms in warm water for 20 minutes to soften. If using fresh, unshucked scallops, open the shells, take the scallops off the shell, trim off and discard all but the white muscle (the round "cushion" of flesh) and the orange roe, and rinse thoroughly under running cold water. If using frozen scallops, only the white meat is present: thaw completely. Sprinkle the scallops with a pinch each of salt and monosodium glutamate (if used) and leave to stand for 15 minutes. Trim the asparagus, leaving only the tender tips about 1½–2 in long (do not use canned asparagus). Drain the mushrooms, cut off their stalks, and discard; cut each cap in half. Cut the asparagus, bamboo shoots, and peeled carrot into very thin slices. Heat a little oil in the wok, just enough to stir-fry the scallops for 30 seconds on each side over moderate heat; set them aside, draining well. Pour a little fresh oil into the wok and stir-fry the mushrooms and thinly sliced vegetables for 1 minute. Remove and

121

Straw mushrooms are very widely used; they are egg-shaped, have a slightly slippery, viscous texture, a very delicate flavor and can be used whole or sliced. Wood ear fungus (also called tree ear, cloud ears or black fungus) is also very popular; as its names would suggest, it grows on tree trunks and has a bland flavor with a slightly musky aroma. These have to be soaked in hot water for about 20 minutes and they double in volume when reconstituted. Trim off any tough, pithy parts and rinse well to eliminate any grit or sand. These decorative, nutritious, and inexpensive fungi are added to all sorts of dishes, especially casseroles and other slow-cooked recipes. This fungus also grows outside China, in woods throughout

Europe, as far south as the Mediterranean.
Tung ku (dong gu) or "winter mushrooms" are highly prized and quite expensive. The best come from south China; they are gathered during the winter months and dried in the sun, in the open air. They are never eaten fresh or canned, always dried, and sold in small packets. Soak the mushrooms in hot water for at least 20–30 minutes with their stems on to give a stronger flavor, but trim these stems off and discard when you drain the mushrooms as they are tough. The water is used by some cooks to flavor sauces and soups. The mushroom caps can be fairly pale with little irregular bumps, or darker and wrinkled.

ger would toughen them). Drain the clams and transfer to a serving dish or individual bowls. Mix all the sauce ingredients and divide between tiny bowls, for each person to dip the clams. If canned or frozen, cooked clams are used (thaw the latter first), blanch for 30 seconds in the *court bouillon*, then prepare as for fresh clams.

SEA CUCUMBERS WITH MUSHROOMS AND SPINACH*
冬菇扒海参
dōng gū pá hǎi shēn

12 sea cucumbers
12 tung ku (dong gu) mushrooms
¹/₄ lb spinach or Swiss chard leaves
3 tbsp oil
¹/₃ cup dark soy sauce
¹/₂–1 tsp monosodium glutamate (optional)
¹/₂–1 tsp sugar
¹/₂–1 tsp salt
3 tbsp light soy sauce
7 cups broth
4 thin slivers fresh ginger
2 scallions, sliced into short lengths
¹/₃ cup rice wine
1 tbsp cornstarch
water chestnut powder or potato flour

Time: 1 hour + 3–5 days soaking time for the sea cucumbers

Scrub the dried sea cucumbers under running cold water, then soak for a minimum of 3 days, preferably 5, to soften and reconstitute them, changing the water frequently. Slit vertically down the smooth section, gut them, and rinse thoroughly. Cut each one in half, place them in a pan of cold water, and bring to a boil. Boil over moderate heat for 2 hours.
Heat 3 tbsp oil in the wok, stir-fry the sea cucumbers for 1 minute, then add the soy sauce, monosodium glutamate (if used), sugar, salt, broth, ginger, scallions, and wine. Simmer gently for 30 minutes. Soak the dried mushrooms in warm water for 20 minutes, cut off the stalks and discard. Blanch the caps in boiling water for a few minutes together with the well-washed spinach. Drain very thoroughly and place on a serving platter. Place the sea cucumbers on top. Pour ³/₄ cup of the liquid in the wok into a small pan, stir in the thickening agent (mixed with a very little cold water) and cook until slightly reduced and thickened. Pour over the sea cucumbers and vegetables.
If preferred, preserve the flavor of the mushrooms by stir-frying them briefly with the sea cucumbers and removing them before adding the cooking liquid and simmering the sea cucumbers.

set aside. Heat 3 tbsp fresh oil and sauté the ginger briefly. Return the scallops and vegetables to the wok, sprinkle with the remaining salt (and monosodium glutamate, if used), the pepper, wine, sesame seed oil, and broth. Cook for a few minutes and serve.

STIR-FRIED CLAMS
炒蚝
chǎo háo

1¹/₄ lb razor shell clams or any other small fresh clams in the shell
1 scallion
1 sprig parsley
2 thin slices fresh ginger
2¹/₂ tbsp rice wine

1 tsp salt
pinch freshly ground ginger

For the sauce:
3 tbsp wine vinegar
1¹/₂ tsp very finely chopped scallion
1 tsp finely chopped fresh ginger
1 tsp finely chopped parsley
1¹/₂ tbsp sesame seed oil

Time: 15 minutes + time to prepare clams if fresh

Wash the fresh (raw) clams well, place in a large bowl of cold, salted water for 2 hours to eliminate any sand inside the shells.
Bring 1 quart water to a boil with the scallion, parsley, ginger, rice wine, salt, and pepper. Add the clams and cook for only 1 minute after the water has returned to a boil (any lon-

124

HAKE WITH GINGER AND SCALLIONS *

葱姜海鳗
cōng jiāng hǎi mán

1 thick steak or middle cut piece of hake (or cod) weighing 1¹/₄ lb
4 thin slices fresh ginger
1 scallion
3 tbsp rice wine
1¹/₂ tbsp sugar

For the sauce:
¹/₄ cup dark Chinkiang vinegar
3 tbsp white wine vinegar
2 thin slices fresh ginger, shredded

Time: 30 minutes

Mix the ginger, scallion, wine, and sugar and place in a glazed earthenware or Pyrex dish that will fit in the steamer leaving a little space all round it. Lay the fish on top and turn to coat all over with the mixture. Place the dish in the steamer, cover, and place over boiling water. Steam for 15 minutes.

Take up the fish, remove the skin, and take the flesh off the bones. Cut into fairly thin pieces measuring about 1¹/₂ × ³/₄ in; transfer these pieces to a serving plate.

Mix the vinegars and ginger and serve in tiny bowls, for each person to dip pieces of fish.

SQUIRREL FISH

松鼠鱼
sōng shǔ yú

1 very fresh whole fish (e.g. porgy, sea bass, trout, or salmon trout) weighing approx. 2¹/₄ lb
1 cup all-purpose flour
oil for frying
1 tbsp fresh or frozen peas
1¹/₂ tbsp pine nuts

For the marinade:
1 tbsp salt
generous pinch freshly ground pepper
3 tbsp rice wine
1 tbsp cornstarch

For the sauce:
1¹/₂ tbsp oil
1 cup chicken broth
¹/₂–1 tsp salt
1 tbsp sugar
2¹/₂ tbsp tomato ketchup
1¹/₂ tbsp red wine vinegar
pinch freshly ground pepper

*1¹/₂ tbsp cornstarch, water chestnut powder or
    potato flour*

Time: 45 minutes

Descale the fish, slit right down its belly and
gut it. Open out flat, remove the backbone and
attached bones, score the fish deeply 4 times
right across the fleshy side; do not cut through
the skin. (Some cooks make a certain number
of slashes on one side, and fewer on the other
to add to the curling effect.) Mix the marinade
in a dish large enough to take the fish, stirring
the cornstarch into a little water beforehand,
and turn these 3 pieces to coat evenly with the
marinade. Leave to stand while you cook the
peas in boiling water until just tender. Drain.
Fry the pine nuts in oil for 1–2 minutes until
pale golden brown.

   Coat the marinated fish all over with the
flour, shaking off excess. Heat plenty of oil in
the stabilized wok or deep-fryer until very hot;
lower the fish into the oil, and fry until golden
brown all over. The tail should curl but it does
not matter if it fails to do so. Remove from the
wok, draining well, and place on a serving
platter, skin side uppermost. The upwardly
curved tail is considered reminiscent of a
squirrel shape by the Chinese.

   While the fish is cooking, make the sauce:
heat the oil and all the sauce ingredients in the
wok, and boil until reduced slightly; stir in the
thickening agent mixed with a very little cold
water. Pour this sauce over the fish, sprinkle
with the peas and pine nuts, and serve at once.

SMOKED FISH *

熏 鱼
xūn yú

*1 porgy weighing approx. 1³/₄ lb
4 thin slices fresh ginger
2 scallions
1 small piece cinnamon bark (or pinch
    ground cinnamon)
2 cloves
3 tbsp rice wine
pinch salt
pinch monosodium glutamate (optional)
generous pinch sugar
6 tbsp soy sauce
generous pinch five-spice powder
oil for frying*

*For the marinade:
1¹/₂ tbsp soy sauce
1 tsp salt
1¹/₂ tsp rice wine*

Time: 1 hour 10 minutes

126

Cut off the fish's head and tail; slit right down the belly and gut. Wash well, dry, and cut right down the backbone. Work the two halves or sides of the fish off the bones as neatly as possible. Mix the soy sauce, salt, and rice wine and marinate the fish in this for 10 minutes.

Bring 1 pint water to a boil in a small saucepan and add the ginger, scallion, cinnamon, cloves, wine, salt, monosodium glutamate (if used), sugar, and soy sauce. Simmer, uncovered, for 15 minutes. Set aside. Heat enough oil to semi deep-fry (or more to deep-fry) in the wok or a deep-fryer. Lower the fish into the oil when very hot and fry for 6 minutes. Remove the fish from the oil, draining well, transfer to a deep dish and pour the reduced flavored liquid over it; leave to stand for 15 minutes. Drain well and transfer to a serving plate. Slice diagonally into fairly thin slices and sprinkle with the five-spice powder. Serve.

In this context "smoked" refers only to the darkened appearance of the fish when it has been marinated.

BABY COD WITH CIE CIAI (PICKLED MUSTARD GREENS)

雪菜川塘鳕鱼
xuě cài chuān táng xuě yú

14 oz small cod (preferably several baby cod, known as scrod or schrod)
1 oz pickled mustard greens (cie ciai)
1 oz bamboo shoots
3 tbsp oil or shortening
2 thin slices fresh ginger
1/2 scallion
1 1/2 tsp rice wine
2 1/4 cups chicken broth
1/2–1 tsp salt
pinch monosodium glutamate (optional)

Time: 1 hour

If you are using whole baby cod, remove their fins and gills and gut them. Rinse the pickled mustard cabbage or greens under running cold water to get rid of excess salt. Shred these and the bamboo shoots.

Heat the oil or shortening in the wok and stir-fry the chopped ginger and scallion. Sprinkle in the wine and add the fish and bamboo shoots; pour in the broth. Bring to a boil and skim off any scum on the surface; simmer for up to 10 minutes or until the fish is very nearly done, add the pickled mustard greens, salt, and monosodium glutamate (if used), return to a boil, and simmer for 1 further minute. Transfer to a serving platter and sprinkle with a little of the cooking liquid.

HONEYED COD *

蜜汁牙鳕鱼
mì zhí yá xuě yú

1 3/4 lb cod (preferably 1 whole fish or several baby cod, known as scrod or schrod)
1/2–1 tsp salt
generous pinch freshly ground pepper
1 1/2 tbsp soy sauce
oil for deep-frying

For the sauce:
3 tbsp oil
1 1/2 tsp finely chopped fresh ginger
1 1/2 tsp finely chopped scallion
1 1/2 tbsp rice wine
1 tbsp sugar
2 1/2 tbsp soy sauce
1 tbsp sesame seed oil
1 tbsp cornstarch

Time: 45 minutes

Trim, gut, wash, and dry the fish. Season with the salt and pepper, sprinkle with the soy sauce and leave to flavor for 10 minutes.

Heat the oil in the wok (on its stand) or preferably in an electric deep-fryer to 300°F or just above and fry the fish for 10 minutes or until crisp and golden on the outside and done, but still moist, on the inside. Drain the fish well and set aside on paper towels. Make the sauce: heat the oil in the wok or an oval fish skillet, stir-fry the scallion and ginger briefly, then add all the other sauce ingredients except for the thickening agent; boil to reduce a little, then blend the cornstarch (or alternative) with a little cold water and stir into the skillet to thicken the sauce. Place the fish in this sauce, turn carefully once or twice to heat and coat thoroughly with the sauce, then transfer to a heated serving platter.

The name of this dish was chosen by Chinese cooks to describe its gently sweetened taste although no honey is actually used.

PORGY WITH LEEKS AND GINGER

姜葱烧鱼
jiāng cōng shāo yú

1 porgy weighing 2 1/4–2 1/2 lb
1 large piece fresh ginger approx. 2 in long
3 leeks
salt
3 tbsp all-purpose flour
1/3 cup oil
3 tbsp soy sauce

3 tbsp rice wine
¹/₂ cup vegetable broth
1¹/₂ tsp cornstarch
freshly ground pepper
1 sprig fresh coriander leaves
2 lemons, sliced

Time: 45 minutes

Peel the ginger and grate it finely. Take off the outer layer of the leek, trim off the root end and tough green leaves, wash the white part thoroughly, and slice into thin rounds. Descale the porgy, trim, gut, and wash well inside and out. Make deep diagonal cuts on both sides. Pat dry, rub all over inside and out with salt, and sprinkle all over with the flour to coat. Heat the oil in a wok or in an oval skillet large enough to take the porgy lying flat. Fry the fish over fairly high heat for 10 minutes on each side, until crisp and golden brown. Remove and keep warm. Lower the heat and stir-fry the leek and ginger in the oil and juices in the pan. Mix the soy sauce, wine, broth, cornstarch, and pepper in a small bowl; stir into the pan. Return the fish to the pan and coat with sauce; transfer to a serving dish and decorate with coriander leaves and lemon slices.

FISH AND LOTUS ROOT SAVORY STEAMED PUDDING

蒸鱼饼
zhěng yú bǐng

¹/₂ lb white fish fillets (flounder or similar)
1 lb lotus roots (fresh or canned)
1 tbsp wine vinegar
¹/₄ cup butter, softened
1 tbsp rice wine
1 tsp cornstarch or potato flour
salt
1 piece fresh root ginger approx. 1¹/₂ in long
1 sprig fresh coriander leaves

Time: 45 minutes

Cut the fish fillets into small pieces then process to a smooth paste in the food processor and transfer to a mixing bowl. If fresh lotus roots are used, peel; grate fresh or canned lotus root finely and sprinkle with the vinegar. Mix well with the fish, add ¹/₄ cup of the butter, the wine and cornstarch or potato flour and salt. Stir thoroughly. Melt the remaining butter (about 1 tbsp) and use to grease a heatproof plate which will fit into the steamer leaving a little space all round its edges. Spread the mixture out on the plate, smoothing level with a spatula dipped in cold water and place a disk of waxed paper loosely on top. Cover and steam for 20 minutes. Decorate with ginger strips and coriander leaves.

BRAISED FISH HEAD

砂锅大鱼头
shā guō dà yú tóu

1 very fresh fish head (from a very large carp
  or porgy) weighing approx. 1³/₄ lb
oil for frying
3 tbsp oil
3 thin slices fresh ginger
1 scallion
3 tbsp rice wine
¹/₂–1 tsp sugar
5 tbsp soy sauce
1 quart fish stock or vegetable or chicken
  broth
¹/₄ lb fresh bacon or pork belly
4 tung ku (dong gu) mushrooms
1¹/₂ oz bamboo shoots
red food coloring (optional)
pinch monosodium glutamate (optional)
1 tsp salt
4 dried soybean leaves (phen pi), soaked in

warm water
1 tbsp sesame seed oil

Time: 1 hour 20 minutes

In China or Hong Kong, this dish would traditionally be made with a pomfret or garoupa head. There is plenty of delicious (white) flesh on many white fish heads, a much neglected delicacy in the West, the cheeks being particularly tasty. Rinse the fish head thoroughly, sprinkle all over with 1 tbsp soy sauce, and leave to stand. Heat a little oil in the wok and fry the fish head, turning frequently until golden brown all over.

Pour 3 tbsp oil into a fireproof earthenware casserole dish; sauté the ginger and scallion, both cut into very small pieces, add the fish head, sprinkle with the wine, and cover. Cook over very low heat for about 5 minutes, then add the sugar, remaining soy sauce, broth, and the bacon or pork belly cut into thin pieces measuring about 1¹/₄ × ³/₄ in. Bring to a boil, then reduce to a simmer, cover, and cook

for 30 minutes. Meanwhile, soak the mushrooms in warm water until soft, drain, remove their stalks and cut the caps into thin strips; cut the bamboo shoots into strips of the same size; snip the pre-soaked soy leaves into small, even-sized pieces. Add these three ingredients to the fish, followed by all the remaining ingredients except for the sesame seed oil. Simmer for 10 minutes longer, sprinkle with the sesame seed oil and serve.

BRAISED ABALONE WITH MUSHROOMS *

干烧鱼翅

hóng shāo má hào

12 dried or canned abalone
10 tung ku (dong gu) mushrooms
5 oz fresh button mushrooms
4 thin slices fresh ginger
2 scallions
2 star anises
6 tbsp rice wine
$^{1}/_{2}$ tsp monosodium glutamate (optional)
6 tbsp soy sauce
$^{1}/_{2}$–1 tbsp salt
1 tbsp sugar
7 cups water
3 tbsp sesame seed oil
$1^{1}/_{2}$ tbsp oyster sauce
1 tbsp cornstarch, water chestnut powder or
   potato flour
oil

Time: 2 hours + soaking time for dried
   abalone

If dried abalone are used, soak these mollusks in cold water for several hours or overnight, then bring to a boil in plenty of water, reduce the heat, and simmer very gently for 6–7 hours or until they are soft and elastic. If using canned abalone, simply drain, reserving the juice if wished.

Soak the dried mushrooms in warm water for 20 minutes, cut off their stalks. Wipe and trim the fresh mushrooms; blanch both sorts briefly in boiling water.

Heat 3 tbsp oil in a deep, heavy pan or cooking pot, fry the ginger and scallion, and add the anise, wine, monosodium glutamate (if used), soy sauce, salt, water, sesame seed oil, and the abalone. Bring to a boil, reduce the heat and simmer, uncovered, for 50 minutes. Add the mushrooms and simmer for a further 15 minutes. Remove the abalone and mushrooms with a slotted spoon and arrange on a serving plate. Pour 1 cup of the cooking liquid (strained) into a small saucepan, stir in the oyster sauce, boil until slightly reduced, then stir in the thickening agent mixed with a little water and cook for 1–2 minutes. Coat the mollusks and mushrooms with this sauce.

Abalone, or sea ears as they are sometimes called (due to the shell's whorls suggesting the shape of the human ear), are sometimes available fresh in California but most are now imported, canned.

FISH WITH GINGER AND CHINESE GHERKINS *

酱瓜鱼丝
jiàng guā yú sī

10 oz fillets of white fish (flounder, sole etc.)
2 oz sweet-pickled or mild-pickled Chinese

gherkins (canned)
2 egg whites
3 tbsp cornstarch
3 tbsp oil
3 thin slices fresh ginger
¹/₂ scallion
1 tsp salt
1¹/₂ tbsp sesame seed oil

1¹/₂ tbsp rice wine
6 tbsp fish stock, chicken broth or water
oil for frying

Time: 30 minutes

Cut across the fish fillets, slicing them into strips with the knife held at an oblique angle. Beat the egg whites, beat in 1¹/₂ tbsp cornstarch, and mix the fish strips thoroughly with this to coat all over. Shred the gherkins. Peel and trim the ginger and scallion and slice very thinly. Heat plenty of oil in the wok (or deep-fryer) until very hot, fry the fish for 30 seconds, then remove, draining well, and pour off the oil from the wok, if used. Heat 3 tbsp fresh oil in the wok and stir-fry the scallion, ginger, and gherkins for 2 minutes over moderate heat; add the fish, salt, sesame seed oil, wine, and broth or water; simmer slowly for 10 minutes; mix the remaining cornstarch (1 1/2 tbsp) with a little cold water and stir gently into the contents of the wok. Serve.

Mild- or sweet-pickled Chinese gherkins are sold canned in Oriental foodstores and are a must for Eastern Chinese dishes. They should not be cooked for too long or they lose their pleasant crispness.

FILLETS OF SOLE WITH JUJUBES *

枣泥鱼卷

zǎo ní yú jiǔan

10 oz fillets of sole or flounder
7 oz jujubes
2 egg whites
1/2 cup cornstarch or potato flour
oil for deep-frying

For the marinade:
1 1/2 tbsp rice wine
generous pinch freshly ground pepper
pinch salt

Time: 45 minutes

Cut the fish fillets into strips measuring 1 1/2 × 3/4 in and season with salt and pepper; mix the marinade ingredients and add the fillets, making sure they are all coated; leave to stand for a few minutes. Steam the jujubes for 5 minutes. Drain excess marinade from fish and transfer to the working surface. Pit the jujubes and chop them finely. Place a little of the chopped jujube on each fish strip, roll up firmly, dip in the stiffly beaten egg whites, and then coat with cornstarch, shaking off excess carefully. Heat the oil in the wok or deep-fryer and fry the rolls a few at a time for 3–4 minutes or until golden brown. They can also be shallow-fried.

Finely chopped marrons glacés (candied chestnuts) can be used instead of jujubes as the filling for these little rolls. Some cooks prefer the natural fish taste to come through more directly and omit the marinating stage.

132

Chopsticks are known to have been in use during the Shang dynasty (1766–1123 B.C.). There are two sizes: shorter, eating implements measuring about 10 in, made of bamboo, plastic or ivory. Table chopsticks are sometimes lacquered and highly decorated.

Longer, kitchen chopsticks, usually made of bamboo, 14 in long, are used for beating eggs, stirring sauces or turning foods as they cook in the wok. Since most foods are cut up into small pieces to ensure that they cook as quickly as possible, thus saving fuel, only one morsel can usually be ferried from bowl to mouth at a time with the chopsticks; it is perfectly proper to

hold your eating bowl close to your mouth, especially in southern China.

When meat etc. is cooked and served in large pieces, it is always very tender, so that pieces can be detached easily with chopsticks, even from the bones. The only time chopsticks are not used, of course, is when eating soup, when the traditional porcelain spoon is used. By the age of three or four, Chinese children are already acquiring the skill of eating with chopsticks. Most Westerners learn quickly once shown the correct way of holding and manipulating these implements.

FRIED EEL IN SAUCE WITH SESAME DRESSING

脆 鳝

cuì shàn

2¹/₄ lb medium-sized young eels
oil for deep-frying
6 thin slices fresh ginger
1 cup chicken broth
3 tbsp light soy sauce
1¹/₂ tbsp rice wine
1 tsp sugar
1 tsp cornstarch
1¹/₂ tbsp sesame seed oil
¹/₂ tbsp freshly ground white pepper

Time: 40 minutes

Blanch the eels in boiling water for a few seconds and skin as directed for Stir-fried eel (qīng chǎo shàn hú) on p. 112. Cut off the heads below the gills, cut the eel into 2-in lengths, take the flesh off the bones as neatly as possible, and cut these 2-in lengths into matchstick strips approx. ³/₈ in thick. Heat plenty of oil in the wok or deep-fryer to about 340°F, lower the pieces of eel into the oil, and fry until crisp and golden brown. Drain well and set aside.

Drain the wok and wipe, if already used for frying; heat the peeled ginger slivers, chicken broth, and soy sauce in it together with the wine and sugar; when the liquid reaches boiling point, add the fried eel pieces, cover, and simmer gently for 3 minutes. Stir in the cornstarch mixed with a very little cold water to thicken; transfer to a serving dish, arranging in a ring with a little well in the middle. Heat the

sesame seed oil in a small saucepan until very hot, pour into the well, and then sprinkle the white pepper all over the eels. The hot sesame seed oil spreads out on the dish below the eels and imparts its unmistakable scent and flavor.

PERCH WITH CHILI PEPPER

辣 豆 瓣 鱼

là dòu bàn ý

1 perch weighing 1–1¹/₄ lb
oil for frying
2 scallions
6 thin slices ginger
2 chili peppers
3 tbsp oil
1¹/₂ tbsp hot soy paste (dou ban jiang)
1¹/₂ tbsp rice wine
1 tbsp sugar
1 tbsp dark Chinkiang vinegar

Time: 40 minutes

Trim and descale the fish, then gut it drawing the entrails out through the gill aperture. Rinse inside and out and pat dry with paper towels. Heat plenty of oil in the wok or deep-fryer to 300°F or a little hotter, and fry the fish until crisp and golden brown all over (turn once if shallow-frying). Remove and set aside. Prepare the scallion, peel the ginger, and shred both into very thin matchstick strips; cut the stalks off the chili peppers, remove and discard the seeds and inner pith, and chop coarsely. Empty the oil used to fry the fish from the wok, wipe clean, and heat 3 tbsp fresh oil; stir-fry the scallion and ginger gently until they give off a good, full aroma, then stir in the soy paste, chili peppers, rice wine, and sugar.

Cook gently for 1 minute, stirring, then mix in 1 cup hot water or broth and bring to a boil. Add the fried fish, cover, and cook for 3 minutes; remove the lid, turn the fish very carefully to avoid breaking it up and cook, uncovered, for a few minutes more to reduce the sauce a little.

Transfer the fish to a serving dish, coat with the sauce, and sprinkle with the Chinkiang vinegar.

FOUR-COLOR FILLETS OF FISH *

四色鱼丝

sì sè yú sī

1 porgy, sea bass or other white fish
   weighing approx. 1¹/₄ lb
1¹/₂ tbsp fresh ginger juice (see method
   below)
1¹/₂ tbsp rice wine
2 egg whites
2¹/₂ tbsp cornstarch or alternative
oil for deep-frying
1 green bell pepper (capsicum)
1¹/₄ lb York ham
1 whole egg

For the sauce:
3 tbsp sesame seed oil
1¹/₂ tbsp rice wine
pinch salt
pinch monosodium glutamate (optional)
1¹/₂ tbsp light soy sauce
1 cup fish stock or chicken broth
1¹/₂ tbsp cornstarch

Time: 2 hours

Trim and gut the fish, slitting it right down the belly. Descale it if necessary and cut into 3 parts: head; middle cut or body; tapering end of the body and tail. Cut the underside of the head lengthwise so that the head can be opened out flat. Bring a pan of water to a boil with the ginger juice (obtained by mincing a piece of ginger through a garlic crusher) and the wine; blanch the head and tail in this for 2 minutes. Remove, drain, and place at either end of an oval serving dish.

Open the fish body out flat and remove the backbone and attached bones from what was the inside, working with the skin side downward. Cut into thin strips, across the width of the fish. Beat the egg whites until stiff. Dip the fish strips in the egg white, then coat with cornstarch. Deep-fry for 1 minute.

Shred the pepper and blanch in boiling water for 1 minute. Drain well. Shred the ham. Break the egg into a bowl, beat lightly, and use to make a very thin omelet; shred.

Fill up the space on the serving platter between the head and tail by alternating strips of pepper, fish, ham, fish and omelet, in that order, repeating until all are used. Make the sauce: heat the sesame oil in the wok, add the wine, salt, monosodium glutamate (if used), soy sauce, and broth. Boil gently until somewhat reduced; mix your chosen thickening agent with a little cold water, stir into the sauce, and cook for 1–2 minutes. Pour the sauce all over the fish and serve.

133

STEAMED FISH WITH EGGS

鱼片蒸蛋

yú piàn zhēng dàn

134

1 very fresh carp (or similar, white fleshed fish) weighing approx. 14 oz–1 lb
3 eggs
1 cup chicken broth
¹/₂–1 tsp salt
1 slice Jin hua ham (or Smithfield ham, Virginia ham or Westphalian ham)

Time: 30 minutes

Trim, gut, and descale the fish. Using a very sharp knife, make deep diagonal, parallel slashes on both sides about 1–1¹/₄ in apart.

Beat the eggs lightly with the salt in a bowl; stir in the broth. Grease the inside of a dish lightly with oil. Pour the egg mixture into this dish and then carefully place the fish flat in it; the egg mixture should come almost halfway up the fish.

Place the dish in the steamer compartment, cover, and steam for about 15 minutes or until cooked; the egg mixture will have set by this time. Sprinkle with the shredded ham and serve.

THREE-FLAVOR FISH ROLLS *

三丝鱼卷

sān sī yú juǎn

1¹/₄ lb fish fillets (e.g. English Dover sole or flounder)
4 tung ku (dong gu) mushrooms
¹/₂ red bell pepper
2 scallions
¹/₄ lb York ham
2¹/₂ tbsp fresh ginger juice (see below)
¹/₂–1 tsp salt
3 egg whites
¹/₂ cup cornstarch
oil for frying

For the sauce:
1¹/₂ tbsp oil
¹/₂ cup fish stock, chicken broth or water
1 tbsp sugar
3 tbsp wine vinegar
3 tbsp sesame seed oil
3 tbsp soy sauce
1 tbsp cornstarch

Time: 1 hour

Soak the dried mushrooms in warm water for 20 minutes. Cut the fish fillets across into strips measuring about 2¹/₂ × ³/₄ in. Trim off the stalk, seeds, and inner pith from the sweet red pepper and shred into strips; do likewise with the scallions and ham. Cut the stalks off the softened mushrooms and discard; cut the caps into thin strips. Mix the fish strips with the salt and ginger juice (this can be extracted by grating the fresh ginger, place in a small piece of damp, clean cloth, twist the cloth round and round, putting pressure on the ginger, which will then release its juice; or by squeezing the ginger in a garlic press). Place a little bundle of vegetable and ham strips near the end of each fish strip and roll up from that end. Beat the egg whites stiffly, dip the rolls in this, and then coat with the cornstarch.

Heat plenty of oil in the stabilized wok or, preferably, in an electric deep-fryer, to 325°F, lower the rolls in batches into the hot oil in a frying basket, and fry until golden brown (about 2 minutes for each batch). Remove the rolls, draining well, place on a serving plate and keep warm, uncovered. Heat 1¹/₂ tbsp fresh oil in the wok (having poured off the frying oil if the wok was used for this), pour in the broth, add the sugar, vinegar, sesame seed oil, and soy sauce. Simmer, uncovered, until considerably reduced; mix the cornstarch with a very little water and stir in.

Sprinkle this sauce over the rolls or serve separately in a bowl with a spoon for each person to add as desired.

FISH FILLETS QI LIN*

蒸鱼饼

qí lín shí bān yú

14 oz fish fillets (e.g. sole, perch, flounder
  etc.)
6 tung ku (dong gu) mushrooms
2 egg whites
pinch freshly ground pepper
$^1/_2$–1 tsp salt
1$^1/_2$ tbsp cornstarch
6 bamboo shoots, thinly sliced
$^1/_4$ lb thinly sliced York ham
1 scallion, finely chopped
1 red and 1 yellow sweet pepper

4 thin slices fresh ginger, finely chopped

For the sauce:
1$^1/_2$ tbsp rice wine
$^1/_2$–1 tsp salt
pinch monosodium glutamate (optional)
1 tbsp sesame seed oil
1 tbsp cornstarch

Time: 1 hour

Soak the dried mushrooms in warm water for
at least 20 minutes. Cut the fish fillets into
pieces measuring approximately 1$^1/_4$ × 1$^1/_2$ in.
Beat the egg whites lightly with the pepper,
salt, and the first quantity of cornstarch and
add the fish pieces, turning them to coat all

over. Leave to stand. Drain the mushrooms,
cut off and discard the stalks; chop the caps.
Chop the bamboo shoots and the ham.

Arrange these three prepared ingredients in
a heatproof dish that will fit in your steamer,
alternating the pieces (fish, mushroom, bamboo shoot, ham). Sprinkle with the chopped
scallion and ginger. Place in the steamer over
fast boiling water, cover, and cook for 10 minutes.

Heat the rice wine, salt, monosodium glutamate (if used) and sesame seed oil very gently;
mix the cornstarch with a very little cold water
and stir into the sauce to thicken and simmer
for a few minutes. Sprinkle all over the surface
of the cooked fish mixture and serve, decorated with the shredded peppers.

BRAISED DUCK WITH SOY SAUCE

酱鸭
jiàng yā

1 oven-ready duck (weighing approx. 4¹/₂ lb)
8 thin slices fresh ginger
3 scallions
3 cloves
1 small piece cinnamon (or pinch ground cinnamon)
6 tbsp rice wine
¹/₂ cup soy sauce
¹/₂–1 tsp monosodium glutamate (optional)
1 tbsp salt
1 tbsp sugar
¹/₄ cup sesame seed oil
1¹/₂ tbsp cornstarch, water chestnut powder or potato flour

Time: 2¹/₂ hours

Sprinkle the duck inside and out with salt and leave to stand for 15 minutes. Rinse inside and out under running cold water and place in a pot large enough to take it lying flat, breast uppermost, with the ginger, scallions, cloves, cinnamon, wine, soy sauce, monosodium glutamate (if used), salt, and sugar. Add sufficient water to cover the duck, bring to a gentle boil, and then simmer for 1¹/₂ hours or until the duck is done and very tender.

Take up the duck, drain well, and cut into fairly small pieces (bone and all) using a heavy cleaver; coat each piece lightly all over with sesame seed oil, using a pastry brush. Arrange on a serving plate.

Use a ladle to scoop off the top, rather fatty layer of the cooking liquid and discard; strain about 1¹/₂ cups of the skimmed liquid into a pan and boil hard to reduce. Mix your chosen thickening agent with a very little cold water and stir into the liquid to thicken. Pour over the duck pieces and serve.

EIGHT-TREASURE DUCK *

八宝全鸭
bā bǎo quán yā

¹/₄ lb dried scallops, pre-soaked in warm water
1 duck weighing about 4¹/₂ lb, boned
3 thin slices fresh ginger
1 scallion
2 tung ku (dong gu) mushrooms
1¹/₂ oz bamboo shoots
1¹/₂ oz Chinese raw smoked ham or Westphalian ham
2 tbsp lotus seeds

²/₃ cup fresh or frozen peas
¹/₄ lb chicken breasts
¹/₂ cup peeled shrimp
¹/₂–1 tsp salt
¹/₂ tsp monosodium glutamate (optional)
3 tbsp rice wine
1¹/₂ tbsp soy sauce
1¹/₂ tbsp cornstarch

Time: 4¹/₂ hours

Soak the scallops for several hours in warm water to reconstitute. Place the boned duck in a large pan of boiling water and blanch for a few minutes only. Drain.

Soak the mushrooms in warm water for 20 minutes to soften and reconstitute them, then drain; cut off and discard their stems. Trim and peel the bamboo shoots if fresh, drain if canned. Blanch the lotus seeds and, if using fresh, remove the hard central core. Cut the mushroom caps into ¹/₄–1¹/₂-in cubes; do likewise with the bamboo shoots, lotus seeds, chicken breasts, shrimp (as far as possible), and the drained scallops. Blanch all these ingredients in boiling water for a few minutes, then drain and use to stuff the duck. Sew the vent and neck openings closed and sew up the long central seam right down the middle. Place the stuffed duck in a dish which will fit into your steamer. Sprinkle the ginger and scallions below and over the duck. Steam for 3 hours, replacing the water in the pan below whenever necessary. Transfer the cooked duck to a serving dish and carefully remove the string. Strain all the juices and fat left behind in the cooking dish, mix in a small saucepan with the salt, monosodium glutamate (if used), rice wine, and soy sauce. Mix the cornstarch with a little cold water, and stir into the sauce. Cook for a few minutes, pour over the duck, and serve.

DUCK WITH FISH DUMPLING ROLLS

馄 饨 鸭
hún tūn yā

1 oven-ready duck (or 1–2 mallard, wild duck) weighing approx. 4¹/₂ lb
1 tsp salt
¹/₄ cup rice wine
1 scallion
5 thin slices fresh ginger

For the wonton (dumplings):
14 oz very fresh, whole white fish fillets (preferably from large flatfish e.g. flounder)
¹/₂ cup shrimp

1 egg white
pinch salt
¹/₂ tbsp very finely chopped fresh ginger
1 tbsp finely chopped scallion
1 tbsp rice wine
pinch monosodium glutamate (optional)
1 heaping tbsp cornstarch

Time: 1¹/₂ hours

Place the duck in a pot with the salt, wine, scallion, and ginger; add 7 cups water or enough to cover the duck and bring to a boil; boil gently for 1 hour or until the duck flesh is very tender. Skim off any scum.

Meanwhile, prepare the wonton dumplings: chop the shrimp very finely and mix with the egg white, salt, ginger, scallion, rice wine, and monosodium glutamate (if used). Cut the fish fillets into pieces measuring 2¹/₂ in square. Sprinkle these with cornstarch and press to flatten and make thinner without breaking them up. Place a little of the shrimp mixture in the center of each piece and roll up secure with small steel skewers if wished. Place in the steamer, on a sheet of waxed paper and steam for 5–6 minutes. Carefully remove the skewers.

Transfer the cooked, drained duck to a large serving platter and surround with the fish rolls; sprinkle the duck and fish with a little of the cooking liquid.

QUAILS IN SWEET SAVORY SAUCE

油 焖 鹌 鹑
yóu mèn ān chún

4 oven-ready quails
2¹/₂ tbsp soy sauce
2¹/₂ tbsp rice wine
oil for frying
1 tbsp finely chopped fresh ginger
1 tbsp finely chopped scallion
1¹/₂ tbsp oil
2 oz bamboo shoots
1 tbsp sugar
1 tsp monosodium glutamate (optional)
1 cup chicken broth
1 heaping tbsp cornstarch

Time: 1¹/₄ hours

Joint each quail into 4 quarters. Sprinkle 1¹/₂ tbsp each soy sauce and rice wine over all these pieces, turn them to flavor evenly, and leave to stand for 15 minutes. Cut the drained canned bamboo shoots into equilateral triangles, their bases measuring about ³/₄ in. Deep-fry the quail pieces for 1 minute. Remove, draining well, and set aside. Heat 1¹/₂ tbsp fresh oil in the emptied wok or a skillet

and fry the ginger and scallion just long enough for them to release their aromas. Add the remaining soy sauce and rice wine (1 tbsp each), the sugar, monosodium glutamate (if used), bamboo shoots, chicken broth, and the quails. Cover and simmer over low heat for 40 minutes, checking every now and then to ensure that the liquid does not reduce too much. When the quails are done and very tender, stir in the cornstarch mixed with a little cold water, cook for a few minutes more, and serve.

WHITE JADE CHICKEN (CHICKEN IN ASPIC)

白 玉 冻 鸡
bái yú dòng jī

1 oven-ready boiling (or roasting) chicken
   weighing approx. 3¹/₂ lb
2 oz York ham, cut into long, thin strips
2 sprigs parsley or coriander
2 leaves isinglass
3 thin slices fresh ginger
1 tbsp salt
¹/₂ tsp monosodium glutamate (optional)
2¹/₂ tbsp rice wine
1 scallion, trimmed

Time: 1¹/₂ hours + cooling and setting time

Wash the chicken and remove any pieces of fat just inside the vent. Bring to a boil in 7 cups water in a deep pot with the ginger, salt, monosodium glutamate (if used), wine and scallion, then simmer for about 45 minutes or until done. Take up the chicken from the pan, draining well (leaving all the liquid in the pot), and remove all the skin. Take the flesh off the bones and shred it. Strain the cooking liquid and pour into a clean saucepan, melt the isinglass in it by boiling until dissolved. Leave to cool. Rinse a very large bowl or mold (approx. 3 quarts capacity) with cold water and line with the ham strips and the parsley leaves.

Arrange the chicken in the bowl or mold. When the gelatin begins to set, ladle it very carefully into the bowl. Refrigerate for several hours to set firmly. Just before serving, run the point of a knife round the inside rim of the bowl, place a very large plate upside down on top of the bowl or mold and then turn the plate right side up, holding the two tightly together. Place on the working surface and unmold.

EIGHT-PIECE FRIED CHICKEN

炸 八 块
zhá bā kuài

1 young cockerel, pullet or young roasting

chicken weighing approx. 1¹/₄–1¹/₂ lb
1 tsp finely chopped fresh ginger
1 tbsp light soy sauce
1 tbsp sesame seed oil
pinch freshly ground pepper
generous pinch sugar
oil for frying

For the sauce:
3 tbsp rice wine
1¹/₂ tbsp light soy sauce

Special condiment:
1 tsp ground Szechwan pepper
1 tsp fairly fine sea salt
pinch monosodium glutamate (optional)

Time: 50 minutes

Joint the chicken into eight sections with a cleaver or carving knife as follows: 2 thighs, 2 drumsticks, the 2 breasts, taken off the carcass and each cut across into 2 pieces (i.e. not lengthwise). In a large, shallow dish mix the ginger, scallion, rice wine, soy sauce, sesame seed oil, pepper, salt, and sugar and marinate the chicken pieces in this, coating evenly all over, for 20 minutes. Heat plenty of oil in a wok (use the stand for stability) or deep-fryer until very hot and fry the chicken pieces until crisp and golden brown. Drain well. In the emptied and wiped wok or a skillet, heat the sauce ingredients together briefly while stirring; add the fried chicken pieces, simmering and turning for 2 minutes to flavor. Serve. Have one or more little dishes containing the condiment on the table for each person to dip pieces of chicken into if wished.

An alternative version of this recipe omits the sauce and instead the marinade is mixed with 2 lightly beaten eggs; once the chicken pieces have been thoroughly covered in this, they are coated with a mixture of all-purpose flour mixed with either cornstarch or potato flour and then deep-fried.

BEGGAR'S CHICKEN

教 化 鸡
jiào huà jī

1 young, oven-ready roasting chicken
   weighing approx. 2¹/₄ lb
1 tsp finely chopped fresh ginger
1 finely chopped scallion
1¹/₂ tbsp rice wine
1¹/₂ tbsp soy sauce
1 tsp salt
pinch monosodium glutamate (optional)
1 pig's caul (see method below)
2 dried lotus leaves
1 cup rice wine or dry white wine
pinch salt

138

Duck is one of the most popular poultry meats in China and duck rearing is a very large industry. It usually features on the menu in some guise or other on festive occasions.

Poultry farmers have developed (and are still perfecting) breeds ideally suited to favorite dishes and expanding production to satisfy demand.

Peking duck, for which only the crisp skin is used (the flesh is not wasted), is only one of countless ways of preparing this favorite, served with special sauces and accompaniments. In the traditional recipe air is pumped between the skin and flesh to separate them, which makes the skin crisp up more effectively. The duck is usually rubbed inside and out with spices and seasonings. Roast duck is sold in special roast meat shops, and the skin and flesh are eaten together.

Once killed, the ducks are hung up in a cool, well ventilated place, then dipped in a malt mixture to coat or lacquer them before they are roasted. Duck is often served with vegetables or added to soups.

Szechwan duck is a delicious dish, the flesh so tender that it falls away from the bones when picked up with chopsticks.

Salted duck is an expensive delicacy: the bird is cut in half, flattened, dried in the sun, sprinkled with salt, and preserved. When winter comes the duck is steamed to reconstitute it and keep all the flavor intact. Duck eggs cooked in tea, the so-called porcelain eggs, are popular and easy to prepare.

139

seal. Bake the chicken for 1½ hours at 350°F. Place the hardened clay case, still with the foil underneath it, on a thick towel on the work surface. Gently crack open the clay casing with a mallet or hammer and remove all the small pieces of clay. Peel away the lotus leaves sufficiently to gain access to the moist, succulent chicken inside. Serve immediately.

CHICKEN FU RONG

芙蓉鸡米
fú róng jī mǐ

2 cups very finely chopped chicken breasts
2½ tbsp rice wine
1 tsp salt
2½ tsp cornstarch or potato flour
5 egg whites
2½ tbsp sesame seed oil
¼ cup chicken broth
pinch monosodium glutamate (optional)
2 cups oil for frying
1½ tbsp soy sauce
1 tsp sugar
¼ cup (2 oz) finely chopped ham
1 finely chopped scallion
1 tbsp finely chopped parsley

Time: 45 minutes

Mix the chopped chicken with half the wine, a pinch of salt, 1 heaping tsp cornstarch or potato flour, 1 egg white, and the monosodium glutamate (if used). Beat well.

Beat the remaining 4 egg whites with 2½ tbsp of the broth, add a pinch of salt, and transfer this mixture to a fairly deep dish which will fit in the steamer. Cover with waxed paper and steam for 6–7 minutes.

Heat the frying oil until very hot in the wok or a large skillet until very hot; draw aside from the heat and add tablespoons of the chicken mixture, carefully sliding them into the hot oil down the sides of the wok or skillet. Once in the oil, the mixture will firm up. Turn after 10 seconds, and fry for a further 10 seconds. Drain on paper towels.

Stir in the soy sauce, remaining rice wine, pinch of salt, remaining broth, and the sugar into the wok. Return the chicken to the wok and cook for a few minutes to reduce the liquid a little; mix the remaining cornstarch with a little cold water and stir into the wok. Remove from the heat.

Sprinkle the sesame oil over the contents of the wok, then transfer them to a heatproof dish which will fit in the steamer; leave a well in the center of the chicken mixture and fill this with the steamed egg whites; sprinkle with the chopped ham, scallion, and parsley, cover, and steam for 10 minutes.

Time: 4 hours

In this recipe the chicken is cooked in a clay chicken brick or in a traditional homemade clay casing, for which you will need 6 lb moist ceramic clay.

Rinse the chicken and dry. Mix the ginger, scallion, rice wine, soy sauce, salt and monosodium glutamate (if used) and pour all over the chicken, inside and out; leave to stand for 30 minutes or longer (the marinating can last for several hours or overnight) to enable the flavors to penetrate, turning frequently.

Soak the pig's caul briefly in warm (not hot) water to which a little vinegar or salt has been added; this will make the caul easier to handle and less likely to tear. Wrap the chicken in the caul; soak a chicken brick according to the manufacturer's instructions, drain, and place the caul-wrapped chicken in it. If using moist clay, pre-soak the lotus leaves in cold water to soften and enfold the caul-wrapped chicken with them so that it is completely enclosed. (If lotus leaves are unavailable – they may be found in Oriental foodstores – substitute foil.)

Using a rolling pin, roll out half the moist ceramic clay into a sheet approx. ½ in thick. Cover a large cookie sheet or baking tray with a sheet of strong aluminum foil and transfer the rolled out sheet of clay very carefully onto it. Place the wrapped chicken on the clay. Roll out the other half of the clay in the same way, cover the chicken with this, pressing the edges to the bottom sheet of clay all the way round to

SESAME SEED CHICKEN ROLLS

芝麻鸡卷

zhī má jī jiuǎn

14 oz chicken breasts
$^1/_2$ lb pork belly
3 tbsp rice wine
$1^1/_2$ tbsp light soy sauce
1 tsp ground Szechwan pepper
$^1/_2$–1 tsp salt
$^1/_2$ tsp monosodium glutamate (optional)
4 egg whites
1 cup cornstarch, water chestnut powder or
    potato flour
approx. $^1/_3$ cup sesame seeds
oil for frying

Time: 1 hour

Slice the chicken into thin rectangular pieces measuring about 2 × $1^1/_2$ in; blanch for a few seconds in boiling water. Cut the pork belly into thin slices measuring about $1^1/_4$ × $^3/_4$ in. Mix the wine, soy sauce, pepper, salt, and monosodium glutamate (if used) and stir well with both the chicken and pork belly in a bowl; leave for stand for 10 minutes.

Place a piece of pork belly on top of a piece of chicken and roll up tightly; do likewise with all the other pieces and dip each roll in the stiffly beaten egg whites, then coat lightly with cornflour (or alternative); roll in the sesame seeds, pressing firmly so that they adhere.

Deep-fry at about 290°F or shallow-fry (turning 2 or 3 times) until golden brown on the outside and cooked inside (about 10 minutes).

CHICKEN WITH TUBEROSES

夜来香花炒鸡丝

yè lái xiāng huā chǎo jī sī

$^1/_2$ lb chicken breasts
3 egg whites
$^1/_2$–1 tsp salt
$1^1/_2$ tbsp cornstarch, water chestnut powder or
    potato flour
oil for frying
3 tbsp oil
$1^1/_2$ tbsp rice wine
3 tbsp chicken broth
5 tuberose flowers

Time: 30 minutes

Skin the chicken and cut into matchstick strips. Whisk the egg whites with the salt and fold in the cornstarch (or alternative). Add the chicken pieces to this.

Heat about $^1/_4$ cup oil over high heat, add the chicken, and fry over high heat until pale golden brown; remove from the oil, draining well, and place on a serving dish. Drain off the oil from the wok, wipe clean, and heat 3 tbsp fresh oil in it; add the wine and chicken broth. Boil gently to reduce a little, add the tuberose petals, stir and pour over the chicken strips.

CHICKEN XIĀNG ZĀO

香糟鸡

xiāng zāo jī

1 oven-ready chicken weighing approx. $2^1/_4$ lb
1 finely chopped scallion
2 slices fresh ginger, finely chopped
1 tsp sugar
1 tsp salt
$^1/_2$ tsp monosodium glutamate (optional)
pinch ground Szechwan pepper
1 cup Shian ciao (Xiāng zāo) rice wine

Time: 4 hours

Bring a large, deep pot two-thirds full of water to a fast boil, add the whole chicken to it, and allow to return to boiling point; reduce the heat and simmer for 5 minutes. Remove the chicken and rinse in cold water. Empty the pot, rinse, and pour in 2 quarts fresh water; bring this to a boil, add the chicken and simmer for 10 minutes once the liquid has returned to boiling point. Use a ladle to remove just over 1 pint of the cooking liquid, pour this into a small saucepan, add the scallion, ginger, sugar, salt, monosodium glutamate (if used), and Szechwan pepper and simmer gently for a few minutes. Leave to cool. Continue cooking the chicken over moderate heat for a further 20 minutes.

Add the wine to the cold, flavored broth, stir well, and strain into a soup tureen or deep dish. Take the chicken out of the pot, draining well, and leave to cool. Use a cleaver or poultry scissors to cut the chicken into quarters, place these in the liquid in the tureen, cover, and leave to stand at cool room temperature for 2–3 hours before serving.

CHICKEN AND WHITE CHINESE MUSHROOM DUMPLINGS

鸡饺银耳

jī jiāo yín ěr

2 oz dried white Chinese mushrooms
14 oz chicken breasts

2 egg whites
$^1/_2$–1 tbsp salt
$^1/_2$ tsp monosodium glutamate (optional)
$2^1/_2$ tbsp rice wine
approx. 5 tbsp cornstarch
7 cups chicken broth

Time: 1 hour

Soak the dried mushrooms in warm water for 20 minutes, drain, then cut off and discard their stalks. Simmer the caps in gently boiling water (or steam them) for 15 minutes.

Finely chop the mushrooms and the skinned chicken breasts. Beat the egg whites until frothy and mix with the mushrooms, chicken, salt, monosodium glutamate (if used), wine, and just enough cornstarch until firm enough to shape into small balls a little smaller than a ping-pong ball (if you find you have added too much cornstarch, work in a little cold water). Bring the broth to a boil, add the dumplings, and simmer for 10 minutes, removing any scum which forms on the surface of the broth. Add a little salt to the broth, if needed, and a little pepper to taste. Serve each person with 2–3 dumplings and a ladleful of broth in a small bowl.

BRAISED CHICKEN AND SEAWEED *

砂煲海带鸡

shā bāo hǎi dài jī

1 young pullet or cockerel weighing about
    $2^1/_4$ lb
3 nori seaweed leaves, pre-soaked
1 scallion
6 tbsp sesame seed oil
$2^1/_2$ tbsp wine vinegar
6 tbsp soy sauce
$^1/_2$ tbsp salt
$^1/_2$ tbsp sugar
1 cup chicken broth

Time: $1^3/_4$ hours

Wash and dry the chicken; take all the flesh off the bones and cut it into fairly thick pieces approx. $1^1/_2$ in square. Shred the scallion. Heat the sesame seed oil gently in a fireproof casserole dish (preferably glazed earthenware), fry the scallion briefly, then add the chicken pieces and stir-fry for a minute; pour in the wine, vinegar, soy sauce, salt, sugar, and broth. Cover and simmer very gently for 1 hour. Rinse the seaweed under running cold water; tear into small pieces and add to the casserole, stirring well. Cook over slightly higher heat for 2 minutes then serve.

CHICKEN WITH SOY SAUCE

鸡 骨 酱

jī gǔ jiàng

142

1 oven-ready chicken weighing 2¹/₄–2¹/₂ lb
oil for frying
3 tbsp oil

2 thin slices fresh ginger
1 tsp salt
1 tbsp sugar
1 cup chicken broth
6 tbsp soy sauce
3 tbsp rice wine
1 tbsp cornstarch or potato flour

Time: 45 minutes

Wash and dry the chicken; use a cleaver to chop it into small pieces (bone and all) mea-suring about 1 × ³/₄ in. Heat plenty of oil in the wok or deep-fryer and fry these chicken pieces for 10 minutes or until golden brown.

Empty the oil out of the wok if used for frying the chicken, wipe the inside clean, and heat 3 tbsp fresh oil to fry the finely chopped ginger; as soon as this gives off its aroma, add the fried chicken pieces, followed by the salt, sugar, broth, soy sauce, and rice wine. Cook over moderate heat for 15 minutes, turning the chicken pieces several times. Mix the thickening agent with a very little cold water, stir into the wok to thicken the sauce and juices, and serve.

BRAISED LAMB LEG

煨羊肉
wēi yáng ròu

1 lamb or mutton leg, weighing approx. 3¼ lb
3 thin slices fresh ginger
2 scallions
1 leek
3 tbsp rice wine
1 quart vegetable or light meat broth
1 sprig fresh coriander leaves
2 star anises
1 tbsp fennel seeds
3 tbsp soy sauce
3 tbsp sugar
pinch monosodium glutamate (optional)
pinch salt
3 tbsp sesame seed oil

Time: 2 hours + soaking time if using mutton

Slit open the inner side of the lamb leg and gradually work the meat away from the bone. Discard the bone, or reserve to make broth, if wished. (If using mutton you may wish to soak the meat in a bowl of cold water, with running cold water dripping onto it very slowly, for 4 hours to eliminate any excessively strong taste.) Drain the meat, tie up neatly in a shape approaching its original unboned shape, and place in a large flameproof earthenware or enameled iron casserole dish with the ginger and finely sliced scallion and leek. Pour in the wine and broth, add the coriander, star anises, and fennel seeds. Bring to a boil, reduce the heat, and cover. Simmer, skimming any scum off the surface at intervals, until the meat is very tender (at least 1½ hours).

When the meat is cooked, add the soy sauce, sugar, monosodium glutamate (if used) and the salt; increase the heat and boil gently, uncovered, to reduce the liquid and thicken it somewhat. Take up the lamb, remove the string, and place the meat on a serving dish. Stir the sesame seed oil into the liquid in the casserole dish, pour over the lamb, and serve. Garnish with very thin strips of raw leek if wished.

SWEET AND SOUR PORK SPARERIBS

糖醋排骨
táng cù pǎi gǔ

14 oz pork spareribs
1½ tbsp soy sauce
½–1 tbsp sugar
½ tbsp salt
1½ tbsp rice wine
oil for frying

For the sauce:
1½ tbsp oil
½ cup sugar
3 tbsp wine vinegar
1½ tbsp rice wine
3 tbsp light soy sauce
1½ tbsp tomato ketchup

Time: 1 hour

Have your butcher saw the spareribs into sections approx. 1½ in long, or do this yourself with a cleaver. Mix them with the soy sauce, sugar, salt, and rice wine in a bowl; leave to marinate for 20 minutes.

Heat sufficient oil in the wok for semi deep-frying to about 300°F and fry the spareribs until pale golden brown on the outside and just done. Do not overcook or the meat will become tough. Remove the spareribs from the wok and drain off the oil. Heat 1½ tbsp fresh oil in the wok, add the sugar, vinegar, wine, soy sauce, ketchup, and 1 cup water; stir well, then return the fried spareribs to the wok and simmer for 10 minutes. Increase the heat and cook fast for a few minutes to reduce the liquid; serve.

PORK IN LOTUS LEAF PARCELS

荷叶粉蒸肉
hé yé fěn zhēng ròu

1 lb pork belly
3 tbsp soy sauce
1 tsp sugar
½ tsp salt
1½ tbsp rice wine
2 thin slices fresh ginger
½ scallion
pinch five-spice powder
4 lotus leaves, pre-soaked in warm water
1¼ cups rice flour

Time: 2½ hours

Slice the pork belly thinly (or have your butcher do this for you). Shred these slices in turn into short, narrow strips and coat all over with the rice flour, shaking off any excess. Mix well in a bowl with the soy sauce, sugar, salt, wine, finely chopped ginger, and scallion.

Blanch the lotus leaves in boiling water for a few minutes, cut each leaf into quarters, and place a little of the mixture on each quarter. Roll up to form a neat, secure parcel and tie each parcel with string.

Arrange these parcels in a heatproof dish in the steamer, cover, and steam for 2 hours. Serve very hot.

BAY TREE PORK

桂花肉
guì huā ròu

¾ lb pork tenderloin
¼ cup rice wine
pinch salt
pinch monosodium glutamate (optional)
2 eggs
½ cup cornstarch, water chestnut powder or potato flour
oil for frying
1½ tbsp oil
1½ tsp finely chopped scallion
1½ tbsp sesame seed oil
generous pinch Szechwan salt
generous pinch sugar
½ cup bay tree flowers (or generous pinch powdered dried bay leaves)

For the sauce:
2½ tbsp sugar
1½ tbsp soy sauce
1½ tbsp wine vinegar
1½ tsp cornstarch

Time: 1 hour

Cut the pork into thin slices, holding the knife at an oblique angle; place these slices between two sheets of waxed paper and beat them lightly with a mallet or rolling pin; cut the slices into narrow strips 1½ in long. Mix these with 3 tbsp of the rice wine, the salt, and the monosodium glutamate (if used) and leave to marinate for a few minutes. Beat the eggs lightly, dip the meat in the beaten egg, and then coat each piece with cornstarch, shaking off excess. Heat sufficient oil in the wok to semi deep-fry the meat and when very hot add the meat and fry for 1 minute (fry in 2 batches, preferably, to keep the oil temperature from falling too low). Remove the meat from the

wok with a slotted spoon, draining well, and set aside. Drain off the oil, wipe the wok, and heat 1½ tbsp fresh oil. Fry the scallion, add the remaining rice wine, followed by the sesame seed oil; add the fried meat and stir. Transfer the contents of the wok to a serving plate and sprinkle with the Szechwan salt and the sugar (and the powdered bay leaves if used). Scatter the bay tree flowers over the top. Mix all the sauce ingredients in a small saucepan and heat; stir in the cornstarch mixed with a little cold water and cook for 1 minute. Serve this sauce separately in a bowl with a deep ceramic spoon.

Three types of bay tree are native to China, bearing silvery white, yellowish-gold or red blossom. The Chinese prefer the yellow-gold blooms for this dish as they are particularly beautiful and highly scented.

Szechwan salt is salt seasoned with five-spice powder and pepper.

SPICED PORK LEG

水 晶 肴 肉
shuǐ jīng yáo ròu

For salting the meat:
1 boned pork leg or shoulder weighing
approx. 3¼ lb
½ tsp Chile saltpeter (sodium nitrite)
2 oz–¼ cup salt

For cooking the meat:
½ cup salt
¼ cup rice wine
3 star anises
1 small piece cinnamon bark (or 1 tsp ground cinnamon)

Time: 4 hours (+ salting and cooling time)

Carefully cut off the skin (or rind) of the pork, leaving only the thinnest layer of fat on the meat. Use a skewer to pierce the meat very deeply all over. Mix the salt and saltpeter thoroughly and use to rub well into the surface of the meat and into the holes you have pierced in it. Tie up the leg or shoulder as far as possible into its original shape before boning and set aside in a cool place (e.g. a larder or larder refrigerator on not too cold a setting; a normal refrigerator is too cold) for 48 hours. The salt and saltpeter will prevent the normal processes of decay from setting in. After these 48 hours have passed, soak the pork in cold water for 2 hours, changing the water once or twice. Rinse well and dry.

Place the pork in a large, deep pot and pour in enough cold water to cover. Add the salt, wine, sugar, scallion, ginger, star anises, and cinnamon, bring to a boil and then simmer for 30 minutes. Remove the pork, drain well, strain the cooking liquid into a clean pot, place the pork in it, and cover. Once the liquid has returned to a boil, reduce the heat to very low, cover again, and weight down the lid to prevent any steam escaping. The liquid must be kept at the gentlest possible simmer for 3 hours. Remove the lid only to skim off any scum which collects on the surface. Lift out the pork, leave to cool and then slice and serve, placing a tiny bowl of ginger-flavored wine vinegar beside each place setting.

This pork recipe is also delicious jellied: use a light homemade broth (instead of water) with about 14 oz of the skin removed from the pork joint, cut into small dice, for the second, longer simmering. When the pork is done, transfer to a large, deep, straight-sided dish or mold, add sufficient cooking liquid to cover the meat by about ¾ in, and leave to cool. Refrigerate when cold to set the liquid into a firm aspic or jelly.

SHANGHAI SPARERIBS *

椒 盐 排 骨
Jiāo yán pái gǔ

3¼ lb pork spareribs
1 heaping tsp sugar
1½ tbsp rice wine
1½ tbsp soy sauce
½ tsp monosodium glutamate (optional)
½–1 tsp ground Szechwan pepper
1 egg
½ cup lotus root powder (or fine breadcrumbs)
oil for frying

For the condiment:
½–1 tbsp five-spice powder
5 tbsp salt
½ tsp monosodium glutamate (optional)

Time: 1 hour

Have your butcher saw the spareribs into 2-in lengths or chop them yourself with a cleaver. Beat the egg with the wine, soy sauce, sugar, monosodium glutamate (if used), and Szechwan pepper; mix the spareribs with this mixture and then leave to marinate in it for 30 minutes, turning occasionally. Remove the spareribs, draining briefly, and coat with the lotus flour (or breadcrumbs). Deep-fry in plenty of hot oil heated to about 340°F until golden brown.

Remove from the oil, draining well; serve without delay, providing each person with a tiny bowl or saucer of the condiment (see above). A bowl of rice wine vinegar is an optional extra.

144

145

FRESH PORK BELLY IN SOY SAUCE

酱肉
jiāng ròu

1¼ lb pork belly with the skin (rind) on
5 thin slices fresh ginger
2 scallions
1 small piece cinnamon bark
4 cloves
3 tbsp rice wine
3 tbsp light soy sauce
½ tsp monosodium glutamate (optional)
3 tbsp sugar
3 tbsp salt
1½ tbsp cornstarch, water chestnut powder or
    potato flour

Time: 2½ hours

Wash the pork belly, sprinkle with all but
approx. 1 tsp salt, and leave to stand for 1
hour, then add to a large, deep pot of boiling
water. Allow to return to a boil, reduce the
heat, and simmer for 10 minutes. Take the
meat out of the pot and make shallow parallel
cuts across the skin or rind just under ¼ in
deep. Pour 1 quart water into the wok or a saucepan, add the meat, ginger, whole (trimmed)
scallions, cinnamon, and cloves; bring to a
boil then simmer for 20 minutes. Add the
wine, soy sauce, monosodium glutamate (if
used), sugar, and the remaining salt. Continue
simmering gently for a further 1½ hours, then
take up the meat, slice it, and arrange on a
serving dish. Use a slotted spoon to remove
and discard the ginger slices and the scallions; mix your chosen thickening agent with a
very little cold water and stir into the liquid in
the wok or pan. Cook for a few minutes more,
then pour the sauce all over the sliced pork.

PORK BELLY WITH FERMENTED TOFU

南乳汁肉
nán rǔ zhī ròu

1¾ lb pork belly with the skin (rind) on
3 oz red fermented tofu (bean curd)
¼ cup sugar
1 small piece cinnamon bark (or generous
    pinch ground cinnamon)
1 star anise
1 scallion
1½ tbsp rice wine
2 slices fresh ginger
½–1 tsp salt
red food coloring

Time: 2½ hours

Rinse the pork well and add to a pot of boiling
water; simmer for 15 minutes, then remove
and drain. Score through the rind and fat with
¾ in-deep parallel cuts; place the pork in the
wok or a saucepan with the fermented tofu
(fermented in rice wine and salt, this is available in cans and jars), the sugar, cinnamon,
star anise, trimmed scallion, rice wine, ginger,
salt, and food coloring. Add sufficient cold
water to cover the meat. Bring to a boil, reduce
the heat, cover and simmer gently for 1 hour.
Remove the pork from the pot, place in a heatproof dish (rind or skin downward) which will
fit easily into the steamer, strain the cooking
liquid, and pour over the pork. Wrap the dish
in foil, place in the steamer, cover, and steam
for 1 hour. Take the pork out of the dish, place
on the serving dish, skin side uppermost, and
pour the cooking liquid and juices over it.

In Shanghai this dish is called "Pork belly
and fermented tofu first class style." In the
Mandarin hierarchy "first class" was equivalent to Prime Minister or President, and the
dish was named after Cia Se Tao who wielded
power under the Song dynasty. He was such a
tyrannical and malevolent high functionary
that the people longed to be free of him; every
time they ate this dish, with its strong, aggress-
ive, almost harsh flavor of fermented tofu, they
could imagine they were devouring their tor-
mentor.

FRIED PORK BALLS *

炸肉丸子
zhà ròu wáw zi

1¾ cups ground or finely chopped pork
    tenderloin
1 cup finely chopped pork belly
1 finely chopped scallion
2 thin slices fresh ginger, finely chopped
½–1 tsp salt
½–1 tsp sugar
3 tbsp dark soy sauce
3 tbsp sesame seed oil
3 tbsp rice wine
generous pinch freshly ground pepper
½ tsp monosodium glutamate (optional)
3 tbsp light soy sauce
¼ cup cornstarch, water chestnut powder or
    potato flour
¼ cup all-purpose flour
¼ lb water chestnuts, finely chopped
2 eggs
1 cup cornstarch
oil for frying

Time: 1 hour

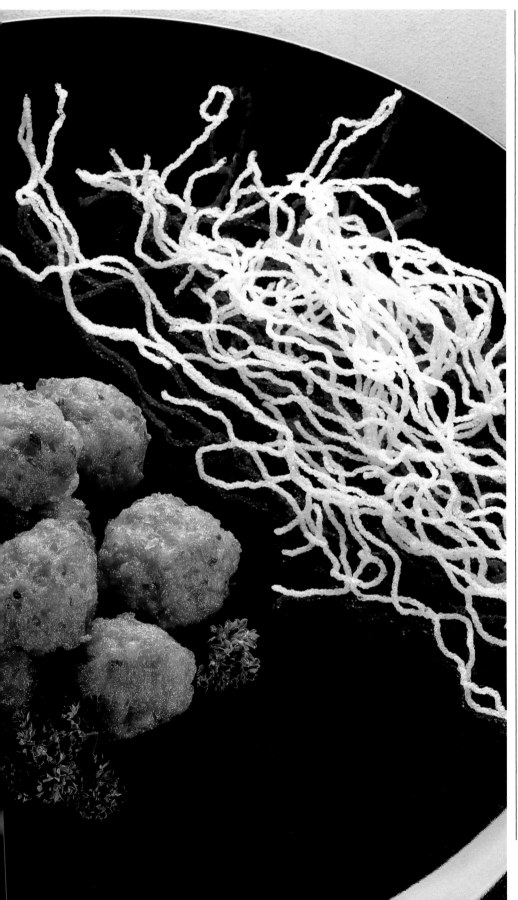

Thoroughly mix all the ingredients listed above except for the last three (eggs, cornstarch, and oil). Shape this mixture firmly into small, compact balls, dip in the lightly beaten eggs to moisten all over, then roll in the cornstarch to coat; shake off excess.

Heat plenty of oil in the wok or deep-fryer to 340°F and fry the meatballs until golden brown all over. Remove from the oil with a slotted spoon, draining well; place on paper towels to finish draining and then serve.

PORK TENDERLOIN WITH WOLFBERRIES

枸杞肉丝
gǒu qǐ ròu sī

1 lb pork tenderloin
3 oz wolfberries (goumi fruit)
1/4 cup oil, melted pork fat or shortening
3 oz bamboo shoots
1 1/2 tbsp rice wine
1/2–1 tsp sugar
1 tsp salt
pinch monosodium glutamate (optional)
1 1/2 tbsp soy sauce
3 tbsp chicken broth
1 1/2 tbsp cornstarch, water chestnut powder or
   potato flour
1 1/2 tbsp sesame seed oil

Time: 30 minutes

Slice the pork into thick strips measuring 1 1/4 × 1/2 in. Do likewise with the bamboo shoots. Heat the oil, pork fat or shortening in the wok and stir-fry the meat and bamboo shoots for 5 minutes or until the bamboo shoots are tender but still crisp; add the wine, sugar, salt, monosodium glutamate (if used), soy sauce, and broth and boil. Add the goumi fruits and cook briefly; stir in the thickening agent mixed with a little cold water. Cook for about 1 minute, sprinkle in the sesame seed oil, stir, and serve.

Greenish-white wolfberries (also known as goumi fruit) come from a plant related to the honeysuckle and turn red when cooked. The Chinese make use of these pleasantly sour-tasting fruits in cooking but also use them for medicinal purposes, to make a cooling draught.

PORK AND CHICKEN SOUP

金银蹄膀鸡汤

jīn yín tí pǎng jī tāng

148

1 hock or half ham (lower, tapering cut) of
   pork weighing approx. 1³/₄ lb
1 boiling fowl weighing 2¹/₄–2¹/₂ lb
1 14-oz piece Chinese raw cured ham
   (Jin Hua huo tui) or Virginia ham
4 thin slices fresh ginger
1 scallion
5 tbsp rice wine
salt

Time: 2¹/₂ hours

Rinse and dry the pork and the chicken and
place both in a very large glazed earthenware
or enameled cast-iron cooking pot or casserole dish with the ham. Add the ginger, scallion, and rice wine, pour in sufficient water to
cover the meat, and cover tightly first with foil
then with the lid (if there is one). Cook over
very gentle heat so that the liquid just simmers; do not remove the foil during cooking
time (approx. 2 hours). When this time has
passed, remove the foil, skim any scum off the
surface, add a little salt if needed, strain the
broth, and pour some into individual bowls.
Serve the meats in the casserole dish. The flavorsome broth is drunk at the same time.

KIDNEYS WITH SESAME PASTE

芝麻腰片

zhī má yāo piàn

14 oz pig's kidneys
3 tbsp sesame paste
1 tsp salt
¹/₄ cup sesame seed oil
3 tbsp wine vinegar
¹/₄ cup rice wine
1¹/₂ tsp finely chopped scallion

Time: 30 minutes

Remove the protective suet covering from
around the kidneys if still present. Peel off the
delicate outer skin or membrane. Cut the kidneys horizontally in half; use a very sharp
pointed knife and scissors to cut out the white
bits of gristle. Slice approx. ¹/₄ in thick. Rinse
then soak in cold water for 10 minutes.
   Bring 1 quart cold water to a boil, add the
kidneys and remove after 1 minute (more
would toughen them). Drain well and place in
a serving dish. Mix the sesame paste with

approx. ¹/₄ cup cold water; blend in the salt,
sesame oil, vinegar, and rice wine; sprinkle
this dressing all over the kidneys. Decorate
with the chopped scallion.

TRICOLOR MOLD *

扣三丝

kòu sān sī

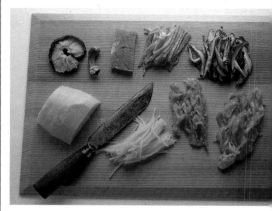

6 oz pork tenderloin
2 oz boneless chicken breast
2 oz York ham
2 oz bamboo shoots
3 large tung ku (dong gu) mushrooms
1 scallion
2 thin slices fresh ginger
¹/₂ tbsp salt
1 tsp monosodium glutamate (optional)
1¹/₂ tbsp rice wine
¹/₂ cup chicken broth
1¹/₂ tbsp cornstarch

Time: 2 hours 10 minutes

Soak the dried mushrooms in warm water for
20 minutes. Add the pork and chicken to a
large pot of boiling water, allow to return to a
boil, and reduce the heat to a simmer. After 10
minutes remove the chicken, draining well.
After a further 20 minutes, remove the meat.
Drain the mushrooms, cut off their stalks, and
discard; keep the caps whole. Cut the pork,
chicken, ham, and bamboo shoots into strips
2 in long, keeping each ingredient separate.
   Choose a large heatproof bowl which will fit
into your steamer with the lid on. Place a
whole mushroom cap in the center of the
bowl, at the bottom. Cover the mushroom and
bottom of the dish with parallel strips of pork,
heaping these up in several layers. Arrange the
chicken, ham, and bamboo strips in vertical
parallel lines all round the inside of the bowl,
pressing them against the sides to begin with
and then building up the thickness of these
sections toward the center of the bowl (alternate the bamboo and ham twice, so that you
have 6 sections, each "color" or ingredient
repeated once. Cover the top with the two
remaining mushroom caps and lay the ginger
slices and trimmed scallion flat on top. Sprinkle with salt and monosodium glutamate (if
used). Pour the wine and broth all over the
top.
   Place the bowl in the steamer and steam for
approx. 1 hour. Remove the ginger and scallion, place a plate which will fit inside the rim
of the bowl on top of the contents, and hold it
against the contents as you tip out all the
juices into a small saucepan. Mix the cornstarch with a little cold water, stir into the
juices and heat to boiling point; keep warm
while you place a serving plate upside down

over the mold then, holding the mold and plate together, turn over and release the mold. Pour over the sauce and serve.

150

LION'S HEAD PORK BALLS

清炖狮子头
qīng dùn shī zǐ tóu

1³/₄ cups pork tenderloin, very finely chopped
1³/₄ cups pork belly, very finely chopped
1 tbsp finely chopped fresh ginger
1 tbsp finely chopped scallion
1 tbsp rice wine
2¹/₂ tsp salt
pinch monosodium glutamate (optional)
2¹/₄ lb Chinese white cabbage
3 tbsp melted fresh pork fat or shortening
1 pint chicken broth

Time: 2¹/₂ hours

Mix the meats with the ginger, scallion, rice wine, 1 tsp salt, and monosodium glutamate (if used). Shape into 8 large, firm meatballs.

Rinse, drain, and shred the cabbage; melt the pork fat or shortening and stir-fry the cabbage, adding 1 tsp salt, for 1–2 minutes. Pour in the broth, bring to a boil and add the meatballs. Cover and simmer gently for 2 hours, skimming any scum off the surface from time to time.

Arrange half the cabbage on the serving platter, place the meatballs on top, and cover with the remaining cabbage.

FROGS' LEGS
WITH SOYBEAN PASTE *

酱爆田鸡腿
jiàng bào tián jī tuǐ

1¹/₄ lb frogs' legs
1 cup cornstarch, water chestnut powder or
*   potato flour*
oil for frying
3 tbsp oil
1 tbsp finely chopped scallion
1 tbsp finely chopped garlic
¹/₂–1 tbsp sugar
3 tbsp rice wine
3 tbsp sweet soybean paste
3 tbsp soy sauce

Time: 30 minutes

Wash and drain the frogs' legs, cutting each pair in two at the top where they join; dry with paper towels and coat with cornstarch or

alternative, shaking off excess. Heat plenty of oil in the wok (for semi deep-frying) or in the deep-fryer (to about 340°F) and fry the frogs' legs for 2–3 minutes or until pale golden brown (fry in several batches). Remove from the oil with a slotted ladle, draining well, and set aside to finish draining on paper towels. Pour the oil out of the wok, wipe the wok and heat 3 tbsp fresh oil; fry the scallion and garlic gently until they are tender; add the sugar, wine, soybean paste, and soy sauce; stir well over moderate heat.

Return the frogs' legs to the wok and stir to coat well with the sauce. Serve.

BRAISED TURTLE

炒樱桃

hóng shāo bīng táng jiǎ yú

1 lb canned (or ³/₄ lb dried) turtle flesh
¹/₂ cup shortening or butter
4 thin slices ginger
1 spring onion
5 tbsp rice wine
1¹/₂ tbsp fresh pork fat
5 tbsp soy sauce
1 heaping tbsp sugar
1 tbsp wine vinegar
1¹/₂ tbsp cornstarch
1 tsp sesame seed oil

Time: 1 hour 40 minutes

The turtle is a rare and protected species in many countries. Turtle farming is now being developed, however, and this is where your turtle meat should come from, if you are using fresh. You may, however, prefer to use canned or dried (and soaked, reconstituted) turtle meat.

Melt the shortening in the wok, stir-fry the ginger slices and the coarsely chopped scallion; once they release their scent, add the turtle meat and fry gently, turning frequently, for 6 minutes. Add the rice wine, just over 2¹/₄ cups water and the finely chopped pork fat; bring to a boil, reduce the heat, and simmer for 30 minutes, skimming off any scum when it rises to the surface.

Stir in the soy sauce and sugar and simmer for another 30 minutes. Increase the heat, add the vinegar and the thickening agent mixed with a very little cold water; stir well. Finally, add the sesame seed oil.

Remove the pieces of turtle meat from the wok, place them on a serving dish and sprinkle with the liquid from the wok (remove and discard the ginger and most of the scallion pieces).

SIMMERED FROGS' LEGS

红烧冰糖甲鱼

chǎo yīng táo

14 oz frogs' legs
¹/₄ cup oil
1¹/₂ tbsp finely chopped fresh ginger
1¹/₂ tbsp finely chopped scallion
1¹/₂ tbsp rice wine
1¹/₂ tbsp soy sauce
1 cup chicken broth
1¹/₂ tbsp sugar
pinch monosodium glutamate (optional)
1¹/₂ tbsp wine vinegar
pinch five-spice powder
1¹/₂ tbsp sesame seed oil

Time: 20 minutes

Heat the oil in the wok and fry the ginger and scallion until they begin to release their aroma. Add the frogs' legs and fry briefly. Add the wine, soy sauce, broth, sugar, monosodium glutamate (if used), bring to a boil, then reduce the heat and simmer for 3 minutes. Increase the heat again and cook, uncovered, to reduce the liquid a little. Sprinkle in the vinegar and the five-spice powder, followed by the sesame seed oil. Stir once and serve.

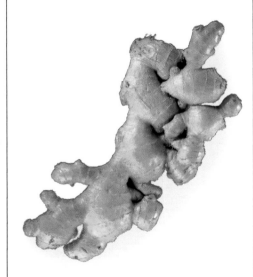

CRAB OMELET

蟹肉炒蛋
xiè ròu chǎo dàn

152

6 very fresh eggs
1 cup fresh, frozen or canned crabmeat
1 slice fresh ginger approx. 1 in thick
2 scallions
salt
few lettuce leaves
1 firm, ripe tomato
¹/₄ cup oil
1 tbsp rice wine
1 tbsp light soy sauce
1 tbsp sugar
1 grape

Time: 20 minutes

Peel the ginger and cut into very thin, short matchstick strips. Trim off the roots of the scallion, remove the outermost layer, trim off the very top of the green leaves and discard; cut the white part into thin rings and chop the green leaves very finely, keeping the two separate.

Break the eggs into a bowl and beat lightly with a pinch of salt; beat in the chopped green part of the scallion. Rinse, dry, and shred the lettuce leaves. Cut the tomato horizontally in half, crosswise, cutting a zigzag line all the way round to achieve a decorative effect. Heat the oil in the wok (or skillet), gently fry the white scallion rings with the ginger until just tender; add the crabmeat and stir. Add the wine and when this has evaporated, stir in the soy sauce and sugar. Pour in the eggs and cook until completely set. Slide the omelet onto a heated serving plate, surround with the shredded lettuce, place the grape in the center of one of the tomato halves, position in the center of the omelet, and serve at once.

PEA SHOOTS SHENG BIAN

生煸豆苗
shēng biān dòu miáo

³/₄ lb pea shoots
1 oz bamboo shoots
6 tung ku (dong gu) mushrooms
¹/₄ cup oil
pinch salt
pinch monosodium glutamate
(optional)

Time: 30 minutes

Soak the dried mushrooms in warm water for 20 minutes. Rinse the pea shoots thoroughly and chop them coarsely; do likewise with the bamboo shoots. Drain the mushrooms, cut off their stalks and discard; cut the caps into small pieces. Heat the oil in the wok, stir-fry the pea shoots very briefly, then add the mushrooms and bamboo shoots and continue stir-frying until the pea shoots and bamboo shoots are tender but still crisp. Sprinkle in the salt and monosodium glutamate (if used), stir-fry for no more than 1 minute, then serve straight away.

If pea shoots are unavailable, use soybean sprouts or very young snow peas.

HUNDRED-YEAR EGG PIE

皮 蛋 鲜 蛋 糕
pí dān xiān dàn gāo

5 hundred-year eggs
5 fresh eggs
1/2 cup chicken broth
pinch salt
pinch monosodium glutamate (optional)
1 1/2 tbsp oil or shortening

Time: 30 minutes

Soak the hundred-year eggs in cold water; when the outer covering has softened to a muddy consistency, scrape it away carefully with a knife. Wash the eggs very thoroughly under running cold water, then shell and chop finely. Break the fresh eggs into a bowl and beat lightly. Mix in the hundred-year eggs, the broth, salt, and monosodium glutamate (if used). Grease a heatproof dish with the shortening, pour the egg mixture into it, and place in the steamer. Cover and cook for 20 minutes. Remove from the steamer and leave to cool. When cold, turn a serving plate upside down over the dish, turn over, releasing the mold or "pie". Serve cold, in slices.

Hundred-year eggs (actually nearer 100-day-old eggs) are difficult to buy outside China but you may be lucky if your city boasts a "Chinatown" with Oriental foodstores. Raw duck eggs are preserved with a mixture of lime, pine ash and salt (not to be attempted at home!). Their taste is slightly fishy.

TEA EGGS

茶 叶 蛋
chá yè dàn

4 fresh eggs
1 cup water
1 1/2 tbsp black tea leaves
1 star anise
1 tsp sugar
1 tsp salt
1 tsp soy sauce

Time: 45 minutes

Bring plenty of water to a boil in a small saucepan; add the eggs (have these at room temperature) and boil for 5 minutes (timed from the moment the water returns to a boil). Remove the eggs from the water, place in a bowl, and run cold water on them to cool; tap their shells all over just hard enough to crack them, with the handle of a large knife, but not

hard enough to dislodge any of the shell. These tiny, irregular cracks all over the egg will enable the tea to stain the surface of the thin membrane inside the shell with a most attractive pattern, like the "crackle" effect seen on old Chinese porcelain. Heat the above-listed quantity of fresh water in the saucepan, add the tea (use several strong tea bags if you prefer), star anise, sugar, salt, and soy sauce; allow to return to a boil, add the eggs, and simmer for up to 1 hour. Allow to cool completely in the liquid (once cold they can be stored short-term in the refrigerator) and peel just before serving. Take care to remove the eggshell without puncturing or removing the very thin membranous skin beneath it. Serve whole, with a garnish of cucumber, sweet peppers or cooked spinach dressed with a mixture of sesame seed oil and soy sauce.

SCRAMBLED EGGS WITH FISH

蛋 花 鱼 丝
dàn huā yú sī

4 fresh eggs
1/2 lb fish fillets (e.g. sole, flounder or other white fish, or trout)
salt
3 tbsp rice wine
1 small bunch chives
3 tbsp cornstarch or potato flour
1 tbsp fresh ginger, peeled and chopped to a paste
oil for frying
1/4 cup shortening

Time: 30 minutes

Separate the eggs. Reserve 3 tbsp of the egg white; mix the rest of the whites with a pinch of salt. Add the rice wine and a generous pinch of salt to the bowl containing the egg yolks. Mix well. Chop the chives or cut into very short lengths. Cut the fish into small pieces; beat the reserved 3 tbsp egg white lightly with the cornstarch, ginger, and a pinch of salt; dip the fish pieces in this mixture, coating well, then fry them briefly in plenty of very hot oil. Heat half the shortening in the wok or skillet, add the larger quantity of salted egg whites, and cook until set, stirring lightly with a fork to scramble as it cooks. Remove from the wok and set aside. Heat the remaining shortening and add the egg yolks; cook until just set, scrambling them with a fork. Return the scrambled whites and the fried fish to the wok, sprinkle with the chives, stir and turn gently but thoroughly, and serve at once, while very hot.

XIE FEN MIXED VEGETABLES

素 炒 蟹 粉
sù chǎo xiè fěn

1 1/2 oz tung ku (dong gu) mushrooms
1 oz mo ha mushrooms (tree ear fungus)
6 oz potatoes
4 oz carrots
4 tbsp oil
1 tbsp very finely chopped fresh ginger
1 heaping tbsp finely chopped scallion
4 eggs
1/2 tbsp salt
pinch monosodium glutamate (optional)
1 tbsp wine vinegar

Time: 1 1/2 hours

Soak both kinds of dried mushrooms in warm water for 20 minutes to reconstitute and soften; drain, cut off the stalks and discard; chop the caps finely. Peel the potatoes and carrots and boil separately; when the potatoes are tender, drain thoroughly and push through a fine sieve while still hot. When the carrots are tender but still crisp chop finely, then squeeze out any lingering moisture.

Heat 1/4 cup oil in the wok and stir-fry the ginger and scallion; when they start to release their aroma, add the carrot, potato, and the mushrooms and stir-fry over fairly high heat for 2 minutes. Beat the eggs lightly and add a little at a time, stirring them so that they scramble. Sprinkle in the salt, monosodium glutamate (if used), and the vinegar. Stir well and serve.

LUO HAN VEGETABLE MEDLEY

罗 汉 香
luó hàn zhāi

2 oz small button mushrooms
2 oz straw mushrooms (canned)
2 oz oyster or abalone white mushrooms (canned or dried)
2 oz tung ku (dong gu) mushrooms
2 oz mo ha dried mushrooms (tree ear fungus)
2 oz ciun sun dried mushrooms (curly black Chinese fungus)
2 oz whole blanched, peeled almonds
2 oz carrots
2 oz potatoes
2 oz broccoli
2 oz soy flour noodles
2 oz fresh firm tofu (bean curd)
2 oz bamboo shoots

seeds. Blanch the bean shoots in boiling salted water for 1 minute only; drain well and refresh under running cold water. Drain again. Wash the leek thoroughly, trim off the ends and outer leaves, and slice into very thin rings; place these in a large salad bowl and mix well with a dressing made with the vinegar, salt, sugar, sesame oil, soy sauce, and monosodium glutamate (if used).

Add the bean threads and bean sprouts. Mix thoroughly and chill in the refrigerator for 30 minutes. Serve.

GREEN BEANS SHANGHAI STYLE *

金 华 四 季 豆

jīn huá sì jì dòu

14 oz French beans (fresh or frozen)
¹/₄ cup finely chopped York ham
¹/₄ cup oil
1 clove garlic
2 thin slices fresh ginger
1 tsp salt
1¹/₂ tsp rice wine
1 tbsp cornstarch, water chestnut powder or
    potato flour
¹/₂ cup chicken or vegetable broth
1 tbsp melted chicken fat (optional)

Time: 30 minutes

Rinse the beans if fresh and trim off the ends. Cut the beans (whether fresh or frozen) into 2¹/₄-in lengths. Heat 2 tbsp of the oil until very hot and fry the ham until crisp; drain and set aside.

Boil the beans in unsalted water for 5 minutes (or until just tender but still crisp); drain. Pour the remaining oil into the wok and gently fry the peeled, lightly minced garlic clove and the peeled ginger slices. Add the beans and stir-fry for 1 minute; remove and discard the garlic clove and ginger slices. Add the salt, wine, chicken fat (if used), and the thickening agent mixed with the cold broth and cook until the liquid has reduced and thickened slightly. Transfer to a serving dish and sprinkle with the fried ham.

¹/₂ cup oil
2¹/₂ tbsp soy sauce
1 tbsp sugar
1 tbsp salt
pinch monosodium glutamate (optional)
1 tbsp rice wine
2¹/₄ cups water
1¹/₂ tbsp cornstarch
1 tbsp sesame seed oil

Time: 1 hour

Soak all the dried mushrooms in warm water for 20–30 minutes or longer to soften and reconstitute them. Drain the canned items (if used) thoroughly. Peel the carrot and potato and slice into small, thin pieces, cutting them with the knife held at an oblique angle. Soak the noodles in warm water for a few minutes before you use them; snip into short lengths.

Cut off the stalks from the dried mushrooms where present and discard. Cut all the mushrooms into small pieces. Heat the oil in the wok and stir-fry all the ingredients over high heat. Add the soy sauce, sugar, salt, monosodium glutamate (if used), rice wine, and water. Cover and simmer over low heat for 30 minutes. Mix the cornstarch with a little cold water and stir into the contents of the wok. Cook for a further 1–2 minutes, sprinkle with the sesame seed oil, and serve.

SPECIAL BEAN SPROUT SALAD

凉 拌 豆 芽

liáng bàn dòu yá

14 oz soybean sprouts or mung bean sprouts
approx. ¹/₄ lb bean threads
1 leek
¹/₄ cup wine vinegar
¹/₂ tbsp salt
1 heaping tsp sugar
1 tbsp sesame oil
1 tbsp soy sauce
pinch monosodium glutamate (optional)

Time: 30 minutes

Pour plenty of boiling water from the kettle into a large heatproof bowl, add the bean threads and soak for 15–30 minutes or until they become transparent and tender; they will expand a good deal. Take care not to soak them for too long or they will become rubbery. Drain and snip them into approx. 2-in lengths with scissors. While the bean threads are soaking, wash the bean sprouts under running cold water; pick off all the empty seed cases as these are bitter, discard any unsprouted

STIR-FRIED MIXED MUSHROOMS *

蟹 肉 白 菜

hóng shāo èr gū

12 tung ku (dong gu) mushrooms
1/4 lb small button mushrooms
1 romaine lettuce
1 pint chicken or vegetable broth
1/3 cup oil

For the sauce:
1/2–1 tbsp sugar
1/2–1 tsp salt
6 tbsp soy sauce
1 tbsp oyster sauce

1 tbsp rice wine
1 tbsp sesame seed oil

Time: 45 minutes

Soak the tung ku mushrooms in warm water until soft. Remove and discard their stalks. Wipe the button mushrooms with a clean, damp cloth. Detach all the lettuce leaves from the stem, discard any that are wilted or damaged and rinse the rest; dry and cut across the strips not longer than about 3 in. Bring the broth to a boil in a small pan, add the drained tung ku mushrooms, reduce the heat, and simmer for 20 minutes.

Heat 1/4 cup oil in the wok and stir-fry the lettuce for 30 seconds, adding a pinch of salt. Remove the lettuce and set aside; heat 3 tbsp fresh oil in the wok and stir-fry the button mushrooms for 3 minutes. Mix the sauce ingredients in a small saucepan and heat gently. Arrange the lettuce leaves in a broad diagonal band across a serving platter; to one side place the tung ku mushrooms, on the other the button mushrooms. Sprinkle the sauce all over the ingredients and serve.

HAM AND VEGETABLE BUNDLES *

酱爆田鸡腿
qīng jiāo fà cài juǎn

3 oz York ham
3 oz cucumber
3 oz carrot
3 oz bamboo shoots
3 oz red sweet bell pepper (capsicum)
1/4 lb chicken breasts
3 tung ku (dong gu) mushrooms
2 oz dried fa cai moss
1 quart chicken broth
3 thin slices fresh ginger
1 scallion
1 tsp salt

For the sauce:
1/2 tsp monosodium glutamate (optional)
1/2–1 tsp salt
1 tbsp rice wine
1 tbsp sesame seed oil
generous pinch freshly ground pepper
1 tbsp cornstarch, water chestnut powder or
    potato flour

Time: 1 hour

Soak the dried mushrooms in warm water for
20–30 minutes; drain, then cut off and discard
their stalks. Soak the dried moss until reconstituted, and drain.

Cut the ham into matchstick strips 1/8 in wide
and 1 1/4 in long. Do likewise with the prepared
cucumber, carrot, bamboo shoots, red pepper, chicken, and mushrooms.

Bring the broth to a boil with the peeled ginger and trimmed scallion; blanch one at a
time, the chicken and the various vegetables,
mushrooms and moss, removing each batch
from the broth with a slotted ladle after 2 minutes and draining well. (The ham is not to be
blanched.) Using a selection of all the prepared ingredients, including the ham, make
up bundles and tie round the middle with the
moss. Heat the sauce ingredients gently
together in a small saucepan, mixing the
thickening agent with a little cold water before
stirring it in. Simmer for a few minutes to
reduce somewhat and then pour over the bundles, coating them evenly.

Fa cai is a hair-fine, dark purple sea moss,
black when dried. It is served as a symbol of
prosperity, particularly at Chinese New Year
celebrations and business dinners.

EIGHT-TREASURE RICE

八宝饭
bā bǎo fàn

1 1/2 cups glutinous rice
1/2 cup sugar
1/2 cup (2 oz) melted fresh pork fat, shortening
    or butter
1/2 oz candied lotus seeds
1/2 oz seedless white raisins
2 oz candied winter melon, cut into thin
    strips
2 oz candied watermelon, cut into thin strips
2 oz candied jujubes, red dates or dried
    prunes
2 oz candied gingko nuts
1 cup soy conserve or sweet red bean paste

Time: 1 1/4 hours + soaking time

All the above ingredients can be bought at
good Chinese foodstores and at many of the
larger Oriental specialty shops.

Place the rice in a sieve, rinse well under
running cold water then leave to soak in a
bowl of cold water for 5–6 hours; drain. Bring 7
cups water to a boil in a large saucepan, add
the sugar, and boil until dissolved. Sprinkle
the rice into the boiling water and boil until
very tender (approx. 20 minutes). Alternatively, place the rice in a bowl lightly greased
with butter and steam over a small amount of
water. When the rice is done, drain well and
stir in the melted pork fat or shortening.
Grease a deep bowl or mold generously with
shortening or butter (choose a container
which will fit in your steamer) and place a
selection of the candied fruits and nuts attractively over the base and sides. Pack half the rice
fairly firmly in a thick layer over the bottom
and sides, taking care not to dislodge the candied ingredients. Place the conserve or sweet
bean paste in the central well of the rice, then
cover with the remaining rice, again packing it
fairly firmly.

Place in the steamer, cover, and steam for
30 minutes. Turn out carefully onto a serving
plate; eat hot or cold, sliced like a pie.

CHON YANG CAKE

重阳糕
chóng yáng gāo

2 1/4 lb (9 cups) glutinous rice flour
2 1/4 cups sugar
10 oz (approx. 2 cups) very finely chopped
    dates or candied chestnuts (marrons
    glacés)
1/2 cup + 2 tbsp melted fresh pork fat,
    shortening or butter
3 oz sesame seeds

Chinese snake wine is a spirit distilled from one or more types of cereal grain. The alcoholic content is difficult to determine, but it is safe always to assume that it is quite high, more than 30 degrees. It can be flavored with herbs, aromatic roots or scented with flowers. The most famous snake wines are Sanshejiu (three snakes wine) and Wushejiu (five snakes wine). Large glass jars containing some

Chinese "wine" are filled with three types or five types of snake, definitely whole and preferably live! More wine is added until the jar is completely full. The jar is sealed and left for at least 40 days. The liquid is then poured off and strained. The wine is pale yellow in color, pleasant tasting and reputed to be an excellent remedy for rheumatism.

WINTER RICE PUDDING

腊 八 粥
là bā zhōu

3/4 cup glutinous rice
1 tbsp fresh, unroasted peanuts
1 tbsp pine nuts
1 tbsp green soy bean sprouts
1 tbsp red soy bean sprouts
1 tbsp dried lotus seeds (or 2 tbsp drained, canned lotus seeds)
1/4 lb candied jujubes
2 oz candied green winter melon
2 oz candied water melon
1/2 cup sugar

Time: 1 hour 10 minutes + soaking time

Place the rice in a sieve and rinse well under running cold water. Place in a bowl of cold water and soak for 4 hours. Soak the peanuts, pine nuts, and lotus seeds (if using dried lotus seeds) in a separate bowl of cold water for the same length of time. Pour scant 4 1/2 cups water into the wok and add the sugar; boil until dissolved, then stir in the drained rice, nuts, and lotus seeds (if canned seeds are used, drain them also). Add the soy bean sprouts, and chopped candied fruit. Bring to a boil, then simmer very gently for about 1 hour until tender, stirring frequently.

La ba zhou rice pudding was traditionally eaten on the eighth day of the twelfth month of the lunar calendar, the day of Là when sacrifices wer made to the gods. Legend has it that this dish was also given to those condemned to death, as their last meal before they were executed.

1 1/2 oz pine nuts
1 1/2 oz quaz ren (roasted melon seeds)
2 candied green plums, chopped
2 candied red plums, chopped
small pinch powdered bay leaves

Time: 1 hour

Mix together the rice flour, sugar, and dates (or chestnuts). Set aside one third of this mixture and work in the melted pork fat or shortening. Mix just enough cold water into the remaining two thirds of the mixture to make a firm, smooth but fairly soft dough. Divide the dough mixed with fat in two; use one half to line the bottom of a greased cake pan or pie dish (make sure this is not too deep to fit in the steamer with the lid on). Cover with all the dough mixed with water, spreading this out so that it covers the bottom layer of dough in a thick layer. Finally, spread out the remaining half of the dough containing fat, to cover the middle layer.

Sprinkle the surface with the sesame seeds, melon seeds, pine nuts, and the chopped candied plums; finally, sprinkle over the bay leaf powder. Use a knife dipped in cold water to mark out slices on the surface of the cake, making shallow incisions radiating outward from the center.

Place in the steamer, cover, and steam for 20 minutes. This cake is traditional fare for the feast of Ion Ion, held on September 9: Ion Ion was a hermit and soothsayer active during the Han dynasty who had warned that this date was inauspicious. As time went by the custom gradually developed of visiting the temples in order to spend the whole of this "unlucky" day praying for protection. A picnic was taken and eaten as part of the traditional proceedings; this substantial cake was one of several foods which it was customary to eat on such occasions.

GREEN SOYBEAN FLOUR CAKE

绿 豆 糕
lü dòu gāo

5 cups green soybean flour
2 1/2 cups sugar
3/4 cup all-purpose flour
1/2 cup sesame seed oil
1 oz powdered bay leaves
1/2 cup soy conserve or sweet red bean paste

Time: 45 minutes

Mix both types of flour with the sugar and work in just enough sesame seed oil to form a soft, smooth dough which will hold its own shape. Grease the inside of a cake pan with a little sesame oil and sprinkle the bottom and sides with the powdered bay leaves. Divide the dough into four equal parts; use one to cover the bottom of the cake pan. Spread one third of the soybean conserve all over the dough. Cover with the second quarter of dough, pressing down quite firmly to adhere to the conserve. Repeat these two steps until all the ingredients have been used; the last, top, layer of the cake will be a dough layer.

Place the pan in the steamer, cover, and steam for 15 minutes.

When the cake is cooked but still hot, a little more sesame seed oil can be sprinkled over the surface.

PEANUTS WITH SEAWEED *

苔菜花生
tái cài huā shēng

1/2 lb roasted peanuts
4 seaweed leaves
3 tbsp sugar
3 tbsp oil

Time: 10 minutes

Heat the seaweed leaves on a griddle or under the broiler at low heat until they are completely dry. Heat the oil in the wok or skillet, fry the peanuts over high heat for 2 minutes, stirring and turning continuously; crumble the nori leaves into the wok or pan, and stir-fry briefly; remove the nuts and seaweed from the wok or pan, draining well, and mix with the sugar. This preparation is served between courses at a Chinese meal or eaten with tea as a sweet snack between meals.

159

SOUTHERN CHINA

華南菜

THE SOUTHERN SCHOOL:
"CANTONESE" COOKING

162

Southern China, and especially the coastal areas along the South China Sea, benefit from a climate which varies from tropical to sub-tropical and enables several crops of an enormous variety of foodstuffs to be grown each year from astonishingly fertile agricultural land. The Hsi Chiang (Pearl River) in Guangdong province and the coastal plains of Fukien are among the most productive areas. In this southern region, as in the eastern region, population is particularly dense along the coasts, in Kwangsi, Kuangtung, and Fukien; the great cities of Canton (Guangzhou), Nanning, Macao, and Anjoy are particularly crowded, and nowhere more so than Hong Kong, where successive waves of enterprising and hardworking immigrants from China (including vast numbers of economic and political refugees over the years as well as more recent highly publicized non-Chinese migrants) have prospered and swelled the already teeming Chinese population, keeping Kowloon, Victoria, and the entire colony, despite its years as a British Crown possession, very much a Chinese city. Hong

Kong is a melting pot in which all the regions of China meet and mingle, typified by its cuisine which draws on the varied, heterogeneous, and cosmopolitan inhabitants.

Not only is the land amazingly prodigal in South China, the sea teems with seafood and fish farms produce large quantities of freshwater fish and other water creatures; pig rearing is practised on a large scale, as is poultry farming, all providing a seemingly endless supply of fresh basic materials which are sent to the markets of the towns and cities.

The fact that this region of China has long been open to foreign influences has added another dimension to the existing flair and enthusiasm of its native people for superb cooking; not only have they been influenced over the centuries by Arabs and Europeans but, of course, also by visitors from the other regions of China. Adopting only the best from each culture, the cooks of this area have evolved tremendous skill and have become famous not only for preparing dishes from their own native province but for perfecting

those from elsewhere in China. Considerable numbers of Chinese from the Pearl River delta (once the haunt of pirates) emigrated all over the world during the nineteenth and twentieth centuries. Driven by hardship, political or other types of persecution and by a spirit of adventure they have founded communities in the United States, Canada, Australia, New Zealand, and other countries all over the world; many of their descendants live in "Chinatowns" in the great cities of their adopted lands and they have remained faithful to the cooking which their forefathers brought with them, often opening restaurants which spread the popularity of Cantonese cooking, to the point where many Westerners equate the southern school of cooking with Chinese cuisine in general.

Only the most carefully selected leaves are gathered to make one of the most highly prized varieties of tea, known as "silver needles."

Two centuries of British rule have left their mark on the cooking in Hong Kong in particular, betrayed by the presence in many dishes of Worcestershire sauce, tomato ketchup, and other Anglo-Saxon favorites assimilated and developed with that particular flair which characterizes the cooks of this region.

Some foodstuffs are basic to the diet of the area: rice is the most important cereal crop grown in the south and is the main everyday food and staple for the people. Indeed, a common southern greeting, equivalent to "Good morning!" or "How are you?" is "Have you had rice?", with the same resonance as an allusion to "daily bread" for a Westerner. The exceptionally favorable climate for rice growing means that several crops can be harvested each year. This same hot climate, varying little between summer and winter, with plentiful summer rains, turns the area into one vast greenhouse, where vegetables, tropical, citrus and many other fruits, including bananas and lychees, grow in profusion. Fukien is famous for its tea plantations, producing a very high-quality product. The indented coastline, with its many creeks, coves and bays, offers particularly good fishing, especially between the large islands of Hainan and Taiwan: fish are caught in nets strung between reefs or hung between stakes set in the seabed, while crustaceans are lured by lamps shining into the sea from small sampans. Deep-sea fishing accounts for the great majority of fish and seafood caught: the fishermen live with their families aboard sailing junks and sampans and have passed on their skill from generation to generation. Their boats, wind-powered with their great sails, although often nowadays with the addition of engine power, still have to confront the terrifying typhoons which can blow up so suddenly in this area. A salient characteristic of Cantonese food is that the creatures used to provide meat and fish etc. are brought to market live, purchased live, and only killed just before they are to be cooked. This is most important to the south Chinese, for they recognize that fish, seafood, and most other flesh tastes sweeter and better if cooked at its peak of freshness. This also helps to explain why Cantonese food is so often a pale shadow of its true nature when prepared elsewhere, in countries where it is difficult to buy vegetables gathered only hours before and where the other raw materials may have been stored for some considerable time. The recipes in this section are those which can be very successfully prepared at home by the Western cook and will help to illustrate why the cooks of Canton (Guangzhou) are considered the most inventive and inspired of all the practitioners of this art in China. The Cantonese have certainly mastered the

Fishermen intent on landing a good night's catch, illuminated by the faint glow of their oil lamps as they fish from little bamboo rafts.

art of stir-frying and the expression "fragrance of the wok" hails from this part of China: ingredients are cooked in a little oil over high heat while being turned repeatedly; they are added to the wok in the correct order so that each will end up cooked to just the right point (although some may already have been quickly cooked in oil or briefly blanched in water). This deliciously refined fare, the ultimate expression of "fast food", with its insistence on the freshest ingredients and

164

flavored with the bare minimum of additions such as ginger and onion in order to complement and enhance, rather than overwhelm, the superb natural flavor of the raw materials, also lends itself to other more complicated and time-consuming preparations and techniques such as pre-cooking in various forms and "slow cooking". Many varied flavors, go to make a sauce; the use of sugar, vinegar, wines, spices in various combinations, with the addition of commercially prepared sauces (some of which are Western in origin) and the combination of all sorts of apparently disparate flavors, lead to such delicious end results as sweet-sour sauces.

One of the best illustrations of the Cantonese cooks' skills is provided by the myriad versions of dim-sum, those delectable, delicate morsels which seem to be as much an art form as food, usually steamed and then enjoyed for breakfast or snacks and for which most people who have tried them acquire a permanent fondness. Southern Chinese cooking certainly seems to offer the best of all culinary worlds.

Rice fields near Guilin. This is a unique landscape, a strange configuration of tall, narrow limestone towers with pointed tips caused by a geological upheaval which lifted the seabed out of the sea, only to be gradually worn away into these shapes by 300 million years of erosion. Guilin was founded by Shi Huangdi in 214 B.C.

SPRING ROLLS *

春卷

chūn juǎn

Makes approx. 8 spring roll wrappers:
1 cup fine cake flour or all-purpose flour
1 cup unbleached bread flour
1 cup water
pinch salt
oil for greasing

Filling (first version):
¼ lb shredded chicken or lean pork
1½ tbsp cornstarch or potato flour
¼ cup oil
2 oz shredded bamboo shoots
2 tung ku (dong gu) mushrooms, pre-soaked, stems removed, caps cut into thin strips
1 small leek or 2 scallions, shredded
1 tbsp sugar
pinch salt
½ tsp monosodium glutamate (optional)
1½ tsp dark soy sauce
1½ tsp light soy sauce
3 tbsp chicken broth
3 tbsp rice wine

Filling (second version):
2 oz meat (pork, chicken or beef)
1 tbsp cornstarch or all-purpose flour
¼ cup oil
¼ lb Chinese cabbage (or ordinary white cabbage)
1 oz bamboo shoots
½ medium-sized onion
2 tung ku (dong gu) mushrooms
3 tbsp rice wine

To assemble and cook the spring rolls:
1½ tbsp all-purpose flour
1½ tbsp water
oil for frying

Time: 1 hour + 1 hour resting time for the batter

Mix and then sift the two types of flour and the salt together into a large mixing bowl; gradually work in as much of the water as is required to make a fairly thick pouring batter; leave to stand for at least 1 hour. Soak the mushrooms in warm water for 20–30 minutes.

Prepare the meat, mix with the cornstarch to coat thoroughly but very lightly, and shake off any excess; leave to stand for 5 minutes.

For the first type of filling: trim and shred the bamboo shoots (or drain and shred if canned); drain the mushrooms, remove and discard the stalks, and cut the caps into very thin strips. Finely chop the leek. Heat the oil in the wok and stir-fry the meat briefly over high heat, add the bamboo shoots and mushrooms and continue stir-frying for 1 minute.

Mix all the remaining ingredients listed under this first filling, add to the wok, and continue stir-frying until all the liquid has evaporated; stir in the chopped leek and draw aside from the heat. Leave to cool.

For the second filling: mix the meat with the cornstarch or all-purpose flour as in the first choice of filling. Stir-fry the meat briefly as for the first version, then add the prepared and finely shredded cabbage, bamboo shoots, mushrooms, and onions; stir-fry for a further 2 minutes, add the rice wine and cook until this has evaporated completely; set aside to cool.

Make the wrappers: use a cast-iron or non-stick omelet skillet about 6 in in diameter. If using a cast-iron skillet, lightly rub the inside with fine sandpaper, wipe with a clean dry cloth, then heat until the iron gives off a very little smoke and the surface acquires faint rainbow reflections. Dip a clean cloth in oil and grease the inside of the skillet. Nonstick pans should not be overheated and need no preparing other than, perhaps, a wipe inside with the cloth dipped in oil. Pour about ¼ cup of the prepared and rested pancake batter into the skillet and immediately tilt this way and that to make sure the batter forms the thinnest possible skin of even thickness all over the bottom of the skillet; turn once the batter has

set (but not colored) and finish cooking or simply continue cooking for a little longer on the first side and then slide out of the pan. Repeat this operation until all the batter has been used, stacking the wrappers on top of one another and wiping the skillet with the oil-dipped cloth at frequent intervals. Packets of good spring roll wrappers (usually called spring roll skins) are sold in most Oriental stores.

Assemble the spring rolls: place a wrapper or skin on the work surface (if using square skins, have a corner facing toward you); place 1–1½ tbsp of the prepared filling fairly close to the edge or corner nearest you, spreading the mixture in a fairly thick oval or rectangle. Fold the edge nearest you over the filling and roll away from you, folding both right and left "sides" inward to form a neat packet. Make a paste by mixing 1½ tbsp flour with 1½ tbsp cold water, stir in 3 tbsp boiling water and brush this around the edges of the exposed surface of the "top" section of the wrapper before completing the wrapping of the roll; this will seal it securely. Heat sufficient oil to semi deep-fry or deep-fry until very hot (350–360°F) and fry the spring rolls 2 or 3 at a time so that they have room to float in the oil for 5 minutes or until pale golden brown and crisp. Serve without delay, while still very hot.

Spring rolls provide a good example of frugal Chinese cooking which has become part of the great classical repertoire. The filling of the original, poor man's spring rolls consisted mainly of vegetables, in the traditional Cantonese tradition. Fillings can vary greatly according to region and preference. One version adds crabmeat to the vegetable base given above. Wrappers are sometimes made with a richer batter: 2 cups flour, 3 eggs, a pinch of salt and 2 tbsp sesame oil, diluted if necessary into a pouring batter with a little water or soy milk. Wrappers can also be made from an egg pasta dough, rolled out and cut to size, not pre-fried as pancakes. Spring rolls can be pre-fried in hot oil for 3 or 4 minutes until very pale golden brown, then removed and drained, and re-fried in hotter oil for 1–2 minutes until golden brown and crisp.

STEAMED VEGETARIAN DUMPLINGS WITH SOY FLOUR NOODLES

粉丝素饺
fěn sī sù jiǎo

For the wrapper dough:
1³/₄ cups rice flour (tian mian)
1 cup hot water
pinch salt
1 tbsp oil

For the filling:
2 oz soy flour noodles
4 tung ku (dong gu) mushrooms
1 oz mu er mushrooms
2 oz carrots
1 scallion
2 oz Savoy cabbage
2 oz bamboo shoots
1 tbsp cornstarch or potato flour

For the sauce:
¹/₂ tbsp salt
¹/₂ tsp monosodium glutamate (optional)
1¹/₂ tbsp soy sauce
1¹/₂ tbsp sesame seed oil
1¹/₂ tbsp rice wine
generous pinch freshly ground pepper

Time: 1 hour 10 minutes

Soak both kinds of mushrooms in warm water for 20–30 minutes. Soak the soy flour noodles in water for 10 minutes. Mix just enough water into the flour and salt to make a smooth, elastic dough which can be kneaded easily. Leave to rest for a few minutes, then add the oil and knead well. Leave to rest again for a few minutes.

Finely chop the scallion. Wash, dry, and trim the cabbage; peel the carrot and bamboo shoots where necessary; if using canned bamboo shoots, drain well; blanch these three vegetables in boiling water for 2 minutes, drain well, and chop finely.

Chop the soy flour noodles into very short lengths. Drain the mushrooms and remove and discard the stems; chop the caps very finely. Mix all these ingredients thoroughly with the cornstarch (or alternative).

Roll out the dough into a very thin sheet and cut out into disks about 3–3¹/₂ in in diameter. Place a little of the filling just below the center of each disk, enclose the filling and pinch together to seal.

Mix the sauce ingredients in a small saucepan and heat gently.

Place the dumplings in the steamer compartment, cover, and steam for 10 minutes. Serve, sprinkled with the sauce.

CANTONESE DUMPLINGS *
虾 饺
xiā jiāo

For the wrappers:
1³/₄ cups rice flour (tian mian)
1 cup boiling water
pinch salt
1 tsp oil

For the filling:
1 cup peeled shrimp
¹/₄ lb bamboo shoots
2 oz fresh pork belly
¹/₂ tsp monosodium glutamate (optional)
¹/₂ tsp salt
1 tbsp cornstarch or potato flour
1 tbsp sesame seed oil
pinch pepper
pinch sugar

Time: 1¹/₂ hours

Mix sufficient boiling water with the flour and salt to make a smooth, elastic dough; when well mixed, leave to stand for a few minutes then work in the oil; knead thoroughly. Leave to rest in a bowl, covered with a clean cloth. Add the pork belly to a saucepan full of boiling water and boil gently for 30 minutes; drain and dry then cut into tiny dice. Cut the bamboo shoots into dice of the same size.

Rinse and dry the shrimp if wished and chop very finely. Mix the meat, bamboo shoots, and shrimp and stir in the monosodium glutamate (if used), salt, cornstarch, sesame oil, pepper, and sugar.

Roll out the dough into a very thin sheet on a lightly floured board with a floured rolling pin; cut out into disks approx. 3–3¹/₂ in in diameter using a cookie cutter or the rim of a glass. Place a little of the filling just below the center of each disk and bring the edges of the disk together, pleating the fuller side and pinching them together to secure.

Line one or more steamer compartments with a clean cloth, or cabbage leaves, place the dumplings on this lining, pinched edges uppermost in a single layer, cover, and steam for 10 minutes.

This is one item in the famous Chinese dim sum range, eaten as snacks or as part of light meals; the Cantonese style of cooking, light and full of variety, lends itself well to these irresistible tidbits.

minutes. Skin the chicken breasts and remove any gristly strings or tough filaments; chop very finely. Trim the scallion and chop very finely together with the water chestnuts and the peeled carrot. Drain the mushrooms well, cut off the stalks and discard, and chop the caps coarsely. Heat the oil in the wok, stir-fry the scallion briefly, add the chicken and stir-fry; add the water chestnuts, carrots, peas, and mushrooms and continue stir-frying for a minute or so. Mix all the remaining ingredients with the cornstarch and stir into the contents of the wok; cook over lower heat for 5 minutes, then remove and leave to cool.

Sift the rice flour, cornstarch or alternative and the salt into a bowl; mix in sufficient boiling water to make a firm, very smooth dough. Leave to rest for a few minutes, then work in the oil. Knead well, then leave to rest again for a few minutes. Roll out into a very thin sheet on a lightly floured board; cut out into disks 3–3½ in in diameter using a cookie cutter or a glass. Place a little of the filling just below the center of each disk and enclose as described in the previous recipe. Line the steamer compartment with cabbage, lettuce leaves, waxed paper or a clean cloth. Arrange the dumplings in a single layer, cover, and steam for 6–7 minutes, by which time the dough of the wrappers should have turned almost transparent and be very glossy. This is another item in the dim sum range.

SLOW BRAISED YUN TUN

馄饨汤
Yún tūng tāng

For the wrapper dough:
2 cups all-purpose flour
1 cup hot water
pinch salt
2½ tbsp shortening
1 egg yolk

For the filling:
½ cup peeled shrimp
½ cup very finely chopped lean pork
½ tsp salt
½ tsp monosodium glutamate (optional)
1 heaping tsp cornstarch or potato flour
1 tbsp finely chopped bamboo shoots
1 tbsp finely chopped water chestnuts
1 tbsp finely chopped raw chicken

For cooking and extra flavoring:
1 leek
2 tung ku (dong gu) mushrooms
¼ cup oil
½ cup water

Time: 1 hour 20 minutes

CANDIED DUMPLINGS WITH CHICKEN *

鸡丁水晶包
jī dīng shǔi jīng bāo

For the filling:
10 oz chicken breasts
½ scallion
¼ cup oil
3 tung ku (dong gu) mushrooms
3 water chestnuts
1 medium-sized carrot
⅓ cup peas
1 tsp sugar

½ tsp monosodium glutamate (optional)
1 tsp salt
1 tsp light soy sauce
1 tsp sesame seed oil
pinch freshly ground ginger
1 tsp cornstarch or potato flour

For the dough:
1¾ cups rice flour (tian mian)
¼ cup cornstarch or potato flour
1 tsp salt
1 cup boiling water
2½ tbsp oil

Time: 1 hour 10 minutes

Soak the mushrooms in warm water for 20–30

Soak the tung ku mushrooms in warm water to soften and reconstitute while you prepare and finely chop all the filling ingredients. Combine all the wrapper dough ingredients and knead to a very smooth dough (you may need a little less or more water, depending on the flour used). Leave the dough to stand for a few minutes, then roll out into a fairly thin sheet; cut out into disks 3–3½ in in diameter using a cookie cutter or the rim of a glass tumbler or cup. (If preferred, use bought wonton wrappers.) Mix all the filling ingredients together to make a smooth mixture. Place a little of this in the center of each disk and enclose, bringing the edges of the disks together, pinching the edges gently together to seal the dumplings securely. Drain the mushrooms, cut off the stems and discard; cut each cap into quarters. Trim the leek and wash thoroughly; dry and cut into very thin, short strips. Heat ¼ cup oil in a fireproof casserole dish or earthenware cooking pot; fry the leeks briefly then add ½ cup water and cover the bottom of the dish or pot with the dumplings (pinched edges uppermost). When the liquid has reached boiling point cover and simmer gently for 10 minutes.

CELLOPHANE NOODLES WITH CHOPPED SHRIMP *

粉丝虾肉

fěn sī xiā ròu

¼ lb cellophane noodles (bean threads)
1 cup peeled, chopped shrimp
¼ lb crisp lettuce or Savoy cabbage
1 tbsp finely chopped scallion
1 tsp finely chopped fresh ginger
6 tbsp oil
1 tsp salt
pinch monosodium glutamate (optional)
1 tbsp light soy sauce
1 tbsp sesame seed oil
¼ cup chicken broth

Time: 40 minutes

Soak the cellophane noodles (bean threads) in water for 10 minutes and drain well. Heat the oil in the wok and sweat the scallion and ginger; add the shrimp and the washed, dried, and very finely chopped lettuce or cabbage. Mix in all the flavorings. Add 1 quart water and when this has come to a boil, add the noodles; stir and leave to simmer, uncovered, over moderate heat until the liquid has considerably reduced. Serve.

171

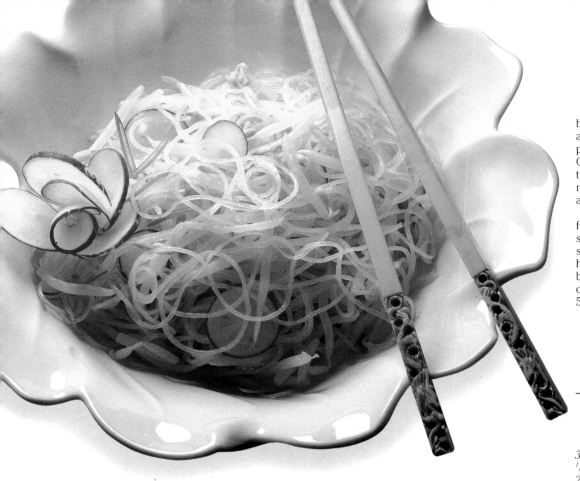

be visible on the surface which will have the appearance of being pitted with shallow "dimples" where the air bubbles have escaped. Once you have grown used to cooking a particular variety of rice by this method, you will not need to lift the lid to check even this once; accurate timing is the key to success.

Turn out the heat, and leave covered for a further 5–10 minutes, by which time the rice should have absorbed all the moisture and should be tender. If cooking on solid electric hotplates which take a long time to cool, it is best to remove the saucepan from the source of heat or use a heat-diffusing pad for the final 5–10 minutes' absorption.

FRIED RICE WITH SHRIMP

虾仁什锦炒饭
xiā rén shí jǐn chǎo fàn

3 cups plain boiled rice (see left)
$^1/_2$ cup peeled shrimp
2 oz fresh button mushrooms
1 zucchini
$^1/_2$ carrot
5 or 6 French beans
$^1/_2$ scallion
$^1/_3$ cup oil
$^1/_2$ tsp salt
$^1/_2$ tsp monosodium glutamate (optional)
generous pinch freshly ground pepper
1 tsp light soy sauce
1 tbsp rice wine

Time: 30 minutes

Wipe the button mushrooms with a damp cloth, wash and trim the zucchini, and peel the carrot; slice all these vegetables thinly. Cut the French beans into short lengths. Heat 3 tbsp of the oil in the wok and stir-fry the shrimp for 1 minute; remove and set aside. Add the remaining oil to the wok and sweat the shredded scallion; add the mushrooms and other vegetables and stir-fry for 3 or 4 minutes over high heat. Return the shrimp to the wok and add the flavorings and seasonings, continuing to stir-fry. Add the rice and stir-fry until very hot; serve.

SOY FLOUR NOODLES FRIED WITH SOYBEAN SPROUTS *

粉丝拌豆芽
fěn sī chǎo dòu yá

$^1/_4$ lb soy flour noodles
$^1/_4$ lb soybean sprouts
1 scallion
1 clove garlic
$^1/_4$ cup oil
2 cups chicken broth or water
$^1/_2$ tsp salt
pinch monosodium glutamate (optional)
1 tbsp rice wine

Time: 35 minutes

Soak the noodles in water for 10 minutes, then drain. Rinse the soybean sprouts and trim off their root ends. Trim and shred the scallion. Heat the oil in the wok, fry the whole peeled, lightly minced garlic clove for 1 minute to flavor the oil, then remove and discard the clove. Add the scallion and stir-fry briefly. Add the soybean sprouts and stir-fry over high heat for 1 minute. Add the noodles, quickly followed by the broth or water then stir in the salt, monosodium glutamate (if used), and the rice wine. Allow to boil for a few minutes until the liquid has reduced and the noodles are very tender (this will not take long). Serve.

PLAIN BOILED RICE

白饭
bái fàn

Desired quantity of Chinese long-grain rice or other good-quality long-grain rice (e.g. Indian basmati rice); allow $2^1/_4$ cups water to every 1 lb uncooked rice, or 1 cup water to 1 cup rice. 1 cup uncooked rice should yield at least $1^1/_4$ times (i.e. more than double) its uncooked bulk, but many varieties expand more.

Time: 30 minutes

Place the rice in a large sieve and hold under running cold water, moving the sieve from side to side and backward and forward to rinse the grains thoroughly. Drain and transfer to a heavy-bottomed saucepan with the appropriate volume of water as above for the absorption method. Do not add any salt. Bring to a boil, stir briefly but thoroughly, and cover with a tight-fitting lid. Turn down the heat extremely low and cook very gently for 12 minutes. Do not remove the lid during this time. By the end of this cooking time, the rice should have absorbed nearly all the liquid, none will

SHRIMP WITH CRISPY RICE

纸包鸡

guō bā xiā rén

1³/₄ cups peeled small shrimp
¹/₃ cup fresh or frozen peas, cooked
8 small crisp rice cakes (guo ba)
oil for frying

Marinade for the shrimp:
1 egg white
¹/₂ tsp salt
¹/₂ tsp sugar
¹/₂ tsp monosodium glutamate (optional)
1 tsp cornstarch or potato flour
1 tbsp cold water

For the sauce:
3 tbsp oil
¹/₄ cup tomato ketchup
1 tsp salt
1 tsp sugar
¹/₂ tsp monosodium glutamate (optional)
pinch freshly ground pepper
1¹/₂ tbsp wine vinegar
1 cup stock
1 tbsp rice wine
1¹/₂ tbsp cornstarch or potato flour

Time: 45 minutes

Rinse and dry the shrimp. Whisk the egg whites and fold in the salt, sugar, monosodium glutamate (if used), and the cornstarch or potato flour mixed with the cold water. Add the shrimp to this frothy mixture and leave them to marinate for 10 minutes.

Heat plenty of oil in the wok or deep-fryer until very hot but not smoking; fry the shrimp in this for 1 minute only. Remove.

Empty the wok and heat 3 tbsp fresh oil; add the shrimp and peas together, stir in the ketchup, salt, sugar, monosodium glutamate (if used), and pepper. Add the vinegar, broth, and rice wine. Continue cooking for a few minutes, uncovered, to allow the liquid to reduce a little then stir in the cornstarch mixed with a little cold water. Cook for a minute or two longer, then serve in a heated dish with the fried rice cakes on top.

Rice cakes: semi deep-fry or deep-fry the rice cakes in very hot oil: they will puff up and turn golden brown. Take them out of the oil with a slotted spoon and drain well. Keep warm while you prepare the dish and then place on top of the shrimp, peas, and sauce.

174

RICE IN LOTUS LEAVES

什锦荷叶饭
shí jīn hé yè fàn

2 tung ku (dong gu) mushrooms
6 tbsp oil
¹/₂ cup peeled shrimp
2 oz pork tenderloin
2 oz roast pork tenderloin (see p. 218)
2 oz Cantonese duck (see p. 211)
2 eggs
1 tbsp finely chopped scallion
approx. 4 cups plain boiled rice (see p. 172)
1 tsp salt
pinch sugar
1 tsp monosodium glutamate (optional)
1 tbsp light soy sauce
pinch pepper
1 tbsp rice wine
1 tbsp sesame seed oil
1 tsp oyster sauce
4 lotus leaves, pre-soaked in warm water

Time: 40 minutes

Soak the mushrooms in warm water for 20 minutes; when they are soft, remove and discard the stalks and chop the caps roughly. Chop the shrimp coarsely and do likewise with the raw and roast meats. Heat the oil in the wok and fry the shrimp and the raw pork.

Beat the eggs in a bowl with the scallion, add the roast meats, the fried pork and shrimp, the rice, mushrooms, salt, sugar, monosodium glutamate (if used), soy sauce, pepper, wine, sesame seed oil, and oyster sauce. Mix very well.

Blanch the lotus leaves in a large pan of boiling water until soft and pliable, drain, and carefully spread out flat on the working surface; place one quarter of the prepared filling in the center of each leaf, fold up to form neat parcels, tie with kitchen string or raffia (not too tightly) and place in the steamer; cover and steam for 10 minutes.

HE FEN RICE NOODLES

干炒牛肉河粉
gàn chǎo niú ròu hé fěn

¹/₂ lb rice noodles
approx. 2 cups oil
¹/₂ lb lean beef
pinch bicarbonate of soda
pinch baking soda
1¹/₂ tsp cornstarch or potato flour
1 egg white
¹/₄ cup soy sauce

1 tbsp fermented black soybeans
2 oz bean sprouts
2 oz bamboo shoots
1 scallion
2 thin slices fresh ginger
oil for frying
pinch salt
pinch freshly ground pepper
pinch monosodium glutamate (optional)
¹/₂ cup broth
1¹/₂ tbsp cornstarch or potato flour
1 tbsp sesame seed oil

Time: 1 hour

Add the noodles to a saucepan full of boiling water and cook for 2 minutes; drain, refresh under running cold water, drain again, and turn into a bowl containing about 1 tbsp oil; stir to coat the noodles lightly.

Cut the meat into very thin slices measuring 1¹/₄ × 2 in; mix the bicarbonate of soda, baking soda, cornstarch or alternative, egg white, and 1¹/₂ tbsp of the soy sauce, add the beef to this, and mix. Leave to marinate for 30 minutes.

Rinse the bean sprouts, pick off any ungerminated seeds and empty seed cases, and chop the sprouts. Rinse the bamboo shoots if fresh, drain if canned; cut the scallion, ginger, and bamboo shoots into thin strips.

Heat the oil in the wok until very hot; fry the beef for 5 minutes and remove with a slotted spoon, draining well. Pour all but 3 tbsp of the oil out of the wok and stir-fry half the scallion and ginger in this remaining oil; add the soy sprouts, noodles, salt, and pepper and stir-fry briefly; transfer to the serving dish. Wipe the inside of the wok and heat just over 1 tbsp oil; stir-fry the soybeans and the remaining scallion and ginger; add the meat, the remaining soy sauce, the monosodium glutamate (if used), and broth and cook over high heat until the liquid has somewhat reduced. Stir in the cornstarch mixed with a very little cold water to thicken the remaining liquid, add the sesame seed oil, stir and spoon over the noodles.

SESAME-STUFFED GLUTINOUS RICE BALLS *

麻蓉汤圆
má róng tān yuán

For the filling:
1 cup sesame seeds
¹/₂ cup chopped unroasted, unsalted peanuts
¹/₂ cup sugar
¹/₄ lb sesame seed paste

For the dough:
3¹/₂ cups glutinous rice flour

¹/₂ cup rice flour (tian mian)
1 cup boiling water

For the sweet broth:
1¹/₄ cups sugar
4 thin slices fresh ginger
¹/₂ tsp pure vanilla extract

Time: 1¹/₂ hours

Heat 2¹/₂ tbsp oil in the wok and fry the sesame seeds and the peanuts until lightly colored and the sesame seeds start to release their distinctive aroma. Turn off the heat and immediately stir in the sugar and the sesame seed paste, blending together very thoroughly. Sift the glutinous rice flour and the low-gluten rice flour together into a bowl; mix in sufficient boiling water to give a smooth dough that can be handled easily. Knead well, then leave to rest for approx. 20–30 minutes. Roll out the dough into a thin sheet on a lightly floured surface; cut out into disks approx. 3–3¹/₂ in in diameter, using a cookie cutter. Place a little of the filling in the center of each and completely enclose, forming a ball.

Pour 6 cups water into a large saucepan, add the sugar, ginger, and vanilla, bring to a boil, then add the dumplings and boil until they bob up to the surface (3–4 minutes); remove, drain, and serve.

PROSPERITY BROTH
状元及第汤
zhuàng yuán jí dì tāng

6 tung ku (dong gu) mushrooms
3 thin slices fresh ginger
1 crisp medium-sized carrot
¹/₄ lb Chinese cabbage
6 scallops (fresh or frozen)
¹/₂ cup peeled shrimp
2 oz canned abalone
¹/₄ lb prepared squid (fresh or frozen)
2 duck gizzards (optional)
2 oz gristle (tendons) from pig's trotter (optional)
¹/₄ lb pork tenderloin
2 quarts broth
1 tsp salt
1 tsp monosodium glutamate (optional)
pinch freshly ground pepper
1 tbsp sesame seed oil

Time: 1 hour

Soak the mushrooms for 20 minutes in warm water; when they are soft and reconstituted, remove and discard their stalks. Wash, trim, and peel the carrot if necessary; cut into very thin slices. Rinse, dry, and shred the cabbage;

176

cut the peeled fresh ginger slices into very small, thin strips. Coarsely chop the shrimp. Wash the scallops; if using fresh, take them off their shells, and use both the white "cushion" of meat and the orange coral; if using frozen, thaw first (only the white meat will be present). Cut the scallops, the drained abalone, and the squid into thin strips. Do likewise with the gizzards and tendons (if used) and the pork; the Chinese like the contrast between the very tender ingredients and the last four, more chewy, items; blanch these (or only the pork if you opt to use it without the gizzards and tendons) for a few minutes in a large pan of boiling water to tenderize. The blanching water can then be used to blanch all the other

ingredients for 2 minutes; remove and drain well. Discard the water.

Bring the broth to a boil in the large saucepan, add all the ingredients (blanched or not), the salt, monosodium glutamate (if used), pepper, and sesame seed oil. Simmer for 15 minutes, skimming off any scum which rises to the surface. The resulting soup, full of interesting contrasting and complementary tastes and textures, is served hot.

In ancient China a state competition was held every three years to decide who would be awarded the top ministerial posts (zhuang yuang means "winner"). Part of the prize was the offer of one of the emperor's daughters in matrimony.

CHICKEN AND GINSENG BROTH

人参鸡汤

rén shēn jī tāng

1 chicken weighing approx. 2¹/₄ lb
1 oz dried ginseng root
2 quarts full-flavored broth (e.g. chicken, ham etc.)
¹/₂–1 tsp salt
¹/₂ tsp monosodium glutamate (optional)
¹/₂–1 tsp sugar

Time: 2¹/₂ hours

Soak the ginseng root in cold water for 30 minutes, then chop. Take all the chicken meat off the bone, cut into small pieces, and blanch for a minute or two in boiling water; drain.

Bring the broth to a boil, add the chicken pieces and the ginseng, and simmer over low heat for 2 hours. Shortly before this time is up, add the salt, monosodium glutamate (if used), and sugar. Ladle into small bowls and serve.

SWALLOWS' NEST SOUP

馄饨汤

yàn wō tāng

2 oz dried swallows' nests
2 thin slices fresh ginger
1 scallion
3 cups concentrated homemade chicken,
  pork and ham broth
1 heaping tbsp cornstarch
salt
1 cup chicken velvet (see below)
¹/₂ oz Chinese Gold Coin ham, Virginia ham
  or Westphalian ham

For the chicken velvet:
2 chicken breasts
¹/₂ tbsp salt
2¹/₂ tbsp iced water
2¹/₂ tbsp cornstarch
1 egg white

Time: 1¹/₂ hours

Whole dried swallows' nests are not necessary for this recipe, dried fragments of swallows' nests will do very well and are less expensive; both can be bought in Chinese foodstores. Fill a bowl with warm water, plunge the swallows' nests into it, and soak overnight. Use tweezers to pick out any foreign bodies and then rinse under running hot water (place in a sieve if necessary).

Put the nests in a small saucepan with the ginger, trimmed and coarsely chopped scallion, and just over 1 cup boiling water. Bring back to a boil and simmer for 10 minutes; remove and discard the ginger slices and scallion pieces and drain briefly but not too thoroughly.

Pour the broth into a saucepan and add the nests; bring to a boil, then reduce the heat to a simmer; mix the cornstarch with a very little cold water and stir into the broth; simmer for a few minutes to allow the cornstarch to cook thoroughly and to reduce the liquid a little. Add a little salt if necessary.

Make the chicken velvet: remove the skin, any trace of fat, cartilage or sinews; place the breasts on the chopping board and use a very

sharp, heavy kitchen knife to chop the chicken, adding a few drops of iced water at intervals as you chop it and continuously scooping the chopped chicken back to the center to be chopped again; grinding does not achieve the ideal texture but you can use the food processor to save time (remember to add a few drops of iced water while you process the chicken); when the chicken has been reduced almost to a stiff purée, it is ready.

Transfer the chicken to a bowl and gradually mix in the cornstarch and egg white, stirring continuously; the result will be a feather-light, smooth purée: chicken velvet.

Mix 1 cup of the hot broth gradually with the chicken velvet to moisten it; pour this mixture into the soup and bring back to a boil, stirring continuously. By the time the soup has come to a boil, the chicken will have cooked sufficiently; ladle the soup into a tureen and sprinkle the surface with the finely chopped ham.

You can prepare the first few stages of this soup well in advance: the cooked nests and the chicken velvet can be kept for several hours in the refrigerator until needed.

PORK AND CARROT SOUP

萝卜肉片汤

luó bo ròu pián tāng

¹/₂ lb lean pork
1 tbsp light soy sauce
1 tbsp sesame seed oil
1¹/₂ tsp cornstarch
¹/₂ lb carrots
6¹/₄ cups meat broth
1 stick celery
salt and pepper
1 sprig coriander

Time: 30 minutes

Chop the pork very finely (do not grind) and place in a bowl with the soy sauce, sesame seed oil, and cornstarch. Mix well and leave to stand for 10 minutes. Meanwhile, trim and peel the carrots and cut them into thin round slices. Pour the broth into a large saucepan, add the carrots and the celery stick (cut in half if wished), add a pinch of salt, bring to a boil, and boil for 5 minutes. Add the meat and simmer until the meat and the carrots are tender. Remove and discard the celery and stir in a little more salt if necessary.

Wash, dry, and snip the coriander leaves coarsely with scissors; ladle the soup into bowls or serve in a large tureen, with the coriander and a little freshly ground black pepper sprinkled over the surface.

VELVETY CHICKEN SOUP *

鸡蓉玉米汤

jī róng yù mǐ tāng

5 oz chicken breasts
1 tbsp oil
¹/₂ cup cornstarch
2 quarts (4¹/₄ cups) boiling meat or chicken
  broth
1 tsp salt
¹/₂–1 tsp sugar
¹/₂ tsp monosodium glutamate (optional)
1 tsp sesame seed oil
generous pinch freshly ground white pepper
1 tbsp rice wine
2 egg whites

Time: 30 minutes

Take the skin off the chicken breasts, remove any muscle or tendon strings, cartilage etc. and chop finely with a very sharp heavy knife (do not grind). Heat the wok, add the oil to coat the inside and stir-fry the chicken until it turns white and opaque. Add the boiling hot broth; stir in the cornstarch mixed with ¹/₂ cup cold water. Add the salt, sugar, monosodium glutamate (if used), sesame seed oil, pepper, and rice wine.

Simmer for 15 minutes, stirring continuously. Beat the egg whites until stiff, then whisk vigorously into the soup, adding 1 heaping tbsp at a time. Serve immediately, while very hot.

EGG AND CRAB SOUP

蟹肉蛋花汤

xiè ròu dàn huā tāng

1 crab weighing 1¹/₄–1³/₄ lb or 14 oz (1¹/₂ cups)
  drained canned crabmeat
4 very fresh eggs
3³/₄ cups vegetable broth
pinch monosodium glutamate (optional)
salt
4 chives
1 tbsp rice wine
pinch sugar
1 tbsp cornstarch

Time: 1 hour

If cooking fresh crab yourself, kill it first by pushing a skewer between the eyes and the mouth parts; stuff pieces of dry bread into any openings, broken claws etc., then add to a large pan of boiling salted water and simmer for 15–20 minutes, depending on the size. Leave to cool completely, then pick out all the flesh, remove the grayish feathery gills ("dead men's fingers") and the stomach parts. For this recipe you will not be using the dark, creamy flesh but this is excellent for spreads, sauces etc. Make very sure that you have eliminated any stray pieces of broken shell and cartilage.

Break the eggs into a bowl and stir with a balloon whisk or fork to break up the yolks and mix them with the whites without beating them. Gradually stir in all but 1 cup of the broth, a pinch of monosodium glutamate (if used), and a pinch of salt; do not beat or whisk. Pour this mixture through a fine sieve into a fairly deep heatproof bowl or dish which will fit in your steamer with the lid on (you may have to use 2 receptacles and 2 compartments). Steam for 15 minutes. Flake the crabmeat (drain well if canned) and snip the chives into very short lengths. Bring the remaining broth to a boil in a small saucepan, stir in the rice wine, sugar, and salt; reduce the heat and add the crabmeat, when this is very hot, stir in the cornstarch mixed with a very little cold water and sprinkle in the chives. Stir, then add to the egg broth mixture when this has been steamed; serve.

HÚN TÚN SOUP
馄饨汤
hún tūn tāng

For the wrapper dough:
2 cups all-purpose flour
approx. 1 cup hot water
pinch salt
2¹/₂ tsp shortening

For the filling:
¹/₂ cup peeled shrimp
¹/₂ tsp salt
pinch freshly ground pepper
1¹/₂ tsp cornstarch or potato flour
1 tbsp finely diced bamboo shoots
1 tsp finely chopped fresh ginger
pinch monosodium glutamate (optional)

For the soup:
1 quart (4¹/₄ cups) good chicken broth
pinch salt
1 tbsp sesame seed oil
1 tbsp light soy sauce
1 tbsp finely chopped scallion
pinch freshly ground pepper
8 fresh, crisp lettuce leaves

Time: 1 hour

Mix just enough hot water into the flour and salt to make a firm but not too stiff dough;

work in the shortening, kneading thoroughly until you have a smooth, easily handled, elastic dough; roll out into a thin sheet on a lightly floured work surface and cut out into disks approx. 3–3¹/₂ in in diameter with a cookie cutter or the rim of a glass.

Chop the shrimp or prawns; cut the bamboo shoots into tiny dice and chop the fresh ginger very finely; mix these three ingredients and stir in the other ingredients of the filling until very well blended. Place 1 tsp of this mixture just below the center of each disk and bring the two edges of the disk together with the edges facing upward; you will need to gather or "pleat" one half of the disk; moisten around the edges before pressing together for a very secure seal. Bring the broth to a boil; add the salt, sesame oil, soy sauce, chopped scallion, and pepper. Add the well washed lettuce leaves and the dumplings; when the latter rise to the surface they are done. Ladle some yun tun dumplings, a lettuce leaf, and some broth into each individual bowl.

PORK-STUFFED WONTON IN CHICKEN BROTH *
馄饨汤
hún tún tǎng

For the dough:
1³/₄ cups all-purpose flour
1 egg
pinch salt
cold water as required

For the chicken broth:
chicken neck, feet (if available), carcass, and
  giblets (all raw); if not available use a
  good concentrated chicken consommé or
  best-quality instant chicken broth cubes
5³/₄ cups water
4 black peppercorns
2 small pieces fresh ginger
1 stick celery
1¹/₂ tsp rice wine
salt
¹/₂ leek

For the filling:
1 cup very finely chopped lean pork (e.g
  tenderloin)
¹/₄ cup very finely chopped peeled shrimp
2 finely chopped scallions
1 tbsp soy sauce
1 tbsp minced or grated fresh ginger
1 lightly beaten egg
¹/₂ tsp monosodium glutamate (optional)
2–3 drops sesame seed oil
salt to taste

For the broth:
1 quart chicken broth (made with above
  ingredients)
¹/₄ lb watercress (or same quantity leek)
2¹/₂ tsp soy sauce
¹/₂ tsp monosodium glutamate (optional)
salt
water

Time: 2 hours 50 minutes

Sift the flour into a mound on a large pastry board or working surface; make a well in the center and place in it the lightly beaten egg, salt, and a very little water. Gradually mix these into the flour, stirring round and round with your slightly cupped hand (fingers held together) or use a wooden spoon. Add more cold water, a very little at a time, if required. The resulting dough should be easy to knead, smooth, and firm. Knead for about 10 minutes. Cover with a clean cloth and leave to rest for at least 2 hours. Knead the dough again briefly shortly before using it; roll out into an extremely thin sheet with a rolling pin on a lightly floured surface. Cut out into disks 3 in in diameter. If preferred, use ready-to-use, bought, wonton wrappers.

While the pasta dough is resting, bring a large pan of water to a boil, add the chicken carcass, giblets, and other pieces, boil hard for 1 minute, remove the carcass etc. with a slotted spoon, and discard the water. Place the blanched chicken pieces in a sieve and rinse under running cold water; place in a large, heavy-bottomed saucepan with the 5³/₄ cups cold water, the peppercorns, peeled ginger, trimmed celery, the rice wine, salt, and leek. Bring to a boil, then simmer for 1 hour, skimming off any scum that rises to the surface. Strain the broth through a fine-weave cloth placed in a sieve into a saucepan; bring to a boil and then keep at a simmer. Prepare the filling: mix the ingredients well in a bowl. Place 1 tsp of the filling in the center of each dough disk and fold these disks in half, enclosing the filling (moisten along the edges with a little egg yolk before pressing them together with your fingertips to achieve a perfect seal). Pour the broth into a large saucepan and bring to a boil; at the same time set a large pan three-quarters full of salted water to come to a boil more quickly, add the dumplings (hún tún) and boil until they bob up to the surface; drain well and add to the pan full of boiling broth. Add the chopped watercress or washed and finely shredded leek, soy sauce, monosodium glutamate (if used), and salt to taste. Boil for 2 minutes, then ladle the broth and the hún tún into bowls and serve while very hot.

SESAME SHRIMP

芝麻虾多士

zhī má xiā duŏ shì

180

4 fairly thick slices small pan loaf
1/4 lb (1/2 cup) peeled shrimp
2–3 oz white fish fillets (e.g. English Dover
*   sole or flounder)*
2 eggs
salt
freshly ground pepper
1 cup fine breadcrumbs
1 cup sesame seeds
oil for frying
4 very small tomatoes
4 whole, unpeeled small shrimp

Time: 35 minutes

Cut the crusts off the bread and fry the slices in a little oil until they are golden brown on both sides. Chop the shrimp and the white fish fillets very finely, season with salt and pepper, and mix thoroughly with 1 lightly beaten egg. Carefully cut the fried slices of bread horizontally in half, spread one half slice with the shrimp and fish mixture and place the other half slice on top; repeat with the other 3 slices. Dip these sandwiches in lightly beaten egg and then coat with the well mixed breadcrumbs and sesame seeds, pressing lightly to make the mixture adhere. Deep-fry, or shallow-fry, turning once, until golden brown, then drain well and serve, garnished with the tomatoes and the whole shrimp.

BABY SQUID WITH VEGETABLES

杂锦炒鲜鱿

zá jǐn chǎo xiān yóu

1 lb small or baby squid
1/2 oz mu er mushrooms (cloud ear fungus)
1 1/2 tbsp rice wine
1 1/2 tbsp cornstarch
1 tbsp minced or grated fresh ginger
1/2 lb broccoli
2 leeks
2 carrots
6 tbsp peanut oil
pinch sugar
salt
2 1/2 tsp sesame seed oil

Time: 35 minutes + marinating time

Soak the mushrooms in a small bowl of warm water for 20–30 minutes. Prepare the squid. If bought whole, pull the tentacles away from the body sacs, use scissors to snip out the hard mouth parts; discard the innards and the small quill and retain only the body sacs and tentacles. Rub the thin skin off the bodies under running cold water. Dry, place in a bowl and pour a mixture of the rice wine, the cornstarch and half the fresh ginger over them; mix well and leave for 20 minutes. Wash the broccoli and use only the florets. Wash the leeks thoroughly and slice into fairly thick rings; peel the carrots and cut into thin round slices. Drain the mushrooms, cut off any tough, hard parts and divide into small pieces. Heat 3 tbsp oil in the wok and stir-fry the leeks with the remaining fresh ginger for a few minutes, add the broccoli florets and carrots and continue stir-frying, then add the mushrooms. Increase the heat, sprinkle with the sugar and salt, and stir-fry until the vegetables are tender but still have plenty of bite to them. Remove the vegetables from the wok, draining off any oil, and keep warm. Wipe the inside of the wok, heat 3 tbsp fresh oil, add the squid and stir-fry for 1–2 minutes only. Return the vegetables to the wok, sprinkle with the sesame seed oil, add a little more salt if needed, and stir briefly before serving.

STIR-FRIED SQUID WITH JELLY FISH

鲜鱿海蜇

xiān yóu hǎi zhē

2 large fresh squid, cleaned and prepared
3 or 4 tung ku (dong gu) mushrooms
1/4 lb carrots
1 stick celery
1/4 lb snow peas
6 tbsp oil
salt
2 tsp sugar
1 tbsp soy sauce
1 tbsp rice wine
1 1/4 lb long white radish (Daikon root)
1/4 lb dried jellyfish
1/4 cup wine vinegar
1 tbsp sesame seed oil

Time: 45 minutes + 3 days preparation for
*   the jellyfish*

Unfold the piece of dried jellyfish to enable you to wash off excess salt (or buy the prepared type, already cut into strips).

Rinse the jellyfish thoroughly under running cold water, squeezing to eliminate the salt. Soak in a large bowl of cold water for 3 days, changing the water twice a day and squeezing well to eliminate the salty taste. When you are ready to cook the jellyfish, soak the dried mushrooms in warm water for 20–30 minutes. Drain, remove and discard the stems, and cut each cap in half. While the mushrooms are soaking, boil the prepared squid lightly in unsalted water and cut into small, bite-sized pieces. Slice the carrot into thin rounds and finely chop the celery. Trim the snow peas and stir-fry in 3 tbsp of the oil for about half a minute over very high heat, then add 1/2 cup water and a pinch of salt and continue stir-frying, until the snow peas are tender but still crisp. Draw aside from the heat.

Stir-fry the carrots and celery separately in the remaining oil; while they are still crisp add the mushrooms, the squid, and the snow peas, half the sugar, the soy sauce, and the rice wine. Add a little more salt to taste if wished and stir-fry until the vegetables are tender but still crisp. Set aside.

Peel the Daikon and cut into thin matchstick strips; place these in a large bowl, sprinkle with 1 heaping tsp salt, stir well, and leave to stand. Drain the water from the jellyfish, squeeze tightly, and slice into strips about 1/8 in wide; place these in a bowl, pour sufficient boiling water over them to cover, then immediately turn into a sieve, draining off all the hot water. Rinse under running cold water. Mix the remaining sugar with the vinegar and sesame seed oil in a large bowl; add the thoroughly drained jellyfish strips, stir, then add the Daikon strips and mix well with the jellyfish and dressing. Serve with the cooked squid and vegetable mixture.

RAZOR SHELL CLAMS WITH LEMON AND GINGER *

盐水蛏子

yán shuĭ chēng zĭ

1 1/4 lb razor shell clams (or any small fresh
*   clams, preferably unshucked)*
1 scallion
2 thin slices fresh ginger
3 tbsp rice wine
1 tbsp salt
12 black peppercorns

For the sauce:
3 tbsp lemon juice
1 tsp fresh garlic juice
1 fresh ginger juice
1 tbsp finely chopped parsley
2 1/2 tbsp dark soy sauce
2 1/2 tbsp oil
1 tsp sesame seed oil

Time: 15 minutes + 2 hours soaking time for
*   the clams*

182

Soak the clams in enough cold, salted water to completely submerge them for 2 hours in order to eliminate any sand etc. Rinse under running cold water.

Bring just over 1 quart water to a boil in a large saucepan with the trimmed and peeled scallion, peeled ginger slices, rice wine, salt, and peppercorns. Add the clams and cook for 2 minutes only. Drain quickly. Transfer, in their shells, to individual serving plates or bowls.

Mix the sauce ingredients in a bowl. Serve the sauce as a dip for the clams.

FISH CUBES WITH PINE NUTS *

松子鱼米

sōng zǐ yù nǐ

2 tung ku (dong gu) mushrooms
1 lb very fresh thick white fish fillets (e.g. pikeperch, sea bass or any white fish that remains firm when cooked)
1 egg white
¹/₂ cup (¹/₄ lb) pine nuts
¹/₂ small red bell pepper
¹/₂ small green bell pepper
1 oz bamboo shoots
1 scallion
¹/₂ tbsp finely chopped fresh ginger
1 tbsp rice wine

¹/₂ tsp salt
pinch pepper
oil for frying

Time: 45 minutes

Soak the mushrooms in warm water for 2 hours. Cut the fish fillets into cubes (or into squares if they are not very thick) and mix in a bowl together with the egg white lightly beaten with a pinch of salt. Fry the pine nuts in oil until pale golden brown; drain and reserve.

Cut the stalks off the mushrooms and discard. Cut the caps into small squares; do likewise with the peppers and the bamboo shoots. Trim the scallion and cut half of it into short lengths.

Semi deep-fry or deep-fry the fish pieces in very hot oil for 30 seconds only; remove with a fine mesh wire ladle or slotted spoon and

drain well. Heat 3 tbsp fresh oil in a clean wok or skillet and stir-fry the ginger and the finely chopped remaining half scallion until they release their aromas. Add the vegetables and stir-fry, add the fish pieces, reducing the heat, and season with salt and pepper. Sprinkle with the wine and cook for a minute or two to allow the wine to evaporate. Transfer to a heated serving dish and surround with the pine nuts (or sprinkle these all over the dish).

THREE-FLAVOR FISH FILLETS *

三丝鱼片
sǎn sī yú jiàn

1 lb fish fillets (e.g. English Dover sole,
*   flounder or any very firm white flat fish)*
2 egg whites
¹/₄ cup cornstarch or potato flour
oil for frying
4 tung ku (dong gu) mushrooms
¹/₄ lb bamboo shoots
1 red or green bell pepper
1 scallion
3 thin slices fresh ginger
¹/₄ cup oil

For the sauce:
1¹/₂ tbsp rice wine
¹/₂–1 tsp salt
pinch freshly ground pepper
1¹/₂ tsp sesame seed oil
1¹/₂ tsp light soy sauce

Time: 40 minutes

Soak the dried mushrooms in warm water for 20–30 minutes. Cut the fish fillets into fairly narrow, short strips, dip in the stiffly beaten egg whites and then coat lightly with the cornstarch or potato flour. Heat plenty of oil for semi deep-frying in the wok or use a deep-fryer; when the oil is very hot (but not smoking) fry the fish strips briefly until pale golden brown; remove with a mesh ladle and leave to finish draining on kitchen paper. Cut off the mushroom stalks and discard them; slice the caps into strips. Blanch the shredded bamboo shoots in boiling water for a few minutes and drain well. Shred the sweet pepper, the scallion, and the ginger.

Heat ¹/₄ cup oil in the wok, stir-fry the ginger and scallion, then add the fried fish strips, mushrooms, bamboo shoots, and sweet pepper and stir-fry over high heat for 1 minute. Transfer to a heated serving dish.

Mix all the sauce ingredients together in a small saucepan; heat quickly, stirring continuously, and pour over the fish dish, decorating with some chopped coriander if wished.

SHRIMP WITH PEAS

青豆虾仁
qīng dòu xiā rén

1³/₄ cups (14 oz) peeled shrimp
¹/₂ cup fresh or frozen peas
1 egg white
3 tbsp rice wine
1 tsp salt
1 tbsp cornstarch or potato flour
1 tsp monosodium glutamate (optional)
oil for frying

Time: 30 minutes

Rinse and dry the shrimp, removing the black vein (the alimentary tract) which runs down their backs, if wished. Whisk the egg white stiffly and fold in the 1¹/₂ tbsp of the rice wine, the salt, cornstarch or alternative, and monosodium glutamate (if used). Fold in the shrimp and leave to stand for a few minutes.

Boil the peas in unsalted water until just tender and drain. Heat plenty of oil in the wok (or deep-fryer) to 340°F and fry the shrimp for 1 minute until a delicate golden brown. Remove with a wire mesh ladle or slotted ladle, drain-

ing well, and place on paper towels. Heat 3 tbsp fresh oil in a clean skillet and add the shrimp and peas; add the remaining 1¹/₂ tbsp rice wine, a pinch more monosodium glutamate (if wished), stir-fry for a minute, and serve.

SHRIMP WITH PINE NUTS *

松子虾仁
sōng zǐ xiā rén

1 lb shrimp
1 egg white
¹/₂ cup pine nuts
¹/₂ small red bell pepper
¹/₂ small green bell pepper
2 tung ku (dong gu) mushrooms
1 oz bamboo shoots
1 scallion
¹/₂ tbsp finely chopped fresh ginger
1 tbsp rice wine
¹/₂–1 tsp salt
pinch freshly ground pepper
¹/₂ cup oil

Time: 50 minutes

lion and cut into thin slices. Heat 3 tbsp oil in the wok and stir-fry the shrimp for 1–2 minutes; remove, draining well, and set aside. Wipe the inside of the wok, add ¼ cup fresh oil and stir-fry the scallion briefly; return the shrimp to the wok, add the mushrooms followed by the monosodium glutamate (if used), the sugar, soy sauce, pepper, and rice wine. Stir-fry for 1 minute and serve.

DEEP-FRIED SHRIMP WITH SPICY SALT DIP

凤尾虾

fèng wěi xiā

1¼ lb shrimp
1½ tsp rice wine
1 fairly thick slice fresh ginger, finely
  chopped, or 1½ tsp fresh ginger juice
oil for frying
fine salt and coarse sea salt
freshly ground black pepper, cayenne pepper
  or crumbled dried chili pepper

For the batter:
2 egg whites
salt
⅓ cup cornstarch or potato flour

Time: 40 minutes

Peel the shrimp except for the last section or "ring" of shell nearest the tail and leave the tail flippers in place; remove the black alimentary tract that runs down their backs; rinse and dry and place in a fairly deep dish. Mix the ginger with the rice wine (if you wish to use ginger juice, use a garlic crusher to extract it from small peeled pieces of ginger or chop the ginger and squeeze tightly in a piece of damp cloth by twisting the free folds of the cloth round and round). Sprinkle the shrimp with this mixture and mix well; leave to marinate for 10 minutes.

Whisk the egg whites stiffly with a pinch of salt; fold in 3 tbsp cornstarch or potato flour. Drain the marinade from the prawns, coat them all over with the cornstarch or alternative, shaking off any excess. Heat plenty of oil in the wok or deep-fryer until very hot but not smoking; dip the prawns in the egg white and cornstarch batter one by one; deep-fry them in several batches until they are crisp and golden brown on the outside (they will brown quite quickly); remove from the oil and drain on paper towels. Serve without delay while still very hot and have one or more bowls of seasoned salt placed on the table for each person to dip the crispy fried shrimp, holding them by their tails in your fingers or with chopsticks.

Soak the dried mushrooms in warm water for 20 minutes. Coarsely chop the shrimp; beat the egg white lightly with a pinch of salt and mix the shrimp with this; leave to stand for 10 minutes. Fry the pine nuts briefly in 1½ tbsp oil until pale golden brown. Drain and set aside. Drain the mushrooms; cut off their stalks and discard.

Cut the peppers, mushroom caps, bamboo shoots, and half the scallion (mainly the white part) into tiny dice. Stir-fry the shrimp in ¼ cup very hot oil for 30 seconds; remove from the wok with a slotted or wire ladle and set aside to finish draining on kitchen towels. Heat 3 tbsp fresh oil in the wok, stir-fry the fresh ginger and the finely chopped remaining half scallion, and add the diced vegetables and the fried shrimp; season with salt and pepper, sprinkle with the rice wine and stir-fry briefly until the wine has evaporated.

Transfer to a heated serving plate, surrounding the shrimp and vegetables with a ring of pine nuts. Alternatively, sprinkle these all over the top if wished, finely chop another scallion and sprinkle over the dish for decoration.

SHRIMP WITH SCALLIONS

葱爆虾仁

cóng bào xiā rén

1¾ cups (14 oz) peeled shrimp
2½ tsp salt
2 tung ku (dong gu) mushrooms
2 scallions
⅓ cup oil
½ tsp monosodium glutamate (optional)
½–1 tsp sugar
1½ tbsp light soy sauce
pinch freshly ground pepper
1½ tbsp rice wine

Time: 30 minutes

Raw (fresh or thawed frozen) shrimp are recommended for this dish, but cooked shrimp can also be used successfully. Rinse and dry the shrimp and sprinkle them with salt. Soak the mushrooms in warm water for about 20–30 minutes, then cut off their stalks and discard them; cut the caps into quarters. Trim the scal-

To make the dipping salt: mix fine salt with cayenne pepper or freshly ground black pepper to taste or, better still, heat coarse flakes of sea salt in the wok with peppercorns (Szechwan or ordinary black peppercorns) or dried crumbled chili pepper; when hot place in a mortar or bowl and pound gently with a pestle or the end of a wooden rolling pin (alternatively, process in the food processor or coffee grinder).

For a simpler version of this dish, omit the marinating stage and make the frying batter with all-purpose flour and a pinch of baking powder; mix with the egg whites and salt and leave to stand for 1 hour.

SHRIMP WITH MUSTARD *

芥末虾片
jiè mò xiā piàn

12 jumbo shrimp
1 tbsp white mustard powder
2¹/₂ tbsp rice wine
1 tsp finely chopped fresh ginger
¹/₂ tsp salt
¹/₂ tsp sugar
¹/₂ tsp monosodium glutamate (optional)
1 tbsp wine vinegar

Time: 30 minutes

Peel the shrimp and remove the black thread-like alimentary tract that runs down their backs. If raw shrimp are used, blanch in boiling water for 2 minutes and drain. Slice the cooked shrimp into fairly thin sections, cutting across their bodies. Mix the mustard powder with 1 tbsp cold water in a bowl and then work in the wine, ginger, salt, sugar, monosodium glutamate (if used), and the vinegar. Add the shrimp to this mixture and stir well or, if preferred, serve the shrimp on their own and hand round the sauce separately.

STIR-FRIED SHRIMP
WITH TOMATO

茄汁虾仁
gié zhī xiā rén

1¹/₄ lb medium-sized shrimp in the shell or
  ³/₄–1 lb peeled shrimp
¹/₂–1 tsp salt
1 lb firm, ripe tomatoes
¹/₂ cup oil
4 cloves garlic
4 scallions
4–5 tbsp dark soy sauce
1 heaping tbsp sugar

1 heaping tbsp cornstarch

Time: 45 minutes

Peel the shrimp if necessary. Remove the black vein that runs down the back. Pat dry with kitchen towels and place in a bowl, sprinkle with the salt, stir, and leave to stand for 15 minutes. Blanch the tomatoes then peel and slice them. Peel and finely chop the garlic; cut the white parts of the scallions into approx. 1-in lengths, reserving the green parts.

Heat the oil in the wok until hot. Add the garlic and half the white part of the scallions; stir-fry until they give off a full aroma, then add the shrimp. Stir-fry for about 30 seconds. Remove with a slotted spoon and transfer to a heated dish. Add the remaining white part of the scallions to the wok, add the tomatoes, a pinch of salt, the soy sauce, and the sugar. Cover and leave to cook over lower heat for 2–3 minutes. Mix the cornstarch with a very little cold water and stir into the wok to thicken the liquid. Return the shrimp to the wok, add the green parts of the scallions, increase the heat, stir-fry briefly, and serve.

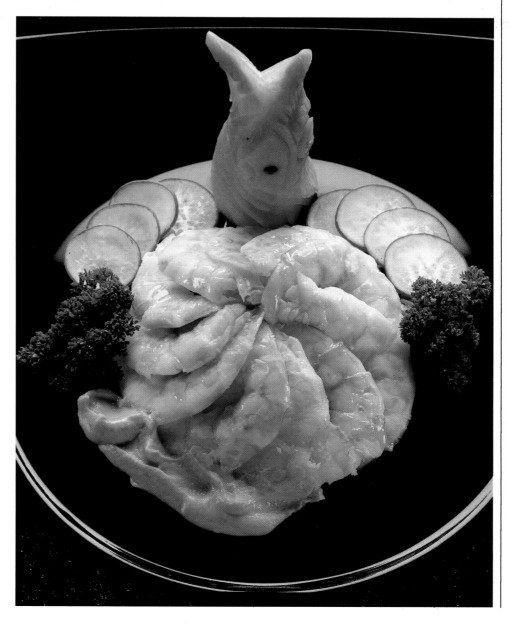

CHILI JUMBO SHRIMP *

白灼虾
bái zhuó xiā

186

12 jumbo shrimp

For the sauce:
1 tbsp finely chopped fresh ginger
1 tbsp finely chopped scallion
1 tsp finely chopped garlic

¹/₂ cup soy sauce
2¹/₂ tbsp sesame seed oil
¹/₂–1 tsp salt
2¹/₂ tbsp hot chili plum sauce
¹/₂ tsp–¹/₂ tbsp chopped fresh chilis

Time: 25 minutes

Trim off the shrimp's feelers and legs with very sharp pointed scissors and cut right down the center of the shrimp's backs, opening just enough to extract the black intestinal tract.

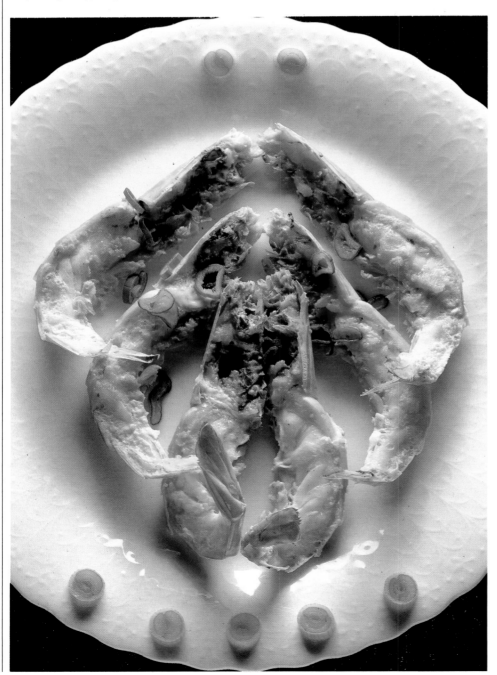

Leave the shells on. If raw shrimp are used, boil for 5 minutes. Pre-cooked shrimp can also be used, in which case omit this boiling stage. Mix the sauce ingredients, adjusting the amount of finely chopped fresh chilis according to taste. Serve this delicious dipping sauce in one or more bowls.

JUMBO SHRIMP WITH LEMON SAUCE *

柠檬虾
níng méng xiā

12 jumbo shrimp
1 lemon

For the shrimp seasoning and marinade:
1 tsp salt
¹/₂–1 tsp sugar
¹/₂ tsp monosodium glutamate (optional)
1 tsp sesame seed oil
pinch freshly ground pepper
1 egg, lightly beaten
¹/₄ cup cornstarch or potato flour
oil for frying

For the sauce:
¹/₂ medium-sized onion
3 tbsp oil
1 tsp salt
2¹/₂ tbsp sugar
1¹/₂ tbsp tomato ketchup
1¹/₂ tbsp sesame seed oil
1¹/₂ tbsp Worcestershire sauce
juice of 1 lemon
1¹/₂ tbsp cornstarch or potato flour

Time: 1 hour

Peel the shrimp, carefully remove the black, thread-like alimentary tract from their backs, cut deeper all the way down their backs taking care not to cut them in half, and open them out almost flat. Beat the egg lightly with the salt, sugar, monosodium glutamate (if used), sesame seed oil, pepper, and cornstarch; add the shrimp to this mixture and stir gently to coat all over; leave to stand and marinate for 30 minutes.

Make the sauce: peel the half onion and cut into wafer-thin slices; heat 3 tbsp oil in a skillet and stir-fry the onion; add the salt, sugar, ketchup, sesame seed oil, Worcestershire sauce, and lemon juice, stir well, and cook over fairly high heat to reduce a little. Mix the cornstarch or potato flour with a very little cold water and stir into the sauce to thicken. Heat plenty of oil in the wok or deep-fryer to 340°F; drain off excess marinade and fry the shrimp for 3–4 minutes or until golden brown; take them out of the oil, draining well, and place on paper towels.

Slice the lemon very thinly into rounds; add these to the piping hot sauce together with the shrimp, stir briefly to mix well, and serve at once.

STEAMED SHRIMP WITH GARLIC AND GINGER

姜蒜蒸虾球

jiāng suàn zhěng xiā qíu

2¹/₄ lb jumbo shrimp
1 tbsp finely chopped fresh ginger
1 tbsp finely chopped garlic
3 tbsp oil
1 large scallion or 2 medium-sized scallions, finely chopped

For the sauce:
3 tbsp light chicken broth
1¹/₂ tbsp light soy sauce
¹/₂ tbsp monosodium glutamate (optional)
¹/₂–1 tbsp sugar
3 tbsp sesame seed oil
1¹/₂ tbsp oyster sauce
pinch freshly ground pepper
1¹/₂ tbsp rice wine

Time: 30 minutes

Use sharp, pointed scissors to trim off the shrimps' antennae and legs and to cut neatly down the center of their backs and extract the black intestinal tract; place them in a heat-proof dish that will fit in your steamer compartment, sprinkle them with the garlic, ginger, and oil, mix briefly, cover, and steam for 3–4 minutes. Mix all the sauce ingredients in a small saucepan and stir over fairly high heat until reduced by half in volume. Transfer the cooked shrimp to a heated serving platter, pour the sauce all over them, and sprinkle with the finely chopped scallion.

CANTONESE SHRIMP *

盐酥虾

yán sū xiā

12 jumbo shrimp
3 tbsp all-purpose flour
oil for frying
1 scallion
4 thin slices fresh ginger
¹/₂ cup chicken broth or water

¹/₂–1 tsp salt
1 tsp five-spice powder
1 tsp monosodium glutamate (optional)
1¹/₂ tbsp rice wine
1¹/₂ tbsp sesame seed oil
pinch sugar

Time: 45 minutes

Use sharp, pointed scissors to snip off the shrimp's feelers and legs and to cut down the middle of their backs in order to extract the

black alimentary tract. Leave the shells on. Wash and dry the shrimp and coat with flour.

Heat plenty of oil in the wok for semi deep-frying or use a deep-fryer; when this has reached 325°F or a little hotter, fry until lightly browned, then drain well and set aside. Heat 3 tbsp fresh oil in a clean wok (empty out the oil and wipe the inside of the wok if used for frying) and stir-fry the coarsely chopped ginger and scallion until they release their aromas.

Pour in the broth or water and add the salt, five-spice powder, monosodium glutamate (if

used), rice wine, sesame seed oil, and sugar. Bring to a boil and boil hard to reduce a little; remove and discard the ginger and scallion pieces, add the shrimp, and stir for a few minutes over high heat, allowing the liquid to reduce further.

CANTONESE STUFFED SHRIMP *

百花虾
bǎi huā xiā

8 extra large jumbo shrimp
1¹/₄ cups (10 oz) peeled small shrimp
¹/₄ lb pork belly
¹/₂–1 tsp salt
¹/₂ tsp monosodium glutamate (optional)
1¹/₂ tbsp rice wine
1 tbsp sesame seed oil
2¹/₂ tbsp cornstarch
¹/₂ cup fresh or frozen peas
¹/₂ medium-sized red bell pepper

1 egg white
oil

Time: 1 hour

Peel the jumbo shrimp leaving on the last section of shell (nearest the tail) and the tail flippers; carefully remove the black alimentary tract that runs down their backs. Flatten their peeled bodies and mold them as much as possible into the shape of a fish.

Chop the small shrimp and pork belly together very finely; work in the salt, monosodium glutamate (if used), the rice wine, sesame seed oil, and cornstarch.

Dry the large shrimp with paper towels. Press a small quantity of the mixture over it; press a pea into place to represent the fishes'

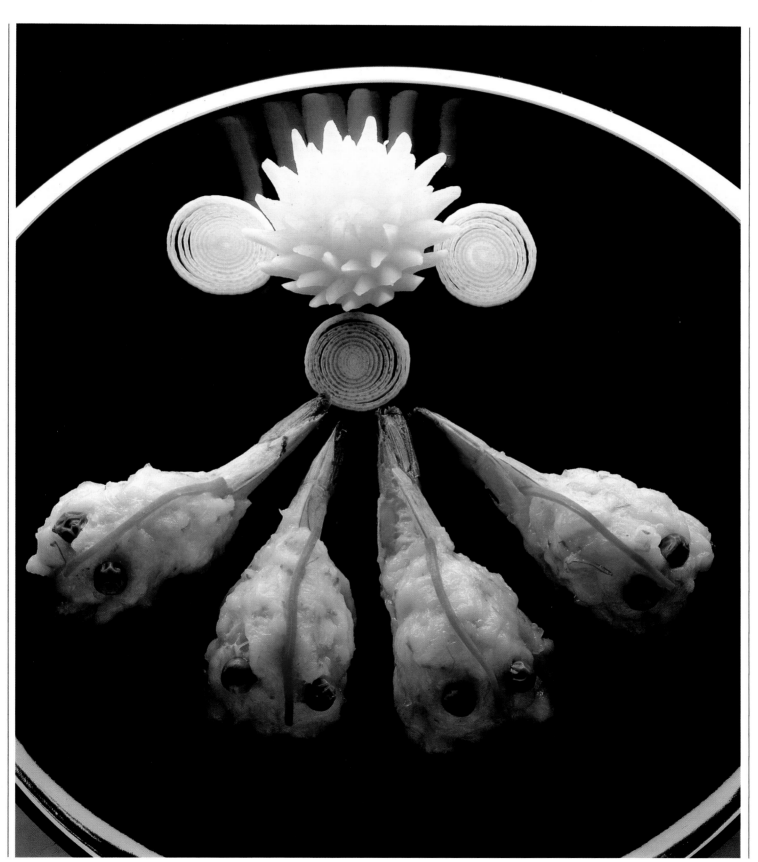

190

eyes, and push in the pieces of finely shredded pepper to represent dorsal fins. Place the "fish" in a wide, fairly shallow heatproof dish that will fit in your steamer compartment, cover, and steam for 10 minutes. Beat the egg white very lightly with a few drops of cold water; heat 1 tbsp oil in a nonstick skillet and cook the egg whites over moderate heat, scrambling them with a fork until set. Arrange the shrimp "fish" on a dish, with the egg white dotted here and there to represent crests of waves.

SHRIMP WITH BLACK SOYBEANS *

豉 椒 虾 球
chǐ jiāo xiā qiú

12 jumbo shrimp
$^1/_2$ medium-sized green bell pepper
$^1/_2$ medium-sized red bell pepper
2 tung ku (dong gu) mushrooms
12 bamboo shoots
oil for frying

Seasoning and marinade for the shrimp:

1 egg white
$1^1/_2$ tbsp rice wine
$^1/_2$ tsp salt
$^1/_2$ tsp sugar
$^1/_2$ tsp monosodium glutamate (optional)
pinch freshly ground pepper

For the sauce:
$^1/_4$ cup oil
1 tbsp fermented black soybeans
1 tsp finely chopped fresh ginger
1 tsp finely chopped garlic
$1^1/_2$ tbsp rice wine
1 tbsp wine vinegar
1 tbsp sesame seed oil
$^1/_2$ tsp salt

¹/₂ tsp sugar
¹/₂ tsp monosodium glutamate (optional)
1 tbsp cornstarch

Time: 1 hour

Soak the dried mushrooms in warm water for 20 minutes or more. Remove the heads from the shrimp if still present; snip in a straight line through their shells along the center of their backs and extract the black alimentary tract. Rinse and dry. Whisk the egg white, stir in the rice wine, salt, sugar, monosodium glutamate (if used), and the pepper and stir in the shrimp. Marinate for about 10 minutes.

Cut the stalks off the drained mushrooms and discard. Cut the peppers (remove the seeds and pith), the mushroom caps, and the bamboo shoots into short thin strips. Heat plenty of oil in the wok or deep-fryer to 340°F and fry the shrimp and peppers for 1 minute; take out of the oil, draining well. Crush the fermented soybeans. Heat ¹/₄ cup fresh oil in the cleaned wok or a large skillet, add the soybeans and cook until they release their distinctive aroma; add the finely chopped ginger and garlic, stirring well. Add the shredded mushrooms, bamboo shoots and the fried shrimp and peppers, then the rice wine, vinegar, sesame seed oil, salt, sugar, and monosodium glutamate (if used); stir-fry over fairly high heat; when the bamboo shoots are tender but still crisp, mix the cornstarch with a little cold water and stir into the wok.

FRIED ABALONE *

金 钱 鲍 鱼

jīn yín bào yú

12 abalone (dried, pre-soaked or canned)
3 tbsp oil
4 thin slices fresh ginger
6 tbsp rice wine
¹/₂ tsp monosodium glutamate (optional)
6 tbsp dark soy sauce
¹/₂–1 tsp salt
¹/₂–1 tsp sugar
1¹/₂ tbsp oyster sauce
1¹/₂ tbsp sesame seed oil
¹/₂–1 tsp five-spice powder (optional)
1¹/₂ tbsp cornstarch or potato flour

Time: 4 hours + 1 day for soaking and
cooking the abalone if dried variety is used

Soak the dried abalone in cold water for about 12 hours or overnight; drain off the water and bring to a boil in fresh water; simmer very slowly for 6–7 hours, adding more boiling water every so often to make sure they are always submerged. You may prefer to use canned abalone (reserve the liquid and dilute with an equal quantity of water).

Heat the oil in the wok, stir-fry the ginger, add the rice wine, monosodium glutamate (if used), soy sauce, salt, sugar, oyster sauce, sesame seed oil, and the five-spice powder (if used) with the well drained abalone and their cooking liquid. Simmer gently for 3–4 hours. Take the abalone out of the cooking liquid and transfer to a heated serving dish. Pour about ³/₄ cup of the cooking liquid from the wok into a small saucepan; mix the cornstarch or potato flour with a little cold water and stir into the liquid over moderate heat until cooked and thickened; coat the abalone with this sauce.

FRIED OYSTERS

酥 炸 生 蚝

sū zhà shēng háo

24 oysters or approx. 10 oz net weight
shucked mollusks
1 leek
1 thin slice fresh ginger
3 tbsp cornstarch or potato flour
1 nori seaweed leaf
oil for frying

For the frying batter:
2 eggs
³/₄ cup all-purpose flour
1 tsp salt

Time: 30 minutes

Shuck the oysters and remove the mollusks from their shells; place in a bowl of lightly salted water for a few minutes; transfer to a sieve and rinse under running cold water, then, keeping them in the sieve, pour a kettleful of boiling water all over them. Drain well and leave to cool in a bowl. Finely chop one quarter of the well washed leek and all the ginger and mix with the oysters. Leave to stand for about 5–10 minutes. Coat the oysters with the cornstarch or potato flour, without brushing off any ginger or leek which clings to them.

Make the coating batter: sift the flour into a bowl, make a well in the center, and gradually mix in the lightly beaten eggs and salt; add a little cold water as necessary to make a fairly thick coating of batter. Heat the nori seaweed leaf under the broiler set to moderate heat and when crisp but not at all scorched, wrap in a clean cloth, break up, and add the finely crumbled pieces to the batter; stir well. Heat plenty of oil in the wok or in the deep-fryer until very hot but not smoking; dip the oysters in the batter to coat all over and add to the oil; fry until crisp and pale golden brown on the outside, taking care not to overcook. Drain well and transfer to a heated serving platter.

192

Have the garnish ready prepared in advance: clean the remaining leek, keeping it in one piece; hold vertically upright and use a very sharp knife to make a number of cuts and cross cuts into the top, to produce a plumed, feathered effect; soak the leek in iced water: the fronds will open out to look like a flower. Place this leek flower in the center of the plate of oysters as decoration.

OYSTERS WITH BASIL KE CIA

客家炒蚝
Kè jiā chǎo háo

24 large oysters or approx. 10 oz net weight
   small shucked oysters
2 scallions
2 cloves garlic
2 chili peppers
oil
pinch salt
pinch monosodium glutamate (optional)
1 tbsp soy sauce
1 cup chicken or vegetable broth
1 1/2 tbsp cornstarch or potato flour
20 fresh basil leaves

Time: 30 minutes

Shuck the oysters, save the liquor if wished, straining through a very fine mesh sieve, and place the detached mollusks in a bowl. Peel and lightly mince the garlic cloves with the flat of a heavy knife blade, trim the scallion, remove and discard the stalk, seeds and pith from the chilis and cut both into very thin, short strips. Heat 1/4 cup oil in the wok and stir-fry the oysters, scallions, garlic, and chili for 1 minute only before adding the salt, monosodium glutamate (if used), soy sauce, and all but 3 tbsp of the broth. Cook briefly to reduce the liquid a little; mix the thickening agent with the reserved broth and stir into the wok to thicken the broth. Immediately afterward, stir in the basil leaves and serve.

STIR-FRIED OYSTERS
AND TOFU

鲜蚝豆腐
xiān háo dòu fǔ

10 oz firm tofu (bean curd)

10 oz shucked and detached small oysters
1 leek
1 1-in thick piece fresh ginger
2 tbsp fermented soybean paste
6 tbsp peanut oil
2 1/2 tbsp light soy sauce
1/2–1 tsp sugar
2 1/2 tbsp sesame seed oil

Time: 30 minutes

Bring a large pan half full of water to a boil with half the washed leek and the peeled piece of ginger. Boil for 5 minutes. Place the oysters in a sieve and rinse well under running cold water then blanch in the flavored boiling water for 1 minute only. Drain and reserve.

Cut the tofu into cubes; cook in the flavored, gently boiling water for 1 minute; remove and set aside. Chop the remaining half leek finely.

Mix the soy sauce in a bowl with the fermented soybean paste, the sugar, and the sesame seed oil and blend into a smooth sauce. Heat the peanut oil in the wok or in a skillet and stir-fry the chopped leek; add the oysters and tofu cubes and stir-fry briefly.

Add the sauce and cook, stirring, for 1–2 minutes, then transfer to a serving dish.

STEAMED FISH *

清蒸鱼
qīng zhěng yú

1 whole fish weighing approx. 1 3/4 lb (e.g. sea
   bass, pikeperch, porgy or similar)
1/2–1 tsp salt
4 thin slices fresh ginger, finely chopped
1 scallion, finely chopped
pinch freshly ground pepper
1/2 tbsp sugar
pinch monosodium glutamate (optional)
2 1/2 tbsp light soy sauce
1 1/2 tbsp sesame seed oil
1 1/2 tbsp rice wine

For added garnish and flavor:
1 scallion
5 thin slices fresh ginger
1/4 cup peanut oil

Time: 40 minutes

Trim the fins off the fish, remove the scales if present, and gut the fish either by slitting open right down the belly or by removing the entrails through the gill opening. Rinse and dry. Mix the salt, ginger, and scallion, sprinkle all over the outside and inside of the fish and place in a heatproof dish; leave to stand for 10 minutes, turning the fish once or twice, and then place in the steamer compartment,

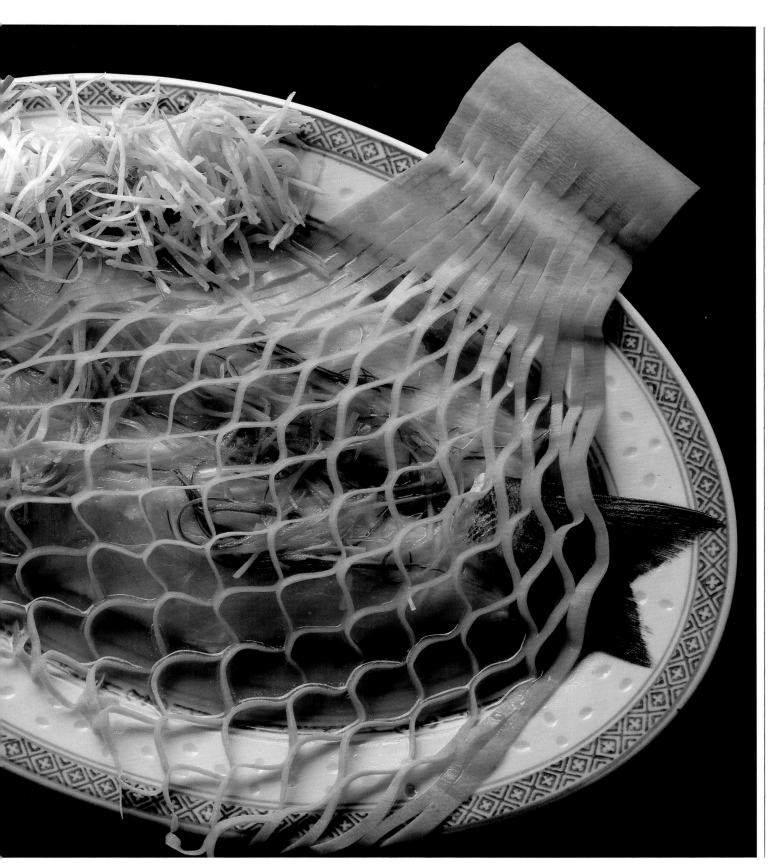

A free market in Fujian. In 1970 rice was rationed and the Chinese people often went hungry as a result. Now supplies are plentiful, as they should be in this warm, humid climate, which is ideal for growing two crops a year. Apart from this staple, meats, poultry, and fish are on sale, as well as various types of noodles. Here and there along the roads to market are small eating houses serving dumplings and other snacks; the Canton area is famous for the

classic shrimp-filled dim sum.
Fujian is one of the most picturesque parts of China, with 2,000 miles of coastline, the antithesis of the desolate steppes of Mongolia. The women of this region still use a plough of ancient design, without wheels, to till the fields; they also weave bamboo baskets and other products, while their children sell sugar cane and tropical fruit such as pineapples and lychees.

cover, and steam for 10 minutes or longer if necessary. Make a small cut right down to the backbone and check whether the fish is cooked through. Transfer to an oval heated serving dish. Save all the cooking juices which have collected in the heatproof dish and pour these into the wok; mix in the pepper, sugar, monosodium glutamate (if used), the soy sauce, sesame seed oil, and rice wine; cook to reduce the liquid a little and then pour all over the fish. Sprinkle the fish with the finely shredded ginger and scallion.

Heat the peanut oil and pour all over the fish.

STEAMED FISH WITH XIAN CAI

咸 菜 蒸 鱼

xián cài zhěng yú

1 whole fish weighing approx. 2¹/₄ lb (e.g. sea bass, pikeperch, porgy or gilt-head bream, small cod or hake etc.)
4 tung ku (dong gu) mushrooms
1 oz pork belly
1¹/₂ oz brine-pickled Chinese greens (xian

cai)
1 large fresh chili pepper
2 slices fresh ginger
3 sprigs coriander
1 scallion
3 tbsp peanut oil

For the sauce:
¹/₂–1 tsp salt
¹/₂ tsp monosodium glutamate (optional)
¹/₂–1 tsp sugar
1¹/₂ tbsp light soy sauce
1¹/₂ tbsp sesame seed oil
pinch freshly ground pepper
3 tbsp water

Time: 1 hour

Trim, descale (if necessary), and gut the fish; wash and dry. Soak the dried mushrooms in warm water for at least 20 minutes, drain, squeeze out excess water, then cut off and discard their stalks. Place the xian cai in a sieve and rinse very thoroughly under running cold water; drain very well. Cut the mushroom caps, pork belly, the xian cai, chili pepper, and ginger into very thin strips. Rinse, dry, and chop the coriander; trim and finely chop the scallion. Mix all the sauce ingredients in a small saucepan and boil gently until the liquid has reduced a little. Place the fish in a heatproof dish that will fit in your steamer compartment, sprinkle the sauce all over the fish, and place all the shredded ingredients on top of it. Cover and steam for 15 minutes or until the fish is cooked through (see previous recipe). Just before you serve the fish, sprinkle it with the coriander and chopped scallion, heat the peanut oil in the wok or a small saucepan until very hot but not smoking, and immediately pour all over the fish.

Xian cai, a pickled vegetable not unlike fennel, is available canned from most Chinese and many Oriental foodstores.

STEAMED CRAB CLAWS

清 蒸 蟹 肉

qǐng zhēng xiè ròu

1³/₄ lb crab claws
1 scallion
1 slice fresh ginger
1 tbsp salt

For the sauce:
3 tbsp soy sauce
1¹/₂ tbsp sesame seed oil
1 tbsp finely chopped fresh ginger
1 tbsp finely chopped scallion

Time: 45 minutes

Break open the crab claws by placing newspaper on top and tapping with a hammer. Carefully extract the flesh, discarding any pieces of shell and cartilage. Transfer to a bowl and flake the flesh with a fork. Mix the peeled and finely chopped ginger and the finely chopped scallion with the crabmeat and place in a heatproof dish that will fit easily in your steamer. Cover and steam for 15 minutes.

Mix the sauce ingredients and hand round separately with the steamed crab claws.

Southern China is famous for its crabs.

SHARK'S FINS WITH CHRYSANTHEMUMS *

炒桂花翅
chǎi guì huā chì

1/4 lb dried shark's fins
3 tung ku (dong gu) mushrooms
1 crab weighing 1 lb
2 oz bamboo shoots
2 scallions
4 thin slices fresh ginger
1/4 cup rice wine
4 eggs
1/2–1 tsp salt
1/2 tsp monosodium glutamate (optional)
1/2 tbsp sugar
2 1/2 tsp light soy sauce
1 tsp sesame seed oil
pinch freshly ground pepper
3 tbsp oil

Time: 4 1/2 hours

Soak the shark's fin in several changes of cold water over 24 hours, to soften. Rinse well under running cold water in a sieve. Add the shark's fins to a large saucepan of cold water; bring to a boil and simmer for 2–2 1/2 hours. Drain, rinse well in a sieve under running cold water and place in the cleaned saucepan in fresh cold water; leave to stand for 2 hours. Soak the dried mushrooms for 20 minutes or more in warm water; drain, cut off and discard the stalks, and cut the caps into thin strips. Boil the crab or crabs until cooked, drain, allow to cool and then take all the flesh out of the shells, discarding the feathery gills and stomach sac. If preferred, use 1/2 lb thawed frozen or canned cooked crabmeat and drain well. Blanch the bamboo shoots in boiling water for a few minutes; drain and shred. Place the shark's fins in yet another change of fresh cold water (enough to cover them again) and add the scallion, ginger, and 3 tbsp of the rice wine and boil gently for 30 minutes. Drain. Beat the eggs lightly with the salt, mono-

196

sodium glutamate (if used), sugar, soy sauce, sesame seed oil, pepper, and the remaining rice wine; heat the oil in the wok, add the egg mixture, and scramble the eggs. Arrange the shark's fins, crabmeat, mushrooms, and bamboo shoots attractively on a serving platter; place small quantities of the scrambled egg over the other ingredients. Serve.

The chrysanthemums of the title are suggested by the appearance of the dish, thought by the Chinese to resemble them.

BRAISED SHARK'S FIN *

干烧鱼翅

gàn shāo yú chì

1 lb dried shark's fin
6 slices fresh ginger
2 scallions
1 boiling chicken weighing approx. 2 lb
10 oz ham, in one piece
2¹/₂ tbsp soy sauce
2¹/₂ tbsp rice wine
1¹/₂ tsp sesame seed oil
pinch monosodium glutamate (optional)
pinch salt
pinch sugar
pinch freshly ground pepper
¹/₄ lb soybean sprouts, blanched
1 tbsp cornstarch or potato flour

Time: 6¹/₂ hours + soaking time

Pre-soak the shark's fins in several changes of cold water for 24 hours, drain, rinse under running cold water, and then place in a saucepan full of cold water, bring to a gentle boil, and simmer for 4 hours. Drain and soak in a bowl of fresh, cold water for about 6 hours or longer. Bring a large saucepan of water to a boil with 3 of the ginger slices, 1 scallion, and the shark's fins; simmer for a further 4 hours. Take the fins out of the cooking liquid, rinse again under running cold water, picking off any pieces of skin, etc. Dry the fins and wrap them securely in a clean piece of cheesecloth, tying the parcel up securely. Poach the chicken gently for 2 hours in water with the ham, the remaining ginger and scallion, and the wrapped shark's fins. When this time is up, remove the wrapped shark's fins and unwrap. Pour 1 cup of the cooking liquid in a smaller saucepan with the soy sauce, rice wine, sesame seed oil, monosodium glutamate (if used), the salt, sugar, and pepper. Add the shark's fins to this flavored liquid and heat through; after the liquid has reduced considerably, stir in the cornstarch or potato flour mixed with a little cold water and cook for a few minutes more. Place the shark's fin and sauce on a plate and surround with the bean sprouts.

Fishermen selling their catch in Xiamen market. These weatherbeaten men with their distinctive yellow headgear usually come from a long line of fisherfolk. They dry the fish they have landed and then sell it with other produce: dried shrimp, squid, cuttlefish, octopus, and oysters for soups and as added protein content in vegetable dishes. Also on offer are lotus seeds, beans, nuts, mushrooms and fungi, and red dates, all sun- and wind-dried.

China has been slow to introduce refrigerated storage of food, but many foodstuffs keep just as well when dried or pickled in brine. The Chinese alternative to preserving is to sell live fish, poultry etc., and

vegetables harvested daily so they are very fresh.

Between the large islands of Hainan and Taiwan, the coastline of southern China is a succession of small bays, teeming with fish; nets are strung across these inlets from the rocks, or barriers are constructed, fixed to the seabed, while crustaceans are trapped by the lights of the small sampans. Deep sea fishing is also practised on a large scale by fisherfolk who live at sea, on board their junks, drenched by the monsoon but making the most of its winds, and sometimes at the mercy of the frighteningly violent and sudden typhoons.

place two pieces of chicken, one on top of the other, in the center of each square, and decorate with 1 or 2 sprigs of parsley: wrap up the chicken pieces. Heat plenty of oil in the wok or deep-fryer to 280°F and lower the parcels into it, using a slotted ladle or frying basket; fry for 6 minutes, then turn up the heat to high for a final minute's fast frying.

CURRIED CHICKEN

咖 哩 鸡 块

g lí jī kuài

14 oz chicken breasts
$^1/_2$ cup oil
1 tbsp chopped scallion
$^1/_2$ tbsp peeled and chopped garlic
1 tbsp Chinese curry powder
1 tsp salt
$^1/_2$–1 tsp sugar
pinch freshly ground pepper
$1^1/_2$ tbsp light soy sauce
$1^1/_2$ tbsp dark soy sauce
1 tbsp cornstarch or potato flour
4 small, hot red chili peppers

Time: 30 minutes

Remove the skin from the chicken breasts and chop the flesh into small, bite-sized pieces. Heat half the oil in the wok and stir-fry the chicken for 3 minutes; drain and set aside. Trim off the stalks from the chili peppers and remove the seeds. Finely chop and set aside. Heat the remaining fresh oil in the wok, stir-fry the scallion and garlic briefly; add the curry powder, salt, sugar, pepper, and soy sauce. Simmer very gently for 10 minutes, then stir in the cornstarch or potato flour, mixed with a little cold water. Return the chicken pieces to the wok, sprinkle with the very finely chopped chili peppers, stir well, and serve.

FIVE-SPICE AND CURRY CHICKEN IN A PAPER CASE

五 香 咖 哩 纸 包 鸡

wǔ xiāng gā lí zh bāo j

14 oz chicken breasts
1 scallion, finely chopped
1 tbsp finely chopped fresh ginger
$^1/_2$–1 tsp five-spice powder
1 tsp Chinese curry powder
$^1/_2$ tbsp salt

$^1/_2$ tbsp sugar
1 tbsp light soy sauce
$2^1/_2$ tbsp peanut oil
1 sprig parsley
oil for frying

Time: 45 minutes

Skin the chicken breasts, remove any tendons, gristle or pieces of cartilage, and cut into $^3/_8$-in slices measuring about $1^1/_2 \times 2$ in. Mix these with the five-spice powder, curry, salt, sugar, soy sauce, and oil.

Cut the paper into large pieces, 8 in square,

CHICKEN IN A PAPER CASE *

纸 包 鸡

zhǐ bāo jī

1 oven-ready, dressed chicken weighing
    approx. 3 lb
4 tung ku (dong gu) mushrooms
1 scallion
4 thin slices fresh ginger
1 tbsp salt
1 tbsp sugar
$^1/_2$ tbsp monosodium glutamate (optional)
1 tbsp dark soy sauce
1 tbsp light soy sauce

¹/₂ tbsp oyster sauce
1 tbsp cornstarch or potato flour
¹/₄ lb thinly sliced York ham
oil for frying

Time: 1 hour 10 minutes

Soak the mushrooms in warm water for 20 minutes. Take all the flesh off the chicken carcass and cut into small pieces measuring not more than 1 in. Peel and trim the ginger and scallion and shred finely. Drain the mushrooms, squeezing out excess moisture, then cut off and discard the stems. Cut the caps into very thin strips. Mix all these prepared ingredients with the salt, sugar, monosodium glutamate (if used), soy and oyster sauces, and the cornstarch or potato flour. Leave to marinate for 30 minutes.

Cut some waxed paper into square sheets measuring 6 × 6 in; with one of the corners of the square pointing toward you, place 1 tbsp of the prepared mixture toward the corner nearest you, cover with a slice of ham (just large enough to cover the mixture) and wrap up in the paper to form a secure envelope.

Heat plenty of oil in the wok or a deep-fryer to 290°F and lower the parcels into it, using a slotted ladle or frying basket; fry for 10 minutes without increasing the heat, then turn up the heat to high for a final minute's cooking. Remove from the wok or fryer, draining well, and serve; each person unwraps one or more parcels, using chopsticks to do so.

CHICKEN WITH SOYBEAN SPROUTS

银 芽 鸡 丝

yín yá jī sī

2 chicken breasts, weighing approx. 10 oz
*   each*
¹/₄ lb soybean or mungbean sprouts
3 tbsp cornstarch
1 egg white
2¹/₂ tbsp rice wine
1 tsp salt
6 tbsp oil
1 tbsp light soy sauce

Time: 35 minutes

Soak the bean sprouts in enough cold water for them to float in; remove all the sprouts which are still floating on the top; those which have sunk to the bottom should be discarded. Use a very sharp knife to cut the chicken into strips, $1\frac{1}{2}$ in long and $\frac{3}{4}$ in wide. Coat with the cornstarch, shaking off any excess, and place in a bowl. Whisk the egg white until very frothy but not at all stiff. Add to the chicken with the rice wine and the salt. Mix together.

Heat 3 tbsp of the oil in the wok and stir-fry the bean sprouts over high heat for 2 minutes. Remove, draining well, and set aside.

Wipe the inside of the wok; heat the remaining oil and stir-fry the chicken over high heat. Return the bean sprouts to the wok, add the soy sauce, mix briefly, and serve.

CHICKEN WITH ALMONDS

杏仁鸡丁

xìng rén jī dīng

1 lb chicken breasts
$\frac{1}{4}$ lb bamboo shoots
$\frac{1}{2}$ red bell pepper
$\frac{1}{2}$ green bell pepper
oil for frying
$\frac{1}{2}$ medium-sized onion
2 thin slices fresh ginger
$1\frac{1}{2}$ tbsp oil

For the batter:
$\frac{1}{2}$ tsp salt
$\frac{1}{2}$ tsp monosodium glutamate (optional)
1 tsp sugar
$\frac{1}{2}$ tsp bicarbonate of soda
1 egg white
$2\frac{1}{2}$ tbsp cornstarch or potato flour
$2\frac{1}{2}$ tbsp water
1 tbsp oil

For the sauce:
$\frac{1}{2}$ tsp sugar
$\frac{1}{2}$ tsp monosodium glutamate (optional)
$\frac{1}{2}$ tsp salt
1 tbsp oyster sauce
1 tbsp soy sauce
1 tbsp sesame seed oil
1 tbsp rice wine
4 cups broth
$1\frac{1}{2}$ tsp cornstarch or potato flour
1 cup roasted almonds

Time: 1 hour

Cut the chicken breasts into $\frac{3}{4}$-in cubes; mix all the ingredients for the batter very

thoroughly and stir in the chicken cubes; leave to stand for up to 30 minutes.

Cut the bamboo shoots and the peppers into small bite-sized pieces. Heat plenty of oil in the wok and when very hot but not smoking, fry the chicken pieces for 2 minutes; remove, drain well, and set aside. Fry first the peppers and then the bamboo shoots for 2 minutes in the oil, in two separate batches. Drain both batches well.

Peel and shred the ginger; trim and shred the scallion. Pour the frying oil out of the wok and wipe the inside; heat $1\frac{1}{2}$ tbsp fresh oil and stir-fry the ginger and scallion and when they have started to release their aroma, return the chicken, peppers, and bamboo shoots to the wok. Add the sugar, monosodium glutamate (if used), salt, oyster and soy sauces, sesame seed oil, and rice wine, and then stir in the broth.

Continue cooking for a few minutes to reduce the liquid a little, then mix the cornstarch (or alternative) with $\frac{1}{2}$–1 tsp of cold water and stir in to thicken the sauce a little. Serve at once.

FRIED CHICKEN AND SHRIMP BALLS WITH ALMOND COATING

杏仁百花鸡

xìng rén bǎi huā jī

1 lb cooked, unshelled shrimp or 1 cup
  cooked, peeled shrimp
$1\frac{1}{4}$ cups finely chopped chicken meat
$\frac{1}{4}$ cup finely chopped pork belly
1 tsp salt
$\frac{1}{2}$ tsp monosodium glutamate (optional)
$\frac{1}{2}$–1 tbsp sugar
1 tbsp sesame seed oil
pinch freshly ground pepper
1 tbsp rice wine
1 tbsp cornstarch or potato flour
$2\frac{1}{2}$ tbsp all-purpose flour
1 egg
2 cups flaked almonds
oil for frying

Time: 1 hour

If you are using unshelled shrimp, remove their heads and shells. Remove the thin black thread-like alimentary tract which runs down their back. Chop finely. Mix the chopped meats and shrimp thoroughly with the salt, monosodium glutamate (if used), sugar, sesame seed oil, pepper, rice wine, and cornstarch; take tablespoonfuls of this mixture and roll between your palms into balls about the

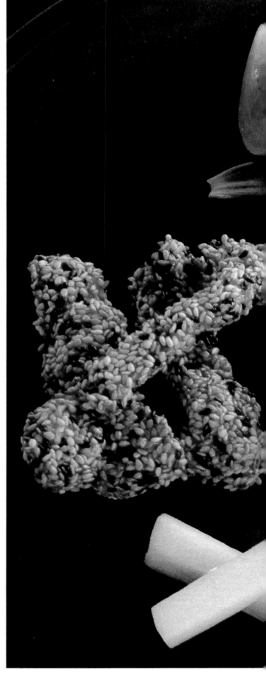

size of an apricot. Coat with the flour and then dip in the lightly beaten egg to coat all over.

Spread the flaked almonds out on a plate and roll the balls in them, pressing quite firmly to make them adhere. Heat plenty of oil in the wok or deep-fryer to 325°F and lower the almond-coated balls into the hot oil a few at a time; fry in batches for 5 minutes, increasing the heat for the last minute's frying to brown lightly if they have not colored enough.

Time: 1 hour 10 minutes

If you have bought a whole chicken, take the flesh off the bone; cut the flesh (or the breasts if you are using these only) into pieces measuring about $3/4 \times 1^1/2$ in. Mix the batter ingredients very thoroughly together in a large bowl and then mix in the chicken pieces well to coat all over. Leave to stand for 30 minutes. Spread out the sesame seeds on a large plate and roll the chicken pieces in them, pressing gently so that they adhere all over.

Heat the oil in the wok to 300°F and fry the chicken pieces, turning them very frequently, until they are golden brown and cooked through (this will take about 10 minutes). If they have not browned sufficiently when they are nearly cooked through, increase the heat for the last 2–3 minutes' frying. Serve on a platter, garnished with slices of cucumber and tomato.

FRIED CHICKEN

炸童子鸡

zhà tóng zǐ jī

2 oven-ready young cockerels or Rock
    Cornish hens, weighing approx. 1 lb each
1 tbsp Chinese rose spirit (mei gui you)
1 tbsp dark soy sauce
2¹/2 tbsp light soy sauce
2 tsp monosodium glutamate (optional)
2¹/2 tsp salt
1 heaping tbsp sugar
2¹/2 tsp fresh ginger juice (see below)
pinch five-spice powder
oil for frying
2 lemons for decoration

Condiment:
6 tbsp salt
1 tsp five-spice powder

Time: 30 minutes + 4 hours marinating time

Mix the rose spirit, soy sauce, monosodium glutamate (if used), the ginger juice (use a garlic crusher to obtain this) and the five-spice powder. Wash the cockerels or Rock Cornish hens, dry well, and then rub all over, inside and out, with this mixture; place in a dish and pour any remaining marinade over them. Leave to stand for 4 hours, turning several times. Heat plenty of oil in the wok or, preferably, in the deep-fryer, to 325°F, add the cockerels and fry until they are golden brown all over; these very young birds are extremely tender, so do not overcook them. Take out of the hot oil, drain well, and use a cleaver or poultry scissors to cut each bird into quarters or, if you are planning to use chopsticks, chop into fairly large bite-sized pieces (bones

CHICKEN WITH SESAME SEEDS AND MUSTARD *

麻辣鸡球

má là jī qiú

1 oven-ready chicken weighing approx.
    1³/4–2 lb or 1³/4 lb chicken breasts
1 cup white sesame seeds
¹/2 cup oil

For the batter:
1 tsp salt
¹/2 tsp sugar
¹/2 tsp monosodium glutamate (optional)
2 egg yolks, lightly beaten
3 tbsp cornstarch or potato flour
1¹/2 tbsp ready-mixed strong mustard
1¹/2 tbsp cold water

For the garnish:
1 cucumber and 2 large tomatoes

included); transfer to a serving plate and decorate with lemon wedges. Mix the condiment ingredients and place in a small bowl or into tiny individual bowls: the chicken pieces are dipped into this as they are eaten.

LEMON CHICKEN *

柠檬鸡
níng méng jī

1¼ lb chicken breasts
1 egg
½–1 tsp salt
½ tsp monosodium glutamate (optional)
1 tbsp sesame seed oil

¼ cup cornstarch or potato flour
oil for frying

For the sauce:
½–1 tsp salt
½–1 tsp sugar
1 tbsp sesame seed oil
1 tbsp lemon juice
1 tbsp cornstarch or potato flour
1 lemon for decoration

Time: 25 minutes

Beat the egg lightly with the salt, monosodium glutamate (if used), and the sesame oil. Cut the chicken breasts horizontally in half and dip in the egg mixture to coat all over; coat with the cornstarch or potato flour and semi deep-fry in the wok or deep-fryer for 6–7 min-

utes once the oil has reached 290°F. Remove from the oil, draining well, and cut into pieces measuring 2½ × ¾ in; place these on a heated serving plate.

Make the sauce: heat the sesame oil with the salt, sugar, and lemon juice, stirring well. Mix the cornstarch or alternative thickening agent with a little cold water and stir into the sauce; cook for a few minutes longer and sprinkle all over the chicken pieces. Decorate with lemon wedges if wished, or arrange thin slices of lemon between the chicken pieces.

202

CHICKEN BAI QIE

白 切 鸡
Bái qiē jī

1 oven-ready chicken weighing 2–2¹/₄ lb
7 cups chicken broth
3 slices fresh ginger
2 scallions
1¹/₂ tbsp peanut oil
1 tsp finely chopped fresh ginger
1 tsp finely chopped scallion
1 tbsp strong mustard (e.g. English)
1 tbsp sesame seed oil
1 tbsp salt

Time: 40 minutes

Wash and dry the chicken. Bring the broth to a boil in a large saucepan, pot or deep fireproof casserole dish and add the chicken, the ginger slices, and the 2 whole trimmed scallions. Cook at a fast boil for 5 minutes. Lower the heat and simmer gently, covered, until the chicken is done (approx. 1–1¹/₂ hours). Test with a fork or skewer inserted into the thigh; if the juices run clear, not pink, the chicken is ready. Take out the chicken; brush all over with a coating of peanut oil and when completely cold, cut into the usual carving sections or cut into much smaller pieces (bones included) using a cleaver.

Place the finely chopped ginger, the chopped scallion, mustard, sesame seed oil, and the salt in individual small bowls or ramekins so that each person can dip pieces of chicken in them before eating them.

CHICKEN WITH LYCHEES *

荔 枝 鸡
lì zhī jī

1 lb boneless chicken meat
10 oz lychees (fresh or canned)
¹/₂ medium-sized mild onion
¹/₂ green bell pepper
¹/₂ red bell pepper
oil for frying

For the batter:
1 tsp salt
¹/₂–1 tsp sugar
1 tbsp sesame seed oil
1 lightly beaten egg
¹/₄ cup cornstarch or potato flour

For the sauce:
3 tbsp oil
3 tbsp sugar

3 tbsp tomato ketchup
¹/₂–1 tsp salt
1¹/₂ tbsp Worcestershire sauce
1¹/₂ tbsp wine vinegar
pinch freshly ground pepper
1¹/₂ tbsp cornstarch or potato flour

Time: 1 hour 10 minutes

Cut the chicken meat into pieces not more than ¹/₂ in thick and just over 1 in long. Beat the sesame seed oil into the egg, followed by the salt, sugar, and cornstarch or potato flour.

Add the chicken pieces to the batter, stir well, and leave to marinate for 30 minutes.

Peel the onion and chop coarsely; chop the peppers into fairly small, even-sized pieces. Peel the lychees if fresh; drain if canned.

Heat plenty of oil in the wok or deep-fryer to 340°F and fry the chicken pieces for 3 or 4 minutes, remove from the oil, draining well, and set aside.

Heat 3 tbsp fresh oil in the emptied and wiped wok or in another skillet and stir-fry the onion and peppers; add the other sauce ingredients (except for the cornstarch or potato flour); add the lychees. Cook until the liquid has reduced a little, then stir in the thickening agent mixed with a little cold water. Return the

chicken pieces to the wok or pan and stir while heating through. Serve.

CHICKEN WITH SOY SAUCE AND ROSE LIQUOR

玫 瑰 油 鸡
méi guì yóu jī

1 oven-ready chicken weighing approx.
*   2–2¹/₄ lb*
¹/₄ cup rose liquor (méi guì yóu)
3 scallions
4 cloves garlic
3 thin slices fresh ginger
3 tbsp oil
1¹/₂ cups soy sauce
3 tbsp sugar
2 star anises
1 tbsp salt
1 tbsp sesame seed oil
1 tbsp cornstarch or potato flour

204

Time: 1 hour

Wash and dry the bird inside and out. Rub all over with 1½ tbsp of the rose liquor and leave to stand while you trim the scallion and chop it finely; peel the garlic and ginger and chop these finely as well. Heat 3 tbsp oil in the wok or in a deep, fireproof casserole dish and stir-fry the chopped mixture until it releases a strong aroma. Add the soy sauce, sugar, anises, salt, and remaining rose liquor.

Add the chicken and pour in sufficient water to cover; bring to a boil, lower the heat and simmer for approx. 1–1½ hours or until done turning at least once during this cooking time. Take the chicken out of the cooking liquid and leave to cool a little, then cut into pieces (use a carving knife and cut into the usual sections or cut the bird up in the Chinese way, bone and flesh together in bite-sized pieces, using a cleaver. Place these on a serving dish. Pour 1 cup of the cooking liquid through a fine sieve into a small saucepan and place over moderate heat; stir in the sesame seed oil; mix the cornstarch or potato flour with a very little cold water and stir into the saucepan to thicken the sauce. Continue cooking for a few minutes while stirring. Pour all over the chicken pieces.

The rose liquor used in this recipe is made from fermented cereal grains; the resulting spirit is scented and flavored with rose petals. Its name, Rose Dew, is misleading as it is a very potent alcoholic drink.

BRAISED CHICKEN WITH TREE EAR FUNGUS
木耳蒸鸡
mu ěr zhěng jī

8 chicken legs
4 large or 6 small mu er mushrooms (tree ear fungus)
1 scallion
¼ lb Savoy cabbage
¼ lb bamboo shoots
1 red bell pepper
⅓ cup oil

For the marinade:
1 tbsp salt
3 tbsp soy sauce
1 tsp sugar
1 tbsp rice wine

For the sauce:
½–1 tsp salt
1½ tbsp soy sauce
1½ tbsp sesame seed oil

1½ tbsp rice wine
1 tbsp wine vinegar

Time: 1 hour

Soak the mushrooms in warm water for 30 minutes or longer. Heat 3 tbsp oil in the wok and fry the chicken legs over high heat, turning frequently, for 2 minutes; take them out of the wok and place in a fairly deep dish. Mix the marinade ingredients thoroughly, pour over the chicken legs, and leave to stand for at least 10 minutes, turning now and then. Return the marinated chicken legs to the wok; save all the marinade, mix a little cold water with it and pour into the wok. Cook over moderate heat for 10 minutes, turning several times. Remove the chicken legs and set aside.

Trim off any tough parts of the well drained mushrooms; trim the scallion, wash and dry the Savoy cabbage, and drain the canned bamboo shoots; cut all these vegetables into fine matchstick strips. Heat ¼ cup oil in the wok and stir-fry the vegetables over high heat for 2 minutes. Mix all the sauce ingredients together, add 3 tbsp cold water and stir into the contents of the wok. Add the chicken legs and stir. Transfer the contents of the wok into a heatproof dish that will fit into your steamer; cover and steam for 10 minutes, then serve.

CHICKEN WITH MANGOES *
芒果鸡丁
máng guǒ jī dīng

1 lb chicken breasts
1 crisp, large carrot
½ red bell pepper
½ green bell pepper
1 ripe mango
¼ lb bamboo shoots
oil for frying

For the chicken marinade:
½ tsp bicarbonate of soda
½ tsp salt
½ tsp monosodium glutamate (optional)
1 tbsp sugar
1 egg white, lightly beaten
2 tbsp water
1 tbsp cornstarch or potato flour

For the sauce:
½ tsp salt
½ tsp monosodium glutamate (optional)
1 tsp sugar
1 tbsp light soy sauce
1 tbsp oyster sauce
1 tbsp sesame seed oil
1 tbsp rice wine
½ tbsp cornstarch or potato flour

Time: 1 hour

Cut the chicken breasts into small bite-sized pieces; mix all the chicken marinade ingredients thoroughly and mix well with the chicken pieces in a bowl. Leave to marinate for 30 minutes.

Trim and peel the carrot; cut into matchstick strips approx. ³/₄ in long and boil for 10 minutes in unsalted water. Cut the peppers and bamboo shoots into strips to match the carrots; cut the mango flesh into small, fairly thin pieces as neatly as possible.

Heat plenty of oil in the wok to 340°F and fry the chicken pieces for 2 minutes; remove from the oil with a slotted ladle, draining well. Add the carrot, peppers, mango, and bamboo shoots to the hot oil and fry in batches; dry for 1 minute each, then remove, draining thoroughly.

Heat 2 tbsp fresh oil in another wok or skillet, add the chicken and vegetables and stir in all the other ingredients listed under the sauce except for the thickening agent; stir-fry briefly, then mix the cornstarch or potato flour with a little cold water and add to the sauce to make it fairly thick and glossy.

FRIED CHICKEN WITH ALMONDS *

杏仁炸鸡
xìng rén zhà jī

1 oven-ready cockerel, pullet or young
    roasting chicken weighing approx. 2¹/₄ lb or
    2 chicken breasts weighing a total of 1¹/₄ lb
1 egg
2¹/₂ tbsp water
1 tsp salt
¹/₂ tsp monosodium glutamate (optional)
¹/₂–1 tsp sugar
1 tbsp light soy sauce
1 tbsp rice wine
pinch freshly ground pepper
1 tsp bicarbonate of soda
2¹/₂ tbsp cornstarch or potato flour
¹/₄ lb/¹/₂ cup blanched, peeled whole almonds
approx. 1 cup oil

Time: 1¹/₂ hours

Place the cockerel on a work surface with the breastbone pointing upward; use poultry scissors to cut from the center of the wishbone right along the breastbone to the vent end, leaving the two halves of the bird joined by the backbone; open the bird out flat and bone carefully, using a very sharp boning knife; cut the boned bird into 4 neat quarters of approximately equal weight (keeping the skin on) and

flatten these slightly with a meat bat or rolling pin. If you opt to use chicken breasts, cut each breast horizontally in half, trim off any remaining pieces of cartilage and remove the tendons, keep the skin on or not as you prefer, and use a meat bat to flatten a little. Place in a single layer in a fairly deep dish.

Lightly beat the egg with the water, salt, monosodium glutamate (if used), sugar, soy sauce, rice wine, pepper, and bicarbonate of soda. Add the cornstarch or potato flour and beat well; pour all over the chicken pieces and turn the pieces to coat thoroughly with this mixture. Leave to marinate for 30 minutes, turning once or twice.

Chop the almonds evenly but fairly coarsely; if you use a food processor, take care to process very briefly or they will be ground far too finely and lose their crunchy texture when used as a coating. Spread out on a plate. Take up the chicken pieces one at a time, drain briefly, then coat all over with the chopped almonds, pressing to make them adhere.

Heat at least $^1/_2$ cup oil in a nonstick skillet or the wok; when the oil is only moderately hot (290–300°F) add the chicken pieces and fry for

7–8 minutes, turning now and then if using a wok to prevent the pieces sticking and add a little more oil if necessary (increase the heat momentarily as you do this to keep the temperature even); turn and fry for another 7–8 minutes; by this time the almonds should be golden brown and the chicken cooked.

BRAISED CHICKEN *
清 蒸 滑 鸡
qīng zhēng huá jī

1 oven-ready chicken weighing approx. 3$^1/_4$ lb
5 tung ku (dong gu) mushrooms
10 thin slices fresh ginger
$^1/_2$ large scallion or 1 whole small scallion

For the marinade:
1 tsp finely chopped fresh ginger
1 tsp monosodium glutamate (optional)

2$^1/_2$ tbsp rice wine
1$^1/_2$ tsp light soy sauce
1 tsp salt
1$^1/_2$ tbsp cornstarch or potato flour mixed with 3 tbsp cold water

Time: 1$^1/_2$ hours

Chop the chicken into small pieces using a cleaver. Place in a fireproof casserole dish. Mix all the marinade ingredients together and pour all over the chicken; mix well and leave to stand for 30 minutes, stirring once or twice. Soak the dried mushrooms in warm water for the same length of time or longer; remove and discard their stalks and cut the caps into thin strips. Shred the peeled ginger slices. Add the mushrooms and ginger to the marinated chicken, stir and then cover with a tight-fitting lid and cook over moderate heat for 15 minutes. Trim and finely chop the scallion. Heat 3 tbsp oil in the wok; transfer the chicken from the casserole dish to the wok, sprinkle the scallion over it and stir-fry over moderate heat for 15 minutes, turning the pieces a few times for them to brown evenly.

CHICKEN WITH XUE CAI AND GINGER

雪菜鸡

xuě cài jī

1 oven-ready chicken weighing approx.
  2–2¹/₄ lb
¹/₄ lb xue cai (brine-pickled rape)
4 thin slices fresh ginger
1 leek
1 scallion
¹/₃ cup oil
1 tsp salt
1 tsp sugar
1 tbsp wine vinegar
1 tbsp rice wine
2¹/₂ tbsp sesame seed oil
1 tsp paprika

Time: 45 minutes

Wash and dry the chicken; use a cleaver or poultry scissors to cut it into fairly small pieces (about 16 pieces). Heat ¹/₄ cup oil in the wok and fry the chicken pieces over high heat for 5 minutes, turning frequently. Take the chicken pieces out of the wok, draining them well. Peel the ginger slices and cut into very thin strips; trim the leek and scallion and shred. Cut or chop the xue cai into fairly small pieces. Add 3 tbsp fresh oil to the wok and stir-fry all the vegetables over high heat for about 3 minutes, or until they are tender.

Return the chicken to the wok, add the salt, sugar, vinegar, rice wine, and sesame seed oil. Simmer for 10 minutes or until the chicken is cooked through, turning several times, then sprinkle with the paprika, stir and serve.

CHICKEN SHI LIU *

石榴鸡

shí liú jī

For the wrapper dough:
2¹/₄ cups all-purpose flour
2 cups (1 pint) water
pinch salt

For the filling:
1 lb boned chicken meat
4 tung ku (dong gu) mushrooms
1 small carrot
6 water chestnuts
1 scallion
¹/₄ lb celery
1 tsp salt
¹/₂ tsp monosodium glutamate (optional)
1 tbsp sesame seed oil

1 tbsp rice wine
pinch freshly ground pepper
1 tbsp soy sauce
1 tbsp cornstarch or potato flour
1 small bunch chives
oil for frying

Time: 2 hours

Gradually mix enough water into the sifted flour and salt to make a smooth elastic dough which is easy to handle; knead for a few minutes and then place in a bowl, covered with a clean cloth, and leave to rest for 1 hour. Soak the dried mushrooms in warm water for 20–30 minutes. Chop all the vegetables very finely. Rinse the chicken, remove any skin and dry; chop very finely. When the mushrooms are fully reconstituted and soft, remove and discard their stalks and chop the caps finely.

Mix all the chopped ingredients together in a bowl very thoroughly; stir in the salt, monosodium glutamate (if used), sesame oil, rice wine, pepper, soy sauce, and cornstarch. Knead the rested dough then roll out into a thin sheet on a lightly floured work surface and cut into 8-in squares. Place a fairly large ball of the filling mixture (about the size of an apricot) in the center of each square sheet; bring the edges of the square up and over the filling and gather on top (have a small "frill" on top, just enough to be easy to tie securely with 1 or 2 strands of chives). Snip off the longer corners and bend back the frill a little (without exposing the filling); this presentation is thought by the Chinese to be reminiscent of a pomegranate (*shi liu* means pomegranate). Heat plenty of oil to 325°F or a little hotter in the wok or deep-fryer and lower the "pomegranates" into it, frying 2 or 3 at a time, until they are golden brown all over (approx. 5 minutes). Drain well and serve hot.

CHICKEN RISSOLES

煎 鸡 饼

jiān jī bǐng

9 oz chicken breasts
4 water chestnuts
2¹/₂ tbsp finely chopped scallion
1¹/₂ tsp finely chopped fresh ginger
1¹/₂ tbsp cornstarch or potato flour
2 egg whites
¹/₂ tbsp salt
¹/₂ tbsp sugar
¹/₂ tsp monosodium glutamate (optional)
1¹/₂ tbsp sesame seed oil
generous pinch freshly ground pepper
1¹/₂ tbsp chopped Chinese Gold Coin ham,
    Virginia ham or Westphalian ham
¹/₃ cup oil

Time: 45 minutes

Skin the chicken breasts, remove the thin tendons between the layers of flesh and any remaining pieces of cartilage, fat etc. Chop the chicken and water chestnuts very finely and mix with 1¹/₂ tbsp of the scallion and all the ginger and the cornstarch or potato flour. Use your hands to shape this mixture into small, firm balls 2 in or smaller in diameter. Whisk the egg whites, fold in the salt, sugar, monosodium glutamate (if used), sesame seed oil, and pepper. Add the meat balls to this mixture and leave for a few minutes; turn them all to coat evenly and leave for a little longer. Mix the remaining scallion with all the ham and roll the rissoles in the mixture, pressing lightly so that it adheres to them.

Heat sufficient oil in the wok to semi deep-or shallow-fry the chicken balls (have this at a moderate heat, 275–290°F); turn them carefully several times so that they brown deeply and evenly all over, by which time they should be well done inside as well as outside.

CHICKEN KABOBS

串 烧 鸡 块

chuàn shāo jī kuài

14 oz chicken breasts

For the marinade:
1 tsp salt
1 tsp sugar
1 tbsp dark soy sauce
1 tbsp light soy sauce
¹/₂ tsp monosodium glutamate (optional)
pinch freshly ground pepper
1 tbsp sesame seed oil
1 tbsp rice wine
pinch five-spice powder

Time: 30 minutes + 1 hour marinating time

Remove any remaining pieces of cartilage etc. from the chicken breasts and cut them lengthwise in half. Remove the very thin, membranous strips of muscle from between the layers of flesh and cut the half breasts across into pieces about 1 in wide.

Mix all the marinade ingredients together in a deep dish or bowl, stir in the chicken pieces, and leave to marinate for 1 hour.

Thread the marinated chicken pieces onto steel skewers (or wood satay sticks) and place these in a shallow roasting pan; cook in a moderate oven for about 10 minutes, then serve. Alternatively, broil under medium heat, turning once or twice.

FRIED CHICKEN MORSELS

软 炸 鸡

ruǎn zhà jī

1 lb chicken breasts
1 tbsp light soy sauce
1 egg, lightly beaten
¹/₂ cup cornstarch or potato flour
oil for frying

For the sauce:
1¹/₂ tbsp rice wine
1¹/₂ tbsp sesame seed oil
¹/₂ tsp monosodium glutamate (optional)
¹/₂ tsp salt
¹/₂ tsp sugar
2¹/₂ tbsp Worcestershire sauce

Time: 30 minutes

Trim off any pieces of cartilage, cut the chicken breasts horizontally in half and remove the thin, stringy strips of muscle. Cut the breasts into pieces measuring about 1 × 2 in and coat with the cornstarch or potato flour, shaking off any excess. Heat plenty of oil in the wok or deep-fryer to 340°F and fry the chicken pieces until golden brown; remove them from the oil, draining well, and place on kitchen paper to finish draining.

Add the sauce ingredients to a clean wok or pan and stir, add the fried chicken pieces, and mix to flavor and moisten evenly.

CHICKEN LIVER PARCEL
WITH OYSTER SAUCE *

网 油 凤 肝 卷

wǎng yóu fèng gān juǎn

1 pig's caul
14 oz chicken livers
¹/₄ lb button mushrooms
¹/₄ lb bamboo shoots
¹/₄ lb York ham
¹/₂ tsp monosodium glutamate (optional)
¹/₂–1 tsp sugar
¹/₂–1 tsp salt
2¹/₂ tbsp oyster sauce
1 tbsp sesame seed oil
1 tbsp rice wine
¹/₂ cup cornstarch or potato flour
oil for frying

Time: 40 minutes

Soften the pig's caul by soaking in warm (not hot) water to which a little wine vinegar or salt

210

has been added. Wipe the mushrooms with a damp cloth; trim off their stalks if necessary; drain the bamboo shoots. Chop the mushrooms and the bamboo shoots into very small pieces. Wash the chicken livers, cut out any discolored parts (often yellowish) and snip out any pieces of gristle; cut these and the ham into small pieces the same size as the vegetables. Stir-fry the mushrooms, bamboo shoots, and chicken livers in a little oil in the wok for a few minutes only; remove from the wok, draining well, and mix in a bowl with the ham, monosodium glutamate (if used), sugar, salt, oyster sauce, sesame seed oil, and rice wine. Wrap the prepared mixture up firmly in the pig's caul, shaping it into a sausage short enough to fit into your wok or deep-fryer easily. Do not make it into too fat a shape or it will take too long to cook through properly and the outside will brown too quickly before it is done in the middle. Mix 1¹/₂ tbsp corn-

starch or alternative with a very little cold water and brush this lightly all over the outside of the bundle to moisten. Coat the bundle all over with the remaining cornstarch or potato flour.

Heat plenty of oil to 325°F or a little higher in the wok or deep-fryer; lower the "sausage" into the hot oil and fry until deep golden brown all over. Slice and serve.

DUCK WITH TANGERINE PEEL

陈 皮 鸭

chén pí yā

1 oven-ready duck weighing approx. 4–4¹/₂ lb
6 tbsp soy sauce
oil for frying
¹/₄ lb pork belly
1 tbsp salt
¹/₂ tsp monosodium glutamate (optional)
1 scallion
3 tbsp rice wine
3 fairly thick slices fresh ginger
2 quarts broth
¹/₄ lb dried Chinese tangerine or orange peel

Time: 3 hours

Wash the duck, having first removed any pieces of fat left behind inside the cavity; dry very thoroughly. Rub half the soy sauce into the surface of the duck (inside and out) and leave to stand for 10 minutes.

Fry the whole duck in plenty of very hot oil, preferably in a deep-fryer. If using a wok take care to see that it is properly stabilized and use less oil than appears necessary as the duck will displace a great deal and it could overflow,

which would be dangerous. Turn the duck if not deep-frying so that all the surface is well browned. Take carefully out of the oil and immediately add to a very large saucepan about two-thirds full of boiling water. Slice the pork belly thinly and cut these slices into pieces measuring about $1^{1}/_{2} \times 2$ in; blanch these for a few minutes in fresh boiling water, then drain well.

Place the duck, breast side uppermost, in a flameproof casserole dish (earthenware or enameled cast iron are best); add the pork belly, the salt, remaining soy sauce, monosodium glutamate (if used), scallion, rice wine, ginger, and the broth. Cover and simmer very gently for 2 hours. About 1 hour 40 minutes into this simmering time, stir the finely shredded tangerine peel into the liquid and continue simmering, uncovered, for the final 20 minutes' cooking time.

CANTONESE DUCK *

广东鸭

guǎng dōng yā

1 oven-ready duck weighing approx. 4–4$^{1}/_{2}$ lb
pinch salt
pinch five-spice powder
$^{1}/_{2}$ tsp very finely chopped fresh ginger
$^{1}/_{2}$ tsp very finely chopped garlic
$^{1}/_{2}$ tbsp hot (peppery chili) soy paste (dou ban jiang)

For the lacquering mixture:
$^{1}/_{2}$ cup hot water
3 tbsp wine vinegar
1$^{1}/_{2}$ tbsp sugar
red food coloring

For the sauce:
$^{1}/_{2}$ cup broth
1 tsp light soy sauce

1 tsp dark soy sauce
$^{1}/_{2}$–1 tsp sugar
$^{1}/_{2}$ tsp monosodium glutamate (optional)
1 tbsp cornstarch or potato flour

Time: 1$^{1}/_{2}$ hours + 6–7 hours drying time after lacquering

Mix the salt, five-spice powder, ginger, garlic, and soy paste, place this mixture inside the duck's cavity, and sew up both ends, using a poultry needle and kitchen string. Mix the lacquering ingredients well and use a pastry brush to brush the entire surface of the duck with the liquid; leave to dry on a rack (breast side uppermost) for 6–7 hours in a cool, dry place. Transfer the duck, still on the rack, to a roasting pan and roast for 1 hour in a hot oven (preheat the oven to 400°F and reduce the heat if the skin begins to burn). Cut into bite-sized pieces. Heat the cooking juices in a small saucepan with the sauce ingredients and hand round separately.

SALTY DUCK

盐 鸭

yán jú yā

1 oven-ready duck weighing approx. 4¹/₂ lb
1 tsp salt
2 fairly thick slices fresh ginger, shredded
1 scallion
2¹/₂ tbsp rice wine
1 small piece cinnamon bark, crumbled
4 star anises
2 dried lotus leaves, pre-soaked in warm
  water
1 tbsp sesame seed oil
3 tbsp shortening, melted
2¹/₂ tbsp oil
1 cup rose liquor or rose spirit (mei kwei lu)
6 cloves
9 lb coarse salt

Time: 6 hours

Sprinkle the duck inside and out with the salt; place in a dish with the ginger, scallion, rice wine, cinnamon, and star anises. Marinate for 2 hours, turning frequently.

Blanch the lotus leaves for a few minutes in boiling water, drain, open out flat, and pat dry with kitchen towels, then brush all over with the sesame seed oil and shortening. Drain off the duck marinade, reserving the scallion and ginger pieces; rinse and dry these.

Heat 3 tbsp oil in a wok and stir-fry the scallion and ginger until they begin to release their full aroma. Add the rose liquor, the cloves and the duck, breast side uppermost; fry gently over low heat; turn the duck after about 5 minutes and continue frying until very lightly colored all over. Remove the duck and place, breast side uppermost, on the oiled side of the lotus leaves, then fold the lotus leaves over the duck and wrap it up, tying with kitchen string. Wrap this parcel in turn in a very large piece of waxed paper or vegetable parchment.

Clean the large casserole dish (or use a large wok) and heat the salt in it; remove half the salt and set aside while you place the duck package on the remaining layer of salt; pack the reserved salt all around the package and on top, to completely enclose the parcel. Place the lid on top and cook in a preheated oven at 350°F for 1 hour, then reduce the heat to 290°F and cook for a further 2 hours. Break open the hardened salt, take out the duck parcel, unwrap the paper wrapping, and serve the duck in its lotus leaf wrapping.

FRIED QUAILS *

炸 禾 花 雀

zhà hé huā què

12 oven-ready quails
oil for frying

For the marinade:
6 tbsp soy sauce
1 heaping tsp freshly ground pepper
1¹/₂ tbsp rice wine
1 tbsp sugar
1 tbsp salt

For the sauce:
¹/₄ cup tomato ketchup
3 tbsp Worcestershire sauce
1¹/₂ tbsp rice wine
1 heaping tsp sugar
1¹/₂ tbsp sesame seed oil

Time: 1 hour

Place the quails in a fairly deep dish in a single layer. Mix the marinade ingredients and pour all over the quails. Leave to marinate for 30 minutes, turning a few times and spooning a little of the marinade inside the cavities of the birds. Heat plenty of oil for semi deep-frying in the wok (or use a deep-fryer); when it has reached 290°F or a little hotter, add the quails and fry the birds in 3 or 4 batches until golden brown all over and cooked. Drain well and keep warm on paper towels. Heat 1¹/₂ tbsp fresh oil in the emptied and wiped wok or in a very large skillet, add all the sauce ingredients and immediately stir in 3 tbsp water. Add the fried quail and cook, turning several times until the sauce has reduced somewhat; serve.

STUFFED BRAISED TOFU *

酿豆腐

níang dòu fǔ

1¼ lb very firm fresh tofu (bean curd)
6 oz pork tenderloin
¼ lb pork belly
1 scallion
½ tsp salt
½ tsp sugar
pinch monosodium glutamate (optional)
1 tbsp soy sauce
1 tbsp sesame seed oil
1 tbsp cornstarch or potato flour
¾ cup all-purpose flour
oil for frying

For the sauce:
½ cup broth
1 tbsp oyster sauce
½ tbsp soy sauce
½ tbsp rice wine
½ tbsp sesame seed oil
1 tbsp cornstarch or potato flour

Time: 1 hour

Cut the tofu into even 2-in square slices ¾ in thick. Grind the pork tenderloin and pork belly; trim and finely chop the scallion. Mix the ground meat very thoroughly with ½ tsp each salt and sugar, a pinch of monosodium glutamate (if used), 1 tbsp each soy sauce, sesame seed oil, and cornstarch or potato flour. Transfer this mixture to a heatproof dish, cover, and steam for 5 minutes. Divide this cooked stuffing mixture into 12 equal portions; press each portion flat, making sure the mixture sticks together, looking almost like a slice of meat loaf; they should be of a size to leave an uncovered border all the way round the tofu square beneath them. Place the flattened filling "slices" on top of 12 of the tofu slices and cover with the remaining 12 slices.

Mix the remaining flour well with just enough cold water to form a thick coating paste or batter (the consistency should be only just liquid enough to pour and just not thick enough to qualify as a "paste"). Press the edges of the tofu "sandwiches" gently together; use a little flour and water paste if wished to make them stick together. Coat carefully with flour and then coat all over with the flour and water batter.

Heat plenty of oil in the wok or use a deep-fryer; when the oil has reached 325°F (medium-high) fry the tofu sandwiches until golden brown all over and little bubbles have started to form on the surface. Use a frying basket if you can as the tofu breaks up fairly easily. Remove from the oil, draining well. Empty the oil out of the wok, wipe the inside, and pour in the broth. Stir in all the other sauce ingredi-ents, stir well until thoroughly heated through, then add the fried tofu sandwiches. Cover and simmer gently for about 5 minutes, then carefully thicken the sauce with the cornstarch or potato flour mixed with a little cold water. Stir the sauce around the tofu and serve.

PLATTER OF ASSORTED COLD MEATS

什锦冷盘

shí jǐn lěng pán

1 tung ku (dong gu) mushroom
¼ lb cold roast pork tenderloin (see p. 218)
1 large, long white radish (Daikon root)
¼ lb Strange-Flavored Chicken (see p. 260)
¼ lb canned abalone
¼ lb thinly sliced York ham
¼ lb Beef in Hot Sauce (see p. 268)
2 large, fat white asparagus spears
1 carrot
1 candied glacé cherry

Time: 40 minutes

Soak the dried mushroom in warm water for 20–30 minutes. Cut the pork into thin slices then cut each slice in half. Peel, wash, and dry the white radish (Daikon root) and shred.

Shred the chicken; drain the abalone and slice very thinly. Trim the sliced ham into oval shapes; cut the beef into thin slices. Boil the asparagus for 5 minutes, then carefully slice lengthwise into three strips, starting from the tip and cutting only one third of the way down each spear. Peel the carrot and take a slice out of the narrower end, cutting obliquely at a very acute angle. Remove and discard the mushroom stalk, then trim the cap into a long, oval shape.

The correct, Chinese way to assemble this platter of assorted meats and vegetables is to imagine you are trying to portray a chicken (viewed in profile): use a very large platter and arrange the shredded white radish in a mounded shape something like the head and neck of a fowl and place the carrot slice in front of this to represent the beak. The mushroom is placed where the eye would be with the cherry (halved so that it will stay in place) placed on top for the eye. Shape the shredded chicken to represent the body; apply the pork, ham and beef slices, overlapping, to look like the bird's wing; the asparagus spears go below the body, with the sliced ends splayed out to represent the feet. The arrangement is often further embellished by a border of sesame shrimp (see p. 180) and bundles of shredded vegetables. The radish and the surrounding vegetables can be dressed with a mixture of oil, wine vinegar, pepper, and salt.

BEEF WITH OYSTER SAUCE

蚝油牛肉

háo yóu niú ròu

1 lb lean beef (e.g. fillet or any tender, prime cut)
1 tbsp cornstarch or potato flour
1 tbsp light soy sauce
½ tsp salt
1 tbsp rice wine
generous pinch freshly ground pepper
½ tsp bicarbonate of soda
1 egg white
6 tbsp oil

For the sauce:
3 thin slices fresh ginger
2½ tbsp oyster sauce
1½ tbsp sesame seed oil
1½ tbsp rice wine
1½ tbsp cornstarch or potato flour

Time: 1 hour 10 minutes

Cut the beef into very thin rectangular slices approx. 1¼–1½ in in size. Mix the cornstarch or potato flour with the soy sauce, salt, rice wine, pepper, bicarbonate of soda, and egg white in a large bowl, add the meat, stir well to coat all the pieces, and leave to marinate for 45 minutes, then drain off any excess moisture. Heat ¼ cup oil in the wok and stir-fry the beef over high heat for only 30 seconds, keeping the slices separate; remove the slices, draining well, and set aside. Heat 3 tbsp fresh oil in the wiped wok and stir-fry the shredded ginger; add the oyster sauce, the sesame seed oil, and rice wine and then return the beef to the wok; stir over gentle heat for 1 minute. Mix the cornstarch or potato flour with a little cold water and stir into the wok to thicken the remaining liquid; serve.

BEEF WITH BLACK PEPPER

黑椒牛柳

hēi jiāo niú liǔ

10 oz beef fillet
⅓ cup soy sauce
1½ tbsp oil
1 tsp cornstarch or potato flour
pinch bicarbonate of soda
5 oz scallions
pinch salt
pinch monosodium glutamate (optional)
pinch sugar
1½ tsp oyster sauce
1 heaping tbsp freshly ground black pepper
oil for frying

Time: 20 minutes + 1 hour marinating time

Cut the beef into rectangular strips approx. $^3/_8$ in thick, $^3/_8$ in wide, and 1–1$^1/_4$ in long. Mix the soy sauce in a large bowl with the oil, the cornstarch or potato flour mixed with a little cold water, and the bicarbonate of soda. Add the beef and stir well to coat all the pieces thoroughly. Leave to marinate for 1 hour. Trim the scallions and shred into short, thin strips. When the beef has been marinated sufficiently, stir-fry it in 3 tbsp hot oil in the wok over high heat for no more than 1 minute; take the beef out of the wok, draining well as you do so, and set aside. Stir-fry the scallions in the same oil for 2 minutes, then set aside.

Add 1$^1/_2$ tbsp fresh oil to the remaining oil and juices in the wok; return the scallions to the wok, add the salt, monosodium glutamate (if used), the sugar, oyster sauce, black pepper, and 3 tbsp water. Stir well. Return the beef to the wok; stir well and quickly, for no longer than it takes to coat and flavor it thoroughly with the sauce and seasonings. Serve with a sprinkling of parsley.

STIR-FRIED BEEF WITH ONIONS *

洋葱牛肉
yáng cōng niú ròu

10 oz lean beef (e.g. fillet or any tender, prime cut)
$^1/_4$ cup soy sauce
14 oz onions
6 tbsp oil
1 egg white
1$^1/_2$ tbsp cornstarch or potato flour
oil for frying
1$^1/_2$ tsp rice wine
1$^1/_2$ tbsp sugar
pinch monosodium glutamate (optional)

Time: 20 minutes + 30 minutes marinating time

Thinly shred the beef and place the strips in a bowl. Add 2 tbsp of the soy sauce, mix well, and leave to marinate for 30 minutes. Cut the onions into thin rings just under $^1/_4$ in thick. Heat the 6 tbsp oil in the wok and stir-fry the sliced onions. Whisk the egg white, fold in the cornstarch or potato flour and then mix well with the marinated beef. Heat plenty of oil for semi deep-frying or deep-frying and when very hot, fry the beef strips briefly until lightly browned using cooking chopsticks or a long-handled fork to keep them from sticking to each other as far as possible. Remove with a wire mesh ladle or slotted spoon and drain well; add to the onions in the wok. Mix well, adding the rice wine, sugar, and monosodium glutamate (if used) for added flavor and stir-fry for a further 1–2 minutes before serving very hot in a heated serving dish.

BEEF WITH BROCCOLI *

芥兰牛肉

jiè lán niú ròu

¹/₂ lb broccoli
14 oz lean beef (e.g. fillet or any tender prime cut)
1 egg white
1 tbsp cornstarch or potato flour
1 tbsp light soy sauce
¹/₂ tsp salt
1 tbsp rice wine
¹/₂ tsp bicarbonate of soda
¹/₃ cup oil

For the sauce:
¹/₄ cup oyster sauce
1¹/₂ tbsp sesame seed oil
1¹/₂ tbsp soy sauce
1¹/₂ tbsp rice wine
¹/₂ tsp monosodium glutamate (optional)
pinch sugar
1¹/₂ tsp cornstarch or potato flour

Time: 40 minutes

Divide the broccoli into small florets with just a short length of stalk attached; wash well and then add to a pan of fast boiling water to blanch for 2 minutes (this means that by the time the dish is ready, they will be just tender but still crunchy, the way the Chinese like most of their green vegetables). Drain well and set aside. Cut the beef into very thin slices, as near to 1¹/₄ in square as possible. Whisk the egg white until stiff, fold in the cornstarch, soy sauce, salt, rice wine, and bicarbonate of soda, then mix in the beef slices to coat all over; leave to marinate for 10 minutes.

Heat ¹/₄ cup oil in the wok and stir-fry the marinated beef over high heat for 30 seconds and no longer; remove from the wok, drain well and set aside. Heat 3 tbsp fresh oil in the wok and stir-fry the broccoli just long enough to coat completely with oil and heat through thoroughly; return the meat to the wok and then add all the sauce ingredients; stir to heat through and flavor the beef and the broccoli thoroughly. Mix the cornstarch or potato flour with a little cold water and stir into the contents of the wok. Serve.

STIR-FRIED BEEF WITH SWEET PEPPERS

青椒牛肉片

qīng jiāo niú ròu pián

1/2 lb lean beef (e.g. fillet or any tender prime cut)
1 tbsp rice wine
1 tbsp cornstarch or potato flour
1 tsp salt
1 tbsp sugar
1 tsp ground chili
1 large green bell pepper
1/4 cup oil
2 scallions, finely chopped
1 tsp finely chopped fresh ginger
2 1/2 tbsp soy sauce

Time: 30 minutes + 20 minutes marinating time

Slice the beef thinly, then cut these slices into thin strips, place in a bowl with the rice wine, cornstarch or potato flour, salt, sugar, and chili powder and stir well; leave to marinate for 20 minutes. Remove the stalk, seeds, and inner pale fibrous parts of the green pepper and cut into thin strips of even length. Heat 1 1/2 tbsp oil in the wok and stir-fry the green pepper until just tender; remove from the wok with a slotted spoon or wire mesh ladle, draining well, and set aside. Add 2 1/2 tbsp fresh oil to the wok and stir-fry the scallions and ginger; add the beef and stir-fry briefly over high heat (err on the side of undercooking or the beef may harden and toughen); add the oyster sauce and the green pepper. Continue stir-frying for 1–2 minutes, then serve.

ROAST PORK TENDERLOIN

叉烧

chā shāo

1 scallion
3 slices fresh ginger
3 tbsp rice wine
3 tbsp soy sauce
1 1/2 tbsp rose liquor or spirit (miei kwei lu)
2 1/2 tbsp sugar
1 tsp salt
1 1/2 tbsp fermented soy paste
1 1/4 lb pork tenderloin, in one piece

Time: 40 minutes + marinating time

Trim the scallion, peel the ginger, and cut both into short, very thin strips; mix these in a fairly deep rectangular or oval ovenproof dish or roasting pan with the rice wine, soy sauce, rose liquor, sugar, salt, and fermented soy paste. Roll the piece of pork in this mixture and leave to marinate for 2–3 hours, turning several times to flavor evenly.

Place the pork, still in the dish, in a pre-heated oven at 300°F for 30 minutes or until cooked through and a good golden brown on the outside. If the pork appears to be cooking too quickly, lower the oven temperature to 285°–290°F.

This is also delicious spit-roasted on a rotisserie, if you have one in your oven.

ROAST PORK BELLY

烧肉

shāo ròu

2 1/4 lb fresh pork belly, in one piece, with the rind on
3 tbsp salt
1 tbsp sugar
2 tsp monosodium glutamate (optional)
2 1/2 tsp five-spice powder

Time: 1 hour or 1 1/2 hours if marinated in vinegar

Add the pork belly to a large saucepan of boiling water and blanch for 3 minutes; take out and drain, place in a bowl or dish; mix all the other ingredients listed above and pour over the meat; turn the meat so that it is evenly coated and flavored. Leave to stand, turning now and then, for 30 minutes.

In China this marinated pork belly is usually threaded on a spit and cooked over glowing embers but it can be cooked almost equally well with the rotisserie unit in your oven if you have one, or roasted on a rack in a roasting pan, skin side uppermost, at 450°F for 20 minutes or until the skin is very crisp and crunchy and the pork belly is cooked through; after the first 5 minutes reduce the oven temperature to 400°F and then, after a further 5 minutes, to 350°F. Slice fairly thickly and serve.

If wished, you can use red food coloring powder to color the pork attractively before roasting it: mix 1/2–1 tbsp red food coloring powder with 3 tbsp hot water and rub all over the pork belly before threading it on the spit or placing on the rack. If you use a rack, start the meat roasting with the skin side uppermost so that it will crisp well. For an even crisper skin, and to run less risk of the rind becoming tough during cooking, sprinkle the blanched, dried piece of pork belly all over with wine vinegar and leave to stand for 30 minutes before marinating.

SWEET AND SOUR PORK *

咕噜肉

gū lū ròu

1 lb pork tenderloin
1 green or red bell pepper
1 large onion
1/4 lb fresh pineapple, peeled, cored, and sliced
2 eggs
pinch bicarbonate of soda
1/2 tsp monosodium glutamate (optional)
1/2 tsp sugar
1 tsp salt
1/4 cup cornstarch or potato flour
oil for frying

For the sauce:
2 tbsp wine vinegar
4 tbsp tomato ketchup
1 1/2 tbsp Worcestershire sauce
1/3 cup sugar
1 1/2 tsp dark soy sauce
1 1/2 tsp light soy sauce
1/2 tsp monosodium glutamate (optional)

Time: 40 minutes

Cut the pork into small, bite-sized pieces; remove the stalk, seeds, and inner white parts of the bell pepper and cut into short, thin strips. Peel the onion and cut into thin strips. Cut the pineapple into thin, bite-sized pieces. Beat the eggs lightly with 1 1/2 tbsp cold water, beat in the bicarbonate of soda, the monosodium glutamate (if used), sugar, and salt, add the pork and mix well, then coat each piece with cornstarch or potato flour, shaking off any excess. Semi deep-fry or deep-fry the pork in very hot oil for 2 minutes. Remove the pork from the oil with a wire mesh ladle or slotted spoon, draining well, and set aside. Fry the green pepper and onion for 1 minute, take out of the oil, and drain well. Heat 3 tbsp fresh oil; add the sauce ingredients and heat through, stirring well. Mix the cornstarch or potato flour with a little cold water and stir into the sauce to thicken. Add the pork, green pepper, onion, and pineapple to this sauce and stir to coat all the ingredients with sauce.

HOT AND SOUR PORK *

酸辣肉煲

suān là ròn bāo

14 oz pork tenderloin
1 egg
pinch bicarbonate of soda
1/2 tsp monosodium glutamate (optional)
1/2–1 tsp salt
1/2–1 tsp sugar

MEAT

¹/₄ cup cornstarch or potato flour
oil for frying
1 red bell pepper
1 scallion
¹/₄ cup oil

220

For the sauce:
3 tbsp wine vinegar
3 tbsp tomato ketchup
2¹/₂ tbsp finely chopped fresh ginger
1¹/₂ tsp dark soy sauce
1¹/₂ tbsp light soy sauce
¹/₂ tbsp monosodium glutamate (optional)
1¹/₂ tbsp hot (chili) soy paste (from Szechwan)
1 tsp salt

Time: 50 minutes

Cut the pork into slices about ³/₈ in thick and cut these into rectangles measuring about 1¹/₄ × 1¹/₂ in; beat the egg lightly with the bicarbonate of soda, monosodium glutamate (if used), salt, sugar, and cornstarch or potato flour. Add the meat to this mixture and stir to coat all the pieces evenly. Leave to stand for 20 minutes. Remove the stalk, seeds, and inner white parts of the red pepper and cut into pieces to match the pork; peel the onion, separate into layers, and cut these to match the size of the red pepper pieces. Heat sufficient oil in the wok for semi deep-frying and fry the pork pieces for 2 minutes. Drain, and set aside.

Heat ¹/₄ cup oil in a fireproof casserole dish and stir-fry the red pepper and scallion for 1 minute. Add all the sauce ingredients and stir in 6 tbsp water; cook, uncovered, for 5 minutes, then add the pork and cook, stirring, for 2–3 minutes then serve.

BRAISED PORK HOCK
红烧元蹄
hóng shāo yúan tí

1 pork hock or shank end of ham weighing approx. 2¹/₄ lb
1¹/₂ tbsp light soy sauce
1¹/₂ tbsp dark soy sauce
7 thin slices fresh ginger
6 scallions

2 star anises
1 small piece cinnamon bark
oil for frying

For the sauce:
2 cups broth or water
¹/₂–1 tsp salt
¹/₂ tsp monosodium glutamate (optional)
1 heaping tbsp sugar
2¹/₂ tsp light soy sauce
2¹/₂ tsp oyster sauce
1 tbsp dark soy sauce
1 tsp cornstarch

Time: 50 minutes

Sprinkle the pork all over with the soy sauce and leave to stand for 15 minutes. Heat approx. ¹/₄ cup oil in the wok or a large skillet and when very hot brown the pork all over. Lift out the pork and place in a colander; pour boiling water all over it, allowing the water to run off the meat, and drain away.

Wipe the wok if used for browning the meat and heat 3 tbsp fresh oil in it (or use the fireproof casserole dish) and stir-fry the peeled and finely chopped ginger and scallions; add

the star anises and cinnamon, stir well, then add all the sauce ingredients except for the cornstarch or potato flour; mix well, add the pork and cook very gently for 2 hours or until very tender. Add a little water to moisten and prevent the meat catching and burning whenever necessary. Slice the pork and arrange on a heated serving plate; strain the cooking juices into a small saucepan and heat. Mix the cornstarch with 1 tsp cold water, and stir into the saucepan to thicken. Pour over the meat.

PORK WITH SOYBEAN SPROUTS
豆芽炒肉丝
dòu yá chǎo ròu sī

14 oz lean pork (e.g. leg or tenderloin)
3 tbsp soy sauce
1¹/₂ tbsp rice wine
1¹/₂ tsp cornstarch
10 oz fresh soybean sprouts (or mungbean
* sprouts)*
2 onions
4 thick slices fresh ginger
1 leek
¹/₄ cup oil
1 tsp salt

Time: 25 minutes + 20 minutes marinating time

Cut the pork into thin slices, then cut these into thin strips and place in a bowl. Add the soy sauce, rice wine, and cornstarch, stir well, and leave to stand and marinate for 20 minutes. Place the soybean sprouts in a large bowl (if unavailable, mungbean sprouts, obtainable fresh all the year round, will do just as well); fill with cold water and leave to stand for a few minutes, then take out the sprouts, discarding any material which has fallen to the bottom of the bowl. Pick off any empty seed cases as well as any ungerminated seeds and discard them. Peel the onions and slice thinly. Peel the ginger and cut into thin strips. Wash the leek thoroughly, dry, and cut lengthwise into thin strips 1¹/₂ in long.

Heat 1¹/₂ tbsp oil in the wok and stir-fry the onion and ginger; when they have softened, add the meat and stir-fry over high heat for only a few minutes. Take the meat and onions and ginger out of the wok, draining well with a wire mesh ladle or slotted spoon, and set aside. Wipe the inside of the wok and heat 3 tbsp fresh oil in it; add the bean sprouts and the leek. Stir-fry for 2 minutes, then add the meat, sprinkle with the salt, and stir well for half a minute. Serve immediately, while still very hot.

Rice fields along the Li Yang river, south of the city of Guilin. The farmers here use oxen and Indian water buffalo to drag their ploughs through the waterlogged rice paddies. This region's rich harvest of rices is spread out to dry in the sun, then gathered into bundles and carried to granaries by field workers riding some of the thousands of bicycles upon which people rely so heavily in China. There it is stored for the winter, still on the stalk.

Apart from these large rice paddies, rice is also grown in terraces, built down the side of steep hills; an inaccessible village is situated atop a series of terraces built 600 years ago by people belonging to China's largest minority, the Zhuang.

During the reign of the Sui dynasty, the Imperial Canal was built, linking three large rivers to facilitate the transport of rice from the fertile south to the less favored north. Also transported are sesame seeds, dried fish, and edible river weed.

STIR-FRIED PORK WITH BAMBOO SHOOTS
冬笋炒肉丝
dōng sǔn chǎo ròu sī

10 oz pork tenderloin
3 tbsp soy sauce
1¹/₂ tbsp rice wine
10 oz bamboo shoots
1 scallion
1 large ripe tomato
¹/₄ cup oil
1 clove garlic
1¹/₂ tbsp wine vinegar

Time: 20 minutes

Chop the pork very finely (do not grind) and place in a mixing bowl; sprinkle with half the soy sauce and with the rice wine, mix well and leave to marinate for 20 minutes. Cut the bamboo shoots into small pieces; trim and peel the scallion and cut into thin rings. Peel and deseed the tomato and cut the flesh into thin strips.

Heat the oil in the wok or in a large skillet with the peeled and half-minced clove of garlic; when the garlic clove has flavored the oil and is turning golden brown, remove and discard it. Add the meat to the flavored oil and stir well while cooking briskly for 1–2 minutes. Add the remaining soy sauce and the bamboo shoots and sprinkle with the vinegar. Continue cooking and stirring until the vinegar has completely evaporated. Serve, decorated with the sliced scallion and tomato strips.

CRAB OMELET

蟹肉炒蛋

xiè ròu chǎo dàn

222

6 very fresh large eggs
1 cup crabmeat
2 scallions
1 slice fresh ginger, 1 1/4 in thick
1 tbsp light soy sauce
1 tbsp rice wine
1 tsp sugar
1/4 cup oil
1 ripe, firm tomato
few crisp lettuce leaves
1 grape
salt

Time: 30 minutes

Peel the ginger and shred finely. Peel the scallions, cut off the green leaf section, and cut into very thin rings; set aside. Slice the white part of the scallion into thin sections. Break the eggs into a large bowl; beat in the green section of the scallions and the salt with a fork. Wash the lettuce leaves then dry and shred them. Cut the tomato horizontally in half with a regular zig-zag cut so that when you separate the two halves they are decoratively saw-toothed. Heat the oil in the wok or a skillet and stir-fry the white part of the scallions over fairly high heat. Add the ginger, stir-fry briefly until it releases its aroma and then add the crabmeat. Sprinkle with the rice wine and cook until this has evaporated. Stir in the soy sauce and the sugar. Lower the heat, give the egg mixture another stir and pour into the wok or skillet. Cook until completely set. Slide the omelet onto a heated serving plate, surround with the shredded lettuce, and place one half of the tomato in the center of the omelet with the grape in its center to represent a flower. Serve.

TOFU OMELET PI PA STYLE *

琵琶豆腐

pí pá dòu fǔ

¹/₂ lb firm tofu (bean curd)
³/₄ cup peeled shrimp
2 tung ku (dong gu) mushrooms
1 scallion
1 stick celery
few sprigs coriander
2 large eggs
¹/₄ lb roast pork tenderloin (see p. 218)
pinch salt
¹/₂ tsp monosodium glutamate (optional)
1 tbsp cornstarch or potato flour

pinch freshly ground pepper
oil

Time: 1 hour

Soak the dried mushrooms in warm water for 20 minutes. Cut the tofu into very small pieces; coarsely chop the shrimp. Chop the scallion, celery, and coriander very finely. Drain the mushrooms, remove and discard their stalks, and chop the caps coarsely. Mix all these ingredients with the lightly beaten eggs, the salt, monosodium glutamate (if used), and the pepper; stir in the cornstarch or potato flour mixed with a little water.

Grease the inside of a skillet generously with oil, heat, and then pour in the omelet mixture. The ideal thickness of this firmly set, thick omelet should be about ³/₄ in. When cooked on the first side, turn the omelet very carefully, adding a little more oil to the pan if necessary; finish cooking, then slide out of the skillet onto a plate and cut into rectangles, approx. ³/₄ × 2¹/₄ in. Heat fresh oil (about ¹/₄ cup) until very hot in the wok and return the omelet pieces to the wok; fry until a good golden brown on both sides, then serve.

OYSTER OMELET CHAO ZHOU STYLE

潮州蚝煎

cháo zhōu háo jiān

¹/₂ lb small, fresh or thawed frozen shucked oysters
¹/₃ cup cornstarch or potato flour
2 scallions
4 eggs
¹/₃ cup all-purpose flour
1 tsp fish sauce
¹/₂ tsp monosodium glutamate (optional)
2 sprigs coriander leaves
oil

Time: 40 minutes

Place the oysters in a plastic bag with 3 tbsp of the cornstarch or potato flour; close and then shake the bag to coat the oysters; transfer them to a sieve and rinse under running cold water. The preliminary flouring makes it easier to clean them more effectively. Finely chop the scallions. Beat the eggs lightly, incorporating the flour, the remaining cornstarch or potato flour mixed with a little water, the chopped scallions, oysters, and the fish sauce. Heat ¹/₄ cup oil until very hot in the wok or in a skillet (if using a nonstick skillet, you will need less oil), draw aside from the heat, and immedi-

ately pour in the omelet mixture. Return to the heat, turned down to low, and cook until the first side is done; turn the omelet carefully, adding more oil to the pan as you do so if this is needed. When the omelet is firmly set, slide out of the skillet and decorate with coriander leaves.

EGGS WITH SHRIMP

滑蛋虾仁

huá dàn xiā rén

1 cup peeled shrimp
pinch salt
pinch freshly ground pepper
4 tung ku (dong gu) mushrooms
few chives
8 eggs
¹/₂ tsp monosodium glutamate (optional)
1 tsp fish sauce
1¹/₂ tbsp rice wine
¹/₃ cup oil
1¹/₂ tbsp sesame seed oil

Time: 40 minutes

Soak the dried mushrooms in warm water for 20 minutes. Chop the shrimp coarsely and season with salt and pepper. Drain the mushrooms, cut off and discard their stalks, and cut the caps into small pieces. Chop the chives. Beat the eggs briefly; stir in the chives, mushrooms, monosodium glutamate (if used), fish sauce, and rice wine. Heat 3 tbsp oil in the wok and stir-fry the shrimp over moderate heat for 1 minute; remove from the wok, draining well, and stir into the egg mixture.

Wipe the wok; heat ¹/₄ cup fresh oil over moderate heat and pour in the egg mixture; scramble this as it cooks for 2 or 3 minutes, stir in the sesame seed oil briefly and serve. The egg mixture should be only just set and still creamy.

SAVORY FRIED BLANCMANGE DA LIANG STYLE

大良炒鲜奶

dà liáng chǎo xian nǎi

8 egg whites
1 cup fresh rich milk
¹/₄ cup cornstarch or potato flour

223

¹/₂–1 tsp salt
¹/₂ tsp monosodium glutamate (optional)
2 oz tiny fresh button mushrooms
¹/₄ cup oil
1 tbsp finely chopped Chinese Gold Coin
  ham, Virginia ham or Westphalian ham

Time: 20 minutes

Whisk the egg whites stiffly; using a metal spoon or mixing spatula fold in the milk, cornstarch or potato flour, salt, and monosodium glutamate (if used). Have the mushrooms ready wiped with a damp cloth and trimmed and add them whole if they are very small, otherwise cut them into small pieces.

Heat the oil in the wok or a skillet and pour in the mixture; scramble it as it cooks, stirring vigorously and continuously with cooking chopsticks, a balloon whisk or a fork. The mixture should thicken and become light and very white.

Serve without delay, sprinkled with the chopped ham. A little crabmeat can be added to the mixture before cooking if wished.

SHRIMP OMELET DA LIANG

大 良 煎 虾 饼

dà líang jiān xiā bǐng

1 cup peeled shrimp
6 tbsp salt
1¹/₂ tbsp bicarbonate of soda
8 eggs
1¹/₂ tbsp finely chopped scallion
¹/₂ tsp monosodium glutamate (optional)
generous pinch freshly ground pepper
1¹/₂ tbsp sesame seed oil
oil for frying

Time: 1 hour

Mix the salt and bicarbonate of soda in a bowl; add the shrimp and stir well; leave to stand for 30 minutes. Transfer to a sieve and rinse well under running cold water. Drain thoroughly and spread out to dry briefly on kitchen towels.

Beat the eggs lightly with the scallion, monosodium glutamate (if used), pepper, and sesame seed oil. Stir-fry the shrimp in 1–2 tbsp hot oil for 1 minute; remove the shrimp from the wok with a slotted spoon, draining well, and add to the egg mixture. Empty the oil from the wok, wipe clean, and heat ¹/₄ cup fresh oil. Pour in the egg mixture and cook over gentle heat until firmly set, turning once when the first side is done and adding a little more oil to prevent the omelet sticking if necessary. Slide the omelet onto a serving plate and cut like cake.

CRAB AND VEGETABLE OMELET *

芙 蓉 虾

fú róng xiè

1³/₄ cups crabmeat (fresh, thawed frozen or
  canned)
¹/₄ lb bamboo shoots, fresh or canned
3 tung ku (dong gu) mushrooms, pre-soaked
1 scallion
5 eggs
1 tsp salt
¹/₂ tsp monosodium glutamate (optional)
pinch freshly ground pepper
1 tsp rice wine
1 tsp sesame seed oil
1¹/₂ tbsp light soy sauce
¹/₄ cup oil

For the sauce:
¹/₄ cup tomato ketchup
1 tsp light soy sauce
¹/₂–1 tsp sugar
1 tsp Worcestershire sauce
3 tbsp broth or water
1 tsp cornstarch or potato flour

Time: 45 minutes

If you decide to cook the crabs yourself, kill them first by inserting a skewer between the eyes and the mouth parts, then boil for about 20 minutes in a large pan of water (you will need a crab or crabs weighing about 2¹/₄ lb to yield enough meat). Remove the meat from the shell, discarding the grayish feathery gills ("dead men's fingers") and the stomach sac. Discard the mushroom stalks and cut the caps into thin strips; do likewise with the bamboo shoots and scallion. Beat the eggs lightly with the salt, monosodium glutamate (if used), pepper, rice wine, sesame seed oil, and soy sauce. Stir in the crabmeat and vegetables.

Heat the oil in a skillet or wok and add the mixture; cook, turning once, until firm on both sides. If preferred, you can scramble the egg mixture as it starts to cook. Heat the sauce ingredients except for the cornstarch or potato flour in a small saucepan until they have reduced a little, mix the thickening agent with a very little cold water and stir into the sauce; cook briefly and then hand round separately in a jug or bowl.

SALTED EGGS WITH PORK

咸 蛋 蒸 肉 饼

xián dàn zheng ròu bǐng

2 salted duck eggs
5 oz finely chopped pork tenderloin
5 oz fresh pork belly, finely chopped
1 egg white
1¹/₂ tbsp cornstarch or potato flour
1¹/₂ tbsp sesame seed oil

Time: 45 minutes

Line your steamer compartment with lettuce or cabbage leaves or vegetable parchment and steam the salted eggs for 10 minutes. Peel the eggs carefully and cut lengthwise in half; take out the yolks and set aside in a bowl; chop the whites very finely and mix in another bowl with the chopped meats, the uncooked egg white and the cornstarch or potato flour; blend very thoroughly.

Grease a small casserole dish with the sesame seed oil (the mixture should form a $^3/_4$-in thick layer when packed firmly all over the bottom of the dish). Break up the cooked egg yolks with a fork and sprinkle al over the surface. Place in the steamer, cover, and steam for 15–20 minutes.

For extra flavor the cooked mixture can be sprinkled with a little more sesame seed oil and finely chopped scallion.

Salted duck eggs can be bought at Chinese foodstores and in many Oriental shops. To prepare your own version make a very strong brine by boiling very heavily salted water, leave to cool, then immerse the very fresh duck eggs in it, cover and leave the eggs for about 2 weeks, by which time they will be preserved by the salt pickle.

CHINESE CABBAGE WITH CRAB'S EGGS

蟹 黄 扒 菜 胆

xiè huáng pá cài dǎn

10 oz heart of Chinese cabbage
3 tbsp oil
2 cups broth
pinch salt
¹/₄ lb crab's eggs
2¹/₂ tbsp sesame seed oil
1¹/₂ tbsp rice wine
1¹/₂ tbsp cornstarch or potato flour

Time: 30 minutes

Wash the cabbage leaves, dry them and cut into bite-sized pieces; stir-fry for 1 minute or less in 3 tbsp oil over high heat, add half the broth and the salt, cover, and simmer for 15 minutes. Remove the cabbage from the wok and transfer to a heated serving dish.

Mix the crab's eggs with 1 tbsp sesame seed oil; stir-fry in the wok in fresh oil for 1 minute, then add the rice wine, the remaining broth, and the cornstarch or potato flour mixed with a very little cold water. Stir well. Sprinkle in the remaining sesame seed oil and pour all over the cabbage. Serve.

MUSHROOMS WITH OYSTER SAUCE

蚝 油 鲜 菇

hóo yóu xiān gū

7 oz straw mushrooms (amanita caesarea),
*   available canned*
oil for frying
2 slices fresh ginger
1¹/₂ tbsp oil
1 cup chicken broth
1¹/₂ tbsp oyster sauce
¹/₂ tsp salt
pinch sugar
pinch freshly ground pepper
1¹/₂ tbsp rice wine
1¹/₂ tbsp cornstarch or potato flour
2 tbsp sesame seed oil

Time: 40 minutes

Drain the mushrooms and cut lengthwise in half. Heat plenty of oil in the wok to about 340°F and fry the mushrooms for 1 minute; take them out of the oil with a wire mesh ladle or slotted spoon and set aside on kitchen towels. This step can be omitted if wished,

especially if canned mushrooms are used.

Peel the ginger and cut into short, thin strips; stir-fry in the wok or a skillet in 1¹/₂ tbsp fresh oil until the aroma is released. Add the mushrooms, broth, oyster sauce, salt, sugar, pepper, and rice wine. Cook, uncovered, over moderate heat to allow the liquid to reduce somewhat. Mix the cornstarch or potato flour with a very little cold water and stir into the wok or pan to thicken the liquid a little. Sprinkle with the sesame seed oil, stir very briefly, and serve.

MEI CAI WITH PORK BELLY

梅 菜 扣 肉

méi cài kòu ròu

14 oz brine-pickled mustard greens (mei cai)
14 oz pork belly, in one piece with the rind on
¹/₂ tsp monosodium glutamate (optional)
2¹/₂ tbsp soy sauce
¹/₂–1 tbsp sugar
1¹/₂ tbsp sesame seed oil

Time: 1¹/₂ hours

Use tweezers to extract the bristles remaining in the rind of the pork belly, wash the piece well, dry, and cut into slices just under ¹/₄ in thick; cut these into rectangles measuring about 1¹/₄ × 2 in.

Rinse the pickled xian cai thoroughly in a sieve under running cold water to eliminate excess salt; drain well and chop finely.

Arrange the pork belly slices in a fairly deep dish in one or more layers, cover with the xian cai, smoothing this with a spatula, and sprinkle with the monosodium glutamate (if used), the soy sauce, sugar, and sesame seed oil. Cover with foil. Place the dish in the steamer compartment, cover, and steam for 1 hour (remember to add more boiling water to the pan below the steamer when necessary). Take the dish out of the steamer, remove the foil and place a large plate upside down on top of the dish; hold the plate and dish tightly together and turn the plate the right way up, releasing the pork and xian cai onto it in one piece like a flan or pie.

Xian cai is a little like fennel and is preserved by salting. It is available canned from Oriental foodstores.

CAULIFLOWER WITH SEAFOOD AND FRESH GINGER *

三 鲜 油 菜 花

sān xiān yóu cài huā

14 oz cauliflower
1 cup peeled shrimp
¹/₂ lb prepared squid or cuttlefish
¹/₂ lb shucked fresh or thawed frozen scallops
¹/₂-1 tsp salt
¹/₂-1 tsp sugar
¹/₂ tsp monosodium glutamate (optional)
1 tsp cornstarch or potato flour
pinch freshly ground pepper
4 thin slices fresh ginger
2 scallions
¹/₂ green bell pepper
¹/₂ red bell pepper
6 tbsp oil

For the sauce:
¹/₂ tsp salt
¹/₂ tsp monosodium glutamate (optional)
1 tbsp sweet soy paste
1 tbsp light soy sauce
1 tsp oyster sauce
1 tbsp sesame seed oil
1 tbsp rice wine
pinch freshly ground pepper
¹/₂ cup broth
1 tbsp cornstarch

Time: 55 minutes

Divide the cauliflower into small florets and boil fast in salted water for 3 minutes. Drain.

Cut the squid into thin strips. Rinse the shrimp and scallops if necessary (you will use only the white cushiony part of the scallop). Mix the salt, sugar, monosodium glutamate (if used), cornstarch, and pepper and stir in the seafood to flavor. Peel and chop the ginger and scallions. Shred the peppers.

Heat 3 tbsp oil in the wok and stir-fry the seafood over high heat for 1 minute; remove with a slotted spoon and set aside; stir-fry the peppers and cauliflower for 1 minute, then remove and set aside.

Wipe the inside of the wok, heat 3 tbsp fresh oil and stir-fry the ginger and scallion gently until they release their aromas.

Return the seafood, cauliflower, and peppers to the wok and stir in the salt, monosodium glutamate (if used), soy paste, soy sauce, oyster sauce, sesame seed oil, rice wine, pepper, and broth. Cook, uncovered, for a few minutes only to reduce the liquid a little; mix the cornstarch with a little cold water and stir into the wok to thicken the sauce a little.

SAVORY COCONUT SHELL CUPS *

海南椰子盅
hǎi nán yē zǐ zhōng

4 coconuts
4 tung ku (dong gu) mushrooms
5 oz chicken breasts
1 tsp salt
pinch monosodium glutamate (optional)
1 tbsp cornstarch or potato flour
2 oz Chinese Gold Coin ham, Virginia ham or
   Westphalian ham
2 cups chicken broth
1 cup milk
¹/₂ cup creamed coconut

Time: 1¹/₂ hours

Soak the mushrooms in warm water for 20 minutes. Use a skewer or similar implement to bore a hole in one of the coconut's three small depressions or "eyes" and empty the coconut juice out of this. (It is not used for this recipe but can be saved for a refreshing drink.) Cut or saw off this end of the coconut to make a "lid".

Drain the mushrooms, remove and discard their stalks, and cut the caps into small pieces. Cut the chicken breasts into small cubes and blanch these in boiling water for 1 minute. Drain well, then roll in the salt mixed with the monosodium glutamate (if used) and the cornstarch or potato flour. Leave to stand and absorb this mixture for 30 minutes. Cut the ham into short, thin strips. Place the coconuts upright in small bowls which will hold them absolutely steady; ladle ¹/₂ cup broth into each one and place in the steamer compartment, cover and steam for 20 minutes to soften the coconut flesh. Take the coconuts, in their bowls, out of the steamer, place equal quantities of mushroom, chicken, and ham inside each and return to the steamer; cover and give them another 30 minutes' steaming. Mix the milk and creamed coconut thoroughly, pour equal quantities of this into the coconuts while they are still in the steamer, cover again, and steam for a further 2 minutes.

STIR-FRIED MIXED VEGETABLES

素什锦
sù shí jīn

3 tung ku (dong gu) mushrooms
1/4 lb carrots
4 or 5 asparagus spears
1/2 green bell pepper
1/2 red bell pepper
2 oz snow peas
2 oz soybean sprouts or mungbean sprouts
1 leek
1 scallion
1 clove garlic
1/4 cup oil

For the sauce:
1 tsp salt
1 tbsp soy sauce
1/2 tsp monosodium glutamate (optional)
1 tbsp sesame seed oil
1 tbsp rice wine

Time: 1 hour

Soak the mushrooms in warm water for 20 minutes. Soak the beans sprouts in cold water. Blanch the asparagus and carrot pieces for 1–2 minutes in boiling water.

Cut the peppers, snow peas, bamboo shoots, carrots, asparagus, leek, and scallion into short, thin sticks no larger than 3/8 × 1 1/4 in.

Drain the mushrooms and squeeze out excess moisture; cut off and discard the stalks, and slice the caps to match the other vegetables. Take the bean sprouts out of the water, discarding any seeds or shoots which have sunk to the bottom of the bowl; remove any empty seed cases and discard. Rinse and drain the bean sprouts well. Heat 1/4 cup oil in the wok and sweat the peeled, minced garlic clove, the leek, and the scallion over very low heat for a few minutes; increase the heat, add the other vegetables, adding the mushrooms and the bean sprouts last of all; stir-fry over high heat for a very few minutes.

When the firmest vegetables are tender but still very crisp, stir in the sauce ingredients and cook for a minute or two longer to reduce the liquid a little. Serve without delay.

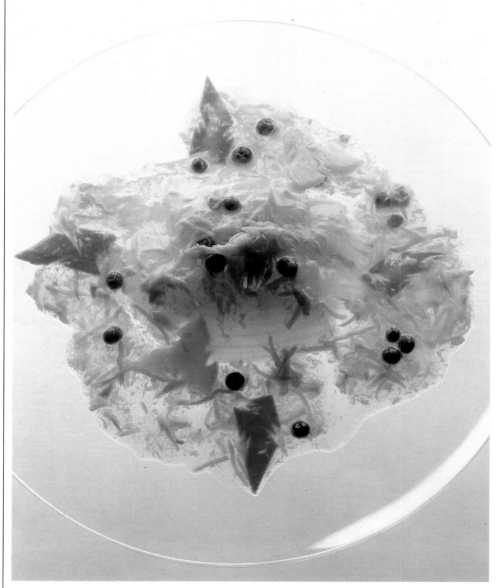

GLUTINOUS RICE CAKES WITH COCONUT

椰蓉糯米糍

yē róng muò mǐ cí

¹/₂ cup teng mien rice flour
1³/₄ cups glutinous rice flour
¹/₂ cup sugar
¹/₄ cup melted shortening
2 cups peanut oil
5 oz chopped peanuts
5 oz grated fresh coconut flesh
10 candied or glacé cherries

Time: 1 hour

Mix the teng mien rice flour with ¹/₄ cup boiling water, using a wooden spoon; mix the glutinous rice flour with 1 cup cold water, ¹/₄ cup sugar, and the shortening. Blend these two mixtures together very thoroughly. Heat the oil in the wok and fry the peanuts over moderate heat; add the remaining sugar, stirring until it has dissolved. Roll out the rice flour dough into a sheet just under ¹/₄ in thick and cut out into disks about 2 in in diameter. Spread the peanut mixture on the disks and shape into sealed rolls. Place these rolls in the steamer compartment (you may need two compartments) and steam for 15 minutes. Take the rolls out of the steamer, roll in the coconut flakes, pressing so that they adhere, and decorate with the candied cherries.

GLUTINOUS RICE CAKES WITH SESAME SEEDS

豆沙煎堆

dòu shā jiān duī

1¹/₂ tbsp shortening
¹/₂ cup sugar
2¹/₂ cups glutinous rice flour
1 cup sweet red bean paste (or sweet lotus seed paste)
1 cup white sesame seeds
oil for frying

Time: 45 minutes

Heat the shortening gently until it has just melted; add the sugar to 1 cup water in a small pan and boil until the sugar has dissolved; combine the shortening and the sugar syrup with the flour, blending very thoroughly. Break

CHINESE CABBAGE WITH CRAB *

蟹肉白菜

xiè ròu bái cài

10 oz Chinese cabbage
10 oz crabmeat
¹/₂ tsp salt
¹/₂ tsp monosodium glutamate (optional)
1¹/₂ tsp rice wine
pinch freshly ground pepper
¹/₂ cup chicken broth
1 tbsp cornstarch or potato flour
2¹/₂ tbsp melted chicken fat (optional)

Time: 30 minutes

Cut the washed and dried cabbage into thin strips about 1¹/₂ in long; add to a large saucepan of boiling water and simmer for about 10 minutes or until tender. Drain well and place on a serving plate. Heat the broth in the wok with the rice wine, salt, monosodium glutamate (if used), and pepper; bring to a boil then stir in the flaked crabmeat, reduce the heat, and simmer for 2 minutes. Mix the cornstarch or potato flour with a very little cold water and stir into the liquid to thicken. Pour this sauce all over the cabbage.

Sprinkle with hot, melted chicken fat if wished.

off small pieces of this mixture, just large enough to shape roughly into 1½-in cubes. Break off much smaller pieces of sweet bean paste and roll these between your palms to form little balls; scoop out a small "plug" of the rice flour dough cubes (or hollow this out with your little finger or a suitable utensil), insert the sweet bean paste ball deep inside, and plug the hole. Roll the cubes between your palms or on the working surface to shape into balls. Roll these balls in the sesame seeds to coat all over, pressing lightly to ensure that they adhere. Heat plenty of oil in the wok for semi deep-frying or in a deep-fryer, to 340°F and fry the rice balls in several batches until golden brown all over; drain well and serve hot or cold.

MANGO PUDDING *

芒果布甸

máng guǒ bù dīng

2 large, ripe mangoes weighing a total of
    about 1 lb
6 tbsp gelatin powder
5 leaves isinglass
1 cup sugar
1 cup milk
1 tsp mango essence (optional)
1 tsp yellow food coloring powder or liquid

Time: 30 minutes + cooling and chilling time

Peel the mangoes and pureé the flesh in a liquidizer or food processor with 1 cup cold water. Bring 2 cups water to a boil in a large, heavy-bottomed saucepan, add the sugar and isinglass, stir until these have completely dissolved, and then draw aside from the heat. Soften the gelatin with a little cold water in a small bowl; stir in a little of the hot liquid from the saucepan and then add the dissolving gelatin to the contents of the saucepan; stir well until the gelatin has completely dissolved. Do not reheat the liquid.

Stir in the mango purée very thoroughly, followed by the milk, mango essence (if used), and the coloring. Rinse a large mold with cold water (or use a glass bowl) and pour the mixture into it.

CRISPY FRIED WATER CHESTNUT CAKE

香 煎 马 蹄 糕

xiān jiān mǎ tī gāo

14 oz water chestnuts (fresh or canned)
2¼ cups water chestnut powder
2½ cups sugar
½–1 tsp pure vanilla extract
3 tbsp cornstarch or potato flour
oil for frying

Time: 1 hour + cooling time

Prepare the water chestnuts if fresh; drain well if canned. Chop very finely. Mix the water chestnut powder with 2 cups water. Bring 2 cups water to a boil in a saucepan, add the chopped chestnuts and the sugar and boil gently, stirring continuously, until the sugar has completely dissolved.

Turn the heat down to very low; stir the mixture of water chestnut powder and water again and add this to the liquid in the saucepan while stirring vigorously. Add the vanilla and continue stirring for a minute or two. Draw aside from the heat. Grease a square or rectangular cake pan with oil and fill with the cooked mixture. Place the cake pan in the steamer, cover, and steam for 30 minutes. Take the cake pan out of the steamer and leave to cool completely. Chill in the refrigerator for 2–3 hours, then unmold and serve just as it is

or you can cut the blancmange into thick, square slices. Coat these all over with the cornstarch or potato flour and deep-fry in plenty of very hot oil until golden brown. Serve at once while still very hot.

COCONUT PUDDING *

椰汁年糕
yē zhī nián gāo

¹/₄ cup milk
2 cups sugar
2 cups creamed coconut
3 tbsp shortening
2¹/₄ cups glutinous rice flour
1 cup tian mian rice flour
oil

Time: 2¹/₂ hours + chilling time

Place the milk, sugar, creamed coconut, and the shortening in a saucepan and heat gradually, stirring, until the sugar has dissolved. Sift the two flours into a large mixing bowl, make a well in the center of the flour, and add the coconut mixture; gradually work this into the flour and mix well.

Grease one large, or 4 small molds with a little oil, fill with the mixture, cover with waxed paper or foil, and steam for 2 hours (remember to keep topping up the boiling water below them).

Take the mold or molds out of the steamer, leave to cool, then chill in the refrigerator. Turn the puddings out onto individual plates or, in the case of the large mold, onto a large plate; this large pudding can then be cut into fairly thick slices. These are then coated with a flour and egg batter and deep- or shallow-fried until golden brown all over; eat while still hot and crisp.

233

LYCHEE AND MANGO SALAD

芒果荔枝
máng guǒ lī zhī

10 oz fresh lychees
1 mango
1 large orange

Time: 20 minutes + chilling time

Peel the lychees. Peel the orange with a very sharp serrated knife, removing the skin and all the white pith. Peel the mango, take the flesh off the pit, and cut into small cubes. Spread the orange slices out over the bottom of a serving dish or shallow bowl and arrange the lychees and mango cubes on top of them so that they alternate. Place in the refrigerator until just before serving. This dish is best eaten well chilled.

The Chinese have cleverly combined three fruits with perfectly complementary tastes for this deliciously refreshing fruit salad. Fresh lychees are best but well drained canned lychees will do just as well.

WESTERN CHINA

華
西
菜

THE WESTERN SCHOOL – THE
COOKING OF SZECHWAN

236

Western China is bordered by several Asian countries: Pakistan, India, Nepal, Burma, Laos, and Vietnam and this long border (part of which is made up by the natural barrier of the Pamir Mountains) marks the westernmost limits of a region which varies greatly in climate and scenery, some parts being remote and inaccessible, mountainous and barren, others well watered, lush, and fertile. For both historical and geographic reasons, western China has mirrored the diversity of the races, creeds, cultures, and customs of its Asian neighbors; it has long been the homeland of many different ethnic groups and the adopted country of many others. Monks and merchants traveled to this region from neighboring lands and were responsible for the spread of Buddhism from northern India across Yunnan. The combination of busy trade routes and missionary zeal helps to account for the similarities in food products and the cooking methods found in this region and those of India, Thailand, and Burma. Moslem influences were also strong and survive to this day.

Western China was a melting pot for traditions and customs of many Asian countries and has adopted and developed these "imports" over the centuries. Szechwan, like other once separate western provinces that are now part of China such as Hunan, had for centuries been an independent country, and a distinctive way of life has survived. This area is an enormous river basin whose streams, rivers, and lakes are fed by the melting ice and snow from the high mountains that dominate the region; its great waterway is, of course, the Yangtze. The river has four main tributaries: the Min, the Jialing, the Yalong, and the To, which have given the province its name, Sihuan meaning "four rivers." These rivers have created the alluvial plains of the Red Basin whose fertility is further enhanced by the favorable climate, warm and humid in summer and mild in winter; from ancient times this long growing season has been further exploited by damming rivers and by the construction of vast and complex canal networks and irrigation channels, especially in the intensively cultivated plain that surrounds the regional capital, Chengdu. Agriculture is extremely productive in this area, rice being the main crop, sustaining and supporting a population of more than 100 million people. Besides rice and other cereals, the region is also famed for its bamboo shoots (which are not only sent to other parts of China and exported but also provide pandas with their sole source of food), for its citrus fruits and cultivated mushrooms.

This Bai fisherman has trained his cormorants well: they will dive for fish in Lake Erhui but a leash round their necks prevents them from swallowing their catch.

Szechwan has given its name to the small, reddish peppercorn, the fruit of a shrub, *Xanthoxylum piperitum*, which bears a similarity to the ordinary peppercorn but with an added acidulated flavor reminiscent of citrus fruit which leaves a tingling sensation in the mouth after it has been eaten.

Such plenty and variety, coupled with the historic prosperity of this province, helps to explain why the cooking of western China is usually described as "Szechwan style cooking." This cuisine is distinguished by the skillful use of a wide range of spices, particularly those which are hot and peppery, and by the absence of real sauces, this being amply compensated by the use of different cooking techniques and the addition of ingredients which contrast pleasantly with each other. Among the cooking methods peculiar to this area is the succession of different cooking phases which food undergoes. Camphor and Tea Smoked Duck is a very good example of this, subjected to four cooking stages: marinating; smoking; steaming and finally frying before it is eaten.

Because of the prevalence of spices and strong flavors in Szechwan and Hunan dishes, the custom is to serve plenty of thirst-quenching and cooling drinks, such as beer, with meals; this is in contrast with usage elsewhere in China. The other regions of western China, Kweichow and Yunnan, have also been influenced by their physical geography, with deep gorges channeled out of the rocks by rushing torrents and rivers, one of the greatest of which, the Mekong, runs through the whole of Yunnan, a province studded with mountains and heavily wooded with great forests. These areas are most remarkable, however, for the racial mix of their inhabitants, among them tribes, some large, some small, who are known to have lived here for thousands of years. Other ethnic groups were literally transplanted from other regions, such as the Mosuo, the descendants of a Mongol settlement established by Kubla Khan, which helps date their presence back to the era of the Yuan or Mongol dynasty (1271–1368). Minorities such as these have brought with them foods and dishes which have Indian, Buddhist, Islamic,

The innately conservative Chinese are expected to live their lives as good Communists while adopting recently reintroduced Western commercial attitudes to trade and industry. In a difficult and uncertain transitional period, these children represent pride in China's achievements and hopes for a "new China."

Vietnamese, and Mongol origins; these are included in the extensive repertoire of western Chinese cuisine served in the increasingly highly regarded restaurants of the capital of Szechwan, Chengdu, where they have joined the pan-Chinese national culinary traditions.

Thai influence is also very strong, particularly through the presence of delicious and resourceful vegetarian dishes introduced by Buddhists. Highly spiced vinegar-pickled vegetables are a specialty of this region, as are the excellent freshwater fish dishes and also, surprisingly for this inland region, saltwater fish recipes (the fish are brought by rail or by the ancient, traditional route by boat

up the Yangtze River, nearly 2,000 miles from where they were caught, to be sold fresh, dried, or salt brine-pickled). Kunming, Yunnan's regional capital, is as famous for an agreeably mild climate as for its excellent restaurants, producing full-flavored, exotic dishes through the plentiful use of herbs and spices, and the local steamed delicacies. Kuei-yang in Kweichow is renowned for its salty dishes, as if to underline man's ingenuity in overcoming the scarcity of sea salt in this area by transporting sufficient quantities over long distances to prepare recipes in which salt is one of the most important ingredients.

With the improvement of communications and transport, interest has grown in Oriental cuisine in general and as a far greater number of people learn more about western China and the area opens up gradually to tourism, this interest has spread to its less widely known, very refined cuisine. The impression that many people initially acquire of very fiery tastes, soon gives way to an appreciation of the subtle and complex mixture of flavors and aromas: western Chinese cuisine makes use of a wide range of basic tastes: sweet, salty, sour, hot, and peppery but it also exploits many aromatic aftertastes, some

The small, thermal lake of Huaqing at Lishan is not far from the mausoleum peopled by vast numbers of terracotta warriors built for the Emperor Qin Shihuangdi. On the left a woman makes her way toward Xishuangbanna market where her produce will be sold alongside all sorts of other goods from the surrounding countryside and further afield. The warm fragrant aromas of these goods include coffee, cocoa, cinnamon, and many medicinal plants.

almost indescribable as the Chinese themselves have found when it came to thinking up such names as "Strange-flavored Chicken"; these are combined with all sorts of contrasting and complementary textures and consistencies, produced naturally or by the cooking techniques employed. This fascinating culinary tradition deserves to be as well known internationally as the hitherto more famous Cantonese and Peking schools.

SHRIMP-STUFFED OPEN DUMPLINGS *

四川烧卖
Sìchuān shāo maì

For the wrappers:
1 cup all-purpose flour
1¹/₂ tbsp cornstarch or potato flour
warm water as required

For the stuffing:
4 or 5 large, crisp lettuce leaves
³/₄ cup peeled shrimp
1¹/₂ tbsp rice wine
1¹/₂ tbsp sesame seed oil
pinch monosodium glutamate (optional)
pinch freshly ground pepper
salt
1¹/₂ tbsp cornstarch or potato flour

Time: 2 hours + resting time for wrapper dough

Gradually add sufficient warm water to the all-purpose flour until you have an easily handled, homogenous dough, which will be just firm enough to be rolled out. Knead well. Place in a bowl, cover with a cloth and leave to rest in a cool place for at least 2 hours.

Blanch the lettuce leaves for 30 seconds in boiling water; drain well and chop finely. Chop the shrimp finely and mix with the chopped lettuce. Stir in the rice wine, sesame seed oil, monosodium glutamate (if used), pepper, and salt. Add 1¹/₂ tbsp cornstarch or potato flour and work in very thoroughly.

Knead the rested dough thoroughly to develop the gluten and make the wrappers elastic and strong; sprinkle lightly with 1¹/₂ tbsp cornstarch or potato flour, sprinkle a little more on a pastry board or work surface and the rolling pin and roll out the dough into a very thin sheet (you should just be able to see the color of your fingertips through it when you place your hand underneath, palm side up). Cut out the sheet into 3-in diameter disks.

Place a disk on the open palm of your left hand (if you are right-handed) then bring your fingers upward to form a cup, without the fingers meeting; this will mold the disk into a shape that is quite easy to fill with a walnut-sized piece of filling. Bring the sides of the disk up and around the filling, pleating and pinching them together as you do so.

Line the steamer compartment(s) with cabbage leaves and place the open dumplings on these. Cover and steam for 10 minutes.

These can be eaten just as they are, or dipped in the usual sauces placed in little bowls on the table (soy sauce, chili oil etc.). If you do not want to make the wrappers yourself, commercially prepared wonton wrappers can be used.

NOODLES WITH BEEF SZECHWAN STYLE *

红烧川味牛肉面

hóng shāo chuān wèi niú ròu
miàn

1 lb beef topside, rump or leg
¹/₄ cup oil
1¹/₂ tbsp sugar
3 tbsp rice wine
¹/₂ cup hot (chili) soybean paste (dou ban
    jiang)
2¹/₂ tbsp chili oil
1 quart beef broth
1 tsp salt
1 tsp monosodium glutamate (optional)
5 oz fresh ginger (preferably in one piece)
4 cloves garlic, minced
14 oz Chinese (wheat flour) noodles

For the sauce:
1 tsp salt
pinch monosodium glutamate (optional)
1 tbsp soy sauce
1 tbsp finely chopped scallion

Time: 3¹/₂ hours

Cut the beef into thin strips about 1¹/₄ in long
and ³/₈ in wide; add these strips to a large saucepan of boiling water, boil for 5 minutes, and
drain well. Heat the oil in the wok, stir in the
sugar until it has dissolved and turned a pale
golden brown, then stir-fry the beef strips. Add
the rice wine, soybean paste and chili oil and
mix well. Pour in the broth (this should cover
the beef) and add the salt, monosodium glutamate (if used), and the minced ginger and garlic; bring to a boil then simmer gently for 3
hours.

Mix the sauce ingredients without heating
them and pour a little into individual bowls
large enough to take portions of noodles and
beef. Cook the noodles until tender in boiling
water (about 10 minutes) then drain and
divide between the bowls; top each serving
with the braised beef strips and moisten with a
little of the cooking liquid.

DAN DAN CHINESE NOODLES SZECHWAN STYLE

四川担担面

Sìchuān dān dān miàn

1 tsp finely chopped fresh ginger
1 tsp finely chopped garlic
1 tsp finely chopped scallion
2 tbsp oil

1 cup finely chopped pork belly
1 cup finely chopped pork tenderloin
2 tbsp soy sauce
1 tsp salt
pinch monosodium glutamate (optional)
14 oz Chinese (wheat flour) noodles
¹/₄ lb bean sprouts (mungbean or soybean)

For the flavored broth:
2 tbsp chili oil
2¹/₂ tbsp soy sauce
2¹/₂ tbsp sesame seed oil
1¹/₂ tbsp finely chopped scallion
2 cups chicken broth

Time: 30 minutes

Heat the oil in the wok and stir-fry the ginger, garlic, and scallion over low heat; add the finely chopped pork belly and stir-fry gently for 1–2 minutes; add the chopped pork. Stir in the soy sauce, salt, and monosodium glutamate

(if used) and continue stir-frying until the meat is done.

Add the noodles to a saucepan of boiling water, cook for 6 minutes at a fast boil, then drain. Meanwhile, blanch the rinsed, drained bean sprouts in another saucepan of boiling water for 30 seconds; drain. As soon as the noodles have been drained, mix quickly with the chili oil, soy sauce, sesame seed oil, and scallion.

Divide into 4 portions and place in 4 individual bowls. Ladle boiling hot chicken broth into each bowl, sprinkle in the meat mixture, and top with the bean sprouts. Serve at once.

Food vendors make their way through the streets of the large cities in Szechwan province, just as they have for centuries, wheeling carts or carrying panniers with all the ingredients for this nourishing meal-in-a-dish which they prepare on the spot when approached by a hungry customer.

SOY FLOUR NOODLES WITH SZECHWAN PORK *

蚂 蚁 上 树

mǎ yǐ shàng shù

¹/₄ lb soy flour noodles
6 tbsp oil
1 cup very finely chopped lean pork
2¹/₂ tbsp finely chopped scallion
1 tbsp finely chopped fresh ginger
1 tbsp hot (chili) soybean paste (dou ban jiang)
1 tbsp soy sauce
1 tbsp finely chopped celery
1 tsp salt
pinch monosodium glutamate (optional)
1 tbsp sesame seed oil
¹/₂ cup broth

Time: 30 minutes

Soak the noodles in warm water for 10 minutes, then drain well. Heat the oil in the wok and sweat 1¹/₂ tbsp of the chopped scallion and all the ginger in it until they release their aromas. Add the meat, stir-fry briefly, then add the noodles, hot soybean paste, soy sauce, celery, salt, monosodium glutamate (if used), sesame seed oil, and the broth. Stir well over slightly lower heat, allowing the liquid to reduce a little. Serve, sprinkled with the remaining chopped scallion.

SZECHWAN STYLE THIN RIBBON NOODLES *

四川炸酱面

Sichuān zhà jiàng miàn

¹/₂ lb very thin ribbon egg noodles
3 tbsp peanut oil
¹/₂ cup finely chopped lean pork
1 oz pickled mustard greens (zha cai)
1 tbsp sweet soybean paste (tian mian jiang)
1¹/₂ tbsp rice wine
pinch salt
pinch monosodium glutamate (optional)
1 scallion
2 oz fresh spinach leaves
¹/₄ cup soy sauce
3 tbsp sesame seed paste
1¹/₂ tsp wine vinegar
1¹/₂ tbsp chili oil
1¹/₂ tbsp sesame seed oil
1 cup hot broth

Time: 45 minutes

Heat the peanut oil to fairly hot in the wok and stir-fry the pork briefly.

Place the zha cai in a sieve and rinse under running cold water to eliminate excess salt; drain and chop finely. Mix the soybean paste, rice wine, salt, monosodium glutamate (if used), the zha cai, and the finely chopped scallion with the pork in the wok; remove from the heat and set aside.

Wash the spinach leaves; cook for 3 minutes only with a very little added boiling water

in a nonmetallic pan. Drain off any liquid and chop the leaves finely; mix with the soy sauce, sesame seed paste, vinegar, chili oil, sesame seed oil, and the monosodium glutamate.

Add the noodles to a saucepan of boiling water and cook for about 4 minutes or until tender; drain and transfer to a heated serving dish or into individual bowls. Mix the spinach mixture with the hot broth and pour over the noodles; top with the pork and serve.

SZECHWAN DUMPLINGS

红油龙抄手

hóng yóu lóng chāo shǒu

For the wrapper dough:
1³/₄ cups all-purpose flour
warm water as required

For the filling:
¹/₂ lb (1 cup) ground pork belly
¹/₂ lb (1 cup) ground pork tenderloin
1¹/₂ tbsp soy sauce
pinch freshly ground pepper
pinch monosodium glutamate (optional)
1 tbsp salt
1¹/₂ tbsp sesame seed oil

1¹/₂ tbsp finely chopped scallion
1¹/₂ tbsp finely chopped fresh ginger

For the sauce:
3 tbsp sweet soy sauce
3 tbsp chili oil
1 tsp finely chopped garlic
1¹/₂ tbsp finely chopped scallion
1¹/₂ tbsp wine vinegar
1 tsp monosodium glutamate (optional)
1 tsp ground Szechwan peppercorns

Time: 1¹/₂ hours

Make the dough in advance to allow time for it to rest: combine sufficient warm water with the flour to make a smooth, easily handled and kneaded dough which will be firm enough to roll out. Place in a bowl, covered with a clean cloth and set aside to rest for an hour or two.

Make the filling: mix the ground meats and all the other ingredients listed under the filling in a large mixing bowl until very well blended. Knead the dough once more briefly and roll out on a lightly floured work surface with a floured rolling pin into a fairly thin sheet. Use a cookie cutter or the rim of a glass to cut out disks approximately 3¹/₂ in in diameter. Place a little of the filling just below the center of each

disk, then fold the disk in half, enclosing the filling and bringing the edges together, pleating the fuller edge and pressing them together to seal well. Dampen the edges slightly with a little cold water if necessary to achieve a good seal.

Bring just over 2 quarts water to a boil in the wok or in a large saucepan; add the dumplings and as soon as they have risen to the surface add 1 cup cold water, pouring it in all at once. Allow the water to return to a boil, with the dumplings bobbing on the surface once more: they will now be perfectly cooked.

Remove the dumplings from the water with a slotted ladle and sprinkle with the well mixed sauce ingredients (unheated). Serve without delay.

NOODLES IN HOT SAUCE

辣酱面

là jiàng miàn

14 oz Chinese noodles
4 tung ku (dong gu) mushrooms
1 scallion
1 carrot
1 leek
6 tbsp oil
1 cup very finely chopped lean pork
1 tsp very finely chopped fresh ginger
3 tbsp hot soybean paste (with chili peppers)
3 tbsp soy sauce
1 cup chicken broth
1¹/₂ tbsp cornstarch
¹/₂–1 tsp salt
¹/₂–1 tsp sugar
¹/₂ tsp monosodium glutamate (optional)
1–1¹/₂ tsp chili oil
1 small bunch chives

Time: 1 hour

Soak the dried mushrooms in warm water for at least 20 minutes. Cook the noodles in lightly salted, boiling water until tender; drain and set aside. Prepare the vegetables and dice. Drain the mushrooms, squeezing out excess moisture, discard the stems, and cut the caps into thin strips. Heat the oil in the wok, stir-fry the meat briefly until it has just colored, then add the mushrooms and other vegetables. Stir-fry for 3–4 minutes. Stir in the ginger, hot soy paste, and soy sauce. Stir the cornstarch into the cold chicken broth and gradually work this into the contents of the wok, stirring the broth just before each addition.

Season with salt, sugar, monosodium glutamate (if used), and chili oil. Stir the noodles into the wok; cook for 2 minutes. Serve sprinkled with finely chopped chives.

THREE-COLOR DUMPLINGS *

三花饺子

sān huā jiǎo zǐ

For the wrapper dough:
1³/₄ cups all-purpose flour
warm water

For the filling:
¹/₂ cup finely chopped lean pork
2 tung ku (dong gu) mushrooms
1 oz bamboo shoots
2 oz York ham
1 egg
1 sprig parsley
1 large scallion
1¹/₂ tbsp soy sauce
1¹/₂ tbsp rice wine
1¹/₂ tbsp sugar
pinch salt
pinch freshly ground pepper
pinch monosodium glutamate (optional)
1¹/₂ tbsp oil

Time: 1 hour + 2¹/₂ hours for making and resting the dough

Sift the flour onto the work surface or marble slab and gradually mix in sufficient warm water to make a smooth, elastic dough that is easy to handle and knead; place this in a bowl, cover with a clean cloth, and leave to rest for about 2 hours.

Make the filling: soak the dried mushrooms in warm water for 20 minutes or longer; drain, cut off and discard the stalks, and chop the caps finely. Chop the scallion; blanch the bamboo shoots, drain and chop finely. Place these chopped ingredients in a bowl with the meat, rice wine, soy sauce, oil, sugar, monosodium glutamate (if used), salt, and pepper; mix very thoroughly. Beat the egg lightly and fry in a small skillet until completely set; chop the resulting omelet into small pieces. Rinse, dry, and finely chop the parsley. Chop the ham. Keep all these ingredients separate from one another.

Knead the dough briefly, then sprinkle lightly with flour and roll out into a very thin, almost transparent sheet on a very lightly floured working surface. Cut the sheet into 3-in disks, using a cookie cutter or the rim of a glass. Place a little of the filling in a small mound in the center of each disk; bring the edges up and around the filling as you do so and gather the edges so that they form 3 little pockets, pinching them together in the center on top of the filling to make them stay in place (see illustration).

Place a pinch of each of the reserved chopped ingredients in these little pockets (ham in one, parsley in another and omelet in the third).

246

Line the steamer compartment or compartments with cabbage or lettuce leaves or vegetable parchment, arrange the dumplings so that they do not touch one another, cover, and steam for 10 minutes. Serve in the steamer compartment, removing the lid at table, or, if you prefer, on a heated plate, accompanied by separate dressings of soy sauce or wine vinegar flavored with shredded fresh ginger.

STUFFED GLUTINOUS RICE DUMPLINGS *

菜肉汤圆
cài ròu tāng yuán

¹/₂ lb Chinese cabbage
1 tbsp salt
¹/₂ cup finely chopped pork
1 tbsp rice wine
1 tsp soy sauce
1 tbsp water
5 tbsp sesame seed oil
pinch salt
pinch freshly ground pepper
pinch monosodium glutamate (optional)
1³/₄ cups glutinous rice flour

Time: 1¹/₄ hours

Wash and dry the cabbage leaves, chop finely, place in a bowl, sprinkle with the salt, and set aside for 10 minutes to wilt and soften.

Mix the meat with the rice wine, soy sauce, water, sesame seed oil, salt, pepper, and the monosodium glutamate (if used).

Place the cabbage in a sieve and rinse thoroughly under running cold water to eliminate the salt. Drain well, spread out on a clean cloth, and squeeze inside the cloth to express excess moisture. Combine the cabbage with the meat mixture.

Gradually stir ¹/₂ cup cold water into the glutinous rice flour, then add ¹/₂ cup very hot water; mix very thoroughly, then knead well to form a smooth, elastic dough. Break off pieces the size of an apricot and press these into 2¹/₄–2¹/₂-in diameter disks, just over ¹/₈ in thick, with your knuckles and fingers. Place a little filling in the center of each disk and wrap the dough around the filling, completely enclosing it. Add these dumplings to a large saucepan of boiling water and cook for 7–8 minutes, removing the dumplings with a slotted spoon as they rise to the surface.

Serve in a deep dish, sprinkled with a little of the cooking liquid.

WINTER MELON AND HAM SOUP

火腿冬瓜汤
huǒ tuǐ dōng guā tāng

*¹/₂ lb prepared winter melon (peeled, with
    seeds and filaments removed)*
*2 oz Chinese Gold Coin ham, Virginia ham or
    Westphalian ham*
2 quarts chicken broth
1 tbsp salt
¹/₂ tsp monosodium glutamate
pinch freshly ground pepper

Time: 50 minutes

Winter melon has a marvelous melting texture
when cooked. Certain types of summer
squash can be successfully used instead but
the texture will not be quite the same. Cut the
winter melon into thin slices measuring about
1¹/₄ × ³/₄ in; cut the ham into thin strips.

Bring the chicken broth to a gentle boil, season with the salt (and monosodium glutamate
if wished), add the winter melon and ham, and
simmer for 40 minutes.

Add a sprinkling of freshly ground black
pepper and serve.

JIAN SHAN SOUP

兼善汤
jiān shàn tāng

¹/₂ lb chicken breasts
*¹/₄ lb Chinese Gold Coin ham, Virginia ham or
    Westphalian ham*
¹/₂ lb squid
2 oz fatty pork
4 tree ears (mu er fungus)
2 oz Chinese celery cabbage
2 tomatoes
2 carrots
1 egg
pinch freshly ground pepper
1¹/₂ tbsp light soy sauce
1¹/₂ tbsp wine vinegar
1¹/₂ tbsp finely chopped scallion
1 tsp salt
1 tsp monosodium glutamate (optional)
2 quarts chicken broth
3 tbsp cornstarch or potato flour

Time: 1 hour

Soak the mushrooms in warm water for at least
20 minutes. Cut the chicken, ham, squid,
pork, all the prepared vegetables and the
soaked, drained tree ears (having first cut off

any tough parts from these fungi) into tiny
dice. Bring the chicken broth to a boil in a
large saucepan or cooking pot, add all the ingredients (reserving only the cornstarch or
potato flour for thickening the soup later) and
simmer gently for 30 minutes. Shortly before
serving, mix the thickening agent with a little
cold water and stir into the soup.

Jian shan means "generosity to all." This
dish, with its abundance of varied ingredients,
is traditionally dedicated to the memory of
Men Zi, who taught that those who rose to
power should not forget others who were less
fortunate, and should have the well-being of
all the people they ruled constantly in mind.

CHICKEN AND GINGER SOUP

老姜子鸡汤
lǎo jiāng zǐ jī tāng

14 oz chicken (preferably leg meat)
4 tree ears (mu er fungus)
1 scallion
15 slices juicy fresh ginger
7 cups water (or chicken broth)
1 tsp salt
¹/₂ tsp monosodium glutamate (optional)
2¹/₂ tbsp rice wine

Time: 50 minutes

Soak the tree ears in warm water for at least 20
minutes. While they are soaking, shred the
chicken meat or cut into very small pieces and
blanch these for a minute in boiling water,
then drain well. Trim the ends off the scallions
and cut them lengthwise in half; peel the ginger slices. Drain the tree ears and cut off any
tough parts; cut into small pieces.

Bring the water (or chicken broth) to a boil
in a large saucepan, add the scallions, ginger,
chicken, and tree ears. Once the liquid returns
to a boil, reduce the heat and simmer gently
for 20 minutes, skimming off any scum.
Shortly before serving stir in the salt, monosodium glutamate (if used), and rice wine, cook
for 1 minute more and then serve.

KIDNEY AND XIAN CAI SOUP

冬菜腰片汤
dōng cài yāo piàn tāng

2 pig's kidneys
1 quart chicken broth
*1 tbsp xian cai (brine pickled mustard
    greens)*
pinch salt
pinch monosodium glutamate (optional)
1 tbsp rice wine

1 tbsp finely chopped scallion
pinch freshly ground pepper

Time: 45 minutes

248

Remove the thin membranous skin from the outside surface of the kidneys; lay them flat on the work surface and cut horizontally in half; use a pair of sharp, pointed scissors to remove pieces of fat and gristle inside them. Add to boiling water and blanch for 1 minute, drain, and cut into thin slices. Rinse these slices in a sieve under running cold water.

Heat the broth to boiling point in the wok or a large saucepan, add the kidneys and the well rinsed, drained and finely chopped xian cai, the salt, monosodium glutamate (if used), and rice wine. Bring back to a boil, reduce the heat, and simmer for 30 minutes, removing any scum that rises to the surface.

Remove the kidney slices with a slotted ladle and place an equal quantity in each individual bowl; pour the broth into the bowls and sprinkle on some freshly ground pepper and top with chopped scallion.

MA LA SOUP

麻 辣 汤
má là tāng

5 oz firm tofu (bean curd)
6 tbsp oil
1/4 cup finely chopped scallions
1 tbsp finely chopped garlic
1/2 cup (1/4 lb) finely chopped beef
1 tbsp chili oil

1 tsp ground chilis
1 tbsp ground Szechwan pepper
1 tbsp hot (chili) soybean paste
1/2–1 tsp salt
1/2 tsp monosodium glutamate (optional)
4 cups broth
1 1/2 tbsp cornstarch or potato flour

Time: 40 minutes

Cut the tofu into 1/2-in cubes. Place in a sieve and lower into boiling water. Blanch for 1–2 minutes, then drain. Heat the oil in the wok, stir-fry 3 tbsp of the scallion and all the garlic; add the meat, followed by the tofu, chili oil, ground chili pepper, Szechwan pepper, soybean paste, salt, monosodium glutamate (if used), and 1/2 cup water. Stir well, then pour in the broth and bring to a boil; simmer uncovered for 10 minutes. Mix the cornstarch or potato flour with a little cold water and stir into the soup to thicken it a little.

Serve very hot, sprinkled with the remaining chopped scallion.

OXTAIL SOUP

清 炖 牛 尾 汤
qīng dùn niú wěi tāng

1 3/4 lb oxtail
1 1/2–1 tbsp sesame seed oil
1 tbsp whole Szechwan peppercorns
6 slices fresh ginger
1 tsp salt
1/2 tsp monosodium glutamate (optional)
3 tbsp rice wine

Time: 2 1/2 hours

Have your butcher cut the upper, thicker part of the oxtail into 2-in thick sections or do this yourself. Use only large, fleshy pieces. Add these to a large saucepan of boiling water and boil for 10 minutes; drain in a colander and rinse well under running cold water. Heat the sesame seed oil in the wok over moderate heat; add the Szechwan peppercorns and cook, stirring, until they give off a spicy aroma; add the peeled ginger slices and stir-fry until they also release their scent. Pour in 2 quarts water, add the pieces of oxtail, salt, monosodium glutamate (if used), and rice wine.

Bring to a boil and then simmer gently for 2 hours or until very tender, skimming any scum off the surface at intervals and adding a little boiling water if necessary. Serve a section of oxtail together with some of the cooking liquid in each bowl. Mix the hot soybean paste with sufficient sesame seed oil to form a thin paste; place a little of this sauce in a bowl. Each person detaches small pieces of the meat from the bone and dips them in the sauce.

HOT AND SOUR SOUP *

酸 辣 汤
suān là tāng

1/2 lb firm tofu (bean curd)
1/4 lb pork
2 tree ear fungus (mu er)
1 tung ku (dong gu) mushroom
1 quart chicken broth
1 egg
1/2–1 tbsp salt
1/2 tsp monosodium glutamate (optional)
1 1/2 tbsp soy sauce
pinch sugar
pinch freshly ground white pepper
1 tbsp finely chopped scallion
1 1/2 tbsp vinegar (ideally hei jiu "black" rice vinegar)
1 1/2 tsp sesame seed oil
1 1/2 tbsp cornstarch or potato flour
1/4 lb pig's or chicken's blood pudding (optional)
1 soaked and prepared sea cucumber (optional)

Time: 40 minutes

Soak the tree ear fungus and the mushroom in warm water for at least 20 minutes (and up to 1 hour if wished). When they are soft, drain well. Trim off any tough parts from the tree ear and cut off and discard the stalk from the tung ku (dong gu) mushroom.

Cut the tofu, meat, fungus, and mushroom, blood pudding and sea cucumber into thin, matchstick strips (have the tofu pieces a little larger as it will break up too much if cut too small) and add to the boiling chicken broth in a large saucepan or cooking pot. Add the salt, monosodium glutamate (if used), soy sauce, sugar, pepper, scallion, vinegar, and sesame seed oil; allow to return to a boil, reduce the heat a little, and stir in the cornstarch or potato flour mixed with a little cold water. Beat the egg until fairly frothy and pour into the soup in a thin stream while stirring so that the egg sets in long tendrils. Draw aside from the heat and serve.

Many Westerners prefer to leave out two of the traditional ingredients of this soup: the blood pudding (which is, however, very flavorsome and versions of which are eaten in many countries outside China) and the sea cucumber, the latter being a dried sea creature which must be well washed and then soaked in water for 3 days to reconstitute it to its original gelatinous self. Slit the sea cucumber down the smooth section, remove the entrails and rinse the inside. Place in a saucepan of cold water and bring to a boil; simmer for about 1 hour or until fairly tender.

YU XIANG FISH FILLETS *

鱼 香 鱼
yú xiāng yú

1 lb firm, fresh white fish fillets
1 tbsp dark soy sauce
1 tbsp cornstarch or potato flour
oil for frying

For the sauce:
2 tbsp oil
1 tbsp finely chopped scallion
1 tbsp finely chopped garlic
1 tbsp finely chopped fresh ginger
1 tbsp hot (chili) soybean paste (dou ban jiang)
pinch salt
1 tsp sugar
1 tsp sesame seed oil
1 tbsp wine vinegar
pinch freshly ground pepper
1 tbsp cornstarch or potato flour

Time: 45 minutes

Cut the fish fillets into thin strips and mix in
the bowl with the dark soy sauce and 1 tbsp
cornstarch or potato flour.

Heat plenty of oil in the wok for semi deep-
frying or in the deep-fryer to 340°F and fry the
fish fillets until pale golden brown; take them
out of the oil with a slotted ladle or wire mesh
ladle and drain well. Empty the wok or use a
clean wok or skillet and heat 3 tbsp fresh oil;
briefly stir-fry the scallion, garlic, and ginger,
add the hot soybean paste, stir, and then
return the fish fillets to the wok; stir carefully
so as not to break up the fish pieces too much,
then add the salt, sugar, sesame seed oil, vinegar, and pepper. Stir briefly but thoroughly,
then cook for a minute or two to allow the
moisture to evaporate a little. Mix the cornstarch or potato flour with a little cold water
and stir gently into the contents of the wok.
Remove from the heat and serve.

Yu xiang means "aroma of fish." This is a
Chinese culinary term to describe a very
widely used cooking technique, particularly
popular in Szechwan; besides fish dishes, the
method is also used for various types of meat
and vegetables.

STEAMED CARP

清 蒸 鱼
qǐng zhěng yú

1 carp (or any other firm-fleshed freshwater
fish) weighing approx. 1¹/₄ lb
1 cup chicken or fish broth
4 tbsp rice wine
4 tbsp light soy sauce
1 tsp salt
5 tung ku (dong gu) mushrooms
10 dried shrimp
1 medium-sized onion
slice fresh ginger, 1³/₄ in thick

Time: 1 hour

Soak the dried mushrooms in warm water for
about 30 minutes. Soak the shrimp in warm
water in a separate bowl. Bring a large saucepan of water (or a fish kettle) to a boil and
while it is heating, trim and scale the fish, gut
it, and wash well inside and out. Peel the
onion and chop finely; peel the ginger and
chop. When the water comes to a fast boil,
lower the fish into it and blanch for only about
10–15 seconds; take the fish out of the water
and drain. Use a very sharp knife to make deep
diagonal slashes along both sides of the fish
(about ³/₄ in apart). Place the fish in a heatproof dish or casserole large enough to take it
lying flat but not so large it will not fit into your
steamer with the steamer lid on.

Drain the mushrooms, and cut off and discard their stalks; drain the shrimp and sprinkle
these over the fish; place the mushroom caps
on the fish. Sprinkle with the onion and ginger.
Mix the broth with the rice wine, soy sauce,
and salt and pour into the casserole dish to
one side of the fish so as not to dislodge the
seasonings.

Place in the steamer, cover, and steam for
30 minutes or place the casserole dish, with its
lid on, in a pan of hot water (to come about
halfway up the sides of the casserole dish) in
the oven and cook for about 35–40 minutes at
350°F.

CARP GAN SHAO

干 烧 鲫 鱼
gàn shāo jì yú

1 carp weighing approx. 1³/₄ lb
oil for frying
1¹/₂ tsp finely chopped fresh ginger
pinch freshly ground pepper
¹/₂ cup finely chopped pork belly
¹/₂ cup finely chopped pork tenderloin
white part of 1 scallion

2 chili peppers (fresh or pickled in brine)
1¹/₂ tbsp soy sauce
1¹/₂ tbsp rice wine
1¹/₂ tbsp sesame seed oil
1¹/₂ tsp sugar
1 cup broth

Time: 1 hour

Clean the fish, trimming off the fins, scales and gutting it through the gill opening or by slitting along the belly. Fry in hot oil to brown lightly all over, remove carefully, and keep warm. Cut the white part of the scallion into thin strips; remove the stalk, seeds, and any pale inner parts from the chilis, and cut into strips. Empty the oil used for frying the fish out of the wok, wipe the inside and heat ¹/₃ cup fresh oil to gently stir-fry the finely chopped ginger and freshly ground pepper (use Szechwan pepper for extra flavor if wished). Add all the meat, stir-frying to cook lightly, then add the scallion and chili peppers. Stir well then add the soy sauce, rice wine, sesame seed oil, and sugar; add the fish to the wok and pour in the broth. Cover and bring to a boil then simmer for 20 minutes or until the fish is done. Carefully transfer the fish to a heated serving dish and pour the reduced liquid all over it as a sauce, removing and discarding the pieces of chili pepper and scallion.

SHRIMP WITH TOFU *

虾仁豆腐
xiā rén dóu fŭ

3 tung ku (dong gu) mushrooms
¹/₂ cup (¹/₄ lb) raw, unpeeled (or cooked, peeled) small shrimp
pinch salt
pinch freshly ground pepper
pinch monosodium glutamate (optional)
2 firm tofu (bean curd) cakes weighing a total of approx. 1¹/₄ lb
2 oz York ham
1 cup peanut oil
1 small piece white part of leek (about 2 in long)
1 thin slice fresh ginger
¹/₂ cup fresh or frozen peas
¹/₂ cup chicken broth
1 tbsp rice wine
¹/₂–1 tsp salt
1 tbsp cornstarch or potato flour
1 tsp sesame seed oil
1 tbsp finely chopped parsley

Time: 50 minutes

Soak the dried mushrooms in warm water for 20–30 minutes. Peel the shrimp, pat dry with

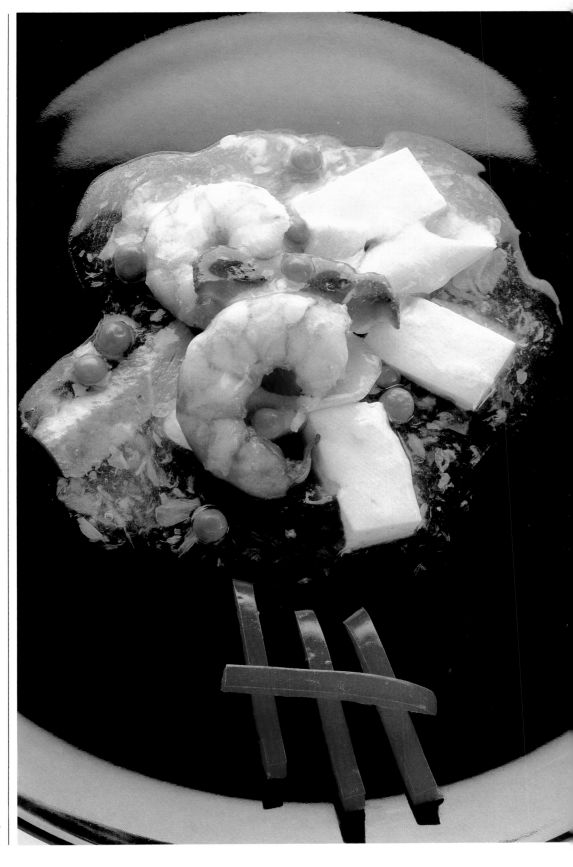

kitchen towels, place in a bowl and mix with the salt, pepper, and monosodium glutamate (if used). Cut the drained tofu and the ham into short, thin strips. Drain the mushrooms, cut off and discard their stems, and cut the caps into thin strips. Heat the peanut oil in the wok and fry the shrimp for 1 minute, then transfer them to a plate, using a slotted spoon and draining well; if you have bought cooked shrimp this frying stage can be omitted.

Empty the wok and wipe the inside. Heat 3 tbsp fresh oil and sweat the well washed, dried and finely chopped leek and the peeled and finely chopped ginger until soft. Add the shrimp, tofu, ham, mushrooms, and peas then pour in the broth mixed with the rice wine. Add salt to taste, allow to come to a boil then stir in the cornstarch or potato flour mixed with a little cold water to thicken the sauce. Cook for 3–4 more minutes.

Transfer to a serving plate. Sprinkle with sesame seed oil and parsley.

SHRIMP IN CHILI SAUCE *

干烧明虾
gàn shāo míng xiā

8 jumbo shrimp, peeled
1¹/₂ cups oil
1 tbsp finely chopped scallion
1 tbsp finely chopped fresh ginger
¹/₄ cup tomato ketchup
1 tbsp hot (chili) soybean paste (dou ban jiang)
1 tbsp rice wine
1 tsp salt
pinch monosodium glutamate (optional)
1 tsp sugar
1 tbsp soy sauce
¹/₄ cup broth
1¹/₂ tsp cornstarch or potato flour
1 tsp sesame seed oil
pinch freshly ground pepper

Time: 45 minutes

Heat 1 cup of the oil in the wok until very hot and fry the shrimp, stirring until they are very lightly browned. Drain well. Empty the oil from the wok.

Wipe the inside of the wok and heat the remaining fresh oil; stir-fry the scallion and ginger until they start to release their aroma, then stir in the ketchup, soybean paste, rice wine, salt, monosodium glutamate (if used), sugar, soy sauce, and broth. Return the shrimp to the wok and cook for a few minutes, while stirring. Mix the cornstarch or potato flour with a little cold water and stir into the contents of the wok to thicken the sauce slightly. Cook for a very few minutes more, uncovered, to reduce the sauce further, then serve.

BRAISED TROUT

茄汁虾仁
guō bā xiā rén

1 trout weighing approx. 1³/₄ lb
¹/₂ tsp salt
4 cloves garlic
1 1¹/₂-in piece fresh ginger
1 cup oil
3 tbsp hot soybean paste (dou ban jiang)
1 tbsp rice wine
¹/₂ tbsp sugar
2 cups chicken broth
1 tbsp chili oil
green part of 2 scallions, chopped

Clean, gut, and dry the trout. Sprinkle with salt inside and out and leave to stand for 15 minutes. Finely chop the garlic and ginger.

Heat the wok until it smokes; pour in the oil and swirl it evenly round the wok to coat, drain off all but 2 tbsp. Place the fish in the wok and cook for 1–2 minutes, then turn carefully, taking care not to break the fish and cook on the other side for 1–2 minutes. Transfer to a plate and set aside.

Heat 2 tbsp fresh oil, fry the garlic and ginger and add the hot soybean paste, the rice wine, and the sugar. Pour in the water or broth and bring to a boil, stirring.

Return the fish to the wok, reduce the heat, cover, and simmer for 15 minutes. Turn the fish carefully, cover, and simmer for 15 minutes. Uncover, baste with the sauce, then take up the trout and place on a heated serving plate. Add the chili oil and the scallions to the sauce in the wok. Heat briefly, and pour over the trout to serve.

252

DEEP-FRIED SOLE AND SHRIMP "SANDWICHES"

金钱鱼饼
jīn qián yú bǐng

10 oz fillets of sole
5 oz peeled small shrimp
$^1/_2$ cup rice wine
1–1$^1/_2$ tbsp soy sauce
1 egg
1 cup fine breadcrumbs
salt
oil for frying

Time: 40 minutes

Chop the shrimp very finely, mix with just enough rice wine and most, or all of the soy sauce, to obtain a thick, spreadable mixture. Spread this on half the sole fillets and cover with the remaining fillets; cut these "sandwiches" across the width into medium-sized pieces. Beat the egg lightly with a pinch of salt; dip the sole "sandwiches" to cover all over, then coat thickly with the breadcrumbs. Deep-fry in plenty of very hot oil until golden brown. Serve hot.

FISH WITH GARLIC SAUCE

川蒜烧鱼
chuān suàn shāo yú

4 very small cod (scrod or schrod), hake or
    whiting
$^1/_2$ cup oil
1 head garlic, divided into cloves, peeled
1 tbsp peeled and finely chopped garlic
1 tbsp finely chopped scallion
1 tbsp finely chopped fresh ginger
2 tbsp hot (chili) soybean paste (dou ban
    jiang)
2 tsp salt
1 tbsp sugar
pinch monosodium glutamate (optional)
2 tbsp soy sauce
2 cups broth
$^1/_4$ cup wine vinegar
1 tbsp chili oil
1 tbsp cornstarch or potato flour
1 scallion, cut into short, very thin strips

Time: 40 minutes

Prepare the fish, trimming, gutting, and washing them inside and out; dry well. Heat $^1/_2$ cup oil in the wok to about 290°F and stir-fry all the whole, peeled cloves of garlic and the chopped garlic together with the scallion and the ginger. Stir in the soybean paste, salt, sugar, monosodium glutamate (if used), soy sauce, and finally the broth. Add the fish. Cook for 15 minutes over low heat once the liquid has reached boiling point, stirring gently to prevent the fish sticking to the wok and turning them carefully halfway through the cooking time. When the fish are cooked, add the vinegar and chili oil; mix the cornstarch or potato flour with a little cold water and stir into the wok to thicken the liquid a little. Serve, garnished with the shredded scallion.

FISH WITH FERMENTED SOYBEAN PASTE

豆瓣鲤鱼
dòu bàn lǐ yú

1 whole fish weighing approx. 2¹/₄ lb (e.g. trout, salmon trout, sea bass or similar)
oil for frying
1 tbsp finely chopped scallion
1 tbsp finely chopped fresh ginger
1 tbsp finely chopped garlic
1 tbsp hot (chili) soybean paste (dou ban jiang)
1 tbsp yellow fermented soybeans
1 tbsp wine vinegar
¹/₂ tsp salt
¹/₂–1 tsp sugar
¹/₂ tsp monosodium glutamate (optional)
1 cup broth
1 tbsp rice wine
1 chili pepper
1 tbsp cornstarch or potato flour
1 scallion cut into very thin strips
1 tbsp sesame seed oil

Time: 1 hour 10 minutes

Prepare the fish, trimming, descaling it if necessary, and gutting it; rinse well and dry. Heat plenty of oil in the wok or in a deep-fryer to 340°F and fry the fish until golden brown all over. Heat ¹/₄ cup fresh oil in another wok or skillet and gently stir-fry the scallion, ginger, and garlic; add the soy sauce, soybeans, vinegar, salt, sugar, monosodium glutamate (if used), broth, rice wine, and the deseeded and chopped chili pepper. Stir well, add the fish, cover, and cook over gentle heat for 30 minutes, turning very carefully just over halfway through this time. Transfer the fish to a heated serving plate; mix the cornstarch or potato flour with a little cold water and stir into the liquid left in the wok to thicken it a little. Sprinkle in the sesame seed oil and the shredded scallion, stir once, and pour over the fish.

CRISPY FISH

脆皮桂鱼
cuì pí guì yú

1 whole fish weighing approx. 2¹/₄ lb (e.g. grouper, porgy, sea bass, carp), gutted
2¹/₂ tsp salt
3 tbsp rice wine
pinch monosodium glutamate (optional)
3 tbsp cornstarch or potato flour
oil for frying

For the sauce:
¹/₄ cup oil
1¹/₂ tbsp finely chopped scallion
1¹/₂ tsp finely chopped ginger
1¹/₂ tbsp sugar
3 tbsp wine vinegar
pinch freshly ground pepper
¹/₃ cup tomato ketchup

Time: 1 hour

Make slanting slashes all down both sides of the fish, about ³/₄ in apart; repeat this operation but in the opposite direction, to achieve a lattice effect. Mix together the salt, rice wine, and 1¹/₂ tbsp of cornstarch or potato flour in a shallow dish large enough to contain the fish. Roll the fish in this mixture until coated all over then leave to stand for 15 minutes, turning several times. Remove the fish from the dish and coat with the remaining cornstarch or potato flour. Heat about ¹/₂ cup oil over fairly high heat, add the fish, and fry over moderate heat for about 15 minutes (turn once very carefully). In a small saucepan, heat ¹/₄ cup fresh oil and stir-fry the finely chopped scallion and ginger; add the sugar, vinegar, pepper, and ketchup and cook, to reduce and thicken. Pour the sauce over the fish.

BRAISED FISH HEAD

砂煲鱼头
shā bāo yú tóu

1 large grouper (or similar fish)
1¹/₂ tbsp salt
1¹/₂ tbsp soy sauce
1¹/₂ tbsp cornstarch or potato flour
oil for frying
¹/₄ lb pork belly
¹/₄ lb pork tenderloin
4 thin slices fresh ginger
3 scallions
10 oz Chinese cabbage, Nappa cabbage or ordinary white cabbage
5 tung ku (dong gu) mushrooms
¹/₄ lb bamboo shoots
1 leek

¹/₄ lb tofu (firm bean curd)

For the sauce:
6 tbsp light soy sauce
3 tbsp dark soy sauce
1¹/₂ tsp sugar
1¹/₂ tsp salt
1 tsp monosodium glutamate (optional)
1¹/₂ tbsp rice wine
pinch freshly ground pepper
1¹/₂ tbsp sesame seed oil

Time: 1 hour 40 minutes

Soak the mushrooms in warm water for 20 minutes. Cut the fish in half across its body, making the cut slightly nearer the head than the middle and leaving quite a long, middle to tail section; you can use this part of the fish for other dishes. The head and fattest part of the body section will be used for this recipe. Remove the scales, slit open the belly and gut the fish. Wash and dry, then cut the fish lengthwise in half: use a very sharp knife to cut along the "top" or back of the fish, right along its backbone, take one half off the backbone and the attached bones that radiate from it and then use a cleaver to continue the cutting right through the head. You will now have two identical halves of the "forward" section.

Mix together the salt, soy sauce, and cornstarch or potato flour and spread this mixture all over the fish. Leave for a few minutes and then deep-fry or semi deep-fry in very hot oil for about 4 minutes. The fish should be golden brown all over Remove from the oil and drain well. Cut the pork belly into thin slices about 1¹/₄ in wide. Cut the ginger and scallions into thin strips. Cut the stalks off the well drained mushrooms and discard, then cut the caps into strips; wash the leek thoroughly and cut into thin rings; cut the bamboo shoots into small pieces. Shred the cabbage. Cut the tofu into ³/₄-in cubes. Stir-fry the meats, mushrooms, leek, bamboo shoots, and tofu in approx. 3 tbsp oil over gentle heat. Heat ¹/₄ cup oil in another wok or skillet and stir-fry the ginger and scallion until they start to release their aromas; add the fish, meat, vegetables, tofu, and all the sauce ingredients. Pour in 6 tbsp boiling water and simmer for 10 minutes.

Transfer all these ingredients to a large, fireproof casserole dish and simmer, tightly covered, over gentle heat for 20 minutes.

EEL GAN BIAN

干煸鳝片
gàn biān shàn piàn

1 eel weighing approx. 1 lb
oil for frying
1 scallion

3 cloves garlic
5 thin slices fresh ginger
4 chili peppers (fresh or pickled in brine)
$^1/_4$ lb celery sticks
$^1/_4$ cup oil
$1^1/_2$ tbsp hot (chili) soybean paste (dou ban jiang)
$1^1/_2$ tbsp soy sauce
$1^1/_2$ tsp sugar
pinch monosodium glutamate (optional)
pinch salt
$^1/_3$ cup chicken broth or water
$1^1/_2$ tsp wine vinegar
$1^1/_2$ tsp sesame seed oil
$1^1/_2$ tbsp cornstarch or potato flour
pinch ground Szechwan pepper

Time: 45 minutes

Have your fishmonger skin the eel for you or do this yourself. Rinse the eel and take the flesh off the bones as neatly as possible, cutting it into pieces approx. $^3/_4 \times 2$ in in size. Trim the ends off the scallion and cut lengthwise into thin strips. peel and thinly slice the garlic. Peel the ginger slices and cut into very small pieces. Remove the seeds, stalk, and any pith from the chili peppers and cut these into very thin strips. Wash the celery, dry, remove any tough strings, and shred.

Heat plenty of oil in the wok or in a deep-fryer to 325°F; add the pieces of eel and fry until golden brown, then remove from the oil, draining well.

Empty and wipe the wok or use another wok or skillet to stir-fry the scallion, garlic, and ginger in $^1/_4$ cup fresh oil. Stir in the soybean paste, the fried eel pieces, celery, and chili peppers. Mix in the soy sauce, sugar, monosodium glutamate (if used), and the salt.

Pour in the broth and cook briefly, uncovered, to reduce the liquid a little; add the vinegar and sesame seed oil for extra flavor and immediately afterward stir in the thickening agent mixed with a little cold water. Cook for about 1 minute more, then sprinkle with freshly ground Szechwan pepper and serve.

BRAISED CHICKEN WINGS *

炖鸡翼

dùn jī yī

12 chicken wings
$1^1/_4$ cups chicken broth
$^1/_2$ leek, washed and finely chopped
1 tbsp finely chopped fresh ginger
$2^1/_2$ tbsp rice wine
$2^1/_2$ tbsp light soy sauce
cornstarch or potato flour as required
oil for frying
1 tsp sugar
$^1/_2$ lb broccoli

3 tbsp oil
pinch salt

Time: 1 hour + 30 minutes marinating time

Cut off the wing tips and use these to make the broth if wished. Mix together the leek, ginger, rice wine, and soy sauce for the marinade.

Place the wings in a deep dish or bowl and sprinkle with the marinade; leave to marinate for 30 minutes, turning several times. Remove the wings from the bowl, draining any excess marinade back into the bowl (reserve the marinade, which will be used later). Pat the wings almost dry with kitchen towels and coat all over with the cornstarch or potato flour. Deep-fry in plenty of very hot oil until crisp and golden brown all over.

Drain well when cooked and set aside. Pour the marinade into a large, heavy-bottomed saucepan or casserole dish, pour in the broth, and add the sugar. Stir well, add the fried chicken wings, and bring to a boil. Lower the heat and simmer, uncovered, for 20 minutes.

Meanwhile, wash the broccoli, trim off the stalks, and blanch the florets in boiling salted water for a few minutes (they should be fairly tender but still very crisp). Drain very thoroughly.

Heat 3 tbsp fresh oil in the wok or a skillet and stir-fry the broccoli. Sprinkle with salt and continue cooking until they are tender but still have plenty of bite to them. Turn off the heat. Arrange the chicken wings and sprinkle with some of the cooking liquid; surround with the broccoli florets. Serve very hot; other cooked vegetables (e.g. carrots) can also be added to the dish with the broccoli.

255

CHICKEN HONG YU STYLE

红烧鸡丁
hóng yóu jī dīng

14 oz boneless chicken
2 oz dried or aged tofu (bean curd cheese)
oil for frying
$1/4$ lb unsalted, roasted peanuts (unpeeled)
1 tbsp finely chopped scallion
$1/2$–1 tsp ground Szechwan pepper
$1/2$–1 tsp sugar
1 tsp sesame seed paste
6 tbsp chicken broth
$1^1/2$ tbsp soy sauce
$1^1/2$ tbsp chili oil
$1^1/2$ tbsp sesame seed oil

Time: 30 minutes

Add the chicken meat to a saucepan of boiling water and boil gently for 10 minutes; drain and cut into small cubes. Cut the tofu into cubes of the same size and deep-fry for a few minutes in very hot oil. Drain well.

Place the chicken and tofu on a serving dish and sprinkle the roasted peanuts all over them.

Mix the scallion, Szechwan pepper, sugar, sesame paste, broth, soy sauce, chili oil, and sesame seed oil in a small saucepan over moderate heat; simmer for 2 minutes then pour over the chicken, peanut, and tofu mixture. Serve cold.

CHICKEN CHENG DU *

成都子鸡
Chéngdū zǐ jī

1 young cockerel, pullet or very young roasting chicken weighing $1^3/4$–$2^1/4$ lb
oil for frying
3 tbsp finely chopped scallion
$1^1/2$ tsp finely chopped fresh ginger
3 tbsp oil
3 tbsp hot (chili) soybean paste (dou ban jiang)
$1^1/2$ tbsp finely chopped red bell pepper
1 tsp salt
1 tsp sugar
$1^1/2$ tbsp rice wine
$1/2$ cup chicken broth
10 oz very young, crisp tender spinach leaves

Time: 50 minutes

If you buy an oven-ready bird, one weighing 1³/₄-lb–2-lb will be sufficient. Cut off the wing tips, rinse the bird well inside and out, and dry well.

Use a cleaver to chop the bird (bones and all) into irregular slices about ³/₄ in thick.

Heat plenty of oil in the wok or in a deep-fryer until very hot and fry the pieces of chicken for 2 minutes in batches; drain each batch well when fried and set aside.

Heat 3 tbsp fresh oil in another wok or skillet and stir-fry 1¹/₂ tsp of the scallion and all the ginger until they release their aromas. Add the fried chicken pieces, the hot soybean paste, finely chopped bell pepper, rice wine, salt, sugar, and broth. Stir well and cook for 5–6 minutes. Transfer to a heated serving dish.

Meanwhile, rinse the spinach leaves and blanch them for 30 seconds in unsalted boiling water. Serve the chicken with a sprinkling of the remaining chopped scallion and surrounded by the spinach leaves. If preferred, broccoli or another green vegetable can replace the spinach. The ancient city of Cheng-du is the historic capital of Szechwan province and has given its name to this full-flavored western dish, typical of the spicy cooking of this region.

LANTERN CHICKEN

灯 笼 鸡

dēng lóng jī

1 oven-ready chicken weighing approx. 2¹/₄ lb
2 slices fresh ginger
1 scallion
1 tsp ground Szechwan pepper
3 tbsp rice wine
1 tsp salt
1 tbsp ground chili
1 tbsp sesame seed oil

Time: 1 hour + time for seasoning

Wash and dry the chicken, removing any pieces of fat left behind just inside the cavity; place the bird on a grid in a fairly shallow heat-proof dish. Peel and finely chop the ginger slices and scallion and mix with the Szechwan pepper. Sprinkle this mixture all over the chicken, inside and out, and rub in. Leave to stand for the flavors to penetrate for 2–3 hours. Bring a kettle of water to a boil and carefully pour all over the chicken, especially over the skin to "set" and tighten it. Drain well. Remove the grid, sprinkle the chicken with the rice wine, salt, and chili pepper.

Place the dish containing the chicken in the steamer (you will need a large, deep, steamer compartment which can accommodate the chicken when the steamer lid is replaced) and steam for 30 minutes or until done over water which is already boiling fast.

Take the chicken out of the steamer, cut into fairly small pieces, bone and all, with a cleaver or carve into Western portions if wished (wing and some breast, drumsticks, thighs, wishbone and two pieces of breast) or keep the bird whole, and use a pastry brush to coat the surface all over with warmed sesame seed oil; transfer to a serving platter and serve.

Usually a bowl (or several tiny bowls) of the following condiment is placed on the table with this dish: mix 2 tbsp salt with 1¹/₂ tbsp ground Szechwan pepper and a pinch of monosodium glutamate (optional). Dip the chicken pieces into this seasoning mixture before eating.

CHICKEN BREASTS IN SHARP SAUCE

醋 溜 鸡 丝

cù liū jī sī

10 oz chicken breasts
1 tsp salt
pinch freshly ground pepper
pinch monosodium glutamate (optional)
1 tbsp rice wine
1 tbsp oil
1 egg white
¹/₄ cup cornstarch or potato flour
oil for frying

For the sauce:
3 tbsp oil
1¹/₂ tsp finely chopped fresh ginger
1¹/₂ tsp finely chopped scallion
1 tsp finely chopped garlic
2 vinegar-pickled chili peppers
3 tbsp wine vinegar
1¹/₂ tbsp tomato ketchup
1¹/₂ tbsp sugar
1 tbsp salt
pinch freshly ground pepper
pinch cornstarch or potato flour

Time: 1 hour

Shred the chicken breasts. Whisk the egg white until stiff in a fairly large bowl and fold in the salt, pepper, monosodium glutamate (if used), rice wine, oil, and cornstarch or potato flour. Add the shredded chicken meat and stir well; leave to stand for 30 minutes.

Heat sufficient oil in the wok or deep-fryer to semi deep-fry or deep-fry; when very hot but not smoking fry the marinated chicken for 3–4 minutes; remove the chicken from the oil, draining well, and set aside.

258

Empty the oil out of the wok if used for semi deep-frying and heat 3 tbsp fresh oil in it; fry the ginger, scallion, garlic, and the finely shredded chili peppers gently.

When these ingredients start to release a full aroma, add the vinegar and then stir in the ketchup, sugar, salt, and pepper; add the chicken and stir well. If the sauce is too liquid and does not coat the chicken strips satisfactorily, mix the cornstarch or potato flour with 1 tsp cold water and stir into the contents of the wok.

BRAISED CHICKEN

黄焖鸡块

huáng mèn jī kuài

1 chicken weighing approx. 2¹/₄ lb
oil for frying
1 tsp finely chopped fresh ginger
1 tbsp finely chopped scallion
3 tbsp oil
1¹/₂ oz bamboo shoots
4 tung ku (dong gu) mushrooms
3 tbsp rice wine
1 tsp monosodium glutamate (optional)
1 tsp salt
3 tbsp soy sauce
¹/₂–1 tsp sugar
1 quart chicken broth
1¹/₂ tbsp cornstarch or potato flour

Time: 1¹/₄ hours

Soak the dried mushrooms in warm water for at least 20 minutes. Drain, discard the stalks, and chop the caps.

Take all the flesh off the chicken and cut into small pieces measuring about ³/₄ × 1¹/₄ in. Heat plenty of oil in the wok or deep-fryer to 340°F and plunge the chicken pieces into it (in several batches) to fry for 1 minute. Remove with a wire mesh or slotted ladle and drain well. Heat 3 tbsp fresh oil in the emptied and wiped wok (or in another wok or skillet) and gently stir-fry the ginger and scallion, then add the thinly sliced bamboo shoots cut into ³/₄ in squares. Stir-fry these briefly, then add the mushrooms. Add the fried chicken, rice wine, monosodium glutamate (if used), salt, soy sauce, sugar, and the chicken broth. Boil gently, uncovered, for 30 minutes. The liquid should reduce by one third; if it does not reduce quickly enough, boil a little harder.

Mix the thickening agent with a very little cold water and stir into the contents of the wok.

CHICKEN WITH SZECHWAN PEPPER

椒麻鸡

jiāo má jī

14 oz boneless chicken
5 oz bean curd skins
1¹/₂ tbsp finely chopped scallion
1¹/₂ tbsp finely chopped fresh ginger
1¹/₂ tbsp soy sauce
1¹/₂ tbsp sesame seed oil
3 tbsp wine vinegar
1 tsp sugar
1 tsp freshly ground Szechwan pepper

Time: 30 minutes

Add the boneless chicken meat to a saucepan of boiling water and boil for 10 minutes; drain well and cut into short, fairly thin batons. Soak the bean curd skins in hot water to soften; cut this into thin strips. Mix the scallion, ginger, soy sauce, sesame seed oil, vinegar, sugar, and Szechwan pepper.

Spread the shredded soybean skins out over a serving dish or large plate; place the chicken pieces on top and sprinkle the sauce all over both. This dish is always eaten cold.

CHICKEN TAI BAI STYLE

太白鸡

Tài Bái jī

10 oz chicken breasts
oil for frying
1 scallion
2 thin slices fresh ginger
3 tbsp oil
5 oz pickled mustard greens (see method)
pinch finely chopped fresh or dried chili
    pepper
generous pinch ground Szechwan pepper
1¹/₂ tbsp rice wine
1¹/₂ tbsp soy sauce
1¹/₂ tbsp wine vinegar
pinch sugar
pinch salt
1¹/₂ tbsp chicken broth

Time: 40 minutes

Cut the chicken breasts into small, bite-sized pieces. Heat plenty of oil in the wok or deep-fryer to 325°F and fry the chicken pieces until golden brown; remove from the oil with a slotted ladle and drain well. Trim the scallion and cut into strips; peel the ginger and cut into thin strips.

Empty and wipe the wok (or use another wok or skillet); heat 3 tbsp fresh oil and sweat the scallion and ginger until they start to release their aromas. Add the fried chicken, the pickled mustard greens, the chili pepper, and all the other seasonings and flavorings. Stir well and simmer to reduce the liquid a little.

Li Tai Bai, better known in the West as Li Po or Li Bai, was a great Chinese poet who lived from 701 to 762 (during the middle of the Tang dynasty, which lasted from 618 to 907). He is said to have been fond of highly spiced dishes, especially those containing the famous Szechwan pepper which besides being peppery has an acidulated, almost citrus note to its flavor and scent. Presumably some well-read cook must have dedicated this dish to him, thinking that the Master would have savored its full, spicy flavor.

CHICKEN GONG BAO *

宫保鸡丁

Gōng Bǎo jī dīng

14 oz chicken breasts
pinch salt
1 egg white
1¹/₂ tsp cornstarch or potato flour
3 tbsp rice wine
oil for frying
3 dried chili peppers
1 clove garlic
2 thin slices fresh ginger
3 tbsp oil
1¹/₂ tbsp soy sauce
pinch monosodium glutamate (optional)
1 tbsp sugar
pinch salt
1¹/₂ tsp wine vinegar
1¹/₂ tsp sesame seed oil
1¹/₂ tsp cornstarch or potato flour
2 tbsp unsalted roasted peanuts

Time: 45 minutes

Cut the chicken breasts into small, bite-sized pieces; whisk the egg white until stiff and fold in the pinch of salt, the cornstarch or potato flour, and rice wine: add the chicken pieces, stir well, and leave to stand for a few minutes.

Crumble the dried chilis; peel and trim the garlic and ginger and cut into thin strips.

Heat plenty of oil in the wok or deep-fryer to 340°F and fry the chicken for 2 minutes; take out of the oil with a wire mesh or slotted ladle and drain well. Empty the wok and wipe the inside (or use another wok or skillet); heat 3 tbsp fresh oil and sweat the chilis, garlic, and

260

BANG BANG CHICKEN

棒 棒 鸡
bàng bàng jī

14 oz chicken breasts
¹/₄ lb tofu (soybean curd) skins (or 1 lettuce)
3 tbsp sesame seed paste
1¹/₂ tbsp soy sauce
1¹/₂ tbsp wine vinegar
¹/₂–1 tsp sugar
pinch monosodium glutamate (optional)
1 tsp chili oil
1¹/₂ tbsp sesame seed oil

Time: 30 minutes

Add the chicken breasts to a pan of unsalted boiling water and boil for 10 minutes, then tear the flesh into shreds by hand. Soak the bean curd skins in hot water to soften or blanch the lettuce leaves for 30 seconds in boiling water and drain. Cut the soybean skins (or the lettuce leaves) into strips ¹/₄ in wide and 2¹/₂ in long. Spread these out on a serving dish. Mix the sesame seed paste with 6 tbsp water and mix with the soy sauce, vinegar, sugar, monosodium glutamate (if used), chili oil, and sesame seed oil.

Spread the shredded chicken on top of the soybean skins or lettuce and sprinkle with the dressing. This is a summer dish and is always eaten cold.

STRANGE-FLAVORED CHICKEN *

怪 味 鸡
guài wèi jī

1 young cockerel, pullet or young roasting
*   chicken weighing approx. 2–2¹/₄ lb*
1 tsp finely chopped fresh ginger
1 tsp finely chopped garlic
¹/₄ cup thick or dark soy sauce
1 tsp salt
1 tsp sugar
pinch monosodium glutamate (optional)
1 tbsp vinegar
1 tbsp sesame seed paste
1 heaping tsp ground Szechwan pepper
1 tbsp chili oil

Time: 1 hour

Wash and dry the chicken, cut off the wing tips and remove any pieces of fat left inside the cavity. Bring a large saucepan of water to a boil, add the chicken and boil for 20 minutes. Remove from the saucepan and immediately plunge into a large bowl of iced water; leave

ginger. As soon as these give off a good, full aroma, add the fried chicken, the soy sauce, the monosodium glutamate (if used), sugar, salt, and vinegar. Cook, stirring, for a few minutes then mix the second quantity of cornstarch or potato flour listed above with a little water and stir into the wok, followed by the sesame seed oil. Mix in the peanuts (rub off their thin, papery skins after roasting them in the oven). Immediately draw aside from the heat, transfer to a heated serving dish, and eat without delay.

Gong Bao was the title given to the tutors of the children of the imperial Qin dynasty (third century B.C.). One of these teachers had a weakness for this dish, hence its name.

for a few minutes, then drain. This process ensures that the chicken is tender.

Mix all the sauce ingredients; if the sugar does not dissolve satisfactorily, heat gently in a small saucepan. Use poultry scissors or a very sharp, heavy knife to cut the chicken open all the way down its backbone; open out flat on a chopping board. Use a cleaver to cut right across the bird, chopping it into strips about ³/₄ in wide; this will make it easy to reassemble the chicken, albeit in a flattened form, on the serving platter, with the strips pushed close together so that the cuts are barely discernible.

Decorate as you wish: flowers or shapes sculpted out of carrots or potatoes or radishes are effective; or tomato skin cut with a thin layer of the flesh attached, and twisted to look like roses; the chicken can be placed on a bed of lettuce leaves. Sprinkle the sauce all over the chicken and serve.

CHICKEN WITH GLUTINOUS RICE STUFFING

糯米鸡
nuò mǐ jī

1 young cockerel, pullet or young roasting chicken weighing approx. 2–2¹/₄ lb
1 oz dried lotus seeds
1 tung ku (dong gu) mushroom
1 oz very small button mushrooms
1 scallion
1 oz bamboo shoots
1 oz peeled small shrimp
1 oz York ham
¹/₂ cup fresh or frozen peas
¹/₂ cup glutinous rice
1¹/₂ tbsp soy sauce
pinch freshly ground pepper
pinch sugar
pinch salt
3 tbsp oil
3 tbsp rice wine

Time: 1 hour 40 minutes

Soak the dried lotus seeds in warm water for 1 hour, or use canned lotus seeds.

Wash and dry the chicken, cutting off the wing tips. Use a very sharp, heavy knife or poultry scissors to split the bird open all along its backbone; open the bird out flat, with the inside facing upward, and bone the bird; start with the wings, then gradually work the flesh off the leg and thigh bones; work the flesh off the ribcage; take care not to puncture the skin at any point during the boning operation.

Soak the dried mushrooms in warm water (20–30 minutes) to soften, drain, then cut off and discard the stalks. Drain the lotus seeds,

A noodle vendor at his stall in a Chengdu street, with his wares draped over bamboo canes. It is fascinating to watch the various types of noodles being made: with lightning speed and skill a lump of dough is transformed into all sorts of shapes. Rice flour noodles, soybean flour and wheat flour noodles are gathered into hanks rather like wool and then hung up in the sun to dry, after which they will keep well. These bundles are then packaged ready for sale and cooked in traditional ways, to be eaten with reconstituted shrimp and mushrooms or meat and sauce, added to soups or fried.

Crispy fried noodles can also be shaped like a fan and eaten as a snack. In Yunnan, dumplings are filled with a mixed vegetable and pork stuffing; another specialty of the region is jiaozi, fried wheat flour triangles filled with sweet soybean paste. These itinerant food sellers are to be found everywhere in China, even in the most isolated villages, setting up their rudimentary stoves and taking cheap, "fast" food to people living in the most out of the way places. Baskets full of surplus home-grown produce are often placed on the stall, also for sale.

peel them and cut out the small, hard central seed (if you use canned lotus seeds this will already have been done). Chop fairly finely. Wipe the button mushrooms with a damp cloth. Trim and coarsely chop the scallion. Cut the mushrooms, bamboo shoots, shrimp, and ham into tiny dice and place in a bowl. Stir in the peas (thawed if frozen). Heat the oil in the wok, stir-fry the scallion until tender, add the diced mixture, the chopped lotus seeds, and the flavorings and seasonings; cook briefly, stirring well. Soak the glutinous rice for 2 minutes in boiling water, drain, and add to

the wok. Stir-fry all these ingredients for a few minutes.

Use this mixture to stuff the chicken; sew up the long slit where the backbone was and sew up any other openings, making the parcel as neat as possible.

Line the steamer compartment of a large steamer with cabbage leaves and place the chicken on top of these; steam for 30 minutes then serve, using a very sharp knife to cut right across the chicken and its stuffing so that the pieces have a border of chicken skin and flesh and a large central area of stuffing.

DA QIAN'S CHICKEN *

大 千 子 鸡
Dà Qiān zǐ jī

262

1 chicken weighing approx. 2–2¹/₄ lb
1 egg white
1¹/₂ tsp soy sauce
1¹/₂ tsp cornstarch or potato flour

oil for frying
1 small green bell pepper
1 small chili pepper, fresh or dried
3 tbsp oil
4 cloves garlic

For the sauce:
1¹/₂ tsp soy sauce
pinch monosodium glutamate (optional)
pinch salt

¹/₂–1 tbsp sugar
¹/₂–1 tbsp wine vinegar
1¹/₂ tbsp sesame seed oil
1¹/₂ tbsp Morello cherry cordial, kirsch or
   Alkermes liqueur
1¹/₂ tbsp cornstarch or potato flour

Time: 1 hour

POULTRY

Wash and dry the chicken; cut off the wing tips. Use a heavy cleaver to chop into bite-sized pieces (cutting through both bone and flesh) about ³/₄ in thick. Remove the stalk, seeds, and pale inner pith from the sweet pepper and cut into bite-sized pieces; prepare the chili pepper and shred. Peel the garlic and slice thinly. Whisk the egg white stiffly in a large bowl and fold in the first amounts of soy sauce and cornstarch or potato flour listed above; add the chicken pieces and mix well.

Heat plenty of oil in the wok for semi deep-frying or use a deep-fryer and when very hot, fry the chicken pieces in several batches for about 4 minutes or until crisp and golden brown, draining well as you remove each batch from the hot oil with a wire mesh or slotted ladle. Empty the wok if used for frying, wipe the inside, and heat 3 tbsp fresh oil. Stir-fry the bell pepper pieces. Add the garlic and the chicken pieces. Continue stir-frying as you add the remaining ingredients in the order listed above except for the second quantity of cornstarch or potato flour.

Mix the cornstarch or potato flour with a little cold water and stir into the contents of the wok; cook for a few minutes more, then serve piping hot.

Zhang Da Qian is one of China's most famous living painters; in a pause from his figurative works of art, he turned his attention to the art of cookery and invented this recipe.

SPICED DUCK

香酥肥鴨
Xiāng sū féi yā

1 oven-ready duck weighing approx. 4–4¹/₂ lb
2¹/₂ tbsp black peppercorns
2¹/₂ tbsp salt
2¹/₂ tbsp finely chopped fresh ginger
3 scallions, finely chopped
2¹/₂ tbsp dark soy sauce
2 tbsp five-spice powder
¹/₂ tsp monosodium glutamate (optional)
oil for frying

Time: 2 hours 40 minutes + 6 hours
marinating time

Remove any pieces of fat which may have been left in the cavity; wash the duck well inside and out and dry thoroughly. Roast the peppercorns for a few minutes over moderate heat in the wok in a heavy-bottomed saucepan, turning them over continually or shaking the saucepan so that they roast evenly and do not burn. Sprinkle with the salt then draw aside from the heat. Pound the peppercorns and salt together in a mortar with a pestle. Mix with the finely chopped ginger and scallion, soy sauce, five-spice powder, and monosodium glutamate (if used).

Rub the duck all over, inside and out, with this mixture; place in a dish, cover with foil, and chill in the refrigerator for 6 hours.

When the duck has had its time for chilling and the seasoning to penetrate, heat the oven to maximum; place a roasting pan three-quarters full of hot water in the bottom, then place the duck carefully on the grid shelf above the roasting pan, breast side up. Cook for 1¹/₂ hours at this very high temperature, turning once halfway through this time. Check to see whether the boiling water in the roasting pan needs topping up from time to time with more boiling water from the kettle. Take the duck out of the oven and check to see that there is no moisture on it (mop up any juices and dampness from the cavity with kitchen towels).

Heat plenty of oil in a deep-fryer until very hot but not smoking. Add the duck and fry, ladling the boiling hot oil continuously over any parts that are not immersed in the oil. The duck should be deep golden brown and very crisp when ready. Remove from the oil, draining well, place on kitchen towels to finish draining, then use 2 forks to break up all the flesh and crisp skin into fairly small pieces, taking them off the bone as you do so (in Chinese restaurants, this is usually done at table). Serve with Mandarin pancakes (see recipe on p. 16) or with plain boiled rice (see p. 172).

SZECHWAN DUCK

香酥鴨
xiāng sū yā

1 oven-ready duck weighing approx. 4–4¹/₂ lb
4 star anises
1 small cinnamon bark
2 cloves
1¹/₂ tsp salt
1 scallion, finely chopped
4 thin slices fresh ginger, finely chopped
1¹/₂ tbsp ground Szechwan pepper
3 tbsp rice wine
1¹/₂ tbsp soy sauce
oil for frying

Time: 3 hours

Rinse the duck thoroughly inside and out and cut off the wing tips. Pound the star anises, cinnamon, and cloves with a pestle and mortar. Mix together the salt, the chopped scallion and ginger, the Szechwan pepper, rice wine, soy sauce, star anises, cinnamon, and cloves and rub the duck inside and out with this seasoning. Place the bird in a pan or heatproof dish, place in the steamer, cover, and steam for 2 hours.

Take the cooked duck out of the steamer and when cool enough to handle, wipe all over with kitchen towels to dry. Heat plenty of oil to 350°F in the wok or in a deep-fryer and fry the duck until the skin is very crisp all over Take out of the oil, drain well, and cut into portions or fairly small pieces with a cleaver, cutting through both the flesh and the bones.

TEA AND CAMPHOR WOOD SMOKED DUCK *

樟 茶 鸭

zhāng chá yā

1 oven-ready duck weighing approx. 4 lb
2¹/₂ tbsp salt
2¹/₂ tbsp Szechwan peppercorns
small pinch saltpeter (sodium nitrate)
1 scallion
2 slices fresh ginger
1 star anise
3 tbsp rice wine

oil for frying

For smoking the duck:
1 cup small pieces of camphor tree bark or
  camphor leaves
2 star anises
4 pieces dried Chinese tangerine or orange
  peel
1¹/₂ tbsp Szechwan peppercorns
2¹/₂ tbsp sugar
2¹/₂ tbsp Ceylon tea leaves

Time: 3 hours + resting time

Heat the peppercorns in the wok over moderate heat, shaking them continuously so that they roast lightly and evenly all over; when they release a spicy aroma, add the salt, stir, and draw aside from the heat.

Cut off the duck's wing tips and remove any large, solid pieces of fat from the cavity; wash inside and out and dry well.

Rub the bird inside and out with the salt and pepper mixture, then rub only the inside with a small pinch of saltpeter. This minute quantity will be sufficient; keep rubbing all over the cavity to make sure it is well distributed. Leave in a cool place, such as a larder or larder refrigerator overnight or for 8–10 hours. The saltpeter and salt and pepper mixture will do their work and the duck will be preserved short-term.

Smoke the duck: rinse the bird thoroughly inside and out under running cold water, then dry very well. Line a large, heavy wok with a high-domed lid with foil (base and lid), allowing plenty of extra foil to overlap the edges of the wok. Place the smoking ingredients in it then lay the duck, breast side uppermost, on a lightly oiled grid resting on the sides of the wok. The duck should only be about 2 in from the smoking ingredients. Place the lid on top and seal all but one section with the extra foil (you will be able to tell whether sufficient smoke is being produced without carbonizing the smoking ingredients by how much smoke comes out of this very small gap). Turn on the heat to moderate or the temperature required to make the smoking ingredients produce a good deal of smoke, and smoke, with the lid on, for 10–15 minutes, then turn off the heat, replenish the smoking ingredients if necessary, and replace the duck on the grid breast side down. Turn the heat on again, cover, and smoke for a further 10–15 minutes. The skin of the duck should be a dark golden brown. (If you are fortunate enough to own a smoking oven, use it in the normal way, substituting the smoking ingredients listed above for your usual materials.)

Trim and chop the scallion; peel and coarsely chop the ginger slices; pound or coarsely grate 1¹/₂ tbsp Szechwan peppercorns and 1 star anise; mix all these with 3 tbsp rice wine. Place the smoked duck, breast side upper-

most, in a roasting pan and sprinkle the cavity with half this mixture; sprinkle or rub the rest all over the outside of the duck.

Place the pan or dish in the steamer compartment, cover, and steam for 1½ hours. (If you have trouble fitting the whole duck into your steamer you may have to cut the bird in quarters at this point and steam in several compartments; the presentation will not be as effective but the taste will be much the same.)

When cooked, leave the duck until sufficiently cool to handle; wipe all over inside and out with kitchen towels to remove the extra pieces of seasoning and flavorings rubbed on before steaming.

Heat plenty of oil in the wok to 350°F (or,

more safely, use a deep-fryer) and fry the duck in the very hot oil until the skin is crisp; it is best lowered into the oil breast downward, and 4 minutes' frying time is usually enough to start the crisping process. Turn the duck carefully if using a wok and ladle the hot oil over any parts that are not submerged by the oil, taking care not to spill any of the oil. After the duck is fried it must be well drained and can then be cut into fairly small sections with a cleaver and then reassembled on a plate.

Place a bowl of sweet soybean paste or hoisin sauce on the table; a bowl of ground Szechwan pepper and a bowl of sesame seed oil for everyone to use as dipping sauces and seasoning for the duck pieces.

DUCK WITH CELERY *

芹菜鴨条
qín cài yā tiáo

½ duck, cooked as for Peking Duck (see p. 40)
10 oz tender sticks celery
½–1 tsp salt
½–1 tsp sugar
½–1 tsp monosodium glutamate (optional)
1½ tbsp sesame seed oil
1 tbsp rice wine

Time: 30 minutes

1¹/₂ tbsp hot (chili) soybean paste
   (dou ban jiang)
1¹/₂ tbsp sweet soybean paste
   (tian mian jiang) or hoisin sauce
1¹/₂ tsp rice wine
1¹/₂ tbsp soy sauce
¹/₂–1 tsp monosodium glutamate (optional)
1 tsp finely chopped garlic
1 tbsp chili oil
¹/₂–1 tsp sugar
pinch salt
1 cup chicken broth
1¹/₂ tbsp cornstarch or potato flour

Time: 40 minutes

Take the cooked duck meat off the bone in as
large pieces as possible; cut these into neat
pieces about ³/₈ × ³/₄ in. Trim and shred the
scallion; peel and shred the ginger slices.
Remove the stalk, seeds, and pale inner parts
of the chili if fresh and shred; if dried, crumble, discarding the seeds.

Heat ¹/₄ cup oil until very hot in the wok and
stir-fry the duck pieces for a few minutes. Set
these aside, draining well. Empty and wipe the
wok; heat 3 tbsp fresh oil in it and stir-fry the
ginger briefly; add the soy pastes, return the
duck pieces to the wok and then stir in the rice
wine, soy sauce, monosodium glutamate (if
used), garlic, chili oil, sugar, and salt.

Stir-fry for a few minutes, then add the
chicken broth; as soon as this comes to a boil,
reduce the heat and simmer, uncovered, for 5
minutes. Increase the heat, add the scallion
and chili, cook fast for 1 minute, then stir in
the cornstarch or potato flour mixed with a little cold water to thicken.

HOUSEWIFE'S TOFU *

家常豆腐
jià cháng dòu fǔ

2 cakes firm tofu (bean curd) weighing a
   total of 1¹/₄ lb
oil for frying
¹/₄ lb lean or fairly lean pork
¹/₂ leek (white part only)
3 tbsp oil
1¹/₂ tbsp sweet soybean paste
   (tian mian jiang)
1¹/₂ tbsp hot (chili) soybean paste
   (dou ban jiang)
¹/₂ cup chicken broth
pinch monosodium glutamate (optional)
pinch freshly ground pepper
pinch salt
3 tbsp rice wine
1¹/₂ tbsp soy sauce
1¹/₂ tsp cornstarch or potato flour

Time: 35 minutes

Wash and dry the celery sticks, removing any
strings; cut into 2-in lengths and blanch in
boiling water for 1 minute. Drain and mix with
the salt, sugar, monosodium glutamate (if
used), sesame seed oil, and rice wine. Take
the flesh off the cooked Peking Duck in as
large pieces as possible then cut these, with
the knife held on the slant, into thin slices.
Arrange the slices in the middle of a serving
plate and surround with the dressed celery.

SALTY DUCK WITH SZECHWAN PEPPER

盐水鸭
yán shiū yā

1 oven-ready duck weighing approx. 4–4¹/₂ lb
1¹/₂ tbsp Szechwan peppercorns
1¹/₂ tbsp salt
8 thin slices fresh ginger
1 scallion
1¹/₂ tbsp rice wine
1¹/₂ tbsp sesame seed oil

Time: 2 hours

Remove any pieces of solid fat left in the
duck's cavity, then wash and dry the bird. Heat

---

the peppercorns in the wok over moderate
heat, shaking the wok continuously so that
they roast evenly and lightly; when they
release their spicy scent, stir in the salt, and
draw aside from the heat. Rub this mixture all
over the duck, inside and out. Place the duck
in a heatproof dish or pan that will fit in your
steamer; lightly mince the peeled ginger
slices, do likewise with the trimmed scallion,
and place some of the ginger slices inside the
duck with the scallion and some of the slices
outside, on top and underneath. Place in the
steamer compartment, cover, and steam for
1¹/₂ hours. When done, carve the duck into portions, reserving all the juices released during
carving and the cooking juices, and place
these on a serving platter.

Heat all the strained juices with the rice
wine and sesame seed oil until they just come
to a boil; pour over the duck and serve.

DUCK WITH GINGER

子姜鸭块
zǐ jiāng yā kuài

1 lb Cantonese duck (see p. 211)
1 scallion
12 thin slices fresh ginger
1 chili pepper (fresh or dried)

Slice the tofu approx. ³/₈–¹/₂ in thick and then cut these slices into 1-in squares. Slice the pork more thinly than the tofu and then cut into squares the same size as the tofu. Wash and dry the leek then shred into thin strips.

Heat plenty of oil in the wok or deep-fryer and when very hot but not smoking, add the tofu pieces and fry until golden brown; remove with a large slotted ladle and drain well. Empty the wok, if used for frying, wipe the inside, and heat 3 tbsp fresh oil; stir-fry the pork until very pale golden brown, add the fried tofu, soybean pastes, broth, leek, monosodium glutamate (if used), pepper, salt, rice wine, and soy sauce. Stir briefly until the broth comes to a boil; mix the cornstarch or potato flour with a little cold water and stir into the contents of the wok. Cook for a further 1–2 minutes and serve.

GRANDMOTHER'S TOFU

麻婆豆腐
má pó dòu fǔ

2 cakes firm tofu (bean curd) weighing a
  total of 1¹/₄ lb
1 clove garlic
1 scallion
3 tbsp oil
¹/₂ cup finely chopped lean pork
1¹/₂ tbsp hot (chili) soybean paste
  (dou ban jiang)
3 tbsp soy sauce
1¹/₂ tbsp sweet soybean paste
  (tian mian jiang)
¹/₂ cup chicken broth
pinch monosodium glutamate (optional)
pinch freshly ground pepper
1 tsp cornstarch or potato flour
pinch ground Szechwan pepper

Time: 30 minutes

Cut the tofu into ³/₄-in cubes. Peel and finely chop the garlic; trim and finely chop the scallion (you may need more than one scallion if they are not large); reserving about 1¹/₂ tbsp of the scallion, mix 1¹/₂ tbsp of it with the garlic. Heat the oil in the wok and stir-fry the pork over high heat for 1 minute. Reduce the heat a little. Add the hot soybean paste, the garlic and scallion mixture, the tofu, soy sauce, and the sweet soybean paste. Mix carefully; pour in the broth and add the monosodium glutamate, if used.

Cook, uncovered, for a few minutes to reduce the liquid. Mix the cornstarch or potato flour with a very little water and stir into the wok; simmer for a few minutes more to reduce the sauce and thicken it further. Sprinkle with the Szechwan pepper and the reserved raw chopped scallion and serve.

268

TWICE-COOKED BEEF

红烧牛腩

hóng shāo niú năn

1¹/₂ lb round of beef or any good casserole
 beef
2 carrots
1 leek
1 scallion
1 thin slice fresh ginger
2–3 cloves garlic
¹/₄ cup oil
¹/₂ cup dark soy sauce
pinch salt
1¹/₂ tbsp sugar
¹/₄ cup rice wine
3 star anises
1¹/₂ tbsp cornstarch or potato flour

Time: 2 hours 10 minutes

Cut the beef into small bite-sized pieces. bring
a large pan containing 7 cups water to a boil,
add the beef, cover and simmer gently for 1¹/₂
hours, skimming off any scum. Remove from
the heat and set aside; do not drain.
 Peel and wash the vegetables where necessary; cut them into small pieces. Peel the ginger
and cut into short, thin strips. Peel and chop
the garlic finely. Heat ¹/₄ cup oil in the wok and
stir-fry these prepared vegetables; when they
are just tender, add the soy sauce, salt, sugar,
rice wine, and the whole star anises. Add the
beef and its broth and stir well. Bring to a boil
then simmer for 30 minutes, by which time the
beef should be very tender and well flavored. A
few minutes before serving, mix the cornstarch or potato flour with a little cold water
and stir into the contents of the wok to thicken.

BEEF WITH DRIED
TANGERINE PEEL

陈皮牛肉

chén pí niú ròu

1¹/₄ lb choice or braising cut of boneless lean
 beef
1¹/₂ tbsp salt
oil for frying
¹/₄ lb dried Chinese tangerine or orange peel
2 dried chili peppers
4 cups broth
¹/₂–1 tsp sugar
3 tbsp rice wine
¹/₂ tsp monosodium glutamate (optional)
1¹/₂ tbsp wine vinegar
1¹/₂ tbsp sesame seed oil

Time: 45 minutes

Slice the beef thinly and then cut these slices
into squares approx. ³/₄ × 1¹/₂ in. Place the beef
in a bowl and sprinkle with half the salt, stir,
and leave to stand for 20 minutes. Heat sufficient oil to semi deep-fry the beef until very
hot, add the beef and fry for 3 minutes, turning
as necessary; remove with a slotted or wire
mesh ladle and drain well. Empty the wok,
wipe the inside, and heat 3 tbsp fresh oil over
moderate heat; add the tangerine peel and the
crumbled chili peppers; add the broth and
then return the fried beef to the wok. Stir in the
sugar, the remaining salt, the rice wine, and
monosodium glutamate (if used). Simmer,
uncovered, until the liquid has reduced, stir in
the vinegar and sesame seed oil, and serve.

BEEF HOME STYLE

家常牛肉丝

jā cháng níu ròu sī

1 lb choice cut lean beef
1¹/₂ tbsp soy sauce
1¹/₂ tsp oyster sauce
1¹/₂ tbsp cornstarch or potato flour
oil for frying
1 celery heart
1 thin slice fresh ginger
1 chili pepper
3 tbsp oil
pinch ground Szechwan pepper

For the sauce:
1¹/₂ tbsp soy sauce
pinch monosodium glutamate (optional)
pinch salt
1¹/₂ tbsp rice wine
1¹/₂ tsp wine vinegar
1¹/₂ tsp sesame seed oil

Time: 30 minutes

Cut the beef into thin slices and then cut these
in turn into rectangles measuring about
³/₄ × 2 in; blend the soy sauce with the oyster
sauce and cornstarch or potato flour in a large
bowl and mix the beef pieces with this mixture
to coat thoroughly. Chop the celery. Peel the
ginger and cut into short, thin strips; shred the
chili pepper.
 Heat about 1 cup oil in the wok (or use more
oil in a deep-fryer) and when very hot, fry the
beef pieces for 2–3 minutes only to seal and
color. Remove from the oil with a slotted ladle
and drain well. If the wok was used for this
stage, empty out the oil and heat 3 tbsp fresh
oil to stir-fry the celery, ginger, and chili gently
for a few minutes. Add the fried beef and stir in
all the sauce ingredients.
 Continue cooking over moderate heat, stirring, for 1 or 2 minutes, sprinkle with the
Szechwan pepper, and serve.

BEEF IN HOT SAUCE *

辣牛肉

là niú ròu

1 lb round of beef or any boneless braising
 cut
3 scallions
5 slices fresh ginger
3 star anises

For the sauce:
4 large, fresh chili peppers
1¹/₂ tbsp rice wine
1 tsp ground Szechwan pepper
1¹/₂ tbsp soy sauce
pinch monosodium glutamate (optional)
1¹/₂ tbsp broth
pinch sugar
¹/₂ tsp sesame seed paste
1¹/₂ tsp chili oil
1¹/₂ tsp sesame seed oil

Time: 1 hour 10 minutes + cooling time

Trim the scallions (if they are small, use double this number). Peel the ginger. Place these
and the star anises in a large pan two-thirds
full of water; bring to a boil and then add the
beef, still in one piece. Allow to return to a boil
then reduce the heat and simmer for 40 minutes. Leave to cool completely in the cooking
liquid, then slice thinly and cut these slices
into 2-in squares. Arrange the beef slices,
slightly overlapping, on a serving plate and
garnish with carrots, tomatoes, and radishes
sculpted or shaped to look like flowers, stars,
etc.
 Place all the sauce ingredients in the wok
(the broth can be the strained liquid from
cooking the beef if you do not have any good
beef or vegetable broth) and heat, stirring, for
1–2 minutes after boiling point is reached.
Serve this sauce separately.

SZECHWAN
TWICE-FRIED BEEF

干炒牛肉丝

gàn chăo niú ròu sī

1¹/₄ lb choice cut of lean beef (e.g. fillet)
5 oz celery
1 large carrot
oil for frying
1¹/₂ tbsp finely chopped scallion
1¹/₂ tbsp finely chopped fresh ginger
1¹/₂ tbsp finely chopped garlic
1¹/₂ tbsp hot (chili) soybean paste
 (dou ban jiang)

1¹/₂ tbsp sweet soybean paste
  (tian mian jiang)
¹/₂–1 tbsp salt
¹/₂–1 tbsp sugar
¹/₂ tsp monosodium glutamate (optional)
1¹/₂ tbsp rice wine
1¹/₂ tbsp chili oil
pinch freshly ground Szechwan pepper

Time: 45 minutes

Cut the beef into little sticks or short, thick strips about 1¹/₄ in long. Trim the scallion, then peel the ginger and garlic and chop finely. Wash and dry the celery, removing any strings; peel the carrot; cut both these vegetables into thin slices. Semi deep-fry or deep-fry the beef in very hot oil; remove from the wok or deep-fryer with a wire mesh or slotted ladle, draining thoroughly. Heat 3 tbsp fresh oil in the emptied wok or a large skillet and stir-fry the scallion, ginger, and garlic until they release their aromas. Add the soybean pastes, salt, sugar, monosodium glutamate (if used), and the rice wine and stir. Add the beef, celery, and carrot and stir-fry briskly. Sprinkle with the chili oil and Szechwan pepper, stir, and serve.

BEEF YU XIANG *

鱼香肉丝
Yú Xiān ròu sī

1 lb beef fillet or similar tender cut
1¹/₂ tbsp dark soy sauce
1¹/₂ tbsp cornstarch or potato flour
oil for frying

For the sauce:
3 tbsp oil
1 tbsp finely chopped scallion
1 tbsp finely chopped fresh ginger
1 tbsp finely chopped garlic
1 tbsp hot (chili) soybean paste
  (dou ban jiang)
pinch salt
1¹/₂ tsp sugar
1¹/₂ tsp sesame seed oil
1¹/₂ tbsp wine vinegar
pinch freshly ground pepper
1 tbsp cornstarch or potato flour

Time: 30 minutes

Cut the beef into thin slices and then into short, narrow strips and mix in a bowl with the soy sauce and 1¹/₂ tbsp cornstarch or potato flour. Heat about 1 cup oil in the wok until very hot and fry the beef strips to seal and lightly cook them (they can be deep-fried for 1–2 minutes if preferred). Remove the beef from the oil with a slotted ladle and drain well. Empty the wok if used for frying the beef and heat 3 tbsp

fresh oil in it over lower heat; stir-fry the scallion, garlic, and ginger then add the soybean paste. Add the fried beef, stir well, and then mix in the salt, sugar, sesame seed oil, vinegar, and pepper. Cook for 2–3 minutes, then mix the cornstarch or potato flour with a very little cold water and stir into the wok to thicken the small amount of liquid and give the beef a glossy appearance.

SLOW-COOKED BEEF

坛 子 肉
tán zī ròn

1 lb beef (e.g. round of beef, braising steak, skirt, flank)
2 oz dried lotus seeds
1 long white radish (Daikon root)
2 carrots
1 tbsp salt
1 tsp monosodium glutamate (optional)
4 cups chicken broth
2 thin slices fresh ginger
1/2 cup rice wine
pinch freshly ground pepper
1/4 cup soy sauce

Time: 20 minutes + soaking time for lotus seeds and slow cooking

Soak the lotus seeds in water for 1 hour. Cut the beef into bite-sized pieces. Peel and dice the radish and carrots. Peel the lotus seeds and, using a cocktail stick, remove the very small, hard pit at the center of the seeds (or buy ready deseeded, prepared canned lotus seeds, in which case you should double the weight used).

Place all the ingredients in a heavy earthenware or cast-iron casserole dish, stir. Cover with foil and then put the lid in place if there is one (as little steam as possible should escape during the long, slow cooking time). Bring slowly to boiling point then simmer very gently for 3–4 hours or until the beef is meltingly tender.

This slow cooking is a traditional Chinese method of making tougher, cheaper cuts of beef into tender, delicious meals.

PORK IN CHILI SAUCE

辣 子 肉 丁
là zī ròu dīng

14 oz pork tenderloin or piece boneless pork leg
1 egg white
1/2–1 tbsp salt
3 1/2 tbsp cornstarch

1 1/2 tbsp rice wine
1 1/2 bamboo shoots
oil for frying
1 small scallion
3 thin slices ginger
1/4 cup oil
1 1/2 tbsp hot (chili) soybean paste (dou ban jiang)
2 fresh chili peppers
1 1/2 tbsp wine vinegar
1/2 tsp monosodium glutamate (optional)
1/2–1 tsp sugar
1 1/2 tbsp soy sauce
1 1/2 tbsp chili oil

Time: 1 hour

Cut the pork into 1/2-in cubes. Whisk the egg white until stiff and fold in the salt, 2 1/2 tbsp cornstarch, and the rice wine; add the cubed pork and stir well; leave to marinate in this mixture for 15 minutes.

Meanwhile, cut the bamboo shoots into small pieces; trim the scallion and cut into thin rounds; peel the ginger and slice into very thin strips. Remove the stalks, seeds, and pale inner parts from the chilis, and chop. Heat sufficient oil in the wok to semi deep-fry the pork (about 1–1 1/2 cups) or use a deep-fryer; when the oil is very hot, add the pork and fry for 3–4 minutes; remove, draining well, and set aside. Fry the bamboo shoots for a slightly shorter time and drain well. If the wok has been used for frying, empty it and wipe the inside; heat 1/4 cup fresh oil and stir-fry the scallion and ginger gently until they soften and emit a good aroma. Stir in the soybean paste and the chilis; add the fried pork and bamboo shoots, stir well, then add the vinegar, monosodium glutamate (if used), sugar, soy sauce, and chili oil. Cook, stirring, for a few minutes more, then mix 1 tbsp cornstarch with a little cold water and stir into the contents of the wok. Serve.

PORK SHUI HU

水 浒 肉
shuǐ hǔ ròu

14 oz pork tenderloin
1 leek
1 egg white
1 1/2 tbsp cornstarch or potato flour
1/4 lb pea shoots or bean sprouts
oil for frying
1 tsp salt
1/2 tsp monosodium glutamate (optional)

For the sauce:
3 tbsp oil
1 dried chili pepper
pinch ground Szechwan pepper
1/2 cup chicken broth

pinch salt
1/2 tsp sugar
1 1/2 tbsp cornstarch or potato flour

Time: 30 minutes

Cut the pork into thin slices and then cut these into rectangles approx. 1 1/4 × 1 1/2 in in size. Wash the leek thoroughly, dry, and slice fairly thinly with the knife held at an acute angle, so the slices are on the slant. Whisk the egg white until stiff and fold in the cornstarch or potato flour. Bring a large saucepan of water to a boil, add the meat, boil for 1 minute, drain very well, then add to the egg and starch mixture. Stir well to coat all the pieces.

Heat 3 tbsp oil in the wok and stir-fry the pea shoots very briefly over high heat, add the salt and monosodium glutamate (if used), stir once more, and transfer to a heated serving plate.

Add a little more oil to the wok if necessary and stir-fry the pork over high heat for 2 minutes; remove from the wok, draining well, and place on top of the pea sprouts. Make the sauce: heat the oil (in a small saucepan or in the emptied, wiped wok) and stir-fry the crumbled chili and the Szechwan pepper, add the broth, salt, and sugar, then stir and boil very briefly to reduce a little. Mix the cornstarch or potato flour with a very little cold water and stir into the sauce to thicken. Pour over the pork and serve.

Some long-forgotten cook dedicated this dish to Shui Hu, a patriot who led a popular uprising during the Song dynasty, at a time when the common people and peasants were undergoing great hardships caused by famine and agrarian mismanagement.

PORK WITH ZHA CAI

榨 菜 肉 丝
zhà cài ròu sī

14 oz pork tenderloin
1 egg white
1 tbsp cornstarch or potato flour
oil for frying
5 oz brine-pickled mustard greens (zha cai)
2 thin slices ginger
1 scallion
3 tbsp oil
1/2 tsp salt
1/2 tsp sugar
1/2 tsp monosodium glutamate (optional)
1 1/2 tsp rice wine
pinch freshly ground pepper
1 tbsp cornstarch or potato flour

Time: 35 minutes

Slice the pork thinly and cut these slices into

narrow strips about $1^1/_2$ in long. Whisk the egg white, beat in the cornstarch or potato flour and mix the pork thoroughly with this. Rinse the zha cai under running cold water to eliminate excess salt; drain well and cut into thin strips about the same length as the pork strips.

Trim the scallion, peel the ginger, and shred both. Heat approx. 1 cup oil in the wok (or deep-fry in a deep-fryer if preferred) and when very hot but not smoking, fry the pork to seal and cook very lightly. Remove the pork with a wire mesh or slotted ladle and drain well. Set aside. Heat 3 tbsp fresh oil in a wok or skillet and stir-fry the ginger and scallion gently; add the fried pork, the zha cai, salt, sugar, monosodium glutamate (if used), rice wine, and pepper. Stir and then leave to cook over moderate heat for 5 minutes; mix the thickening agent with a little cold water and stir into the contents of the wok. Serve.

PORK YU XIANG

鱼香猪肉

yú xiāng zhū ròu

1 lb lean pork
$^1/_2$ oz tree ears (dried mu er fungus)
6 fresh or canned water chestnuts
2 oz canned bamboo shoots
$^1/_3$ cup oil
3 cloves garlic
1 thin slice fresh ginger
4 scallions
1 tbsp Szechwan chili paste or hot soybean paste
$1^1/_2$ tbsp rice wine
$2^1/_2$ tbsp white wine vinegar

For the seasoned flour coating:
pinch salt
$1^1/_2$ tbsp potato flour (or cornstarch)
$1^1/_2$ tbsp oil
1 tbsp sesame seed oil

For the sauce
$1^1/_2$ tbsp cornstarch
6 tbsp light broth or water
1 tbsp light soy sauce
1 tbsp sugar

Time: 45 minutes

Soak the tree ears in warm water for 20–30 minutes. Cut the pork into thin strips measuring about $2^1/_4$ in long and $^1/_4$ in wide. Place these in a bowl, sprinkle with the salt and $1^1/_2$ tbsp potato flour or cornstarch; stir well and leave to stand for 20 minutes. Sprinkle with the two oils and stir well.

Drain the fungus, trim off any tough parts and cut into thin strips. Cut the bamboo shoots and the water chestnuts into strips also. Trim and thinly slice the scallions, keeping the white and green parts separate.

Mix $1^1/_2$ tbsp cornstarch with the cold broth or water then stir in the soy sauce and the chopped green section of the scallions. Set aside.

Peel and finely chop the garlic and the ginger, keeping them separate. Heat the wok, add the oil, swirl this round the inside of the wok and then stir-fry the garlic until it starts to color; add the ginger and the white parts of the scallions; stir-fry briefly until the ginger and scallions release a full scent.

Stir in the Szechwan paste, meat, fungus, and bamboo shoots. Use a spatula to scrape the meat away from the inside of the wok as you turn it continuously while frying gently for 1 minute. Pour in the rice wine, increase the heat and stir-fry for 1–2 minutes, or until all the pork has turned very pale. Stir the reserved sauce, add to the wok, and mix well until thickened. Remove the wok from the heat; sprinkle in the vinegar, stir, and serve in a hot serving dish.

Yu xiang means "aroma of fish," a slightly misleading culinary term for Westerners as there is no fish in this dish to describe a popular Szechwan technique. See also Fish fillets yu xiang (page 250), and Eggplant yu xiang (page 284).

CRISPY ROAST PORK BELLY *

酥烤大方
sū kǎo dà fāng

1 3–3¹/₄-lb piece pork belly, with the rind on
1¹/₂ tbsp ground Szechwan pepper
2¹/₂ tbsp salt
1¹/₂ tbsp finely chopped scallion
1 cup sesame seed oil

For the sauce:
3 tbsp soy sauce
3 tbsp sesame seed oil
pinch ground Szechwan pepper

Time: 1¹/₄ hours

Use tweezers to extract all the bristles you can see from the skin. Use a skewer to make fairly deep incisions in the pork belly, through the skin and about halfway into the flesh. Heat the pepper and salt in the wok over moderate heat, shaking as you heat them; leave to cool. Mix the pepper and salt with the scallion and use most of this mixture for rubbing all over the skin and meat forcing the seasoning into the incisions you have made. Brush the entire surface of the pork belly and the rind with sesame seed oil. Sprinkle a little of the remaining seasoning mixture into a roasting pan, place the pork belly in it, skin side uppermost, and sprinkle the rest of this mixture over the meat. Place in a preheated oven at 400°F and roast until the skin starts to contract, wrinkle, and darken a little. Take the meat out of the oven and wrap it in a clean cloth. Leave to cool; by this time the rind will have softened and you may well find that there are more bristles to be extracted, revealed by the shrinkage of the skin; remove these with tweezers. Brush the entire piece of pork belly once more with sesame seed oil and return to the oven, preheated to 300°F, for 5 minutes.

Repeat the wrapping, cooling, checking for bristles and the brushing with sesame seed oil. Then replace in the oven for a final roasting, this time for 20 minutes (or until done) at 250°F. By this time the skin should have crisped well and the meat should be well cooked right through. Mix all the sauce ingredients without heating them and place in a bowl or in several tiny bowls; each person dips small pieces of the pork belly (and the crispy skin) in this sauce if wished.

The pork belly can also be thinly sliced and served with Mandarin pancakes (see p. 16) and the usual accompaniments, eating the crisp skin first.

STIR-FRIED PORK BELLY *

回锅肉
hiú guō ròu

1 lb pork belly with a good proportion of lean to fat
1 green bell pepper
oil for frying
1 scallion
1 leek
3 tbsp oil
3 tbsp sweet soybean paste (tian mian jiang)
1¹/₂ tbsp hot (chili) soybean paste (dou ban jiang)
3 tbsp broth
1¹/₂ tsp sugar
pinch monosodium glutamate (optional)

Time: 1 hour 10 minutes

Wash the pork belly and extract any bristles with tweezers. Bring a large saucepan of water to a boil and add the bacon; allow to return to a gentle boil and cook for 30 minutes. Drain and set aside to cool. Remove the stalk, seeds, and pale inner parts of the pepper; cut into square, bite-sized pieces. Trim the scallion and leek; wash and dry the leek and cut both these into fairly thick, diagonal slices. As soon as the pork belly is cool enough to handle, cut it into thin slices and then cut these in turn into rectangles, approx. $1\frac{1}{2} \times 2$ in in size. Heat plenty of oil in the wok (or use a deep-fryer) to 340°F or a little hotter and fry the pork belly slices until pale golden brown; add the green pepper pieces and fry them together for another 2 minutes. Remove the meat and peppers from the oil with a wire mesh or slotted ladle and drain well.

Heat 3 tbsp fresh oil in the wok or a large skillet, stir-fry the scallion and leek until they are tender; stir in the soybean pastes, the broth, sugar, and monosodium glutamate (if used). Make sure the oil has completely blended with the pastes. Add the pork belly and peppers and stir for just long enough to enable the bacon to heat through. Serve.

SMOKED PORK SPARERIBS

重排骨
xūn pái gǔ

2¼–2½ lb pork spareribs
1½ tsp ground Szechwan pepper
4 thin slices fresh ginger
1 scallion
1 tbsp salt
¼ cup rice wine
pinch monosodium glutamate (optional)
pinch sugar
1½ tsp sesame seed oil
oil for frying
few large twigs or small branches of pine
   wood (optional)

Time: 1 hour 20 minutes + 2 hours seasoning
   time

Ask your butcher to saw the spareribs into 3-in lengths or do this yourself with a cleaver. Place the ribs in a heatproof dish (although sawn in half across you can leave them attached to one another by the connective strips of flesh); trim, peel and finely chop the scallion and the ginger. Sprinkle the spareribs with the Szechwan pepper, ginger, scallion, and salt and leave to season for 2 hours, turning now and then to flavor all over. Place the dish in the steamer, cover, and steam for 45 minutes. Take the dish out of the steamer and set aside.

Mix the rice wine with the monosodium glutamate (if used), the sugar, and sesame seed oil. Sprinkle this all over the cooked spareribs, turning them to coat evenly. Heat plenty of oil in the deep-fryer until very hot but not smoking; fry the spareribs, preferably still in joined sections of 2 or 3 ribs, in several batches if necessary until crisp and golden brown. Drain well. If you are barbecuing these ribs or using a smoking oven, place small branches and twigs of pine among the embers and place the

spareribs on a grid just above them; smoke the spareribs for about 20–30 minutes, turning halfway through this time. Serve very hot, with barbecue or hoisin sauce.

STIR-FRIED PIG'S LIVER

火爆猪肝
huǒ bào zhū gān

10 oz pig's liver
2 tree ears (mu er fungus)
½ tsp salt
pinch freshly ground pepper
1 tbsp rice wine
1 tbsp cornstarch or potato flour
oil for frying
½ tbsp finely chopped fresh ginger
½ tbsp finely chopped scallion
1 finely chopped clove of garlic
3 tbsp oil
1 oz bamboo shoots
1 tbsp soy sauce
pinch salt
pinch monosodium glutamate (optional)
1 tbsp sesame seed oil
pinch ground Szechwan pepper

Time: 45 minutes

Soak the tree ears in warm water for 20 minutes or longer. Cut the liver into thin slices, then cut these slices into rectangles approx. $1\frac{1}{4} \times 2$ in in size. In a large bowl combine the salt, pepper, rice wine, and half the first quantity of cornstarch or potato flour listed above mixed with a little cold water; add the liver and mix well to coat all the pieces. Leave to stand for 20 minutes.

Mix together the chopped ginger, scallion, and garlic. Cut the bamboo shoots into very thin slices. When the tree ears have softened and reconstituted, drain them well and use kitchen scissors to cut off any remaining tough parts; tear into small pieces.

Heat plenty of oil in the wok for semi deep-frying until very hot (or use a deep-fryer) and add the liver slices; leave in the oil for only 10 seconds (to seal and cook very lightly indeed) then remove in the frying basket or by means of a wire mesh ladle, draining well. Empty and wipe the wok if used for frying. Heat 3 tbsp fresh oil and stir-fry the finely chopped ginger, scallion, and garlic mixture lightly; when these give off a full aroma, add the bamboo shoots and the tree ears. Stir-fry for 2 or 3 minutes then add the soy sauce, salt, and monosodium glutamate (if used). Stir once more then add the pork and mix well. Reduce the heat. Combine the cornstarch or potato flour with a little cold water and stir into the contents of the wok. Sprinkle with the sesame seed oil and the Szechwan pepper, stir, and serve.

STIR-FRIED TRIPE SZECHWAN STYLE *

爆牛肚梁
bào niú dǔ liáng

276

14 oz tripe, cleaned and boiled
1 oz bamboo shoots
¹/₂ leek (white part only)
¹/₂ large scallion
3 thin slices ginger
3 fresh (or brine-pickled) chili peppers
5 tree ears (mu er fungus), soaked and
*   softened*
few celery leaves
1¹/₂ tbsp rice wine
1 tbsp salt
pinch monosodium glutamate (optional)
¹/₃ cup oil
1¹/₂ tbsp soy sauce
1 tsp sugar
¹/₂ cup chicken broth
2¹/₂ tbsp cornstarch or potato flour

Time: 1 hour 40 minutes

Rinse the tripe well under running cold water then add to a large saucepan of boiling water; boil gently for 30 minutes. Drain well, then cut into rectangles measuring about 1¹/₄ × 2 in. Make shallow evenly spaced parallel incisions on the smooth side with the knife held at an acute angle; repeat this operation in the opposite direction to make a lattice of shallow cuts.

Mix the tripe very thoroughly with the rice wine, salt, and monosodium glutamate (if used) in a bowl and leave to stand for 30 minutes.

Soak the fungus for at least 20 minutes in warm water; drain, squeeze out excess moisture, and cut off any tough parts. Cut the bamboo shoots into thin slices and cut these into rectangles measuring about ³/₄ × 1¹/₂ in; cut them with a shallow lattice effect as with the tripe. Trim and clean the leek, scallion, and ginger where necessary and cut into small pieces. Cut the chilis lengthwise in quarters then remove the stalk and seeds. Tear the tree ears into small pieces. Wash and dry the celery leaves and tear into small pieces. Coat the pieces of tripe very lightly with cornstarch or potato flour (1¹/₂ tbsp should be sufficient). Heat ¹/₄ cup oil in the wok and stir-fry the tripe briefly over high heat; remove, draining well, and set aside. Add 3 tbsp fresh oil to the wok and stir-fry the leek, scallion, and ginger until they release their aromas. Add the bamboo shoots, chilis, tree ears, fried tripe, celery leaves, soy sauce, sugar, and broth and cook for a few minutes to allow the liquid to reduce a little. Mix the remaining cornstarch or potato flour with a little cold water and stir into the wok to thicken the sauce. Serve.

PORK SPARERIBS WITH LOTUS LEAVES *

荷叶排骨

Approx. 1³/₄ lb pork spareribs
¹/₄ cup soy sauce
1 heaping tbsp salt
¹/₄ cup rice wine
4–5 large, dried lotus leaves
2¹/₂ tsp five-spice powder
approx. 1¹/₄ cups ground rice or 1³/₄ cups rice
  flour

Time: 2¹/₂ hours

Cut the spareribs into approx. 3-in lengths. Mix the soy sauce, salt, and rice wine and marinate the spareribs in this mixture for 2–3 hours. Pre-soak the lotus leaves in cold water, then, when softened, place in a large bowl of hot water for 2 minutes to soak further; drain and cut the leaves into 6-in squares. Cut down between the spareribs, dividing them into single ribs or pairs. Mix the ground rice or rice flour with the five-spice powder and coat the spareribs all over with this mixture. Wrap the spareribs in pairs or threes in the lotus leaf pieces, making the parcels as neat and secure as possible, tucking in the sides so that they are sealed. Line one or more steamer compartments with cabbage leaves or vegetable parchment and arrange the parcels in the steamer. Cover and steam for 2 hours.

Serve, still wrapped in the lotus leaves, for each person to undo at table.

RABBIT WITH BEAN SPROUTS *

银针兔肉丝
yín zhēn tù roùsi

10 oz boneless rabbit meat
2 thin slices fresh ginger
2 chili peppers
¹/₂ lb bean sprouts (soybean or mungbean)
1 egg white
oil for frying
3 tbsp oil
1¹/₂ tbsp rice wine
pinch salt
pinch monosodium glutamate (optional)
pinch freshly ground pepper
1 tbsp cornstarch or potato flour

Time: 35 minutes

SZECHWAN RABBIT *

鱼 香 酥 皮 兔 糕

Yú Xiāng sū pítù gāo

1¹/₄–1¹/₂ cups (10 oz) very finely chopped
    boneless rabbit meat
3 egg whites
1¹/₂ tbsp cornstarch or potato flour
¹/₄ cup shortening or melted pork fat
pinch salt
oil for frying

For the sauce:
3 tbsp oil
1 tbsp finely chopped garlic
1 tbsp finely chopped fresh ginger
1 tbsp finely chopped scallion
1 tbsp hot (chili) soybean paste
    (dou ban jiang)
1¹/₂ tsp soy sauce
1¹/₂ tsp wine vinegar
pinch salt
pinch sugar
pinch monosodium glutamate (optional)

Time: 1 hour

Place the chopped rabbit meat in a bowl and mix in the egg whites. Mix half the cornstarch or potato flour with approx. 1 tbsp water and add to the bowl. Stir well, then stir in first the melted shortening or pork fat, then the salt and finally ¹/₄ cup more water. Mix until the texture is quite smooth and sticks together well. Spread the rabbit mixture out ³/₈–¹/₂ in thick in a heatproof dish that will fit into your steamer compartment; cover and steam for 20 minutes. Take the dish out of the steamer and leave to cool; when completely cold, cut into rectangles about ³/₄ × 1¹/₂ in; coat these lightly with the remaining cornstarch or potato flour, using a little more if necessary and gently shaking off any excess.

Heat sufficient oil in the wok to semi deep-fry, or use a deep-fryer; when the oil reaches a temperature of 350°F, fry the squares in several batches until golden brown; this will only take a very short time, so take care they do not color too deeply.

Make the sauce: heat 3 tbsp oil in the wok (emptied and wiped if previously used for frying) and sweat the garlic, ginger, and scallion until they release their aromas; stir in all the other sauce ingredients.

Add the fried squares to this sauce, turn carefully to coat lightly with sauce, and heat through. Serve at once, while still very hot.

Cut the rabbit meat into thin strips. Peel and shred the ginger; remove the stalk and seeds from the chilis and shred. Place the bean sprouts in a large bowl full of cold water, stir and mix, then leave to stand. Whisk the egg white, add the rabbit meat to it, and stir well; leave to stand for a few minutes.

Heat about 1–1¹/₂ cups oil in the wok or use a deep-fryer; when very hot fry the rabbit for 1 minute; remove the strips with a wire mesh or slotted ladle and drain well.

Take the bean sprouts out of the water, lifting them out so that any ungerminated seeds or wilted sprouts remain at the bottom of the bowl. Pick off any empty seed cases. Rinse the sprouts in a sieve under running cold water. Drain thoroughly. Empty the wok if used for frying the rabbit, wipe the inside and heat 3 tbsp fresh oil. Stir-fry the ginger until it gives off a good, full scent, then add the chilis, the fried rabbit, and the bean sprouts; stir-fry for just 1 minute over high heat to prevent the sprouts losing their crispness. Mix the rice wine with the salt, monosodium glutamate (if used), and the pepper and add these to the wok; stir-fry for no more than 2 minutes, mix the cornstarch or potato flour with a little cold water, and stir into the wok. Serve. This light, digestible dish is a good summertime recipe.

water; beat in the chives, meats, and bean sprouts. Heat the wok, add 3 tbsp oil and swirl round to coat the inside (or use less oil and cook the omelet in a large nonstick skillet), add the egg mixture, and cook over gentle heat for about 5 minutes or longer, turning once. The omelet should gradually set firmly right through its thickness rather than fry and color; add a little more oil if needed.

OMELET YU XIANG

鱼香烘蛋

yú xiāng hōng dàn

6 eggs
1 scallion
1¹/₂ tsp cornstarch
pinch salt
¹/₄ cup oil

For the sauce:
¹/₄ cup oil
1 scallion
2 thin slices fresh ginger
2 cloves garlic
6 water chestnuts
2¹/₂ tbsp hot (chili) soybean paste
    (dou ban jiang)
¹/₂ tbsp wine vinegar
¹/₂ tbsp sugar
¹/₂ tbsp soy sauce
¹/₂ tbsp sesame seed oil
¹/₂ cup broth
1 tsp salt
pinch monosodium glutamate (optional)
1 tbsp cornstarch

Time: 30 minutes

Trim the ends off the scallion, peel the ginger and garlic, and chop all these and the water chestnuts very finely, keeping them separate.

Make the sauce: heat ¹/₄ cup oil in the wok and stir-fry the equivalent of 1 chopped scallion, all the ginger, and garlic until they release a good, full aroma. Stir in the soybean paste, the water chestnuts, vinegar, sugar, soy sauce, sesame seed oil, broth, salt, and monosodium glutamate (if used). Continue cooking for a few minutes, stirring to allow the liquid to reduce; mix the cornstarch listed in the sauce ingredients with a very little cold water and stir into the sauce to thicken. Keep warm.

Make the omelet: beat the eggs lightly with the cornstarch mixed with a very little cold water; beat in the salt and the remaining chopped scallion. Grease a nonstick omelet skillet with oil and when hot pour in the egg mixture; cook until firmly set, turning once if wished or cook with a lid on; slide the omelet onto a serving plate, pour the sauce all over the top, and serve, cutting the omelet into sections like a pie.

BEAN SPROUT OMELET

豆芽烘蛋

dòu yá hōng dàn

8 eggs
¹/₂ tsp salt
¹/₂ tsp monosodium glutamate (optional)
1¹/₂ tbsp cornstarch or potato flour
1 tbsp finely chopped fresh chives
¹/₂ cup finely chopped lean pork
¹/₂ cup finely chopped fresh pork belly
¹/₄ lb bean sprouts (soybean or mungbean)
approx. ¹/₄ cup oil

Time: 30 minutes

Have all the ingredients that need preparation ready before you start to make the omelet: chop the meats; chop the washed and dried chives; soak the bean sprouts in a large bowl of cold water, swishing them about, then leave to stand. Take out of the bowl and place in a colander. Leave any ungerminated seeds or wilted sprouts at the bottom of the bowl, pick off and discard the empty seed cases, rinse under running cold water, and drain thoroughly. Beat the eggs with the salt, monosodium glutamate (if used), and the cornstarch or potato flour mixed with a little cold

SPECIAL SET EGG WHITES WITH SCALLOPS *

干贝无黄蛋

gàn bèi wú huáng dàn

280

8 eggs
4 dried scallops (conpoy)
1 tbsp rice wine
2 pinches salt
2 pinches monosodium glutamate (optional)
1 cup chicken broth
10 oz broccoli or asparagus spears
3 tbsp oil
1 tbsp sesame seed oil

For the sauce:
1 cup chicken broth
pinch monosodium glutamate (optional)
pinch sugar
1 tbsp oyster sauce
1 tbsp cornstarch or potato flour

Time: 1³/₄ hours

Rinse the scallops, place in a heatproof dish, sprinkle them with the rice wine, cover and steam for 1 hour. Carefully make a small hole in one end of each eggshell and with great care gently pour out the white, followed by the yolk (the yolks are not used for this recipe). Avoid the yolk breaking as you need just the white for this dish. Empty each into a cup before adding its white to the other, successfully extracted whites in a bowl. Beat the egg whites lightly with a fork, adding a pinch of salt and of monosodium glutamate (if used) then gradually beat in 1 cup chicken broth; pour this mixture into a large measuring jug or use a lipped mixing bowl. Rinse the egg shells and carefully fill with the mixture: use a small funnel and stand the eggs, hole uppermost, in egg cups or any heatproof cups or dishes in which they will stand steadily; alternatively, place a fairly thick layer of rice in the steamer compartment and stabilize the eggs in this. Place the eggs, in their containers or nestling in the rice, in the steamer, cover, and steam for 10 minutes, then remove the eggs from the steamer and add to a saucepan of boiling water and boil for 40 minutes.

Place the hard-boiled eggs under running cold water until they are cold, then peel them carefully. While the eggs are boiling, trim the broccoli into florets, discarding the stalks. Wash, drain, and blanch the florets or asparagus spears for 3–4 minutes in boiling water. Drain well. Once the eggs are cooked and cooled, stir-fry the broccoli or asparagus in the wok in 3 tbsp oil with a pinch each of salt and monosodium glutamate (if used). Sprinkle with the sesame seed oil, stir, and transfer to a serving dish. Place the hard-boiled eggs on the

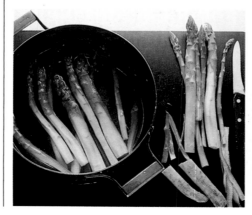

bed of broccoli or asparagus spears.

Drain the cooking juices from the scallops into a small saucepan; cut the scallops into thin strips and arrange decoratively over the eggs. Heat the scallop juices with the remaining 1 cup chicken broth, the monosodium glutamate (if used), sugar, and oyster sauce. Boil briefly, then mix the cornstarch or potato flour with a very little cold water and stir into the sauce to thicken. Pour the sauce over the broccoli or asparagus and serve.

PIGEON'S EGGS DUMPLINGS
溜鸽蛋铰
liū gē dàn jiǎo

12 pigeon's eggs (or 18 quail's eggs)
3 tbsp oil
¹/₄ cup cornstarch or potato flour
oil for frying
2 oz bamboo shoots
2 oz very small, fresh button mushrooms
1 firm, ripe tomato
10 leaves arugula (lamb's tongue lettuce)
3 tbsp chicken broth
¹/₂ tbsp salt
pinch monosodium glutamate (optional)
1 tbsp melted chicken fat

Time: 55 minutes

The vegetable garnish and sauce for this dish are best prepared before starting to cook the eggs (see below).

Select a wide, shallow heatproof plate or dish that will fit into your steamer and grease lightly with oil. Carefully break all the eggs into it, positioning them as they break so that each egg is beside and not on top of the rest; they should be in a neat single layer; take care not to break any of the yolks. Cover and steam for 10 minutes. Take the dish out of the steamer and carefully run a sharp knife between the yolk vertically and then horizontally so that you have neat squares, each with a yolk in the middle of a squared off surround of white. Cut each of these squares diagonally in half (wipe your knife with a clean damp cloth between each cut as otherwise the yolk will stick to the blade and make cutting the next egg more difficult). Now you should have little triangles, with the cut yolk exposed on one side. Coat these lightly and very carefully with cornstarch or potato flour. Semi deep-fry or deep-fry these eggs in very hot but not smoking oil for only 2 minutes or until golden brown all over.

Sauce and vegetable garnish: cut the bamboo shoots into very small pieces; wipe the mushrooms with a damp cloth, leaving them whole; blanch, peel, and cut the tomato into small pieces or thin strips; wash and dry the arugula. Stir-fry all these ingredients briefly in

1¹/₂ tbsp oil in the wok, adding them in the same order as listed above. Add the broth, salt, monosodium glutamate (if used), and chicken fat. Boil uncovered for 1–2 minutes to reduce the liquid a little; mix the cornstarch or potato flour with a very little water and stir into the contents of the wok to thicken the sauce.

As soon as the eggs are fried, transfer them immediately to a heated serving plate and cover with the vegetable and sauce mixture.

PIGEON'S EGGS GUO TIE

锅 贴 鸽 蛋

guō tiē gē dàn

12 pigeon's eggs (or 24 quail's eggs)
3 tbsp oil
¹/₂ lb white fish fillets
2 oz finely chopped pork belly
1 egg white
1¹/₂ tbsp cornstarch or potato flour
pinch salt
pinch sugar
1 tsp finely chopped fresh ginger
1 tsp finely chopped scallion
1 tbsp rice wine
1 tbsp sesame seed oil
2 canned figs
6 slices from a small pan loaf (white)
12 chives (or 12 stems zha cai pickled rape)
12 canned cherries
oil for frying

Time: 40 minutes

Lightly grease 12 small cocotte dishes or small timbale molds with oil; break one pigeon egg into each (if using quail's eggs, you will need 2 per mold) taking care to avoid the yolks breaking. Place these molds in the steamer, cover, and steam for 5 minutes (4 minutes will be enough for the quail's eggs). Chop the fish fillets finely and mix well with the chopped pork belly; whisk the egg white lightly, gradually adding the cornstarch or potato flour, the salt, sugar, ginger, scallion, rice wine, and sesame seed oil; work this into the chopped mixture until it forms a homogenous mixture which will keep its shape. Drain the figs of their syrup and cut into thin strips. Trim the crusts from the bread slices; cut each slice in half and trim these halves to a teardrop shape; spread these shapes with a layer of the prepared mixture, making this layer approximately the same thickness as the bread slice. Arrange the chives or zha cai strips and the figs on the meat and fish spread, shaping these into the top section of a wide exclamation mark (starting at the wider end of the "teardrop" of bread). Place the halved cherries at the narrow end, cut side down, as if to form the full stop of

the exclamation marks. Place these bread slices on one or more lightly oiled plates in one or more compartments of your steamer; cover and steam for 10 minutes.

Heat approx. ¹/₂ cup oil in a very wide skillet and when very hot (about 350°F) place the slices, bread side down, in the oil and fry in batches until crisp and golden brown.

PIGEON'S EGGS WITH WHITE FUNGUS

清 汤 木 耳 鸽 蛋

qīng tāng mú ěr gé dàn

2 oz dried white fungus (tremella),
    sometimes called silver fungus
12 pigeon's eggs (or 18 quail's eggs)
¹/₄ lb chicken breasts
7 cups chicken broth
1 tsp salt
¹/₂ tsp monosodium glutamate (optional)

Time: 1 hour

Soak the white fungus for at least 20 minutes in warm water; when it is soft and fully reconstituted, drain well and snip off any remaining tough parts; tear into small pieces. Hard boil the eggs by placing them in a saucepan of cold water, bringing them to a boil and timing them for 4 minutes after the water boils; drain quickly and immediately place under running cold water to cool rapidly and prevent discoloration of the yolks. When cold, peel.

Finely chop the chicken breasts; add this chopped raw meat to a small saucepan of boiling water, blanch for 1 minute, then remove with a slotted ladle or drain through a fine sieve. Bring the broth to a boil, add the blanched chicken and fungus; stir in the salt and monosodium glutamate (if used) and simmer gently for 20 minutes.

Pour the chicken broth over the eggs and serve.

PICKLED CUCUMBERS

醋 溜 黄 瓜

cù liū huáng guā

14 oz cucumbers
1¹/₂ tbsp salt
¹/₄ cup sesame seed oil
1 tbsp Szechwan peppercorns
3 small pieces chili pepper
1 tbsp finely chopped fresh ginger
1 tbsp finely chopped scallion
3 tbsp wine vinegar
1 tbsp soy sauce

1¹/₂ tbsp sugar
1¹/₂ tbsp cornstarch or potato flour

Time: 45 minutes

Cut the cucumbers lengthwise in half; scoop out the seeds and discard these. Cut the cucumber halves into fairly thick slices, place in a bowl and sprinkle with the salt; stir and turn, then leave to stand for 30 minutes. Drain and dry.

Heat the sesame seed oil in the wok, add the Szechwan peppercorns, chili pieces, ginger, and scallion and stir-fry gently until there is a good, full aroma. Add the cucumber pieces, stir, then add the vinegar, soy sauce, and sugar and stir well while cooking over moderate heat for a few minutes; when the added liquid of the vinegar and soy sauce has reduced, mix the cornstarch or potato flour with a little cold water and stir into the contents of the wok to thicken the remaining liquid and glaze the cucumbers.

BRAISED FRESH SOYBEANS AND CHICKEN

鸡 火 青 豆

jī huǒ qīng dòu

14 oz fresh soybeans (if unavailable, use
    fava beans)
¹/₂ lb chicken breasts
1 egg white
¹/₂–1 tsp salt
1¹/₂ tbsp cornstarch or potato flour
oil for frying
¹/₂ lb York ham, in one piece
1 scallion
2 slices fresh ginger
3 tbsp oil
7 cups broth
¹/₄ cup shortening or melted pork fat
1 tsp salt
pinch monosodium glutamate (optional)
1¹/₂ tbsp cornstarch or potato flour

Time: 1¹/₄ hours

Shuck the beans. Cut the chicken breasts into small cubes. Whisk the egg with the salt and first quantity of cornstarch or potato flour listed above; add the chicken and stir well; leave to stand for a few minutes. Heat approx. ¹/₂ cup oil in the wok to about 340°F (or use more oil and the deep-fryer); fry the chicken cubes until pale golden brown; remove from the oil, draining well, and set aside. Cut the ham into cubes.

Empty the wok if used for frying the chicken and wipe the inside; heat 3 tbsp fresh oil and stir-fry the trimmed, whole scallion and the

1 tsp salt
pinch sugar
1^1/$_2$ tbsp cornstarch or potato flour
3 tbsp melted chicken fat

Time: 20 minutes

Separate the leaves, wash, and then blanch in fast boiling water for 10 seconds only. Drain well. Heat 2 cups oil in the wok (or use more oil and a deep-fryer) and when the oil has reached a temperature of 290°F fry the leaves for 2 minutes. Remove and drain well.

Empty the wok and wipe if used for frying the leaves; pour in the broth, add the leaves, the monosodium glutamate (if used), salt, and sugar; cook over moderate heat for a few minutes, stirring occasionally; mix the cornstarch or potato flour with a little cold water and stir into the wok to thicken the liquid.

"Milky" broth is a mixed meat, and poultry broth made by boiling raw offcuts and carcasses of chicken and duck with the remains of a pork leg (bone, meat, and trotter) for 1^1/$_2$ hours, by which time it assumes an opaque, almost milky look, hence its name.

THREE-FLAVOR BRAISED CABBAGE

三丝白菜炖

sān sī bái cài dùn

5 oz Chinese Gold Coin ham, Virginia ham or Westphalian ham
5 oz chicken breasts
8 tung ku (dong gu) mushrooms
1 Chinese cabbage weighing approx. 2^1/$_4$ lb
7 cups chicken broth
^{1}/$_4$ cup oil
1 tbsp salt
1 tsp monosodium glutamate (optional)
1^1/$_2$ tbsp cornstarch or potato flour

Time: 45 minutes

Shred the ham and chicken. Soak the dried mushrooms in warm water. Wash the cabbage and cut into quarters. Bring the broth to a boil in the wok or a saucepan and boil the cabbage, uncovered, for 30 minutes, turning once or twice during this time; do not worry if the broth reduces considerably. Drain the mushrooms, cut off and discard their stalks and cut the caps into thin strips. Heat ^{1}/$_4$ cup oil in a wok or skillet and stir-fry the chicken and the mushrooms; stir in the salt and monosodium glutamate (if used). The broth will now have reduced considerably; take out the cabbage, drain well and place in a serving dish. Add the ham, chicken, and mushrooms to the broth

A Buddhist monk in Xishuangbanna where once there were 360 Buddhist temples; now there are 220. Buddhism is very widely practised in Xishuangbanna and in Bajiaoting the famous Octagonal Pagoda was built in the hope of deliverance from the huge swarms of wasps that plagued the area. The Mengzhe Buddhist temple is also well known, with its two large, colored stupa or tower-like shrines, and two little monks with their closely shaven heads and limbs tattooed with prayers in the Dai language.

The monks run their communities along self-sufficient lines, with well defined hierarchies. Besides being religious and cultural centers, they protect and cultivate certain botanical species of religious reasons and for ornamental purposes; they also grow fruit trees such as payayas, coconuts, lychees, and tamarinds etc.

Buddhist law lays down four immutable requirements when a temple is built: there must be a statue of Sakyamuni, the founder of Buddhism, and a reliquary for his sacred ashes; at least five monks must be in attendance and an orchard and garden must be established to grow certain plants and thus ensure their survival.

Buddhism offers an oasis of peace and tranquillity and seems to be attracting plenty of novices, especially among young people who are turning away from the superstitions and ancestor-worship of Confucianism to embrace a life of self-denial and austerity.

peeled, whole slices of ginger until they both give off a good aroma and have flavored the oil. Remove the scallion and ginger and discard. Add the chicken to the flavored oil, followed by the ham, beans, broth, shortening or pork fat, salt, and monosodium glutamate (if used). Once the liquid has reached boiling point simmer gently for 40 minutes. Shortly before serving, mix the second quantity of cornstarch or potato flour listed above with a little cold water and stir into the contents of the wok to thicken the remaining liquid.

CHINESE CABBAGE WITH CHICKEN FAT

鸡油菜心

jī yóu cài xīn

14 oz Chinese cabbage
oil for frying
1 cup milky broth (see below)
^{1}/$_2$ tsp monosodium glutamate (optional)

and simmer for a few minutes; mix the cornstarch or potato flour with a little cold water and stir into the liquid and other ingredients to thicken; pour all over the cabbage and serve.

of cold water and stir into the sauce, cooking for 1–2 minutes, to thicken. Pour this sauce over the stuffed peppers.

284

STUFFED PEPPERS
酿青椒
niàng qīng jiāo

6 large red bell peppers
¹/₂ lb lean pork
¹/₄ lb Chinese Gold Coin ham, Virginia ham or
*   Westphalian ham*
¹/₄ lb chicken
1¹/₂ tbsp peeled shrimp
2 water chestnuts
1 tbsp finely chopped scallions
1 tsp finely chopped fresh ginger
pinch freshly ground pepper
¹/₂ tsp sugar
1 egg
1¹/₂ tbsp cornstarch or potato flour
oil for frying

For the sauce:
1¹/₂ tbsp chicken broth
¹/₂ tbsp soy sauce
1¹/₂ tbsp rice wine
1 tbsp sesame seed oil
1 tbsp cornstarch or potato flour

Time: 1¹/₄ hours

Chop the pork very finely (this gives a better texture than grinding it). Chop the ham, chicken, and shrimp finely. Chop the water chestnuts, the trimmed and peeled scallion, and ginger. Mix all these ingredients in a large bowl, add the pepper, sugar, egg, and cornstarch or potato flour. Cut the peppers across in half, remove the seeds and inner pale, pithy parts; stuff both pepper halves with the meat mixture, packing it in securely. Heat plenty of oil in the wok or deep-fryer to about 300°F or slightly higher and carefully fry the stuffed peppers for 4 minutes in several batches to avoid the oil temperature dropping too low. Remove from the oil and drain well. Pour the chicken broth into a fairly deep heatproof dish or into two dishes, large enough to hold the peppers in a single layer but not too large to fit in your steamer.

Place the peppers in this broth, meat side uppermost, and place in the steamer; cover and steam for 20 minutes. Take the peppers out of the steamer, transfer to a serving dish, and pour the remaining broth into a saucepan; stir in the soy sauce, rice wine, and sesame seed oil and boil to reduce a little; mix the cornstarch or potato flour with a small amount

EGGPLANT YU XIANG *
鱼香茄子
Yú Xiāng qié zǔ

2 small eggplants weighing about ¹/₂ lb each
oil for frying

For the sauce:
3 tbsp oil
1 tbsp finely chopped scallion
1 tbsp finely chopped garlic
1 tbsp finely chopped fresh ginger
1 tbsp hot (chili) soybean paste
1 cup finely chopped lean pork
1 tsp salt
1 tsp sugar
1¹/₂ tsp wine vinegar
pinch freshly ground pepper
pinch monosodium glutamate (optional)
1 tbsp soy sauce
¹/₂ cup broth (or water)
1¹/₂ tbsp cornstarch or potato flour

Time: 50 minutes

Wash and dry the eggplants and remove their stalks and calyx. Cut lengthwise into ¹/₂-in thick slices and then cut these slices into strips ³/₄ in wide and 2³/₄ in long. Semi deep-fry or deep-fry the eggplant strips in oil until tender. Drain well.

Heat 3 tbsp fresh oil in the emptied and wiped wok or another, large skillet and stir-fry the garlic, ginger, and scallion until they release a good strong aroma. Stir in the soybean paste, followed by the meat; continue stirring and cooking until the meat is cooked and lightly browned.

Add the fried eggplant, all the other ingredients, including the broth, but leaving out the cornstarch or potato flour, which will be added later. Simmer for 5 minutes, uncovered, stirring 2 or 3 times and allow the liquid to reduce considerably. Mix the thickening agent with a little cold water and stir into the contents of the wok.

Yu Xiang is a technical term for the culinary process of oil-blanching ingredients as a precooking phase. (See Yu Xiang Fish Fillets on p. 250.)

before stuffing peppers, dust the inside of peppers with cornstarch

286

A woman draws water from the well in Yunnan. The geological history of Yunnan, "the land of eternal spring," is probably the most complex and fascinating of all China's landscapes. Two hundred million years ago it lay under the sea, now the Karst-formation stone forest covers more than 190 acres, with villages nestling between the rocks, tiny, narrow alleys winding tortuously between houses with corn cobs hung along their stone walls and strings of chili peppers dangling from the eaves, all drying in the sun while the peach blossom blooms. The monsoon winds from Malaysia blow across the mountain ridges of the high plateau and howl through the deep gorges; frequent earthquakes over the centuries have led to the growth of strange superstitions and propitiatory rites.

The Sani people live in this stone forest, having settled here after the kingdom was conquered by Kubla Khan. The Naxi, another ethnic minority native to this region were responsible for extremely ancient pictorial art showing the exploits of early man. Living in wooden houses, with a peaceable way of life in tune with nature, they practise very crude methods of agriculture, trusting to the auspicious winds from the snow capped mountains, the breath of the Jade Dragon, to bring them good fortune. Change reaches even these remote parts: the Sani women used to be bartered, like chattels, now they have won the right to choose their husbands themselves. Traditional dress is still worn, the babies' caps and the earflaps of the women's bonnets being typical and in keeping with local custom.

leave to stand for 6 hours, with a small plate and weight on top.

Rinse the cabbage in a colander under running cold water, drain, and squeeze out any excess moisture. The cabbage will have gone limp because it has lost much of its water content during the standing and salting process. Place the cabbage strips in a fairly deep, preferably straight-sided nonmetallic dish and place the peeled and shredded ginger and the trimmed and shredded chilis (the fresh or brine-pickled chilis) on top.

Heat the sesame seed oil gently in the wok or in a small pan and fry the Szechwan peppercorns and the crumbled dried chilis in it (remove the seeds from the latter if you do not want the cabbage to be too peppery); when the spices have released their flavor into the oil (about 5 minutes) strain the oil, pouring it over the cabbage. Heat the vinegar with the sugar in a nonmetallic pan until the sugar has dissolved; pour this in turn over the cabbage. Leave to stand for 5 hours before serving.

BRINE-PICKLED VEGETABLES
四川泡菜
Sìchuān pào cài

1 small Savoy cabbage
1 small or ¹/₂ large cucumber
1 small, long white radish (Daikon root)
1 carrot
1 small head or bunch of celery
1 red bell pepper
¹/₄ lb fresh ginger
5 chili peppers (preferably fresh)
6 tbsp wine vinegar
2¹/₂ tbsp salt
2¹/₂ tbsp sugar
3 cups distilled water
2¹/₂ tbsp rice wine

Time: 30 minutes + 2 days pickling time

Separate the cabbage leaves from the stem and cut the leaves into quarters. Peel the cucumber, cut lengthwise in half and scoop out the seeds. Prepare the radish, carrot, celery, and red bell pepper. Cut all the vegetables (except for the quartered cabbage leaves) into matchstick strips. Peel the ginger and shred; cut the stalks off the chili peppers and slice across, keeping the seeds in place.

Place all these vegetables, in equal proportions, into glass preserving jars or jam jars. Mix all the remaining ingredients together and pour into the jar or jars; the liquid should cover all the vegetables. Seal the jar tightly. After 48 hours these vegetables will be ready for eating; they will last well for 1 week.

CHILI-PICKLED CABBAGE
辣白菜
là bái cài

14 oz Chinese cabbage
1 tbsp salt
4 slices fresh ginger
2 chili peppers (fresh or brine-pickled)
¹/₄ cup sesame seed oil
1 tbsp Szechwan peppercorns
5 dried chili peppers
1 cup wine vinegar
¹/₄–¹/₂ cup sugar, to taste

Time: 30 minutes + degorging time for the cabbage and standing time

Cut across the cabbage leaves, slicing into ¹/₄-in wide strips. Wash and dry. Place in a bowl and sprinkle with salt; stir and turn and

BANANAS STUFFED WITH SWEET RED SOYBEAN PASTE *

夹沙香蕉
jiā shā xiāng jiāo

1¹/₄ lb bananas (ripe but not discolored)
2 oz sweet red soybean paste
1¹/₂ tbsp all-purpose flour
1¹/₂ tbsp cornstarch or potato flour
1¹/₂ tbsp sesame seed oil
oil for frying
¹/₂ cup confectioner's sugar

Time: 40 minutes

Peel the bananas, cut lengthwise in half, and then into 2-in lengths, keeping the pieces beside their twins so you will know which half matches which. Crush these very slightly to flatten them a little, using the blunt, flat side of a heavy knife blade.

Spread the cut side of half the slices with red soybean paste and place their matching halves on top. Press gently. Mix the flour and cornstarch or potato flour with the sesame seed oil and dip the bananas in this mixture or coat them with it. Heat oil in the deep-fryer to 340°F and fry the bananas until golden brown all over. Drain well as you remove them with a large slotted ladle from the oil, then finish draining briefly on kitchen towels. Transfer to a heated serving dish and sprinkle all over with sifted confectioner's sugar.

ROSE PETAL FRITTERS

玫瑰窝渣
méi guì wō zhā

1 oz dried rose petals
1 cup all-purpose flour
2 eggs
3 tbsp cornstarch or potato flour
1 cup sugar
oil

Time: 1 hour + cooling time

Chop the rose petals. Mix just over half of them with the flour, just over 2 cups water, the eggs, and half the cornstarch or potato flour. Grease the wok lightly with oil, pour the mixture into it, and cook over very gentle heat, stirring continuously, until it thickens. Transfer to a bowl, leave to cool, and chill in the refrigerator. Take the mixture out of the bowl, place on a pastry board or working surface and roll into a fairly thick sheet about ¹/₄ in thick. Cut into strips

¼ in wide and 2–2¼ in long. Coat these carefully with cornstarch or potato flour and deep-fry in hot oil (heated to 340°F) until golden brown (about 5 minutes). Take out of the oil, draining well, and transfer to a serving dish.

Heat the sugar with about ½ cup water and when the resulting sugar syrup forms bubbles around the edges, pour it all over the rose petal fritters. Sprinkle the remaining rose petals, mixed with a little superfine or confectioner's sugar, on top and serve.

FRIED SESAME SEED COOKIES

芝麻窝渣

zhī má wō zhā

3½ cups all-purpose flour
2½ tbsp cornstarch or potato flour
1 egg
oil
3 tbsp sesame seeds
¼ cup sugar

Time: 45 minutes

Sift the flour into a mound in a large mixing bowl; make a well in the center; mix the cornstarch or potato flour with the lightly beaten egg and pour this into the well; gradually mix the egg mixture into the flour; add sufficient water to make a fairly thick batter. Pour 1 cup water into the wok, bring it to a boil and then add the mixture to the wok; beat vigorously with a wooden spoon or a balloon whisk while cooking over lower heat until the mixture thickens very considerably; this will take about 10 minutes. Transfer the mixture to a lightly oiled plate (it should form a fairly thick sheet) and cut into strips measuring ¼ × 2in. Coat these lightly with the cornstarch and deep-fry in hot oil (340°F) until golden brown. Take out of the oil, draining well, and place on a plate. Roast the sesame seeds over moderate heat, shaking the pan continually, until they start to give off their distinctive nutty scent; sprinkle the fritters with these and then with the sugar.

CANDIED WATER CHESTNUT FRITTERS *

玫瑰马蹄饼

méi guì mǎ tí bīng

1¼ lb water chestnuts
6 tbsp all-purpose flour

2 oz sweet red bean paste
oil for frying
½ cup sugar
1½ tsp cornstarch or potato flour
1½ tbsp rose-scented sugar

Time: 45 minutes

Peel the water chestnuts and chop. Mix with half the flour and shape into balls. Shape the sweet soybean paste into smaller balls. Make a hole in each large ball, insert a smaller ball, and close up. Coat lightly with the remaining flour and deep-fry until golden brown.

Heat the sugar with 1 cup water in a small

saucepan until the sugar has completely dissolved; mix the cornstarch or potato flour with a little cold water and stir into the sugar syrup. Pour this syrup all over the fritters.

Sprinkle the dessert with the rose-scented sugar (sold in Oriental foodstores).

PEACHES WITH MINT

薄荷鲜桃

bò hé xiān táo

4 large, ripe peaches
1¹/₂ oz candied orange peel
¹/₂ cup sugar
15 mint leaves

Time: 30 minutes

Peel the peaches, cut them in half, remove the pit, and slice. Place the peach slices in a heatproof dish. Cut the orange peel into small dice and sprinkle all over the peaches. Heat the sugar with 2 cups water and when the sugar has completely dissolved, pour this light syrup all over the peaches. Cover the peaches with a piece of cheesecloth, scatter the mint leaves, lying flat, on this piece of cheesecloth, and then cover them with another piece of cheesecloth. Press the layers of cheesecloth gently down so that they touch the syrup and become soaked by it. Place the dish in the steamer, cover with the steamer lid and steam for 10 minutes. As they cook the peaches will absorb the flavor of the mint. When the peaches have cooked, take the dish out of the steamer, remove the two layers of cheesecloth, with the leaves between them. Cover with foil and chill.

SWEET BEAN PASTE AND RICE FLOUR PARCELS

端午粽子

buān wǔ zòng zǐ

1¹/₄ cups glutinous rice flour
12 dried bamboo leaves, pre-soaked in cold
    water for several hours
oil
¹/₂ cup sweet red bean paste

Time: 45 minutes

Place the flour in a mixing bowl; sprinkle with ¹/₄ cup boiling water, mix into the flour, then sprinkle in 3 tbsp cold water and mix well. The dough should hold its shape but be soft; add a little more cold water if necessary.

Place the pre-soaked lotus leaves in hot water to soak for a further 5 minutes, then spread out flat on the work surface. Brush the surface of the leaves all over with a thin film of oil. Roll the dough out on a lightly floured surface to a fairly thin sheet; cut this sheet out into 12 disks with a cookie cutter or glass approx. 3 in in diameter. Place just over ¹/₂ tbsp of the sweet bean paste in the center of each disk and either fold in half, pinching the edges together, or enclose the paste as directed for wontons on p. 17.

Place each of these dumplings on a bamboo leaf and wrap up securely but not tightly, tying with string.

Place these parcels in the steamer, cover, and steam for 15 minutes. These parcels are unwrapped at table, and may be eaten hot or cold, dipped in sugar if wished.

The Chinese celebrate the festival of Duan Wu on the fifth day of the fifth month of the Chinese lunar calendar; this festival is held in memory of a famous poet, Qu Yuan (332–295 B.C.), who strove to better the lot of people in the China of his day. He was dismissed from his position at court, and in despair he drowned himself in the Mi Lo river.

Legend has it that the search party sent to recover his body threw rice into the river to attract the fish and stop them eating his corpse. On Duan Wu a ritual is observed in memory of this legend, and parcels of cooked rice wrapped in bamboo leaves or a symbolic representation of them, are thrown into rivers.

SWEET PEASE PUDDING

冰冻豆茸

bīng dòng dòu róng

1¹/₄ lb unshucked peas or 14 oz (approx. 2¹/₂
    cups) fresh or frozen shucked peas
1³/₄ cups sugar
¹/₂ cup cornstarch or potato flour
3 tbsp chopped walnuts

Time: 30 minutes

Cook the shucked peas in boiling water for 5 minutes (cook until just tender if frozen peas are used). Push these peas through a sieve while still very hot. Heat the sugar with 1 quart water over moderate heat (do not allow to boil for this recipe; use a double boiler if wished); when the sugar has dissolved, mix in the pea purée, taking care not to allow the mixture to boil at any time. Mix the cornstarch or potato flour with just sufficient cold water to form a thin paste and stir this into the pease pudding mixture. Continue stirring over gentle heat until the mixture has thickened well, transfer to a pudding bowl, smooth the surface with a palette knife or spatula, and leave to cool. When cold, chill in the refrigerator. Serve in the bowl, or unmolded on a plate, sprinkled with the walnuts.

Added flavor in the form of finely chopped mint leaves or a very little pure vanilla extract can be stirred into the pudding before leaving it to cool.

290

Knowing how to make good basic broths and stocks is a fundamental requirement in all great culinary traditions. The foundation stocks used in international cooking have their equivalents, and possibly also their origins, in the rich broth, concentrated broth and the other, lighter Chinese basic stocks, although the latter differ from their Western counterparts in some respects.

These broths are often categorized as primary broths (which we shall describe as rich broths) and as secondary broths, made with the ingredients left over from making the first, rich broth. It is probably more accurately descriptive to call the primary broths rich, strong broths and the others light, clear broths. These two types of stock are used, among other things, to make two kinds of soup: thick, concentrated soups and clear soups. The clear soups are served as something to drink during the course of a meal. The rich, concentrated broths have a different purpose: they are considered by Chinese cooks to be a concentration of flavors and nourishment, a means of distilling the taste of ingredients, as well as being reviving, regenerating, and invigorating. Cooks all over the world make broths of varying strengths from raw materials specially chosen for the purpose or from raw leftovers and offcuts, trimmings etc.: almost anything can be used to prepare these broths when boiled in water for meat, fish, vegetable and mixed stocks, with high or very low fat contents, flavored by the use of one or more ingredients.

To save time, large quantities of those Chinese broths which take a long time to prepare – although they are all simple to make and do not need constant attention – can be made at the same time and frozen until they are needed. Many other broths are very quickly made, so that the temptation to use cubes and other instant broths can be resisted.

A few general hints on making Chinese broths: start off with all your ingredients cold (water included) and with raw meat, fish or poultry etc.; never add salt. When you want to make a light chicken broth, the most commonly used of all the basic stocks in Chinese cooking, simply bring a saucepan containing equal amounts of chicken and pork spareribs with plenty of cold water to a boil (the water should not only completely cover the meat but come some 1–2 in above the contents of the saucepan) and then simmer for 2 hours, skimming off any scum that rises to the surface at intervals. Strain through a very fine sieve.

Some cooks prefer to use chicken only for chicken broth, without the addition of the pork spareribs; in this case, the chicken is blanched in boiling water for 2 minutes, drained, and the chicken pieces placed in a saucepan of fresh cold water with two slices of fresh ginger and 1 scallion. After it has boiled, it is simmered just as in the other method. Cost-conscious cooks use only the bones and carcasses of chickens, with hardly any meat left on them, with or without the spareribs or calf's feet: The following broth recipes are quite robust in flavor and, depending on the purpose for which they are intended, are made mainly with meat and poultry, fish or vegetables and give a representative selection of classic Chinese broths and stocks.

VEGETABLE BROTH

Equal small quantities of:
tung ku (dong gu) mushrooms
fresh button mushrooms
xian cai (brine-pickled green vegetables)
yellow soybean sprouts

Try using approx. 2 oz of each ingredient to make this broth; if you find it is not quite strong enough, use a little more of each the next time. Soak the dried tung ku (dong gu) mushrooms in warm water for 20–30 minutes. Wipe the fresh mushrooms with a clean, damp cloth. When the dried mushrooms have softened and reconstituted, drain off the water and discard. Rinse the xian cai thoroughly under running cold water to eliminate excess salt. Place both types of mushroom in a large saucepan with the rinsed soybean sprouts and the pickled vegetable. Add sufficient cold water to cover the ingredients and bring to a boil; skim off any scum from the surface, cover and simmer gently for 1 hour. Strain through a fine sieve.

This broth is used in many vegetarian dishes. Mung bean sprouts can be used instead of soybean sprouts if the latter are difficult to find.

CLEAR VEGETABLE BROTH

approx. $^{1}/_{2}$ lb soybean sprouts or mung bean sprouts
2 tbsp oil

Rinse the bean sprouts, pick off any empty seed cases and ungerminated seeds, and drain well. Heat 2 tbsp oil in a saucepan and stir-fry the bean sprouts. As soon as they have started to color, pour in enough water to gen-

erously cover the sprouts. Bring to a boil, reduce the heat to a simmer, cover, and cook gently until the liquid has reduced to half or less of its original volume. Strain through a fine sieve, discarding the contents of the sieve.

Besides being an invaluable broth for all vegetarian dishes, this stock can be used for braising bamboo shoots and other vegetables, intensifying their flavor.

MILKY BROTH

1 chicken or 1 duck
approx. 2–2$^{1}/_{2}$ lb pork hock or hocks
approx. $^{1}/_{2}$ lb pig's tripe
1 pig's trotter

You can use older, boiling fowls or duck for this recipe; medium-sized birds (2–2$^{1}/_{2}$ lb dressed weight) will do. Rinse all the above listed ingredients thoroughly under running cold water then make the broth using the same method as in the preceding recipes. Remember to remove the scum from the surface at intervals while the meat is simmering. After 2 hours' slow cooking, the stock should have acquired a slightly milky, opaque look. To heighten this effect, some cooks add a very little fresh milk.

CONCENTRATED BROTH

10 oz pork tenderloin
10 oz pork spareribs
5 oz raw cured ham (e.g. Jinhua Chinese ham, Virginia ham or Westphalian ham)
2 oz dried shrimp (scie mi)
2 thick slices fresh root ginger, peeled
1 star anise
1 small piece dried Chinese tangerine or orange peel
approx. 6 cups cold water (2$^{1}/_{2}$ pints)

Place the pork in a medium-sized saucepan with the well-rinsed spareribs, the ham, and the other ingredients. Add sufficient water to amply cover all the meat (use more water than suggested above if necessary) and bring to a boil. Remove any scum that has risen to the surface. Reduce the heat, cover with a tight-fitting lid, and simmer gently for 2 hours. This will yield approx. 2 cups of full-flavored broth. Strain through a fine sieve.

The recipe for this broth originated in western China, where the taste is for food with pronounced, agreeably complex, and unexpected flavors, often achieved by an unusual combination of ingredients as in this recipe, with its dried shrimp, tangerine peel, and pork. This broth is also used in other parts of China, to add extra flavor to soups and sauces.

ORIGINAL BROTH

1 oven-ready chicken or 2–2¹/₂ lb lean beef
(e.g. shin)
2 scallions

You can use an older, boiling fowl for this broth. Rinse the bird well inside and out (or rinse the beef, keeping it in one piece). Rinse and trim the scallions. Place the chicken or meat and scallions in a large saucepan or cooking pot, add enough cold water to cover completely, and bring to a boil. Skim off any scum that has risen to the surface, cover tightly and simmer gently for 1¹/₂ hours. (Use foil if wished to make sure that very little steam can escape during this simmering time.) Strain the broth through a fine sieve or through a piece of cheesecloth placed in a sieve.

This basic stock is called "original" broth because it "originates" from only one type of meat. It has a pleasant golden color (especially when made with chicken) and plenty of flavor.

RED BROTH

1 oven-ready chicken weighing approx. 2 lb
1 oven-ready duck weighing approx. 2 lb
1 pork hock (on the bone)
1 pig's trotter
1 lb Jinhua Chinese ham or any good raw,
*   sweet cured ham (e.g. Smithfield ham,*
*   Virginia ham or Westphalian ham)*
³/₄ cup–¹/₄ lb fresh button mushrooms
2 cups rice wine
2¹/₂ tbsp light soy sauce

Wipe the mushrooms with a clean, damp cloth, trim off the ends of the stalks if necessary. Rinse the chicken and duck well inside and out; rinse the pork; use a cleaver to cut the pig's trotter lengthwise in half. Place all the poultry and all the other meats in a very large saucepan or cooking pot and add sufficient water to cover completely (the water should come about 1–2 in above the contents of the saucepan, to allow for evaporation). Bring to a boil; skim off the scum that rises to the surface, removing as little liquid as possible when you do this. Reduce the heat to a simmer, cover and cook gently for 1¹/₂ hours, then add the mushrooms, rice wine, and soy sauce. Cover again and simmer for a further 30 minutes once the liquid has returned to a boil. Strain through a very fine sieve or a piece of cheesecloth placed in the sieve.

This reddish, very full-flavored broth is used for some of the most elaborate and sophisticated Chinese dishes, such as braised shark's fin and shark's fin soup. It is a favorite with restaurant chefs.

FISH BROTH

2–2¹/₂ lb mixed saltwater fish (use very small
*   fish for part of this selection if wished) or*
*   fresh fish heads, bones, and trimmings*
1 scallion
2 slices fresh ginger
3 tbsp shortening
3 tbsp rice wine
1 tsp freshly ground Szechwan peppercorns

Peel and trim the scallion and ginger where necessary; chop coarsely. Melt the shortening in a large, heavy-bottomed saucepan and stir-fry the scallion and ginger until they release a good, full aroma; they will then have flavored the fat well. Remove and discard the ginger and scallion pieces with a slotted spoon, draining as much of the flavored fat as possible back into the saucepan. Add the well-washed, gutted fish or fish pieces and trimmings (do not use any of the fish's innards to make broth) to the saucepan, sprinkle in the wine and add sufficient cold water to cover the fish completely. Bring to a boil, skimming at regular intervals. Reduce the heat, cover, and simmer for 30 minutes. Strain the fish stock through a fine sieve or through a piece of cheesecloth placed in a sieve.

CLEAR CHICKEN BROTH

1 raw chicken carcass and giblets
¹/₂ leek
4 black peppercorns
2 thin slices fresh ginger
1 stick celery
1¹/₂ tbsp rice wine

Add the chicken carcass and giblets to a saucepan of boiling water, blanch for 1 minute, drain, and discard the water. Place the blanched chicken carcass and giblets in a saucepan, add 6 cups cold water, the leek, peppercorns, peeled ginger, celery, and the rice wine. Bring to a boil, skim off any scum, then reduce the heat, cover, and simmer for at least 1 hour, removing the lid every so often to remove any scum. Strain the broth through a piece of cheesecloth placed in a sieve.

This broth is ideal for wonton soup or any of the recipes in this book for clear soup with dumplings.

RICH MIXED MEAT BROTH

1 boiling chicken or 1 duck
2–2¹/₂ lb pork spareribs
1 lb Jinhua Chinese ham or any good raw,
*   sweet cured ham (e.g. Smithfield ham,*
*   Virginia ham or Westphalian ham)*

Rinse all the meats and the chicken (or duck) inside and out under running cold water and then place in a very large saucepan or cooking pot; add sufficient cold water to cover the contents of the pot amply, bring to a boil, and skim off any scum at intervals. Reduce the heat, cover, and simmer for at least 1¹/₂ hours, removing the scum every now and then. Strain through a fine sieve.

This is a much-used basic broth, very popular with restaurant chefs as it adapts well to a wide variety of flavors when additional ingredients are added for various dishes.

GLOSSARY

A number of ingredients used in Chinese cooking are seldom, if ever, used in Western dishes; some are relatively rare in China itself while others are known and used all over the world but are used in a different way in Chinese food.

Among the ingredients that typify all that is exotic and strange about Chinese cooking to us Westerners but which are familiar (although expensive) to Chinese cooks are sea cucumbers, swallows' nests, shark's fins, and jellyfish. Golden needles and galingale are probably even less well known in the West, whereas curry powder, although probably not the Chinese blend of spices, and chili are everyday seasonings.

This theme of the familiar used in an unfamiliar fashion also applies to rice and rice flour, particularly when it comes to glutinous rice, and certain rice preparations such as crispy rice. Most Westerners eat, or at least know of, tofu (bean curd) but there are a number of other products of the soybean (fermented beans, paste, sauces, bean curd skins, etc.) that need some explanation. These unfamiliar ingredients can be fascinating, not only from a culinary point of view but also from the nutritional angle: the Chinese have, after all, been observing and recording the effects of eating certain foods for thousands of years, so we can learn a lot from them. If you are unable to buy certain ingredients, it is sometimes possible to use a Western substitute (in the case of ordinary rice wine, dry white wine can be used); if you cannot find Shao Xing lao jiu, then saké or dry sherry will do. Use ordinary white cabbage if Chinese cabbage is unavailable. On the whole, however, it is better to make every effort to find the correct Chinese ingredients. A few concessions have been made to Western tastes and eating habits in these recipes, especially as regards the quantities of seasonings (particularly with salt, monosodium glutamate, commercially prepared Chinese sauces, and spices) and usually this means that amounts have been reduced.

The Chinese eat a wide variety of foods, having had to develop catholic tastes with such a vast population to feed, especially when suffering from the recurrent famines which have been such a feature of China's history. This tendency to eat such an extraordinarily broad selection of foods also stems from the precepts of Chinese medicine, or philosophy or religion. Some items amaze and appal Westerners because they are simply not part of our culinary tradition. The animal world provides some of the most notorious examples of this: snakes, frogs, dogs, wild cats, and camel's humps. Some recipes in the Chinese repertoire cannot, therefore, be copied even by the most enthusiastic and adventurous Western cook. Chinese housewives and professional cooks find a use for a vast range of comestibles, nothing goes to waste, including those parts of an animal, poultry etc., that we would not dream of eating: tendons or muscle from pig's feet, wing tips and feet from poultry, bird's beaks, chicken's blood … in fact, as the Chinese themselves say, everything may be put to good use, except for the feathers.

Abalone A gastropod belonging to the Aliotid family, this mollusk has a flattened shell shaped rather like a human ear. It attaches itself firmly to rocks buffeted by the waves along the waterline in temperate zones, the most widely distributed types being *Haliotis tuberculata*, the edible variety and *Haliotis lammellosa*.

Abalone is difficult to extract from its shell and tends to be chewy; it has a true taste of the sea and can be eaten raw but is more often cooked and canned. These pale, ivory-colored, canned abalone should only be warmed through or given the briefest cooking or they become sticky and viscous; they should therefore be among the last ingredients to be added when cooking a composite dish. The canning liquid can be added to soups or sauces of recipes which include abalone, to add extra taste. Dried abalone keep almost indefinitely provided they are stored in a very dry place. They are given a lengthy presoaking and cooking before being added to composite dishes to impart extra flavor and contrasting texture.

Agar agar A jelling or setting agent in everyday use in China and in east Asian countries. Also used as a thickening agent, to prevent crystallization of the sugar syrup in ice cream, and for various other uses in the international food industry. Besides using agar agar for sweetmeats, certain types of candy, and jello, the Chinese also soak it in leaf or sheet form in hot water and then serve it cut into strips or variously shaped pieces in salads or cold mixed platters with meat or chicken.

Agar agar is a seaweed extract and still has a very faint scent of the type of seaweed used. Sold in leaves or small sheets, in strips, ribbons or more commonly in bundles of slightly wavy threads. These should be soaked in cold water for 30 minutes and then cooked, or soaked in hot water until tender and used just as it is. When used for setting or thickening, the agar agar is added to boiling water and allowed to dissolve gradually.

Keeps well at room temperature. Can be substituted for isinglass or gelatin. Also available in powder form.

Allspice Fruit of the pimento tree, *Pimenta officinalis*, belonging to the Myrtaceae family, one of the rare spices native to the western hemisphere. It grows profusely in Jamaica and Mexico (between them these two countries account for nearly all the world's supplies) and to a lesser extent in other parts of the Caribbean and Central and South America. The ripe berries are dark purple, about the size of juniper berries; the dried spice is dark reddish brown. Called allspice because its flavor and aroma are reminiscent of a combination of pepper and cloves, with hints of cinnamon and nutmeg.

The whole dried berries keep well in an airtight jar and should be ground as you need them, as once ground they lose their taste and scent quickly.

Bai cai See Cabbage.

Bamboo See Bamboo shoots.

Bamboo leaves Used fresh as a wrapping for all sorts of recipes, to enclose food to be steamed or boiled.

Sold dried, in bunches, the leaves keep well and only have to be soaked in water, drained and then dried, brushed lightly with oil before being used just like the fresh leaves.

Bamboo shoots Hundreds of tropical and subtropical varieties of bamboo grow all over the world, at least 160 of them in Asia. Besides all its other uses, this invaluable huge grass provides a food in the form of its shoots, which are used as a vegetable for cooking on their own or with poultry and meat, with or without a sauce.

These shoots, which grow around the base of the plant, start to grow during the wet season; those gathered during the winter months are considered the best although the spring shoots are also sought after. In the West it is difficult to buy fresh shoots, so canned (whole or sliced) or dried shoots have to be used instead. The canned shoots should be well

293

rinsed before use; they will keep for several days if refrigerated in water provided this is changed daily. Dried bamboo shoots should be soaked in warm water for at least 2 hours and preferably overnight.

294

Bean curd skins See Tofu.

Cabbage In China there are many members of the *Brassica* family in everyday use ranging from the large, rather hard cabbages, enormous numbers of which are grown in the north (the Tianjin cabbage is particularly well known) to the small, tender, sweet, and juicy type grown in the fertile south (especially around Guangdong). Below we give just a few of the many varieties grown and eaten in China:

The cabbage which we in the West think of as the most typical Chinese variety, and often call the Chinese cabbage is *Brassica pekinensis*, often referred to as the Chinese celery cabbage or Chinese leaves.

It is also, as its Latin name would suggest, called Peking cabbage; sometimes Tientsin (Tianjin) cabbage. It is compact, roughly cylindrical in shape, and white with yellowish ribs in its leaves; sometimes these are a light green. Valued for its crunchy texture and mild, agreeable taste, it is used in all sorts of ways: as an ingredient in soups and meat dishes, or on its own, braised or stir-fried.

Chinese broccoli (*Brassica aboglabra*) are full of flavor, similar to Western varieties in appearance, but with oval leaves which have a blueish tinge.

One of the great Chinese favorites, especially in the east and south where it is very widely grown, is choy sum (*Brassica parachinensis*), sprigs of green leaves on green stems about 6 in long with yellow flowers on top. This green vegetable is tender and has a delicate taste. After trimming and rinsing it is cooked briefly to keep its crisp texture and considerable Vitamin C content before it is added to various dishes; also good by itself, blanched in water or stir-fried, when it makes a refreshing accompaniment to other dishes.

Chinese cabbage (*Brassica chinensis*) is also known as bai cai or white cabbage and belongs to the tender, southern, or warm climate types of cabbage. There are many varieties, the most common being about 4–6 in high, with firm, white stalks and tender, bright green leaves. Both the stalks and leaves are juicy and have plenty of mild, sweet taste to them; they should only be cooked for a short time.

Cassia See Cinnamon.

Chicken fat This is just as simple as it sounds; the fat from the inside of the cavity near the vent and other very fatty parts of the chicken such as the tail are heated gently and at length. The melted fat is then rendered and strained and is almost transparent. Used for frying and as a flavoring for certain dishes; added during the cooking or at the very end. Since its aroma is distinctive and quite strong, chicken fat is used in small quantities to avoid drowning other tastes.

Chili sauce See Hot Plum Sauce.

Chinese cauliflower See Vegetables.

Cellophane noodles These very thin white vermicelli-type noodles are made with soy flour, dried and sold in hanks or bundles, tied with a piece of string and/or a band of paper. They have a translucent appearance and should be soaked in water for a short time, then drained, before use. Usually added to sauces and cooked briefly, with or without vegetables, giving the dish a pleasantly slippery, almost gelatinous texture. They are valued for their role as a side dish, served in much the same way as vegetables, and for their consistency and nutritional value.

Cinnamon The dried bark taken from the smaller branches of an evergreen tree belonging to the laurel family, the *Cinnamomum zeylanicum*, a native of the warmer regions of Asia and which grows throughout the tropics. Looking like small, thin cylinders in the natural, dried state, cinnamon is an attractive lightish brown in color and has a well known warm, spicy taste and aroma.

In southern China, however, another type, known as Chinese cinnamon is more common. The cylinders of dried bark from this plant are shorter and more russet, with a stronger, more pronounced flavor and aroma. Extract of *Cinnamomum cassia* is also used as a mild laxative.

Cinnamon is sold as an essential oil and, of course, in ground form. Cinnamon or cassia is an important ingredient in certain spice mixtures (Five-spice powder and Chinese curry powder, among others) and is therefore used in many hot, peppery or salty or savory dishes as well as being very popular in desserts and confectionery.

Coconut milk The juice or thin liquid contained in a coconut, the fruit of the tropical palm, is often referred to as the milk; this is confusing since "coconut milk" is made by grating the coconut flesh, pouring boiling water over it, and leaving it to stand and cool a little before the milk is squeezed out by hand or in a tightly twisted piece of cloth. Can also be made in a liquidizer and with dried shredded coconut instead of the fresh flesh. When freshly picked, the fruits are light green; they then turn dark brown and the surface becomes hairy but the flesh and milk inside stay fresh for a long time provided the coconuts are stored correctly.

Blocks of creamed coconut or coconut cream are available (frozen or simply packaged in waxed paper) with which to make coconut milk of varying thicknesses depending on the amount of hot water added. Check that the creamed coconut has a sweet, true smell of coconut; if at all rancid do not use. Keep refrigerated.

Coriander Vivid green herb with many stems and indented leaves, producing white or russet flowers in an umbelliferous arrangement. *Coriandrum sativum* is often called Chinese parsley because of its fairly close resemblance to this herb. Used a good deal for culinary purposes in China and throughout Asia. The fresh leaves are highly nutritious and are coarsely or finely chopped, or simply cut into sprigs and used for decoration. The taste is strong, acid, with a very distinctive aromatic quality.

This plant is thought to be native to the eastern Mediterranean basin but it grows all over the world. The seeds, looking like grains, about $1/8$ in in diameter are almost spherical and very hard, gray-colored until they are dried when they turn a light russet brown. Ripe coriander seeds have an easily identifiable, pleasing scent and slightly sour, aromatic taste, totally different to that of the leaves; they have been used to flavor food since ancient times and are still used widely in such preparations as cured meats and sausages, preserves, and in alcoholic drinks and liqueurs.

Coriander has gentle, beneficial stimulant and bacteriocidal properties it also aids the digestion.

Cornstarch Corn (maize) is processed to eliminate all but the pure starch content, used for marinades for meat and fish (it has a tenderizing effect on meat and poultry) and for coating, frying batters as well as a thickening agent for sauces. Contains no gluten and therefore has a much reduced tendency to form lumps compared with ordinary wheat flour. Gives a glossy appearance to clear sauces when used to bind and thicken them. You may prefer to use potato flour or water chestnut powder (or even arrowroot for certain uses) instead, which have the same advantages of thickening without forming lumps provided they are mixed with a little cold liquid before being stirred into the hot mixture, and which produce a less noticeable texture. Cornstarch is flavorless but needs to cook for a few minutes to eliminate its "raw" taste.

Creamed coconut See Coconut milk.

Crispy rice This is now commercially prepared and sold in small, flattish cakes, often square, and is not expensive. The traditional and more delicious version can, however, be made at home and is a good way of using up leftover rice. Short-grain, glutinous rice with its high starch content is much better than long-grain rice for this purpose. The poor

people of China used to scrape off the grains that had stuck to the base and sides of the cooking pot, put them to dry in the sun, then fry them. The rice cakes you can buy in Chinese foodstores are called *guo ba*, which means, literally, "leftover rice." For the home-cooked version: steam glutinous rice until very tender; cook enough to spread out in a $^3/_4$-in layer to fill a shallow sided baking tray or Jelly roll pan, pressing down gently but firmly. Some cooks mix a little water with the cooked rice to make it extra sticky before spreading it out, some add a little cornstarch or potato flour. Place in a moderate oven to dry out, which can take several hours, then use as required. Usually served as an accompaniment or garnish in the same way as fried triangles or croûtons in Western cookery. Can be used to make sizzling rice, a famous dish, when the dried rice cake is broken into fairly small, bite-sized pieces, then fried in very hot oil over high heat; the rice grains swell and turn a light yellow color in about 30 seconds; remove and drain. A delicious shrimp sauce is poured over these crisp cakes and the dish is served at once.

Curry powder A blend of spices, the most well known being used for Indian dishes, either made up from freshly ground spices to the individual cook's taste or manufactured on a large scale; usually sold as Hot, Medium and Mild curry powder; many types of curry powder, suited to various dishes, can be bought at Oriental stores.

A commercially prepared version well suited to many Chinese dishes that call for curry powder is available or you can make your own by mixing ground turmeric or saffron, with ground coriander, cumin seeds, cinnamon, cardamom seeds, cloves, nutmeg, black peppercorns, and mace (this is just one example of the many blends possible).

The spices first have to be roasted lightly for about 10 minutes (this varies), cooled and then ground with a pestle and mortar or in, say, a coffee grinder. They are then mixed together. Any surplus from that day's curry can be kept for a few weeks in a sealed jar.

Dou ban jiang See Hot soybean paste.

Dried oysters Once a cheap and plentiful poor man's food, these are now expensive in the West where they are mainly eaten fresh, raw or lightly cooked. In China they are usually dried: large oysters are selected, salted, and dried in the sun. These hard, almost rectangular dried mollusks are not cheap and are regarded as a gourmet food. They impart a very definite, pronounced taste, salty yet subtle, to dishes in which they are used.

Dried oysters keep well provided they are efficiently salted and dried if kept in a cool place but they have a tendency to develop a growth of mold. Checked before use.

Dried scallops or conpoy Although these are not quite the same as the bivalves found in Atlantic and Mediterranean waters (*Pecten maximus* and *Pecten jacobeus*), the Chinese variety is very similar in appearance. The white cushions of meat (very tender despite being the mollusk's muscle, provided it is not overcooked) are dried in the sun all along the coasts of China and particularly in Shandong province on the Yellow Sea.

These dried mollusks are a yellowish or reddish brown color, very light (about $^1/_2$ oz) before being soaked after which they swell up and their mild, sweetish taste adds a pleasant flavor to a variety of dishes. Store in a tightly sealed container in a cool place.

Dried shrimp Even when soaked, these are still very small, hardly ever more than $^3/_4$ in long. The shrimp are salted and then sun-dried. They are a very effective way of adding plenty of flavor to a dish, not only for fish but also for meat, vegetable, and egg dishes.

Fa cai See Vegetables.

Fermented black soybeans Whole black soybeans are mixed with salt and ginger and left to ferment; they develop a very pronounced, almost sour flavor. Often fried in oil with or without garlic and used in small quantities to give a robust taste to a variety of dishes. Can be bought canned in brine, or dried, loose. (The latter are reputed to be the best.)

Fermented yellow soybeans There are over 1,000 varieties of soybean and one of them, a yellow soybean, is used for this preparation. The beans are left whole or only slightly crushed, salt, flour, and sugar are added and the beans left to ferment. Used as an added, salty flavoring (but not as salty, peppery, and pungent as fermented black beans) for certain meat dishes and vegetable dishes. Sold in cans.

Fish sauce A pouring sauce, transparent and with no impurities, amber-gold in color with a salty taste and pronounced aroma and flavor which blend into the dishes to which it is added, and add a very distinctive note to their taste. Keeps well in the re-sealed bottle or jar if refrigerated.

Five-spice powder Mixture of five ground aromatic spices and, like all spice mixtures, the proportions can vary according to taste and availability. Usually comprises: cinnamon (or cassia), star anise, cloves, pepper, and tangerine peel.

Some variations stress a particular constituent: cassia, Szechwan pepper, garlic, fennel, anise, giving a flavor and aroma that is very strong and harsh, or anise, cinnamon, cloves, fennel, and cardamom (with anise being by far the most dominant taste).

Five-spice powder is always very pronounced in taste and scent. It can be added to dishes which are then cooked, or sprinkled over finished dishes, or mixed into meat and fish marinades.

As with all spices, especially when they are ground, it should not be kept for too long or there will be a deterioration in aroma and taste.

Galingale or **Galangal** The rhizome of a perennial plant *Alpinia officinarum*, belonging to the ginger family, native to China but grown in many parts of Asia. Galingale is a knobbly root, reddish brown on the outside, tough and fibrous; the flesh inside varies depending on the variety, from brown to an orange tinge to pale golden color. The aromatic scent is complemented by a strong taste which is something like a blend of ginger and pepper. If galingale is not available, ginger can be substituted. Sold in small, dried pieces which are very hard and can be ground or, alternatively, chopped after at least 1 hour's soaking in hot water.

Ginger One of the most vital ingredients to achieve the true Chinese taste for innumerable dishes. The Chinese are known to have used ginger in their cooking for at least 2,000 years, in combination with scallion, leek or garlic when it works its magic most effectively. It is also credited with being very good for the digestion and general health. When fried gently, it releases an intense, delicious aroma and has a taste which is both strong and yet subtle. Fresh ginger masks or eliminates very strong, otherwise unpleasant, odors. The use of ginger is becoming increasingly common in the Western world. There should, therefore, be no difficulty in buying fresh ginger root, but canned fresh ginger can also be used. Ground ginger is no substitute and will spoil your dish if you use it.

This root is actually a rhizome, of the herbaceous plant belonging to the Zingiberaceae, and its first use dates so far back in history or prehistory that it is difficult to be sure where it originated, although it was probably in a wet and warm region of Asia. This plant (*Zingiber officinale*) is grown in many parts of China to satisfy the enormous demand. The fresh rhizome varies in size and is knobbly, with a pale yellowish brown skin that must be peeled off before use. The flesh inside is a deep creamy or grayish color with a hint of green to it. The peeled ginger is cut into very thin slices and may then be cut into very thin strips or finely chopped. Used in just about every imaginable dish: stir-fried dishes, sauces, to give flavor to liquid for poaching fish or boiling meat. The juice alone may be used (the ginger should be finely chopped then placed in a piece of clean cloth and the cloth gathered together, enclosing the ginger and twisted round and round so that pressure is brought to bear on the ginger

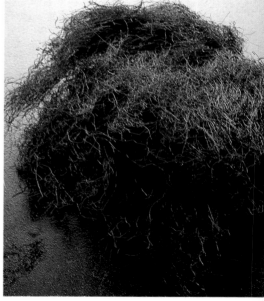

From top to bottom, left to right, a selection of ingredients that are always used dried: tong cong cai vegetables, jujubes, tangerine peel, zha cai, pickled vegetables, and angelica.

From top to bottom, left to right: fruit for both culinary and medicinal use, a dried tiger lily bulb (golden needle) cut into strips, white or silver fungus, mu er mushrooms, and the famous tung ku (dong gu) mushrooms.

and the juice is expelled).

Ginger keeps well in the refrigerator for up to two or three weeks, but it is best to buy frequent fresh supplies.

Candied ginger is excellent eaten on its own or included in cakes, desserts, and puddings.

298

Ginkgo nuts These are enclosed in a fleshy covering which both tastes and smells unpleasant. The nuts are usually extracted, shucked, and peeled before they are sold; here in the West it is certainly best to buy them in cans, when all the work has been done for you. They are also available dried. Ginkgo nuts are also candied and used for cookies, cakes, and desserts. The fruit comes from a very ancient type of deciduous tree, *Ginkgo biloba*, native to northern China but which now grows in many parts of the world. It was once venerated by the Chinese as a sacred tree.

These oval-shaped nuts are a great favorite with Chinese vegetarians who use them in casseroles and soups; they are also added to elaborate dishes containing many ingredients and used for decoration.

Golden needles This is the descriptive Chinese name given to the dried flower buds of tiger lilies, *Hemerocallis fulva*. These grow in most regions of China but are especially common in Szechwan. The dried buds are about 3 in long and the color varies from reddish orange to a bright yellow (the latter color are best in terms of quality). When added to certain dishes, these buds impart a pleasant consistency and a delicate but unmistakable, slightly musky aroma. Use in vegetarian and in meat dishes. Soak in hot water for 20–30 minutes before use to reconstitute, squeeze out excess water, and remove any hard parts or foreign matter if present. Golden needles keep well if stored in a hermetically sealed glass jar.

Guo ba See Crispy rice.

Hoisin sauce See Sweet soybean paste.

Hot plum sauce This peppery sauce is often placed on the table as a dipping condiment for fried or steamed foods. It imparts a very tasty, peppery flavor to dishes. This bright orange-red sauce is made with plums, fresh chilis, vinegar, and salt. Keeps for a long time in the refrigerator. Often called **chili sauce.**

Hot soybean paste Ground soybeans are seasoned and flavored with chili peppers, sugar, and salt. A popular addition to highly spiced dishes, especially in western China; very hot and aromatic. Indispensable for many of Szechwan's most typical dishes (where it is used with shrimp, beef, and pork). Called *dou ban jiang* in China, it is sold in jars or cans and keeps for a long time, especially if refrigerated.

Szechwan produces an even more fiery version of this paste, in which the chilis form the largest, basic constituent and yellow soybeans the subordinate, additional ingredient.

Hundred-year eggs This method of preserving eggs (usually very fresh duck eggs) is very different from the Western method but is based on the same principle of making the shell impermeable. Preserved the Chinese way, (they call these eggs *pi dan*) the egg yolk and white undergo certain changes in appearance (the whites become amber colored and translucent, the yolks turn green), taste, and consistency, in part due to the fact that some of the substances used for the preserving mixture penetrate the shell. Although called Hundred-year eggs, sometimes Thousand-year eggs, they are considered preserved after the coating has been in place for 100 days and will then keep for up to 6 months.

A muddy-looking alkaline paste is made with salt, wood ash, and slaked lime, then plastered over the eggs, covering them completely with a thick layer. This mixture can vary, incorporating tea; the wood ash can be a combination of resinous wood ash and non-resinous wood ash. The eggs are then placed in containers, covered with mud, and left in a cool, dark place.

Very old recipes for Hundred- or Thousand-year eggs have survived and these give detailed instructions to the cook, turning the whole process into something approaching a ritual. Today the eggs are mainly used as an appetizer, combined with a selection of other cold foods, or chopped and mixed with fresh eggs to make omelets.

Before use, they must be soaked to soften the mud covering; this is then scraped off, and the eggs are washed thoroughly and peeled.

Jellyfish Many different types of jellyfish caught in the seas around China are rendered palatable by a salting and drying process and are sold in the form of thin disks or circles, sometimes measuring up to 16 in in diameter, which have been sprinkled with salt, folded up and packaged in plastic.

These sheets of jellyfish are yellowish brown in color, with a sticky texture and keep almost indefinitely provided the seal is not broken.

When it is time to use the jellyfish, the excess salt is brushed or wiped off, the sheet soaked in several changes of cold water, rinsed under running cold water before being immersed once more; this process takes at least 2 days. Ready prepared strips of jellyfish, looking rather like ribbon noodles, are available for certain uses.

Lao jiu See Rice wine.

Longan The fruits of a tree belonging to the

Sapindaceae, *Euphoria longan* also known as *Nephelium longana*, are sometimes known by the evocative name of Dragon's eyes. They resemble lychees in appearance, are round, measure about $^3/_4 \times 1$ in, have leathery yellowish brown skins and a seed or pit enclosed in a fleshy seed-coat. This evergreen tree grows to considerable dimensions, although small trees are raised in large pots or under glass in colder areas, and is probably native to southern India, flourishing in southeastern China.

As with lychees, to which the longan is closely related, it is the fleshy seed-coat that tastes so good, sweetish yet acidulated, juicy, and with an almost gelatinous consistency. These fruits are often candied and used in Chinese patisserie or served as sweet dishes (what we Westerners would call desserts), especially those canned in a light sugar syrup.

Lotus This water lily grows throughout China except, of course, in dry regions such as Tibet and Mongolia. It is considered sacred and is invested with much symbolism by the Chinese; the metaphor being that the plant has its roots in the mud, yet produces such a dazzlingly beautiful flower. Almost all parts of the lotus are put to good gastronomic use: the leaves are used for wrappers when food is cooked in parcels; the roots (fresh or dried) eaten as vegetables or used as one of many ingredients in innumerable dishes, while the seeds or nuts (fresh, canned or dried) are used as an extra ingredient in composite dishes and for decorative purposes, especially for cakes and other sweet preparations.

See also: Lotus leaves; Sweet lotus seed paste; Lotus root; Lotus seeds.

Lotus leaves Used in much the same way as bamboo leaves, fresh or dried; these leaves impart a distinctive, pleasant aroma to the foods cooked in them.

Lotus root When fresh these roots are crisp with a delicate, faintly sweet taste. Hardly ever sold fresh in the West, canned lotus root is widely available and keeps well for a few days if kept covered in water (which should be changed daily) in the refrigerator.

Most frequently used in soups and in vegetable dishes, especially vegetarian dishes, but also used in composite dishes with fish or meat, lotus roots are also available dried and candied. The former need soaking to reconstitute them, while the latter make a delicious sweet snack or ingredient in cakes, desserts, etc.

Lotus seeds Green, turning pale yellow when dried, these are mainly used for garnishes and decorative purposes; they therefore occur in the more elaborate Chinese dishes, especially those which are arranged to look like flowers, animals, and birds, etc. Also available

canned; sometimes called lotus nuts.

Can also be finely chopped or broken into small pieces and used in fillings and stuffings.

Mei gui you See Rose liquor or spirit.

Monosodium glutamate Extracted from seaweed and other vegetable matter and used a great deal in Chinese and Japanese cooking, together with salt and sugar, as a flavor enhancer, hence its alternative name of taste powder. It is not a condiment in itself but brings out the flavor of the ingredients to which it is added. The addition of this chemical to food has caused some controversy in the West, where many people have reportedly had allergic reactions to its presence in their food; Western manufacturers have, however, used monosodium glutamate widely for many years in all sorts of commercially prepared food and especially in instant broth, stock, and soup powders and cubes.

Monosodium glutamate looks a little like salt but the crystals are finer and more translucent and shiny. Each individual cook can decide whether or not to use it; it is best used sparingly and not indiscriminately. It is worth mentioning, however, that monosodium glutamate often makes a good deal of difference to certain Chinese recipes and in some cases does enhance them and make them taste more "authentic."

Mu er See Mushrooms and fungi (tree ears).

Mu er See Seaweed.

Mushrooms and fungi These play a very important role in Chinese cookery. Compared with the number of varieties used in Italian and French cookery, the Chinese selection is small but these favorite types are used very frequently in a wide range of dishes, whether for taste or texture or both. Usually sold dried, they are then soaked until they soften and reconstitute, regaining their original shape and texture.

Fresh or canned mushrooms are often used in the same dish as the dried varieties; among these fresh mushrooms are the button variety, just like those so widely used in international Western cooking, *Psalliota* (or *Agaricus bispora*), pure white or slightly beige-toned skin on their caps, these being smooth or slightly scaly, or a warm brown color (in the case of the *avellanea* variety). These mushrooms should be used when very fresh, not at all wrinkled or discolored and when the caps are still "closed," i.e. still joined to the stem by a thin white stretch of skin or membrane, so that the gills are not yet visible.

The most widely used dried mushroom in China is the so-called Jew's ear, or *Auricularia auricula-judae*. This mushroom grows widely in Europe and elsewhere but is not nearly so popular or well known in the West as it is in

China, perhaps because it does not fry well, being much better suited to cooking in liquid. Also known as cloud (mu er) ears, especially in southern China, tree ears or simply black fungus. When dried, these look ragged and irregular in shape, and the pieces vary from large and reddish brown to medium or smaller, brownish fragments. When soaked, they swell and expand greatly, the "leaves" become frilly and the stalk can just be discerned; often it needs trimming off as it is tough. In their fresh state these fungi are slightly reminiscent of an ear, as their Latin name suggests, their texture is almost elastic and slightly gelatinous but firm and they are brownish violet in color. They grow in large clumps on live or dead trunks of broadleaved trees (such as elder, maple, plane trees, elms, oaks, etc.).

The most generally valued, though not the most expensive, widely used mushroom in Chinese cooking is the *Lentinus edodes* or tung ku (dong gu), black winter mushroom, which the Japanese call shiitake. These also grow in the West but are not widely consumed.

Always sold dried, these mushrooms can vary slightly in color, those with the paler caps and small, irregular bumps giving something like a flower pattern on their surface, are said to be the best; others have thick, wrinkled caps, in varying shades of brown, or with thinner, flatter caps, these second and last types being less sought after and often sold mixed with one another. *Lentinus edodes* is cultivated on oak trunks, in the West it has been grown successfully on artificial trunks made from pressed sawdust. When eaten fresh, these mushrooms are fleshy yet crisp with the suggestion of garlic about them and whether fresh (seldom available) or dried and reconstituted are delicious in soups, sautéed or braised, retaining their shape during prolonged cooking. The stems of these mushrooms are never used, being too tough and woody. As with all these dried mushrooms and fungi, they should be rinsed well then soaked (the soaking water is sometimes strained and used) and any sections which have not lasted well or are tough should be cut away and discarded.

Straw mushrooms, *Volvariella esculenta* (also called *volvacea*), are almost egg-shaped, with a peaked or conical cap; as their English name suggests, they are grown on rice straw, in the rice fields. We usually see these mushrooms canned in the West and they should be drained, discarding the canning liquid, and rinsed briefly in cold water before they are used. They keep well over short periods if immersed in cold water (which should be changed frequently) in the refrigerator. Their taste is almost negligible but they have a very agreeable, firm yet tender texture. When dried (although not widely available in this form in the West) they develop more taste

and aroma and should be soaked in water before being added to vegetable dishes and soups to add flavor.

Among other mushrooms used are dried black mushrooms (xianggu); St. George's mushrooms (koumo), while other fungi include morels, also much prized in the West, and white or silver fungus (tremella) which is rare and expensive and believed to have strong medicinal properties; lastly, staghorn or bamboo fungus (*Dictyophora phalloidea*), an even more costly item; extremely rare and beautiful, having the appearance of white lace and only found in Szechwan; a real delicacy for Buddhist recipes.

Mustard The small round seeds of the *Brassica nigra* or *Sinapis alba* of the Cruciferae family vary in color from white or light brown to dark brown or black. Although this annual is probably native to the Mediterranean region, most the world's supply of mustard is now grown in North America (mainly in Canada) and in Europe.

Mustard is used in Chinese cooking mainly where foreign, especially European, influence has been strong. It is best added ready-mixed and cold to food as a condiment, or mixed into the dish in the last stages of cooking: the enzyme crucial to the release of the main active constituents (alcaloids and glucosides) producing mustard's piquant, aromatic qualities, is neutralized by heat,

The Chinese sometimes use mustard seeds whole, fried in oil (which gives them a nutty flavor) as a basic spice for highly seasoned dishes and also use mustard oil, cooked or just as it is, as a condiment.

Several varieties of a genuinely Chinese mustard plant *Brassica juncea* are grown for use as a fresh vegetable or for salting and preserving, or drying. See also under Pickled cabbage and Vegetables.

Oyster sauce Various qualities of this sauce are sold; buy the best you can afford as a little goes a long way; the flavor of the good-quality product is delicate and goes very well with vegetables, improves many fish and egg dishes and goes well with certain meats and poultry. One very good version is made with oyster extract or liquor, cereal flours such as fermented soy sauce, salt, and sugar; it is fairly thick and darkish, almost "shiny" brown.

Sold in bottles, sometimes in cans; keeps well in the resealed glass bottle in the refrigerator.

Pickled cabbage Known as zha cai; in Szechwan large quantities of *Brassica juncea* are grown, preserved by pickling in a salt brine. Some of the brine is drained off and the cabbage flavored with spices before being canned. This very strongly flavored pickled vegetable should be rinsed well under running cold water to eliminate excess saltiness

before use. It has an agreeably crunchy texture and adds zest and flavor to a dish when cooked with other ingredients.

Pickled vegetables Although these preserved vegetables are popular throughout China, they have historically been vital to the good health of the inhabitants of northern China where the long, bitter cold winters make the growing season for green vegetables very short indeed. During the summer, when supplies are plentiful, vegetables are salted and dried, or brine-pickled in their fresh state, and the resulting pickles are used on their own or with other vegetables, meat, and fish.

Besides the plentiful use of salt, chili peppers are much used both as preservatives and as a flavoring agent. In order to preserve vegetables Chinese style (the vegetables used can be your own choice), see the recipe for Brine-pickled Vegetables in the Western China chapter on page 286.

Out of a wide variety of vegetable preserves here are just a few: xian cai is a little like fennel in taste and is sold canned in the West, in a very concentrated brine. The vegetable must be rinsed thoroughly under running cold water to eliminate excess salt before use. This pickle goes equally well with meat (such as pork belly) or with fish.

Xue cai is made with a variety of *Brassica juncea*, a member of the cabbage family, with its reddish root, and which is called "flower of the snow" because it is hardy enough to shoot and grow when it is still cold enough for snow to be covering the ground. The leaves and the tender stalks are pickled in a brine. This is sold canned in the West and must also be rinsed well before it is eaten, with meat dishes or cooked in soups, or it will be unpleasantly salty.

Xue li liang is an extremely salty preserve, and the larger stems, which are almost always rather tough should be trimmed off and discarded. This is usually added to vegetable dishes to give them a more pronounced flavor. Zha cai is another widely used salt-pickled vegetable.

Pi dan See Hundred-year eggs.

Qua ran or **Qua zi** See Toasted melon seeds.

Red soybean paste A very thick, smooth sweet paste, reddish brown in color, made with ground red soybeans. Used as a filling for various types of steamed dumplings, and dim sum, and in Chinese patisserie, with or without fresh or candied fruit.

Rice Rice must be the staple food upon which the greatest number of people depend to stay alive all over the world and to the Chinese it has always been the most important crop, especially in the vast southern provinces with the hot, humid climate in which this cereal

flourishes.

Rice growing in China dates back to at least twelve centuries before Christ, and many varieties are grown; the Chinese are particularly fond of long-grain rice, with a low starch content to be cooked and eaten just as it is, or fried. A great deal of glutinous (short-grain) rice is also used, opaque when raw, becoming sticky and transparent when cooked and used for cakes, sweet pies, puddings, molds, and stuffings.

A good deal of the Chinese crop is now processed in much the same way as elsewhere in the world, although a considerable amount is still harvested in the age-old way with little or no mechanization, left in shocks to dry in the sun and stored still on the stem, to be threshed and cleaned as it is needed.

Rice is processed in all sorts of ways: into flour with a low-starch content (teng mien), or high-starch content flour, depending on the type of rice used to make it. Many recipes call for a mixture of these two types of rice flour in carefully calculated proportion; the kneading process may vary according to the consistency required. Many types of noodles, both fresh and dried, are marketed which differ considerably from the transparent soy flour noodles and from the wheat flour variety.

Rice flour noodles These are very thin, white noodles of the vermicelli type. They differ from soy (or mung bean) flour noodles, not least because they are not translucent, and almost transparent when soaked in hot water. Sold dried, in hanks, they only need soaking and brief cooking.

Rice wine Known as "lao jiu" by the Chinese and made from the fermentation of sweetened rice must using the action of naturally occurring yeast; aromatic substances may or may not be added to give extra flavor and aroma; the quality, inevitably, varies according to the production methods used and whether the wine is aged or not. Although there are various qualities, the alcoholic content is consistently high (betwen 15 and 20 degrees). The taste is slightly oxidized, sometimes a little smokey in character. Dry or fairly sweet varieties are produced.

Rice wine is classified into the equivalent of *vin de table* and superior wines, perhaps the equivalent of Western "fine wines" although it is difficult to make a comparison. Shaoxing rice wine is a famous type and named after the eastern city Shaoxing, in the Shanghai region. Shao Xing lao jiu is amber tinted or yellow, with a bouquet of varying fullness; it is one of the most important flavorings in many dishes, particularly for specialties from Shanghai and surrounding provinces and is valued and savored throughout China. Also used in fillings, stuffings, marinades, casseroles, soups, and sauces, playing a dominant or supporting role.

Shao Xing lao jiu is also the traditional drink when there are toasts to be drunk, for elegant banquets, and to round off a good meal in style. It is served warm, in porcelain bottles or flasks, poured into small porcelain cups. If you cannot buy Shao Xing, then lao jiu (the equivalent of table wine) can be used instead but will not enhance your dish as much as the better wine; failing this, use dry (fino) sherry.

Shian ciaot (Xiang zao) rice wine is also considered very good. Flavored with sugar and with the flowers of a particular variety of bay tree blossom, its taste is both sweet and acidulated. Also used to flavor certain dishes, especially in the south of China.

Rose liquor or spirit Chinese restaurateurs in the West tend to offer this beverage to customers as a cordial or liqueur at the end of a meal. Often used in sauces, as extra flavoring for marinades and as a very distinctive addition to composite dishes. *Mei gui you* (rose dew) as the Chinese themselves call it, is based on the strong spirit, Kaoliang, distilled from sorghum wheat, a great deal of which is produced and drunk in northern China, to which highly scented rose petals give a strong perfume. Inferior versions of the very aromatic spirit are common, so it is best to make sure you are buying the genuine article.

Sea cucumber This creature's other name, sea slug, is perhaps more descriptive. It belongs to the Holothuria class of the Echinoderm family and has a long, soft body, round in section, protected by calcareous protuberances all over its skin. Many Westerners find its appearance and consistency unpleasant but the Chinese value sea cucumbers not only for providing variety of texture but also as a source of gelatin protein, which is believed to help prevent osteoporosis (brittle bone disease) in elderly people.

The East Asians and the Chinese in particular harvest sea cucumbers from the Indian and Pacific oceans, then dry them in the sun, after which they are called trepang and keep almost indefinitely. They require lengthy preparation; first a careful brushing under running cold water, then soaking for 3–5 days, followed by gutting, rinsing, and boiling, after which they are ready to cook, to be served on their own or as just one among many ingredients in numerous recipes.

Seaweed Many varieties of this sea vegetation are processed in the East to extract such products as monosodium glutamate and agar agar. They are also gathered, dried, and prepared in various ways for consumption still in leaf form.

Vast quantities of seaweed are consumed in Japan where they are prized for their reputed tonic and regenerative properties. Reviving beverages are made with some varieties, such as kombucha or seaweed tea; broths and

basic stocks are another major product of seaweed. The Chinese also use seaweed a great deal in their cooking, sometimes using the same varieties as the Japanese. Nori (the Japanese name for this purplish-black seaweed has been adopted world-wide) is sold in leaves, rectangles, strips, and sometimes chopped. It is full-flavored with a pleasant aroma and needs no cooking as such, being added after the other ingredients shortly before a dish is ready to be served.

Another seaweed, known in Japan as Wakame (sold dried in braided blackish hanks) when soaked in cold or lukewarm water reconstitutes to green, rather slippery leaves; these are trimmed and then need to be cooked briefly.

Other seaweeds, widely sold but called by different names in the various countries where they are marketed, are put to much the same uses. One example is the white seaweed (known as mu er in Hong Kong) which can be used in desserts as well as savory recipes; this is soaked in hot water and then the tough stalks are trimmed off.

At the beginning of spring, the Chinese gather tai tiao seaweed which turns a dark green when dried and has a very agreeable, pronounced taste and unmistakable scent and aroma.

Sesame paste White sesame seeds are crushed or ground, and the resulting yellowish warm brown paste has a delicate, fragrant nutty taste and aroma. Usually sold in jars, it is very thick, about the same consistency as peanut butter which can be substituted for sesame paste provided it is mixed with sesame oil. Usually mixed with a little water or vinegar, soy sauce, etc., to make it into a pourable sauce or condiment, or diluted with broth or other liquid ingredients when added to a dish. Particularly good with poultry, pork, to add extra taste to casseroles, etc., and as an ingredient of dipping sauces, etc.

Sesame seeds Put to all sorts of uses in Chinese cooking: as an outer coating for cakes, small pies, buns or as an ingredient in fillings and stuffings. These very small, flattish seeds can be black, white (actually a creamy white), red or brown and are produced in large quantities inside the two compartments of the oblong seedcase of the herbaceous plant *Sesamum indicum*.

Best stored in hermetically sealed jars.

Sesame seed oil Sesame seeds are pressed and an oil extracted, usually with the aid of certain solvents; this oil is refined and used for cooking.

The type of sesame seed oil used as a condiment or dressing by the Chinese is darker than the sesame seed oil we are familiar with in the West and is thick and aromatic, having been extracted from toasted white sesame seeds.

This oil's organoleptic composition means that it is best used in small quantities, in sauces, pickling brines and preserves, or added to dishes at the end of the cooking process. Only very rarely would it be used as a cooking oil. Buy in small quantities and store in a cool, dark, dry place; if kept too long it will turn rancid.

There is no satisfactory substitute for this oil, with its very distinctive aroma and flavor.

Shark's fin It would be a mistake to imagine that the market for these is a limited and specialist one: the fishing industries of many Asian, European, and South American countries are engaged in satisfying demand. The fins are taken from various types of sharks and the best quality of dried fin comes in long filaments, the lowest quality in odd pieces. Whole fin is the most expensive. Preparation and drying is a lengthy, laborious process, so they are marketed ready prepared and need blanching, soaking, and lengthy cooking to reconstitute them and return them to a gelatinous consistency. They are an expensive delicacy prized not only for their texture and for the fact that they absorb flavors of the ingredients cooked with them, but also, since they are mainly cartilaginous, because they provide a valuable source of gelatin protein, valued by the Chinese for its reputation of helping to prevent osteoporosis (brittle bone disease). The Chinese think it a good idea to start eating more gelatin protein from the age of about 35 onward (sea cucumber, a sort of a sea urchin and swallows' nest, as well as duck's web and tree fungus are some of the other sources).

The most famous shark's fin dish is shark's fin soup, a very costly delicacy, but shark's fin is also used in other dishes, such as Braised Shark's Fin (see page 196).

Shrimp paste or sauce Used as a condiment and made by grinding small crustaceans that have been pickled in brine. This pinkish gray thick sauce or purée has a very pronounced flavor and aroma and is therefore used sparingly and often diluted, in dishes of vegetables, squid, shrimp, and occasionally in soups.

Sold in jars. It keeps well if the lid is replaced securely after use and the jar refrigerated. A much thicker, almost solid, version is sold which has a saltier taste and is used in even smaller quantities.

Soy flour (mung bean flour) noodles Often called cellophane noodles or bean threads, these glasslike threads expand greatly when soaked in hot water. They should not be soaked for long or they become tough.

Soy sauce The most everyday, ubiquitous condiment, indispensable in the Chinese kitchen and synonymous throughout the

world with Chinese cooking. Two main versions are sold: dark and light soy sauce. Dark soy sauce, thicker and more full-bodied, is dark brown, almost black in color, and its taste is sweeter and stronger than the light variety. The latter is thinner, much paler, brownish amber colored and although its taste is more subtle, it is nevertheless pronounced and definitely salty.

Dark soy sauce is mainly used in braised and casseroled dishes, added so that the ingredients cook in it and it is often combined with rice wine; also used to marinate meat before cooking, making the finished dish look very rich and dark. Often used as a condiment at table, to add flavor to such bland foods as plain boiled or steamed rice.

Light soy sauce is often used for marinades, added to mixtures of ingredients that are being stir-fried, and as a flavoring for appetizers and stuffings.

Many recipes call for a carefully proportioned mixture of the two types of soy sauce.

When using this sauce, especially the light variety, little or no added salt is needed.

Soybean The *Glycine soja* or *Glycine ispida* or *Soja ispida*, a legume native to Eastern Asia, has been cultivated in China and Japan for thousands of years. It has a very high nutritional value with a high protein content and is now grown all over the world. It is, however, in Oriental cooking that soy and all its derivants have really been put to full use and they in turn have helped shape the distinctive taste and texture of many of the most typical, traditional dishes.

Soybean sprouts These are used when the seeds of the mung bean variety germinate, best when they are small, not more than 2 in long. Grown and sold all over the world nowadays, they have been valued in China for thousands of years as a rich source of protein and other nutrients and for their crisp, crunchy texture. They have very little taste and are seldom eaten raw in China, much more often briefly stir-fried or blanched and added to dishes, as the only vegetable or combined with several different vegetables.

They must be eaten very fresh, but will keep for a day or two if you have bought very fresh sprouts in a tightly sealed plastic bag or Saran wrap in the refrigerator. The shoots should be very firm, hard and crisp, white, and dry when you buy them; check the bottom of the container if it is the see-through type and if juice has started to collect on the bottom, the shoots are probably not fresh. Avoid using canned bean sprouts as they are far too soft, moist and mushy.

Star anise Fruit of the *Illicium verum*, a broadleaf evergreen plant belonging to the magnolia family, cultivated in many parts of

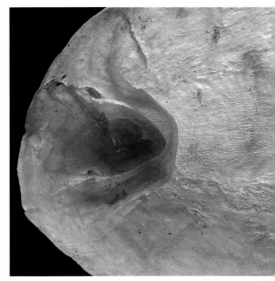

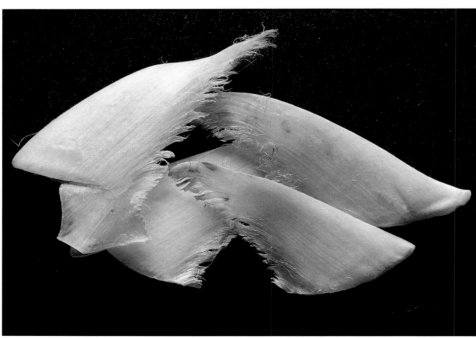

*From top to bottom, left to right, a further selection
of ingredients that are always available dried: sea
cucumber (trepang), shark's fins, swallows' nests,
and lotus seeds.*

A selection of spices. From top to bottom:
cinnamon, Szechwan pepper, nutmeg, and sesame
seeds.

Southeast Asia, particularly in southern China.

The fruit is star-shaped (hence its name) varies from $3/4$ in–$1^1/2$ in in diameter, and is made up of anything from 6 to 12 hard, rough and woody looking pointed seed pods, each containing a flattened, oval seed. The dried fruit is russet on the outside, the seed shiny and yellowish brown or mahogany red.

Apart from being one of the ingredients in commercially prepared seasonings, it is used whole, slightly crushed or ground (in small quantities) as a flavoring for Chinese dishes, particularly with roast meat and poultry, in slow-cooked casseroles etc., as well as for preserved foods, drinks, and sometimes for fish and crustaceans. Star anise also plays a role in herbal medicine. Both the fruit and the plant it comes from have a very strong scent, for they contain anise and other aromatic compounds. The taste is strong, sharp, and persistent with sweet, peppery overtones.

Star anise is included in the ancient Pents'ao pharmacopoeia, and mentioned in Chinese mythology and certain Oriental religions, often as a symbol of long life. Star anise seems to aid the digestion. It is one of the ingredients in five-spice powder, and blends particularly harmoniously with other spices and flavors.

Both the whole star anises and the ground version keep well but, as with all spices, they gradually lose their flavor and aroma, so it is best to buy small quantities frequently and to store them in a hermetically sealed glass jar.

Star anise has some of the same tastes and aromas as the other varieties of anise (such as *Pimpinella anisum* which grows in Mediterranean countries). It is so widely available nowadays in Oriental and ordinary foodstores that it would be a pity to substitute any other type of anise for the real thing.

Swallows' nests The most famous use of these is for soup, a gourmet dish that must be one of the best illustrations of the Chinese determination to use any conceivable substance that is remotely edible and transform the raw material into a superb meal. Nests of the *Collocalia esculenta* swallow, small, dark-plumaged birds with a wide wingspan are gathered (with great danger to life and limb) from the birds' colonies on the rocky coasts of Southeast Asia, the Sonda islands, Polynesia, and Australia. The birds build their cup-shaped nests on the rockfaces, using fragments of seaweed, fish larva and other seaborne material which are glued together with a transparent liquid secreted from the bird's exceptionally well-developed mandible glands during the mating season. This glue hardens on exposure to the air. In their natural state these nests are full of impurities but most of these are taken out from the closely enmeshed fabric of the nests before they are packaged and sold. Understandably, many of the nests break during this difficult and time-consuming process.

Sweet lotus seed paste The lotus nuts or seeds are cooked and crushed, sweetened with sugar and often used instead of sweet red soybean paste or jam for cakes, cookies, sweet steamed buns and other items calling for sweetness.

See also: Lotus; Lotus seeds.

Sweet soybean paste One of the most popular sweet mixtures with Chinese cooks, used in all sorts of ways. This dark brown purée is made from fermented yellow soybeans, to which are added flour, salt, and sometimes sugar and spices. *Hoisin*, often used instead of sweet soybean paste, is reddish brown, thick and sweet-sour in taste, made with more ingredients (garlic, vinegar, chili peppers, sesame oil, etc.) and is most often used with barbecued meats. Sweet soybean paste, or tian mian jiang, is sold in jars or cans and should be refrigerated once opened.

Szechwan pepper Not a true pepper although it does have a hot, peppery taste and its aroma is faintly reminiscent of pepper. Sometimes misleadingly called anise pepper. The dried red berries of a plant belonging to the Rutaceae family, *Xanthoxylum piperitum*, are used as an astringent in medicine and in cooking as a spice and seasoning. Grown and used on a particularly large scale in the western province of Szechwan but also popular throughout China and used in many classical dishes. Besides having an initial taste of pepper, the aftertaste is reminiscent of citrus peel and leaves a strange prickling sensation on the lips and tip of the tongue for a minute or two after it has been eaten. This effect has led to the name Prickly Ash being given to the mixture of roasted and crushed Szechwan peppercorns and sea salt used as a dipping seasoning. An important ingredient in five-spice powder. Often labeled Farchiew spice in Chinese grocery stores.

Tai tiao See Seaweed.

Tangerine peel Small pieces of peel from tangerine or mandarin oranges (which are native to Yunnan province in southern China) turn a brownish color when dried and become hard and friable. When added to meat, especially in casseroles, the peel improves and emphasizes the flavor and when combined with other spices, such as star anise and pepper adds an unmistakable aroma. The little pieces of dried peel can also be eaten just as they are, as tidbits; they keep well if stored in tightly sealed jars in a cool, dry place.

Taro This is the everyday name given to the tuber or rhizome of a plant native to India and Malaysia, *Colcasia antiquorum*, called wo tou in Chinese, which belongs to the Araceae family.

Sometimes called the red-budded taro, only two common varieties are grown: one smaller, and rather like a duck egg in shape, the other larger and oblong. Both have a brown hairy surface and encircling scars. Grown in tropical areas of Asia, the flesh is very pale gray or ivory with reddish tints, and is soft, fine-grained and almost creamy in texture, very digestible when boiled, steamed, baked or deep-fried. The traditional Cantonese way of eating taro is to boil them in their skins, then peel and eat them with the hands, especially during the celebrations held by the light of the full moon at the mid-autumn festival. Also provides a good foil to fatty foods such as pork, goose or duck; sometimes cooked with these in certain dishes.

Teng mien See Rice.

Tian mian jiang See Sweet soybean paste.

Toasted melon seeds Used, together with other seeds and fruits, in Chinese patisserie and sweet preparations. Known in China as qua ran or qua zi.

Tofu (bean curd) Long used in the East as an invaluable cheap, plentiful, and nutritious food, soybean cake or curd is but one of the many by-products of the soybean. Widely used by vegetarians as a good substitute for meat and fish, it is the most nutritionally valuable natural vegetable food known, being rich in protein and many other vital nutrients.

Tofu can be made at home from soybean powder, water, and lemon juice: the powder is mixed with cold water, left to stand for a while with the occasional stir, then brought to a boil, simmered, the lemon juice added to curdle the mixture which is then well stirred. When cold, the curd is hung up in cheesecloth to drain and pressed to express a good deal of the liquid content. The commercially prepared product is now so widely sold in the West and is so inexpensive that few people find this worthwhile. The fresh bean curd or cake will keep for several days in the refrigerator if kept submerged in a bowl of water which should be changed every day.

Tofu is virtually tasteless and has hardly any smell when fresh; if used with other ingredients, it takes on their flavors and can therefore be very useful for "stretching" expensive ingredients and can be adapted for all sorts of preparations.

Fried tofu: little cubes of fresh bean curd are deep-fried, turning golden brown on the outside and acquiring a very light honeycomb texture inside as the air in the curd expands. These cubes soak up some of the flavors and sauces when added to a dish. They keep well when dried and are sold in this form in Chinese foodstores.

Tofu skins or *bean curd skins* or *sheets*: the skin that forms on the surface of the curd during the tofu-making process is removed and dried; these yellowish, translucent sheets are sold dried or semi-dried, folded, rolled up, cut into strips, etc. and must be soaked and spread out before being used as wrappers, whether for non-vegetarian mixtures or wrapped around vegetarian fillings and made to resemble meat. They are soluble when crumbled into water and dissolved for a broth or stock in which other ingredients can be boiled. Not to be confused with dried soybean milk: the skin that forms on bean curd milk is dried and sold in yellowish wrinkled sticks.

Smoked tofu is a specialty of Chengdu in Szechwan and is sold in several shapes, including square blocks or slices; plain smoked or spiced varieties are marketed.

Fermented tofu sometimes called soybean cheese comes in many shapes, colors and versions, the most common being red or white, with a very strong, well-defined flavor, somewhat reminiscent of certain Western cheeses. Production methods may vary but usually entail the use of salt, rice wine, spices and sugar, the "cheese" being left to ferment and ripen for several months.

Used as an extra flavoring or relish with plain boiled or steamed rice or as an added ingredient in certain meat, poultry or vegetable dishes when a very pronounced flavor is required. Usually sold in glass or earthenware jars, it keeps well if refrigerated.

Trepang See Sea cucumber.

Tung ku (dong gu) See Mushrooms and fungi.

Vinegar Vinegar is produced by allowing bacteria to attack alcohol and oxidize it to acetic acid. As these bacteria need oxygen, they grow on the surface and stick to one another, forming a skin; this layer is called vinegar plant or mother of vinegar and can be used as a starter.

The most typical Chinese vinegar is rice wine or malt vinegar. This is colorless and is used for cooking and as a dressing for vegetables. White wine or cider vinegar can be used instead.

Another, milder, red variety is considered more suitable for dipping sauces and a few drops of this type of vinegar are added to shark's fin soup.

Black (hei jiu) vinegar is used a great deal in sweet-sour sauces: it is subtle, not very sharp and full of fragrance and taste. The best comes from Chin Kiang. Balsamic vinegar from Modena, Italy can replace it. (a very expensive substitute). Both red and black Chinese vinegars are less sharp than Western-style red wine vinegar; if you do use this instead, make sure you use the best (Orléans type), reduce the quantity used, and add a pinch of sugar if necessary.

Vegetables Markets in China, especially in the fertile, humid area to the south, east and in Szechwan, even in the north during the summer months, are full of any number of different fresh vegetables and fruit. Many of these are also available in the West and China exports a certain amount of her production.

The overwhelming impression to a Western visitor to these markets is one of amazing variety of produce, with many totally unfamiliar fruits and vegetables. Some of the species and varieties available in the West, often because the Chinese know how to dry them so efficiently, are worth mentioning, even if they represent a tiny proportion of the range used in Chinese cooking:

Fa cai, a sea moss which looks like hair, grows wild in the northern provinces of China, on high hills or mountains, wherever the climate is sufficiently damp and the situation shady. It has its own, faint, distinctive scent but no taste at all; one of its advantages is the ability to absorb the flavors of foods cooked with it. The use of fa cai gives what can only be described as an agreeably slippery consistency to a dish. It is also decorative and can be used to tie up parcels of food or bundles of vegetables very attractively. It cannot be cultivated and the limited supply that grows wild is therefore at a premium. Sold dried in Chinese foodstores: soak in warm water or other liquids (such as broth) to rehydrate and soften. Said to have a high vitamin content and to be effective in lowering blood pressure.

Another curiosity to the Western visitor is the fresh vegetable often called mustard greens in the West (*Brassica juncea*, see under the heading Mustard). This belongs to the cabbage family and both the leaves and the stems are used (unlike another mustard cabbage whose leaves are too strongly flavored and bitter, only the very firm, fleshy, large stems being used). One of the most common types is also known as the sow cabbage, and has large green stems which widen into darker, brighter green oval leaves, and a very agreeable, distinctive smell, making them excellent eating when stir-fried and also when added to soups or stews.

Water chestnuts These are the fruits of a herbaceous plant that grows with its roots in the beds of lakes or slow flowing streams, its leaves floating on the surface. Certain varieties of water chestnut (*Trapa natans* is one of them) grow in Europe, East Asia, Africa, and they have also been naturalized in America.

Consumption of these trilobate chestnuts with their spiky protuberances has been very limited in the West, even when locally grown supplies are available; most of the water chestnuts we eat are canned, imported from China where they are very popular and where several varieties exist (one being *Trapa licornis*). Some sources give *Eleocharis tuberosa* as the name of another variety of Chinese water chestnut.

The type most commonly found in China is reddish, mahogany brown; inside is the white, crisp and very slightly sweet flesh which can be enjoyed raw as well as cooked. Canned water chestnuts are slightly less crisp but very practical as they are ready peeled. Whether fresh or canned, they are an ingredient in many recipes, used whole or sliced in vegetable mixtures etc., or chopped to varying degrees of fineness and mixed with other chopped ingredients for fillings and stuffings.

Water chestnut powder or flour is grayish in color and very fine; it is used as an almost tasteless thickening agent for many sauces and dishes, as well as for desserts and some sweetmeats.

Winter melon A large melon that looks almost like an enormous pear with frosted, greenish skin which, despite its name, is sold throughout the year. The flesh is white enclosing many seeds in the center; size varies from small to very large indeed (more than 88 lb).

When cooked, the flesh becomes almost translucent and has a wonderful melting texture. Used in soups, or cooked with pork and poultry. Often pickled in brine to preserve, and small pieces of winter melon are candied and sold in packets. A whole, uncut winter melon will keep well in a cool place for a month or more. If you buy winter melon in a large, precut piece, wrap it in Saran wrap, foil or waxed paper and refrigerate to prevent it drying out and shrivelling for up to one week only. Once it starts to discolor, usually turning a yellowish color, it is deteriorating.

Wolfberries Chinese wolfberries, called *gouqui* berries in English transliteration of the Chinese character, are widely available in the West, sold dried in packets when they are an attractive coral red, rather wrinkled and oblong in shape, tapering away from the stalk. These are the berries of the matrimony vine, *Lycium Chinense*, a dry prairie shrub that is a member of the honeysuckle family. The berries have a slightly bitter taste and are picked in spring, mainly in eastern China, when they are greenish white; they are used as an extra ingredient and flavoring in food, enhancing the dish with their bright color (they turn red when cooked). They have medicinal properties, and the Chinese drink a soup or infusion of them to relieve headaches and refresh themselves. Also available canned.

Wo tou See Taro.

Xian cai See Pickled vegetables.

Xiang zao See Rice wine.

Xue cai See Pickled vegetables.

Xue li liang See Pickled vegetables.

305

309

Picture sources
All the photographs of the recipes are by
Adriano Brusaferri, Studio Adna, Milan.
Introduction: Mondadori Archives: 14 below,
15, 16–17, 18–19. A. Brusaferri: 22, 24–5, 27;
ⓒ Airone 1988: D. Pellegrini: 21.
Other photographs: E. Bossan, Vicenza:
28–29, 30, 31, 32–33, 42, 69, 83, 86; A.
Brusaferri, Milan: 104, 296, 297, 302, 303;
G. Coato, Verona: 100–101; E. Fazzioli:
122, 132, 158, 215, 217; Magnum, Milan,
E. Arnold: 216; Anderson: 99; Barbey: 98,
160–161, 163, 212–213, 261; Chine
Nouvelle: 72; Hiroji Kubota: 139, 162,
164–5, 194, 198, 221, 283; Lei Zhao/Ana:
37; R. Marcialis: 41, 61, 70–71, 85, 95,
102, 152, 179, 216, 222, 224–5; ⓒ Airone
1988: Daniele Pellegrini: 214; M. Rigo,
Verona: 112.